The fortifications on the Janiculum at the top of the picture and other similar bastions are new.
Otherwise the city is as it was during the Sack.

THE SACK OF
ROME
1527

JUDITH HOOK

THE SACK OF

ROME

1527

MACMILLAN

SBN 333 13272 6

First published 1972 by
MACMILLAN LONDON LIMITED
London and Basingstoke
Associated companies in New York Toronto
Dublin Melbourne Johannesburg and Madras

Printed in Great Britain by
W & J MACKAY LIMITED
Chatham

FOR ANDREW

CONTENTS

LIST OF ILLUSTRATIONS

MAPS

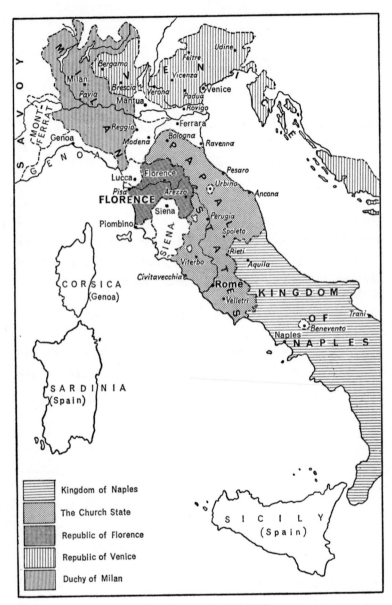

THE ITALIAN STATES

A NOTE ON ITALY

ITALY in the sixteenth century was a geographical area, containing a large number of independent states, franchises and jurisdictions. Each of the Italian states was a highly sophisticated political entity and intensely jealous of its independence. This book is concerned largely with the fortunes of the five largest of these states:

THE KINGDOM OF NAPLES. A monarchy, technically under the suzerainty of the papacy to whom an annual tribute was due from the ruler. Since 1503 Naples (known to the Italians as the *Regno* or Kingdom) had been effectively ruled by the Spanish, although it was claimed, with some justice, by the French. The French attempt to make good this claim in 1494 had precipitated the Italian wars. Within the kingdom of Naples the popes possessed the small state of Benevento.

THE CHURCH STATE. The temporal estates of the church in central Italy. Its boundaries were open to question but, on the whole, were expanding at this date.

FLORENCE. A republic in name, but normally ruled by the Medici family, by a complicated system of management. Between 1527 and 1530 Florence came very close to being a republic in fact as well as name.

VENICE. Also a republic in name, but in fact a closed oligarchy, at the head of which stood the doge (Andrea Gritti). Venice also ruled a large mainland empire in Italy, including Verona, Vicenza, Feltre, Bassano, Padua, Udine, Friuli, Brescia, Bergamo, Ravenna, Crema, Rovigo and the Polesine. She had extensive settlements in Dalmatia and in the eastern Mediterranean, including many of the islands. In the kingdom of Naples she held, until 1530, Trani, Brindisi and Otranto.

MILAN. A duchy, under the overlordship of the emperor, technically ruled at this date by the native duke, Francesco Maria Sforza.

Of the smaller Italian states the most important were the duchy of Savoy, which at this date was outside the mainstream of Italian events; the duchy of Ferrara, ruled by Duke Alfonso d'Este under the joint overlordship of pope and emperor; the Marquessate of Mantua; the Republics of Genoa and Siena; and, within the Church State, the duchy of Urbino. Sardinia had been a province of the crown of Aragon since 1327, and Sicily since 1406.

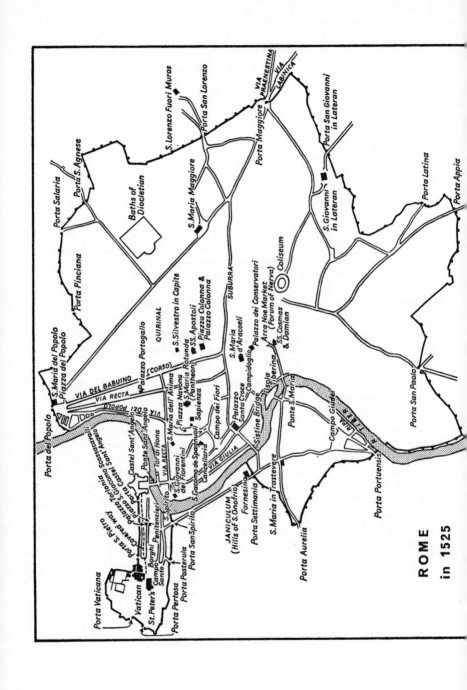

ROME
in 1525

Porta Vaticana
Vatican
St. Peter's
Porta Pertosa
Porta Posterula
Porta San-Spirito
Porta Settimania
Porta Aurelia
Porta S. Pietro
Palazzo S. Giacomo Sant'Angelo
Borghi Penitenzieri
Campo Santo
S. Spirito
JANICULUM (Hills of S. Onofrio)
S. Maria in Trastevere
Porta Portuensis
Porta del Popolo
Porta Trofonio scossacavalli
Porta S. Giacomo Sant'Angelo
Castel Sant'Angelo
Ponte Sant'Angelo
Tor di Nona
S. Giovanni dei Florentini
S. Giacomo de Spagnuoli
Cancellaria
VIA GIULIA
Farnesina
VIA DEL BABUINO
VIA DEL POPOLO
VIA RECTA
S. Maria del Popolo
Piazza del Popolo
S. Maria dell'Anima
Piazza Navona
S. Maria Rotunda (Pantheon)
Sapienza
Campo dei Fiori
Palazzo Santa Croce
Sistine Bridge
Tisola
Ponte S. Maria
Campo Giudeo
Porta San Paolo
Palazzo Portogallo
(CORSO)
QUIRINAL
S. Silvestro in Capite
SS. Apostoli
Piazza Colonna & Palazzo Colonna
S. Maria d'Aracoeli
Campidoglio
Palazzo dei Conservatori
Arca Noe Market (Forum of Nerva)
SS. Cosmas & Damian
Coliseum
SUBURRA
S. Maria Maggiore
Baths of Diocletian
Porta Salaria
Porta S. Agnese
Porta Pinciana
S. Lorenzo Fuori Muras
Porta San Lorenzo
S. Maria Maggiore
Porta Maggiore
VIA PRAENESTINA
VIA LABINICA
Porta San Giovanni in Lateran
S. Giovanni in Lateran
Porta Latina
Porta Appia
Porta San Paolo
TIBER

INTRODUCTION

SINCE there is no modern account of the sack of Rome in English it might seem that there is no need for an apology on behalf of such a book; and, indeed, this introduction is intended largely as an explanation of my purposes and methods. Much of the research was undertaken in preparing a dissertation which was submitted for the degree of Doctor of Philosophy in the University of Edinburgh. My intention at that time was to explore the impact of the sack of Rome on Italy in order to discover, for my own satisfaction, how much the different states into which Italy was divided – Venice, Florence, Milan, Naples, the Church State, Siena, Lucca, Piombino, Mantua, Ferrara, Montferrat, etc. – had in common. Ultimately my interest was in the idea of Italy. Some of this interest is, inevitably and, no doubt, properly, reflected in this book but I have tried not to let it obtrude too much into a description of what happened within Italy between 1525 and 1530.

Most of the sources used originate in Italy because I was anxious to see things from an Italian point of view and to understand the sense of exploitation which clearly underlies all the writings and utterances of contemporaries, faced by the blatant imperialism of France and Spain, who chose to fight out their national conflicts over the battlefields of Italy. There can be little doubt that this use of, in the main, Italian sources, may well have affected the emphasis of my study, for contemporary Italians, with a highly developed sense of the colourful and episodic, limit their reports, observations, histories and remarks to what was regarded as important. Lucca, the little Tuscan republic, for instance, is scarcely mentioned and then only in derogatory terms; and, although Siena was of importance, Italian contemporaries pay scant attention to that city.

Covering this period, there is a wealth of diplomatic material, the vast bulk of it in print, dealing with a succession of delicate

and complicated negotiations, some of which issued in such agreements as the Treaty of Madrid, the League of Cognac, the Treaty
of Barcelona and the Peace of Cambrai, and others which proved
abortive. The League members tended to retain resident ambassadors at the courts of other members and to supplement them with
extraordinary embassies to deal with specific questions; Venice,
for instance, had four resident ambassadors with Clement VII
between 1525 and 1531 – the poet Domenico Venier, Francesco
Pesaro, Antonio Soriano and Marcantonio Venier – but also sent
three extraordinary embassies to the pope during the same period.
There were English ambassadors in Spain and Rome, a papal
nuncio to Francis I and to Venice, another papal nuncio to
Charles V, and representatives of the emperor throughout Europe.
In Italy the emperor had various ambassadors and agents: Carraciolo
and Sanchez at Venice, Sessa at Rome, Lope de Soria at Genoa,
Herrara, Hurtado da Mendoza, Don Hugo da Moncada, and the
abbot of Najera in Lombardy. There were special negotiations
between France and Spain, between France and England, and
between England and Spain. The papal correspondence at this
date, particularly that conducted by Giberti, is especially valuable
since the pope was involved in so many negotiations simultaneously. Many of the most distinguished literary figures were
active in the diplomatic world – Guicciardini, Machiavelli,
Vettori, Castiglione, Navagero and Nerli among them.

There is a vast number of eye-witness accounts of the sack of
Rome. Some are strictly contemporary; the accounts found in
Sanuto's *Diarii*, which, by its very nature, is a compilation of
sources; the letters of Gonzaga, Como and Gattinara; the account
by the Frenchman Jean Cave, or the German Cornelius de Fine.
Others are more literary, the product of later reflection, like
Giovio's account, or the many poetic descriptions of the sack, and
in these the literary quality of the work often tends towards a
perversion of the truth. The most notorious case of this is, of
course, to be found in Cellini's autobiography. Other accounts,
although not by eye-witnesses, make use of materials provided by
those who were. Such an account is that of Brantôme, who claimed
that his material came from oral and written contemporary accounts. A similar type of work is that of Jacopo Buonaparte which,
although not published until 1756 and, apparently, a compilation

of earlier sources, is usually accurate. Contemporary chronicles have been freely used, but they tend to be very parochial in outlook.

Finally, use has been made of the general histories of the period. Guicciardini's monumental *Storia d'Italia,* Paruta's *Dell'Istorie Veneziane,* Varchi's *Storia Fiorentina* and Guazzo's *Historie* are among them. Here allowance has to be made for local and personal bias and inaccuracies – Varchi is notoriously unreliable over dates – but these histories are invaluable in placing the sack of Rome in its Italian perspective and sometimes give detailed information not readily available elsewhere. In the course of this book I quote extensively from these varied sources, and where necessary I have translated fairly freely in order to render their sense in modern English.

Anyone writing on this period and on this subject must do so under two great shadows, that of Ludwig von Pastor and that of Karl Brandi. Of Pastor's *History of the Popes* I can record little more than my admiration, my respect, and a regret that it is a book which, today, is little read. Brandi's biography of *Charles V* remains a masterpiece to which I have had constant recourse, but, for Brandi, the Italian wars were essentially the result of dynastic preoccupations, turning on the question of Charles V's Burgundian inheritance. Italy was no more than a battlefield where the struggle between Hapsburg and Valois was played out. Brandi regarded the imperial idea, so marked in correspondence relating to Italy, as an idea imposed on the emperor by Gattinara. In no sense does he see the struggle between Charles V and Clement VII as an extension of the old papal–imperial struggle which had dominated Italian history for so long. He regarded Burgundy as the key to Charles V's policies, rather than Charles's position as emperor with all that that implied both in a European context and, more particularly, in the Italian political and intellectual world.

According to Lord Acton, 'Nothing causes more error and unfairness in men's view of history than the interest which is inspired by individual characters.' This study of the sack of Rome, in its Italian setting, to some extent modifies the impression left by Brandi's great biography, concentrating less on the personality of Charles V, of Francis I or even of Clement VII, and more on the context within which they were operating and of which they were often curiously ignorant. But the early sixteenth century is an age in which personality does obtrude and is of importance. How else can one explain the position held by Wolsey and the respect felt for him throughout Europe? By showing how limited was his field of action, I have attempted, at least, a partial rehabilitation of Clement VII, who has found few apologists either among his contemporaries or among subsequent scholars.

Money must figure very largely in any account of events between 1525 and 1530, but I have made no attempt to translate sums of money mentioned into modern equivalents. Even if it were possible, I doubt if it would be helpful. When writing about large sums contemporaries were often inaccurate. It is clear that frequently the Venetian and papal ducat, the *scudo*, crown and florin are treated as equivalent in value even when they were not. Yet, when they wanted, the same contemporaries could be very specific and exact about the value of the various currencies they were forced to deal in. Where it is clear that such a specific use is in question I have incorporated it into the text. On all other occasions sums are given in ducats. Weights and measures I have also retained in their contemporary form and, because I have not yet learnt to 'think metric', distances are given in miles. Place-names use the modern spelling, with the exception of Melegnano which, in its sixteenth-century context, is better known as Marignano. Borgo San Donnino is referred to by its modern name of Fidenza, which it acquired in 1907.

I would like to record my thanks to the librarians and archivists who have helped me in my research for this book, among many others the staff of the Bodleian Library, of the university libraries at Bologna, Cambridge, Edinburgh and Princeton. I would also like to thank the Archivio dello Stato at Venice, Modena and Mantua, the National Library of Scotland, the British Museum, the English Public Record Office and the Bibliothèque Nationale. But above all else I would like to mention, with the deepest gratitude, the unfailing courtesy, kindness and intelligent assistance that I have received throughout from the Vatican Library, whose efficient service never ceases to amaze me.

Quite early in the career of this book substantial debts were incurred which I can never repay. Having inspired in a whole generation of Oxford undergraduates, as well as myself, a love of sixteenth-century Italy, Professor John Hale has given me personally every assistance and encouragement, from the day when I first mentioned that I intended to work on the sack of Rome and he handed me his own bibliography on the subject. At the same period my old college of Somerville financed my first year of research, and for this I am very grateful. Since then my greatest debt has been to Professor Denys Hay of the University of Edinburgh, under whom it has been the greatest privilege to work, who, even at his busiest, as chairman of a very large department, has shown constant interest in my research and can indeed be said to have nursed it to completion. He has helped me and inspired me throughout and I am really sensible of my good fortune in having had such a supervisor for a doctoral dissertation. I would like to thank those of my friends and colleagues who have shown interest in my work, in particular Owen Dudley Edwards for his imaginative assistance and for his faith in my abilities and Dr Harry Dickinson who read the manuscript and made many helpful and just criticisms. To Mrs Katie Brown, for her loan of microfilm, and Mrs Rosemary Pesman for her information about the Soderini, I would also like to say thank you; as also to Dr Peter Williams for miscellaneous information about sixteenth-century music. While I have been writing this book my children, Sarah and Caspar, have been patient and forgiving, and for that their mother thanks them. Without their tolerance it could not have been done. I would not want the expression of gratitude to my husband to be regarded as a matter of form. Without his loving-kindness I could not have completed this book; there is little in it that is not already partly his; he has read and reread the manuscript, offering constant advice and encouragement; he has been constantly loving and caring, even when he has been hard-worked and tired. I thank him from the bottom of my heart.

For all of the errors in this book I myself take responsibility, because they are my own.

J. H.

CHAPTER I

CLEMENT VII AND ROME

A papacy composed of compliment,
Debate, consideration, complaisance,
Of 'furthermore', 'then', 'but', 'yet', 'well', 'perchance',
'Haply', and such like terms . . .
Of feet of lead, of tame neutrality. . . .
To speak the truth, you will live to see
Pope Adrian sainted through this papacy.

Francesco Berni

O N 14 September 1523 the man who was the least loved of all the popes died at Rome. Adrian VI, although of exemplary virtue in his personal life and a true reforming pope, was little mourned; indeed, the College of Cardinals and the people of Rome could barely disguise their joy when they learned that he was dead. Qualities which would have endeared Adrian VI to the twentieth century made him hated in the sixteenth. Adrian spent more time at prayer than in conducting the business of the Church; he pursued his own studies for at least two hours every day, putting more energy into them than into running the Church State which, to the constant despair of the cardinals, he seemed quite ready to dismember by giving pieces away to anyone who asked for them; yet he was parsimonious with his money – his food reputedly cost less than a ducat a day and his only servant, who did all his cooking and housework, was an old Flemish woman he had brought to Rome from his own country. To contemporaries it seemed clear that Adrian did not have the first notion of a pope's duties either in the local or international sphere. Afraid of making wrong decisions, he deferred making any. The two outstanding events of his pontificate were both major disasters for Christendom: the loss of Belgrade and the fall of Rhodes to the aggressive Ottoman Turks. But now at last he was dead, and on 1 October, while a thunder-storm was raging, thirty-five electors of the Sacred College of Cardinals met in the Sistine Chapel to choose his successor, determined not to repeat the mistake of electing a foreigner or a saint as pope.

The cardinals were aware that this was likely to be a conclave of unprecedented length. The reasons which had forced them in desperation to elect Adrian VI as a stop-gap pope remained valid. The Sacred College was bitterly divided by the quarrel between Cardinal Colonna and Cardinal Giulio de' Medici – so bitterly divided, in fact, that it was manifestly clear that nothing short of the intervention of the Holy Spirit could hope to produce agreement. The favourite candidate for success was Alessandro Farnese, the most authoritative of the cardinals, and the most important personality in Rome, beloved by the Romans, who considered him as one of themselves. There were, however, other possibilities: the Cardinal de' Medici himself or one of the Colonna candidates – Jacobacci or Soderini, but against Soderini it could be argued that he had been in prison at the time of the late pope's death, for alleged treasonable activities, and had had to be specially released from Castel Sant'Angelo in order to take part in the conclave at all. If money were to count, the most likely candidate was Cardinal Gonzaga. In fact, after the Adrian VI débâcle, it is reasonable to assume that good odds could have been obtained on any of the cardinals that autumn in Rome.

The key to the inevitable long duration of the conclave lay in the ten votes Cardinal de' Medici had in his pocket – enough to prevent the election of anyone else but not enough to ensure his own elevation. He had wanted the papacy in 1521 when his cousin, Leo X, died, but on that occasion Cardinal Colonna had skilfully suggested that if Giulio de' Medici were to succeed his cousin there was a fair chance that the papacy might become a hereditary fief of the Medici family. His failure in the preceding conclave only made Medici more determined to succeed in this.

Yet success was far from certain. The entire French party was opposed to a man who was a known imperialist and, if Medici had staying-power, so did Cardinal Colonna who had at his disposal the votes of several of the older and more authoritative members of the Sacred College, men who disliked Medici as the leader of the group of young cardinals nominated by Leo X. Colonna's initial policy was to force a delay in coming to any decision until the arrival of the French cardinals. Their arrival, he believed, would counteract the influence of the imperial ambassador, the duke of Sessa, who under instruction from Charles V was working actively on behalf of Cardinal de' Medici.

The first scrutiny was to take place on the morning of 6 October; but while the cardinals were still hearing mass they were disturbed by the sudden arrival of the French – Louis de Bourbon, François de Clermont and Jean de Lorraine. Still booted, spurred and travel-stained, the French cardinals entered the conclave, to the intense annoyance of the imperialists. Their arrival determined that the conclave would become an arena for the conflict between rival imperial and French power. In the first scrutiny of 8 October the parties were seen to be so evenly divided that all hope of a speedy end to the conclave was given up. The cardinals, Rome, the Church State and the rest of Europe settled down for a long wait. On 10 October the disturbances, demonstrations and riots, which customarily accompanied a long conclave, began in Rome.

Yet it was clear that the Romans shared the view of the cardinals that the appointment of another foreign pope would be a disaster. When on 12 October the Roman commune told the Sacred College that it must appoint a pope quickly or starve, Cardinal Armellini sent out the answer, 'Since you can put up with a foreign pope, we are almost on the point of giving you one; he lives in England.'[1] The Roman response to such a suggestion was unequivocal. They would have no more foreign popes. So ended Cardinal Wolsey's hopes of attaining the papal tiara.[2]

Still the cardinals were no nearer agreement. Medici's opponents were united only in one thing – they all wished to prevent his attaining the papacy; but on a candidate of their own they could not agree. By 11 November the entire civic life of Rome had ground to a halt. In the Church State, which was effectively without a central government, all the destructive forces which customarily attended a vacancy were at work. The duke of Ferrara attacked Modena and Reggio, cities which he believed had been unjustly taken from him by the popes, and which were governed by the papal lieutenant, Francesco Guicciardini. Guicciardini, against all expectation – for he had no money with which to pay his troops, and the cardinals, engrossed in the conclave, could not even be bothered to answer his letters appealing for help – managed to hold onto Modena, but had to let Reggio and its dependent town Rubiera fall into the hands of the Ferrarese.

Within the conclave itself the Orsini and Colonna families could come to no agreement, but outside the wall the same factions promised to support the Roman commune in starving the cardinals into agreement. The turning-point came when Pompeio Colonna renounced his opposition to Medici. He was already disillusioned with the French, who had consistently refused to support his own candidate Jacobacci, but the real motive for his change of heart was fear. It had temporarily looked as though Cardinal Orsini might be elected. On 17 November Colonna and Medici were publicly reconciled, and two days later Christendom learnt that it had a pope once more. The choice of the Holy Spirit was, after all, Giulio de' Medici who took the name of Clement VII to signify his reconciliation with his enemies.

Chief of these, and yet paradoxically the man whose votes had finally given him the papacy, was Cardinal Pompeio Colonna, the head of the Colonna faction, a man as ambitious and as able as Clement VII himself. It was family obligation combined with personal ambition which made him the new pope's enemy. He had wanted the papacy himself; he had been thwarted by Clement; and Clement was, in addition, a relative of the Orsini, a family which for centuries had been in a state of perpetual conflict with the Colonna. Throughout the preceding century the Colonna–Orsini conflict had presented each succeeding pope with a major political problem.

In the Roman Campagna the Colonna and the Orsini were constantly at war matching sizeable armies against each other. They sheltered fugitives from papal justice and they hindered all economic development. Their power came from their wealth. Between them the two factions commanded an annual revenue which was more than that of the states of Lucca or Piombino. And, inevitably, the Colonna and the Orsini grasped at any opportunity to increase their income. So, when Rome began to grow in size and prosperity in the fifteenth century and a good market developed for meat, the Colonna and the Orsini tended to place more and more of their land under pasture. Previously the Roman populace had been largely fed by wheat grown in the Campagna, but by the beginning of the sixteenth century Rome was totally dependent on imported wheat, and when wheat imports were delayed or reduced the city was quickly reduced to famine level.

To counteract this danger the popes made constant efforts to revive grain production in the Campagna, and these attempts were systematically sabotaged by the Roman barons.[3]

It was with reason that contemporaries spoke of the Orsini or Colonna 'state'. Their territorial rights were extensive and consolidated, carrying with them rights of jurisdication which made the Colonna and the Orsini sovereign within the confines of their own properties. They lived like princes, each of the barons maintaining his own little court. Many played an important role in the development of humanism in Italy and as patrons of the arts. Some surrounded themselves with scholars, even on military campaigns, and several of them turned their hands to writing. From their earliest youth the Roman barons had the best military education available. In this field many showed considerable genius and they were employed as *condottieri*, soldiers of fortune, up and down the Italian peninsula.

Successful marriage alliances enhanced their position. Through complicated structures of relationship the Colonna and the Orsini were united to most of the major families in Italy. On the whole the Orsini married into Guelf, the Colonna into Ghibelline families. The Medici twice married into the Orsini family: in one of the most splendid wedding ceremonies of the fifteenth century Lorenzo the Magnificent, effectual ruler of Florence, had married Clarice Orsini; and their son, Piero, married Alfonsina, the daughter of Roberto Orsini. Henceforward the ties between the Medici and the Orsini families were strong and the Medici had become automatically the enemies of the entire Colonna clan.

Legally, the Colonna and the Orsini were subjects of the pope within the Church State, but they consistently ignored the fact that their obligations as citizens were incompatible with engagements of a military and political nature which they entered into elsewhere. The Colonna normally took service with the Spanish, the Orsini with the French or the Venetians. In relation to the papacy the Orsini were in the less complicated situation, for by the first quarter of the sixteenth century the papacy and the Orsini had entered into an unwritten alliance, based upon significant geographical facts. The Orsini controlled a large territory to the northwest of Rome which included some of the most important

fortresses in the Campagna. Effectively this meant that they controlled all the routes leading north from Rome including the vital
roads to Civitàvecchia and Florence. Even Julius II, often foolhardy in the extreme, had been unable to break with Florence, for
the merchant class of that city fed and clothed Rome. Whatever
happened, then, the road to the north had to be kept open.

It was not for control of territory that the Orsini and Colonna
fought. Conflict between them arose from other causes. The
Colonna were embittered because they had no secure title to their
lands. Their power had had a vast extension in grants made to
them by the Colonna pope, Martin V, who had also persuaded
Giovanna of Naples to grant his brothers rich fiefs in the kingdom
of Naples and so made it an essential factor in the political life of
the Colonna that they remain on good terms with the *de facto*
government of that kingdom. The importance of this became all
the more evident when Eugenius IV revoked all the grants of
Martin V and asked for the restitution of the property of the Holy
See. The Colonna refused to comply with the request, but thereafter held their land in the Church State not of right but by force,
and the history of their relationship with the papacy is the history
of their struggle to legalise their position. When they fought
against the papacy for their rights, the popes naturally turned to
the Orsini who were called in to counterbalance the Colonna
power. It was in this way that the conflict between the Orsini and
the Colonna originated, a conflict which was essentially a struggle
for power, not over the commune of Rome, which no longer had
any real political significance, but in the Curia, the Patrimony and
the kingdom of Naples. By the sixteenth century the struggle was
concentrated in the Curia, the real centre of power in the Church
State.

In all the years of struggle neither family had been able to produce one leader with a coherent political plan – neither, that is,
until Pompeio Colonna emerged from obscurity at the beginning
of the sixteenth century. He was the first of the Roman barons to
understand that the power he sought could best be attained by
using more than military force, though this too had its place.
Rather than by force of arms alone, he hoped to gain his ends by
organising the sympathies of the Roman populace against the
papacy, by appealing beyond the pope to the Church at large and

organising discontent against the Medici and the Orsini throughout Italy.

Pompeio Colonna was a Roman by birth and first made a name for himself as a soldier. It was only pressure from his relatives that induced him to embark on an ecclesiastical career, for which he was eminently unsuited. In 1507, when he was still only twenty-eight, he was already bishop of Rieti and protonotary to the Apostolic Chamber; and in the following year, through family influence, he was made abbot of Subiaco and Grottaferrata. But the greater prize eluded him, for Julius II refused to make him a cardinal. Julius, in fact, refused to create any cardinals from either the Colonna or the Orsini families since, in Machiavelli's words, 'those parties are never at rest when they have cardinals, for they stir up the parties both inside Rome and outside it, and the barons are forced to defend them. Thus from the ambitions of prelates arise the discords and tumults among the barons.'[4] Julius's refusal to grant to Pompeio Colonna the coveted cardinal's hat was a constant source of friction and finally provoked Colonna into a false move. It had always been Colonna policy to seize military control of Rome during moments of crisis and the Colonna family frequently championed the Roman people; in 1494 it had been Prospero Colonna, not the pope, who complained to Charles VIII about the behaviour of French troops in Rome. Pompeio Colonna now turned this tradition of sympathy to political advantage. In 1511 Julius II fell gravely ill, his life was despaired of, and Pompeio Colonna promptly allied with the more republican members of the Roman commune. In an abortive *coup* he tried to seize control of Rome, urging the Roman people to throw off the yoke of papal government and restore their ancient liberties.[5]

The attempt failed. The pope recovered, and for the first time in his career Pompeio was deprived of all his dignities. He continued to cultivate the commune and the people of Rome, and in 1517 Leo X, a Medici pope, restored him to all his former glories and made him a cardinal at last. As a temporary move this proved a successful way of buying Colonna's loyalty. For the remaining years of Leo's pontificate, and throughout the brief reign of Adrian VI, Pompeio played no prominent part in politics. But he continued to hope for the papacy himself; he continued to hate the Orsini–Medici clan; and he included the new pope in his general condemnation of them and all their works. He was embittered by the fact that he had been personally responsible for this election; even the gift of the vice-chancery and the Palazzo Venezia made to him by Clement could not soften the blow. He had wanted to be pope himself and he still intended that he should be. To him it was imperative that the Medici pope be eliminated in one way or another – by deposition, or by death. To both ends he now bent all his energies.

It was clear that many opportunities for intrigue would be open to Colonna. Even a man of more vigour than Giulio de' Medici might have shrunk from assuming the responsibilities of the papacy at this juncture. But, in fact, Clement VII was not a man of vigour, nor was he cast in the heroic mould of a Julius II. He had many very fine qualities. He was extremely handsome. He was tall and graceful with a refined face of regular feature, marred only by a slight squint in his right eye. A just man and personally charitable, Clement was as liberal in his almsgiving as Leo X: in Rome certain conventual houses received Clement's alms regularly throughout the pontificate, and Clement took personal delight in giving charity where it was most needed. He was careful in his observation of the Church's year: throughout Lent he fed only on bread and water and he fasted as faithfully on all the vigils of the feasts of the Virgin. As pope he suffered by contrast with his cousin Leo X, for, essentially, Clement VII, like Adrian VI, was a scholar and disliked the show which accompanied the papal office. He lost popularity at Rome by refusing to say mass in public as frequently as his predecessors, for this had always been an opportunity for the people of Rome to enjoy the pomp of the Church and to experience the benefit of having the popes resident in their city. Clement's court was not simply non-existent, like that of Adrian VI, but neither was it splendid in the style of the Borgias, of Julius II or of Leo X. Clement was popularly famed to be the best musician in Italy, so famed indeed that another musician also named Clement was identified by the surname of Not-pope, and elaborate use was made of music in the celebration of services at the Vatican and St Peter's; but there were no musicians and no secular music at the pope's court. The traditional court-fools no longer entertained the pope at meal-times; Clement preferred the company of learned doctors with whom he discussed health-foods and good diets, of philosophers and theologians who were required to discourse on their own subjects while the pope ate. At the most basic level of his personality Clement was a sophisticated intellectual, and this may explain his failure to charm or to evoke an affectionate response in the majority of those who met him, for he appeared cold and unemotional to all but those who knew him best. It was the same intellectual quality which often made Clement appear indecisive. In approaching any problem he would delay until the matter was perfectly clear to him, no matter what disasters delay might bring in its train. This was a way of thinking which contemporaries recognized and character-ized as Florentine.

It was their experience of the Italian wars since 1494 which had rightly convinced the Florentines that their city was not strong enough to allow them to take the initiative in politics. In any critical situation the customary recommendation was to delay making a decision until the situation clarified, and for this kind of policy they had a phrase – 'to enjoy the benefit of time'.[6] No man was a more faithful disciple of this general Florentine belief, or more true to the habits of his native city, than Clement VII. Delay was the essence of all his policies.

Clement was unfortunate in that very often the one thing he was unable to do was to enjoy the 'benefit of time'. There were, for instance, long-term tendencies already at work in the Church State which would ultimately strengthen the papacy, but in 1523 they were as yet barely discernible. Very gradually papal govern-ment was coming to represent a tradition of good government, opposed to old-fashioned rule by faction and terror. In the terms of the sixteenth century, papal government was good government and was serviced by a highly developed administration. The regions of the Church State were becoming more amenable to central authority, all the more attractive in that it emanated from the centre of the Christian world and a city which drew visitors from all over Europe.

In the first decades of the sixteenth century Rome was acknow-ledged to be the centre of civilization. Venetian diplomats still spoke of the 'mother' or the 'home of us all' when referring to the papal city. Rome was the centre of art, learning, beauty, the heart of the Christian world. Drawn by the patronage of the popes, of the cardinals, of the Florentine merchants and the Roman barons, artists from all over Europe flocked to Rome.[7]

The years before 1526 were, therefore, the great years of papal Rome. Visitors flocked to the city either as traditional pilgrims or to visit the antiquities and the ruins. They came, too, to purchase modern works of art or antique statues and marbles. In the pontificate of Adrian VI, the pope's failure to show interest in such matters depressed the market, and it was possible to pick up a bargain. But such a chance became more and more rare. The citizens of Rome soon developed a sense of the value of any object that could be sold to foreigners, including books and manuscripts.[8]

Throughout Europe there was a popular market in guide-books for visitors to Rome and it was a growing market, despite all Luther's denunciations of the Holy City. Between 1475 and 1600 at least 127 editions of guides to Rome were published, 48 in Latin, 22 in German, 4 in French, 6 in Spanish and 1 in Flemish.[9] In the jubilee years for the quarter-centuries the normal flow of visitors became a torrent, and the resources of Rome were stretched to their fullest to cope with the influx of pilgrims from all over Christendom.

The most striking feature about early maps of Rome is the contrast between the ancient and modern centres of population. Ancient Rome was a city of seven hills on whose slopes it had been built, but when the city was overthrown in the barbarian invasions the aqueducts which had brought water to the hills had been broken. True, a few minor aqueducts survived and there were a few springs which rose on the hills, as well as many ancient cisterns and wells, but these never produced enough water, and so the medieval population of the city was forced down into the less healthy area along the banks of the Tiber.

The limits of the city were still determined by the old city-wall, built by Aurelius (161–80) and Probus (276–82), and restored by Honorius (384–423). The upkeep of this wall was important, for it was vital to the defence of Rome. It was a primary drain on papal finance, for it was never allowed to deteriorate. Nevertheless, for purposes of fortification, by 1520 it was distinctly old-fashioned. Since the boundaries of modern Rome were those of the old capital of the empire, Rome was unique among medieval towns of a comparable size in incorporating villas, vineyards, deer-parks and large areas of waste ground. Many people in Rome found employment as vinedressers, cowherds or gardeners, and every year seasonal employment was provided for peasants who came down from Lombardy to dig the vineyards.

Perpetually involved in baronial feuds, medieval Rome had not been a peaceful city, and the main architectural need before the fifteenth century was for fortification. But in the fifteenth century the popes began rebuilding the city, thereby ultimately weakening its defences. New thoroughfares were driven through Rome to replace the old muddy, dark alleys; new bridges were built; access and communication were improved. As a result, by 1520 Rome was becoming a city of greaty beauty which, by a synthesis of the ancient and the modern, made a fitting centre for the modern Christian world. In the early stages of the Italian wars Rome was immune from the miseries endured by other Italian cities and became a second home for refugees from the north.

In the early sixteenth century the Borgo and Trastevere, the two areas of settlement on the north bank of the Tiber, were still completely separate and to go from one to another it was necessary to go out by Porta Settimania, cross the virtually uninhabited area by the river and enter the Borgo through Porta San Spirito. The traveller who did so would pass by one of the wonders of contemporary Rome, the new villa, now called the Farnesina, built by Peruzzi for the great Sienese banker Agostino Chigi, a villa of which Vasari said that its beauty showed it to have been born, not made.

By the sixteenth century, the Borgo Leonino, the Leonine City, on the north bank of the Tiber in the area around St Peter's was the centre of papal Rome. The Borgo had been favoured at the expense of the old centre of papal authority, the Lateran, because it was independent of the Roman commune and came directly under papal jurisdiction. The Leonine city was not an area of dense population, for, apart from many inns and taverns and apothecaries' shops, it was an aristocratic quarter full of pleasure-gardens and open spaces. Here were the palaces of the great cardinals, built for the most part as recently as the pontificates of Julius II and Leo X, the homes of Orsini, Rangoni, Ridolfi, and of Cardinal Campeggio who occupied Palazzo Torlonia on Piazza San Giacomo Scossacavalli. Cardinal Armellino, the financial adviser of the two Medici popes, had a palace in the Borgo Vecchio, and the cardinal of Ancona had purchased Raphael's house built by Bramante on the Borgo Nuovo. Here, too, were to be found the palaces of Giberti, the datary of Clement VII, and that of the pope's close relative, Filippo Strozzi.

St Peter's, the true heart of the Christian world, was still in the process of being rebuilt according to the grandiose schemes of Julius II, who defied the Sacred College, the commune of Rome and public opinion throughout Christendom when he ordered that the old church be pulled down to make way for a more fitting building. Even during the pontificate of Julius II it had been noted that rebuilding did not move forward very fast, for the whole scheme proved to be appallingly expensive. Whenever war or diplomacy made more pressing demands on the papal treasury the rebuilding of St Peter's was apt to be temporarily abandoned, and in the early sixteenth century warfare was almost a normal condition of life in Italy.

From the square in front of St Peter's ran five roads: Borgo Vecchio, Borgo Sant'Angelo, Borgo Santo Spirito, Borgo Pio and Borgo Nuovo. This last had been built by Alexander VI for the jubilee of 1500 and had been erected in only nine months.

At its far end, on the banks of the Tiber, rose the great papal fortress of Castel Sant'Angelo, which in the time of Alexander VI had been connected to the Vatican palace by a raised corridor down which a pope might flee in time of trouble into his impregnable fortress. For impregnable Sant'Angelo was; if properly supplied it could withstand siege for years. In form a large imposing tower of stone and bricks, Castel Sant'Angelo has played an enduring part in Roman history. It had been built originally not as a fortress but as a tomb, by the Emperor Hadrian, and here all the emperors from Hadrian to Septimius Severus were buried. The first changes in the building were made by Aurelius, who enclosed the powerful building within his city wall, and it became at first a stronghold and then a real fortress which for centuries was to play an important part in the defence of Rome.

Castel Sant'Angelo in its modern dress is largely the creation of Alexander VI and of his favourite architect, Antonio da Sangallo. During Alexander's pontificate the building was completely refortified with parapets and towers, and was surrounded by a wall and ditch. The old gate in the wall of the fortress was replaced by a newer and larger entrance, a strong tower was added to command the bridge over the Tiber, and the outworks of the castle were strengthened.

In the area between St Peter's and Castel Sant'Angelo there were to be found many hospitals, monasteries and hostels for pilgrims. It was a beautiful and distinguished area of the city; Borgo Vecchio and Borgo Nuovo, together with Piazza San Giacomo Scossacavalli, were already enriched by great palaces, among them the Penitenzieri (begun 1480), Palazzo Soderini and Palazzo Castelli (Giraud-Torlonia), the residence of the English ambassadors to Rome, which Bramante had built about 1503. Along Borgo Sant'Angelo stretched many gardens and walks from which one could look out over the Roman countryside.

Leaving the Borgo and crossing over Ponte Sant'Angelo the visitor to Rome entered Rione Ponte. Here two roads would take him into the populated districts: Canale di Ponte and Via di Panico which went as far as Monte Giordano. This was the most lively area of the city. Here was the financial centre of Rome, here were the *banchi*, and here lived bankers, merchants, curialists, *literati*, jewellers, booksellers and the most popular courtesans. Normally the governor of the city resided in Ponte where, in Tor di Nona, were the city dungeons. The most famous engravers, silversmiths and artists also resided in Ponte, for the papal mint was located there and acted as a powerful magnet for the talented. During the pontificate of Leo X many northern Italians settled in the area and erected new buildings of which many were remarkable for their great beauty: Palazzo Cicciaporci, built for Giulio Alteriori in 1521, Palazzo Lante ai Capretari, built by Jacopo Sansovino, and Palazzo Maccaroni, built by Giulio Romano for the Cenci family.

It was in the aristocratic district of Parione, however, that the greatest of the great palaces were to be found: the Cancellaria, the three palaces of the Massimi, Palazzo Millini in Via dell'Anima and Palazzo Sanguigni between San Apollinare and Piazza Navona, the market-place of Rome. This was the famous oblong piazza which had served in antiquity as the field of Domitian's stadium for Greek foot-races or *agones*. By a natural process over the centuries the name *platea in agone* gradually evolved into Piazza

Navona, and the place itself had become the heart of Roman city-life. In the centre of the piazza stood the most famous statue in Rome. In origin probably a Hellenestic Hercules, it had at some time been renamed Pasquino and it became the bulletin board for all the squibs, scandals and lampoons of Renaissance Rome. Around the piazza, in the little streets running behind it, many pastry-cooks, often of French origin, had settled, and supplied luxury goods to the great palaces.

Rione San Eustachio was the home of the University, which dated from the pontificate of Eugenius IV. The university palace, the Sapienza, had been begun during the pontificate of Leo X to a design of Michelangelo, but was as yet unfinished. San Eustachio was also the centre of various industries, most notably of soap manufacture.

The adjoining Rione Pigna was very distinguished; from the earliest times the old Roman nobility, the Altieri, the Astalli and the Leni had their palaces there, and Rione Sant'Angelo which was dominated by the Santa Croce family was scarcely less aristocratic. Ripa, on the other hand, although important as a port and full of ancient ruins, was undistinguished; and the enormous Rione Campitelli which stretched from the Campidoglio to the city-wall was largely uninhabited. Rione Trevi stretched on the right side of what is now the Corso as far as Piazza Colonna and the Quirinal (Monte Cavallo). In the Middle Ages this had been covered by vineyards, but these were gradually being replaced by villas.

Campo Marzio was the area of greatest growth in the sixteenth century. Its development was fostered by the existence of Ripetta, a port with traffic nearly as intense as that of Ripa Grande, and by Clement's development of Piazza del Popolo, Via Lata, Via dei Popoli and Via del Babuino. After 1520 the *rione* became a favoured haunt of artists and artisans, and many new houses and workshops were being built there. By contrast, Rione Monte was virtually uninhabited, while Trastevere, with its many ancient fortified houses, towers and religious buildings retained a characteristically medieval appearance.

Successive popes had done much to make Rome a beautiful city but in doing so they had certainly weakened the city's defences. There were very obvious vulnerable areas. There were too many

Giulio de' Medici, Pope Clement VII, portrait by Sebastiano del Piombo, presumably painted after the Sack of Rome, since it shows him with the long beard which he grew as a sign of mourning

Late fifteenth-century view of Rome, a map for the guidance of pilgrims visiting the city

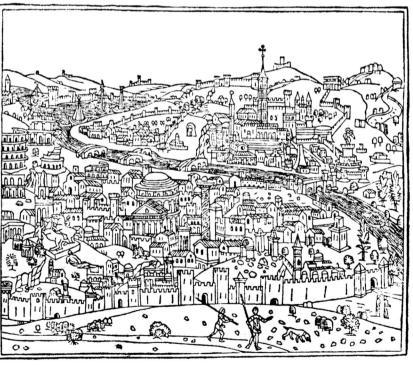

Charles V, by Titian

'The sunset he tilts at is big Venetian stuff,
The true Charles, done by Titian, never lived.
The struggle he rides offstage to is offstage.'
Robert Lowell, *Notebook*

gates for all to be defended adequately, but the very size of Rome made them all essential. There were, after all, many traditional approaches to the city. Travelling from the north or from Ancona by way of Farfa, along the Via Flaminia, a visitor entered the city through Porta del Popolo, the principal entrance to Rome and that traditionally used on ceremonial occasions. To the east, the next gate on the wall, the Pinciana, also gave access to the north. Further east were Porta Salaria and Porta San Agnese through which, after passing the baths of Diocletian, a road ran out to the church of San Agnese in Agone. Stretching south-east for some distance there was a tract of wall before the gate of San Lorenzo fuori Muros. The Via Praenestina and the Via Labinica entered the city from the east through Porta Maggiore, whence a road ran to the populated quarter around Santa Maria Maggiore. South-east, Porta San Giovanni in Lateran gave access to the important church of the same name which lay almost against the city wall. Due south were Porta Latina, and beyond that Porta Appia. The last gate on the Aurelian wall was Porta San Paolo through which travellers to Ostia had to pass.

Of the gates of Trastevere the most southerly was Porta Portuensis, and on the west was the Porta Aurelia. To the north the Lungara, connecting Trastevere with the Borgo Leonino, passed through Porta Settimania which had been rebuilt by Alexander VI. The Lungara entered the Borgo through Porta San Spirito. Beyond this gate to the north was Porta Posterula, and on the northern wall itself were the two gates of the Pertosa and the Vatican. On the east were Porta San Pietro and Porta di Castel Sant'Angelo.

A contemporary military strategist would also have concluded that Rome had too many bridges. North of the city and outside the walls the Tiber was bridged by Ponte Molle (Milvio), a medieval bridge which gave access to the Via Flaminia, the Via Cassia and the Via Clodia. In origin a classical bridge, the ends had been demolished and replaced with wood which could easily be destroyed in time of war. Within the walls of Rome the first bridge was at Castel Sant'Angelo; it gave access to the Borgo from Rome. The Sistine bridge was built on the site of the old Pons Agrippae which fell into disuse in the Middle Ages and had to be rebuilt by Sixtus IV and Julius II. Downstream were the two bridges of the

Isola Tiberina, and immediately below that the Ponte Santa Maria, the largest bridge in Rome, which had frequently been rebuilt, for it was the quickest route from the Campidoglio to Trastevere.

The bridges crossed what was essentially the main commercial thoroughfare of Rome. The Tiber was a vital channel of communication, particularly in the absence of any adequate road to the coast. Large vessels bound for Rome docked at Civitàvecchia where they were unloaded into small boats which made their way to Ostia and up the Tiber.

The Tiber was still the quickest communication-route within the city, but new roads were now being built to replace the medieval maze of alleys and passages. The Campidoglio and the Vatican were linked by two roads, the Via Peregrinorum and the Via Papale. The latter was the road used by the pope after his coronation, when he proceeded from St Peter's to the Lateran in solemn procession for the ceremony known as *il possesso* when he assumed the temporal power of the papacy. The traveller reaching Rome from the north already had the choice of two roads by which to enter the city: the Via Trionfale which led across Monte Mario to the Borgo near the Vatican, or the Flaminia which passed through Porta del Popolo. From Piazza del Popolo the traveller might either pass direct down the Via Lata to the Campidoglio or take the Via dei Popoli to Piazza Navona. This complex of roads was the work of Clement VII, who was largely responsible for its completion. Two roads ran along the Tiber: the Lungara on the north bank of the river, and the Via Giulia on the south, which ran from the new church San Giovanni dei Fiorentini to the Sistine bridge.

Between these main thoroughfares, ran higgledy-piggledy the streets, lanes, *rioni* and alleys where the population of Rome laboured and was housed. It was a population which was probably increasing, having reached a total of about 55,000.[10] This population was essentially cosmopolitan. There was a very large Jewish ghetto, divided between the *rioni* Sant'Angelo, Ripa and Regola. This Jewish community had grown considerably during the pontificates of Alexander VI and Julius II, who had welcomed refugees from Spain, Portugal and Provence. More refugees flooded into Rome in the pontificate of Leo X, who encouraged Jews at the papal court and ordered the Talmud to be printed at the Hebrew printing press in the Piazza Montanara. But the Jews were but one of the foreign elements in this international city. It is possible that as many as one-quarter of the inhabitants of Rome came from outside Italy, and the most important single group were those from the Iberian peninsula. There may have been as many as 7000 Spaniards living in Rome in the pontificate of Clement VII.[11] Germans also were present in Rome in large numbers engaged mainly in the hotel industry or in the meat trade. The first two printers in Rome had been Teutonic in origin, and Germans continued to dominate the printing industry. There were in addition important German bankers, although Clement broke the monopolising hold which the Fugger had held over papal finances since 1495. The papal guard was Swiss, and at least ten per cent of the household of Leo X had been German. If Clement was to engage in a struggle with the emperor who ruled both Spain and Germany he must face the fact that he had a very large potential fifth-column within the weak walls of his city.

CHAPTER II

POPE AND EMPEROR

*I shall go into Italy and revenge myself on those who have injured me,
especially on that poltroon the Pope. Some day, perhaps, Martin Luther
will become a man of weight.*

Charles V

ON the election of Clement VII none could have been more
enthusiastic than the imperial servants of Charles V, king
of Spain and the Indies, Holy Roman Emperor, and ruler
of the Netherlands. At the close of the conclave which elected
Clement, the duke of Sessa wrote to Charles: 'The Pope is entirely
your Majesty's creature. So great is your Majesty's power that you
can change stones into obedient children.'[1] It is strange that it was
not yet understood at the court of the emperor that it was likely
that the very nature of their offices would bring pope and emperor
into conflict. Yet, within months of Clement's election, the in-
evitability of such conflict was obvious, even were the pope to
remain uninvolved in the international struggle between Spain
and France.

Neutrality, although desired by the pope, was likely to prove an
impossibility. There had already been war in Italy for a generation.
Between 1494 and 1519 it was a war between France, Spain and
the Swiss confederation *for* Italy, but in 1519 the nature of the war
changed. In 1516 the Swiss had been finally defeated and had
relinquished their interests in Italy; and three years later Charles,
ruler of the Netherlands, the most prosperous area of Europe
after Italy, and ruler too of Spain, became the Emperor Charles V.
From this date onwards Charles was engaged in a deadly struggle
with Francis I of France for control of the whole of the western
Mediterranean and for dominance in Europe.

It was in the nature of Charles's inheritance that the struggle
should be played out in Italy. Before everything else Charles was
emperor, a man with a dream of justified world dominion that he
had inherited from his medieval ancestors. Charles V lived in a
half-world between the Middle Ages and the modern world, pur-

suing medieval ambitions by modern – often surprisingly modern – means. To the Italians the fact that Charles had imperial claims was all-important, for it meant that in Italy he would have a legal cloak for anything he chose to do. The Italians knew there would be nothing to wonder at if the emperor talked himself into occupying other people's lands. In a certain sense the whole world belonged to him, and the world needed this dominion. Christendom was threatened once more by Islam, by Islam on the offensive, and from the medieval past the idea survived that it was the emperor's duty to defend the civilized world against the barbarian. It was significant that such a role fitted in with the reality of the political world of Charles V, for everywhere the recent successes of the Ottoman Turks had brought them within striking distance of his dominions – in Naples, Sardinia, Sicily, Vienna and even Spain.

Charles's imperial ambitions were not empty. He ruled a larger empire than the world had ever known, and was thus the first emperor powerful enough to make good imperial pretensions in Italy. Here he was already complete master of Sicily, Naples and Sardinia, and, as the two most recent conclaves had shown, he had a controlling voice in the fortunes of the papacy. Nor was the emperor without his Italian supporters. Those who had profited from the anti-Turkish and anti-French policies of Charles V's maternal grandfather, Ferdinand of Aragon, spoke in relation to Charles V of the 'benevolence of Caesar'. Others, more realistic, looked at the success of Spanish armies in Italy and spoke of the emperor's desire for the 'monarchy of Italy'. It was forgotten that at the time of the Catholic monarchs Ferdinand and Isabella, the Spanish had only been drawn reluctantly into Italy to counterbalance the French and to check the developing Turkish seapower, and that at that time the Italians had welcomed Spanish troops in their peninsula.

Those Italians who feared the 'monarchy of Italy', and those who relied on 'benevolence', were united in believing that the emperor was concerned with little except Italy. Like the emperor's own chancellor Gattinara, himself an Italian in origin, they believed that the very nature of emperorship involved Italy as a primary factor. Gattinara was merely expressing a political commonplace of the time when he argued that since God had called Charles to be the first prince in Christendom it was only fitting that he should concern himself first with Italy. 'It seems', said the Florentine Acciauoli, 'that Caesar's appetite is so set on this occupation of Italy that he would rather lose Austria and all its neighbouring provinces than remain the loser in this enterprise, and whatever money he manages to accumulate he will devote first to the subversion of Italy.'[2] It is doubtful whether such high-flown notions of the imperial office were reflected in the political thinking of Charles V who, although he had inherited a vigorous Italian policy from his grandfather, was concerned with Italy only in so far as it affected his plans for dealing with the triple menace of the Turk, the French and Lutheran Germany.

Within Italy no contemporary was able to distinguish between the executive and the administrative powers of the empire. It was generally believed that the emperor's servants always acted under explicit instructions. The emperor certainly aimed to neutralize Italy, and whenever possible Charles gave the fullest possible instructions for achieving that end; but communications were long and untrustworthy – in the winter usually non-existent – and inevitably those operating in the field had to be left the largest possible latitude of action. Even in the summer it took at least five weeks for news to reach Spain from Italy, and in the winter it was not uncommon for imperialists in Italy to be without any message from Spain for two months or more. Their letters home to Spain were full of complaints that they had been forgotten and were neglected. Yet even neglect could be preferable to some instructions. Charles V consistently revealed his total ignorance of Italy; in September 1525 Mendoza had to point out to the emperor that the peace arrangements he had made with the papacy were completely unworkable on practical grounds. Charles had promised to withdraw his troops from the Church State and from the duchy of Milan; but Mantua and Montferrat, which he had designated as quarters for the infantry, had no room for them.[3]

Despite his remoteness, Charles was aware that as emperor he stood in a peculiar historical relationship to Italy where the ancient struggle between pope and emperor, long exhausted in the rest of Europe, was still a reality. In 1522 there were still many people alive who remembered the half-crazed emperor Maximilian, Charles V's paternal grandfather, who had planned to unite in one person the supreme power of both pope and emperor. Charles V's anachronistic pretensions were of more importance in Italy than in Germany, for they enabled him to adopt a peculiarly arrogant view of the papacy and the Church that fitted in ideally with his general political policies.

'You must know', Guicciardini told the pope, 'that the emperor has a special relationship with the Church, so that, in a way, it is in the nature of his office that he should think about the reform and good government of the Church.' In this terrible age, when all the old landmarks seemed to be disappearing, when Christendom was threatened by the twin menace of the Lutheran heresy and the aggressive Islamic empire of the Ottoman Turk, it seemed to many that the pope was incapable of making head against the Protestant revolt, incapable of preventing the total subversion of all things and the end of the established order, and that the emperor was the only possible bulwark against an oncoming storm. All this worked to the advantage of Charles V. To put it even at its lowest level, the emperor was in a position to use against a recalcitrant papacy the very spiritual weapons that the pope himself might hope to use. An arrogant attitude towards the papacy was also fostered by the emperor's belief that Adrian VI and Clement VII were imperial clients, or as contemporaries put it 'the emperor's chaplains', and this basic misconception permanently bedevilled relations between pope and emperor.

From the beginning Charles and Clement quarrelled and quarrelled vigorously over patronage and provisions to benefices in the kingdom of Naples and in Spain. They quarrelled equally vigorously over Clement's choice of friends; Charles disliked Clement's family alliance with the Orsini, but he objected even more strongly to the new pope's choice of advisers.

Since it suited Clement's temperament to delay as long as possible and to consult a wide spectrum of opinion before coming to a decision, he surrounded himself with councillors of conflicting opinions. Unlike other rulers the popes could call on talent from any country in the Christian world to assist in the government of the Church, and throughout his pontificate Clement made full use of this potential. First and foremost, though, came family and clan solidarity, and at the heart of Clement's entourage were the Medici relatives. There were the three cardinal-nephews, Cybo, Ridolfi and Salviati, although only Salviati, a man of considerable wisdom and experience in politics, with a leaning towards the imperialist cause, 'a great servant of the emperor',[4] was regularly used by Clement in council. Both Salviati and Ridolfi favoured Venice and a Venetian alliance.[5] Then there was Filippo Strozzi one of the wealthiest men in Europe, and his wife Clarice de' Medici, the sister of Duke Lorenzo of Urbino, a capable and intelligent woman with a hearty dislike of Clement.

Apart from his family, Clement's most intimate advisers were Schomberg, the datary Giberti, Armellino, Benedetto Accolti, a consistent supporter of the Medici who had first been promoted by Leo X and now became papal secretary, Cardinal Accolti the cardinal of Ancona, who was a close friend of Sadoleto, the Genoese Agostino Foglietta, Alberto Pio, and at a later date Guicciardini. Schomberg was a native of Saxony but had arrived in Italy while he was still young to study law. In Florence he had fallen under the spell of Savonarola and had entered the Dominican order. In 1520 Leo X made him archbishop of Capua, and Clement appointed him as his secretary of state. Schomberg was now in his fifties, a mature and experienced man but a convinced imperialist. Clement's relations with the emperor could often, therefore, be gauged by whether or not Schomberg was being used in government. When Charles was out of favour with the pope Schomberg's work was taken over by Alberto Pio, the dispossessed prince of Carpi. Giovan Matteo Giberti was only half Schomberg's age but held one of the most important offices in the papal administration. In origin the datariat was the office where the date was appended to papal bulls, but in time the datary had acquired responsibility for most of the spiritual affairs of the church. By Giberti's time the datariat was one of the most overworked of papal offices, and the datary had become a person of the greatest importance. As the months passed Clement came to rely more and more on Giberti, and in all matters concerning ecclesiastical questions he accepted Giberti's decisions without question.[6] But Giberti's policies were totally incompatible with those of Schomberg as Giberti gradually came to believe that only the defeat of Charles V by France could save Italy. It was from his father that Giberti inherited a great love of Venice, 'to which I have always been devoted, since I seem to see in her a true image of the ancient greatness and the true liberty of Italy'.[7] It was presumably also his father's influence which convinced Giberti of the necessity of preventing the predominance of any one power in Italy, and that freedom of the state and freedom to reform the Church went hand in hand. By nature Giberti seems to have had little liking for political life, and seems in this respect to have shared many of Clement's feelings. A member of the Oratorio del Divino Amore, he counted among his close friends Sadoleto, Contarini, Gaetano da Thiene, Caraffa, Bembo, Vittoria Colonna and Reginald de la Pole. This last friendship probably explains Giberti's great admiration for England and for Henry VIII from whom he always hoped for much, although these hopes were to prove illusory. For obvious reasons Charles V always disliked Giberti and his influence with the pope and, comparing the position of predominance which Clement had held in his cousin's pontificate to that which he believed was held by Giberti, he remarked that it was strange that 'when the pope was Cardinal de' Medici he was pope, and now that he is pope wants another to be pope in his stead'.[8]

Among the cardinals resident in Rome there were distinct pressure-groups. There were the young cardinals, represented by Farnese, who was anti-imperial and pro-Venetian although he had little sympathy with France, and who had connexions with the Orsini family. Opposed to the Farnese were the Colonna supporters including Jacobacci and dal Monte. There were the legalists like Cardinal Pucci, a great canon-lawyer, famous for his support of established usage, and the pro-English cardinals, Accolti, dal Monte, and Campeggio, the gentle Erasmian who had become well versed in the affairs of the Holy See during the pontificate of Adrian VI. In moments of crisis Clement was quite capable of consulting all these groups, attempting to keep a balance between them. Overwhelmed as he was by work and advice there is little wonder that decision-making was difficult, or that Francesco Gonzaga should compare him to a boat buffeted hither and thither by contrary winds.[9] And every decision which the pope had to make sooner or later was bound to involve his steadily worsening relationship with the emperor.

As it became apparent that Clement VII would not always act according to imperial desires there were open to Charles V two courses. He might use his imperial power, political and spiritual, to depose the pope and replace him by a more compliant one. This was the plan favoured and urged by Pompeio Colonna, who hoped to fill the future role of a compliant imperial pope. The alternative, which for obvious reasons Colonna would not have favoured, was to reduce the papacy to such a state of dependence on the emperor that no pope thereafter would be able to pursue an independent policy. The single prerequisite for either course of action was the capture of Rome and of Clement VII, and the opportunity to implement such a plan depended on the fortunes of the war with France.

Neither Francis I nor Charles V intervened in Italy for the sake of the Italians. They fought out in Italy a much wider struggle: over Burgundy; over control of the western Mediterranean; and, on the part of the French, over the encirclement of their country. It was convenient that this power struggle should be played out in Italy, for the peninsula offered many opportunities to foreign intervention through the divisions and rivalries of the small powers who divided the rule of Italy between them. But, although the peninsula remained politically divided and therefore weak, Italy as a whole was both prosperous and powerful and therefore naturally attractive to the rulers of both Spain and France, who had been struggling since 1494 for control of Naples and Milan.

In later years Charles V was to declare, 'My cousin Francis and I are in complete accord; he wants Milan and so do I.' The importance of Milan lay not so much in her wealth, which a quarter-century of warfare had rendered negligible, as in the strategic interests of other countries in Lombardy. By 1525 this meant the interest of France and Spain, for after 1515 the Swiss were too weak to intervene decisively in Lombardy, although they had a considerable interest in preventing it falling to the emperor, and the Venetians were no longer expanding in the area. But the emperor and the French remained peculiarly obstinate over Milan and neither was prepared to abandon its control to the other. Charles V could not permit France to hold the duchy, for, if she did, a vital link in the internal communications of his vast empire would be lost, together with the possibility of controlling Genoa, on whose shipyards, banking facilities and port he depended. Possession of Milan would enable Charles V to defend Naples, contain Venice and dominate Italy.

The first victory in the duel between Francis I and the Spanish for control of Milan went to Francis, for in 1515, the year of his accession, he led the largest army yet seen in Italy, an army of 40,000 men, over a new Alpine pass into Lombardy. The Swiss, defending the duchy of Milan for its duke, Massimiliano Sforza, came out to meet the French. At Marignano, a few miles from Milan, a furious battle raged for two days; Francis himself fought in the midst of it and was knighted on the spot by the Chevalier de Bayard, the last great chivalric figure of European history. The Swiss left 13,000 dead on the field when they finally acknowledged defeat. With this victory Francis gained complete control over northern Italy, for Massimiliano Sforza surrendered his duchy and and was taken off to an honourable prison in France.

Yet French control of Milan proved ephemeral. In 1513 Leo X had been elected pope, and, although in most of the causes in dispute between the great powers of Europe he was prepared to appear neutral, it was a consistent intention of his policy that Sforza should be restored to Milan. In 1521 combined papal and imperial forces chased the French army from Lombardy. Milan was won with scarcely a blow being struck and was restored to its native line of dukes in the person of the effeminate and weak Francesco Maria Sforza. Over the next three years France was driven onto the defensive until on 12 December 1524, alarmed by the success of the emperor in Italy, Clement VII, Venice and Florence joined in a secret alliance with France, an alliance which became public on 5 January 1525. On the pope's part, at least, the treaty was dictated by expediency; the French commander, John Stuart, duke of Albany, was already marching through the Church State on his way to Naples.

Charles V, however, when he heard of the treaty, would accept none of the arguments of necessity. Such an action on the part of the pope could only be regarded as treachery, a treachery which could not be forgiven, for Clement had been his protégé. 'I shall go into Italy and revenge myself on those who have injured me,' raged the emperor, 'especially on that poltroon the Pope. Some day, perhaps, Martin Luther will become a man of weight.'[10]

Scarcely any alliance has been more ill-timed than this 'Italian League'. With covert support from Venice and the pope, French troops had already re-entered Italy, seized Milan and besieged

Pavia. In February 1525 the French northern army was well entrenched in the park of Mirabello near Pavia; it had everything to gain if it remained stationary. But, contrary to all reason, the French command challenged the imperial army under George von Frundsberg and the marquess of Pescara. In one of the most decisive battles of history the French army was almost annihilated; poor tactics nullified the strong French artillery, and the Spanish troops proved their superiority to the Swiss infantry on which the French army was dependent. No one could question the gallantry of the French king, although they might well have serious reservations about his wisdom. While his troops retreated he pressed forward; his horse was killed under him and he fought on on foot until, totally exhausted, he surrendered to the imperial forces. From the tent, hurriedly provided for him by his embarrassed captors, he wrote to his mother, 'All is lost save honour – and my skin which is safe.'

Pavia was a battle which overnight changed the whole complexion of European affairs. There was no need now for anti-imperial propaganda to convince Italians that, before everything else, they must break the hold of Charles V over Italy. The message was underlined by the kind of noises coming from Spain. Here the ideas of Mercurino Gattinara were temporarily in the ascendant; from the imperial chancery came a flood of propaganda proclaiming the messianic mission of the emperor. Pavia was clearly a divine miracle, for now the emperor would be able to press on to recapture Constantinople and Jerusalem, and the whole world would be united under the just dominion of Charles V.[11]

On a more mundane and realistic level there were certain immediate advantages to be gained from the success at Pavia. For as long as Charles went on fighting Francis I and other Christian princes he would find it difficult to take the offensive against the Turks who were threatening his empire. Charles, too, was unhappy about his German inheritance. In 1521 at the Diet of Worms Luther had raised the standard of revolt against the emperor, or so at least it seemed to Charles. The emperor had forbidden Luther's doctrines within the empire, but they continued to spread. Charles came to believe that an internal reform of the Church could put an end to such heresy and that, for reform to begin, the Church must first call a general council. But a general council would be one in name only if half of Christendom absented itself, and for as long as Charles was at war with his neighbours he knew that they would not come. So his programme must be first a general European peace, then a council of the Church, and, at the last, a crusade against the Turkish empire.

This was the emperor's reasoning, and it seemed that what obstructed him was his inability to control events in Italy. He was thwarted at every turn by the pope and the Venetian Republic. Even Florence was still capable of upsetting the peace of Europe by intriguing with the French and subsidizing French expeditions into Italy. Charles had good advisers on Italian affairs – men like Gattinara, like the great Neapolitan prince and soldier Hugo da Moncada, and the wily Perez, and all of these were agreed in advising Charles V to make himself immediate master of Italy.

The emperor had agents and allies throughout Italy. One of his most important alliances was with the great family of the Colonna, and five days after Pavia the Colonna brought the emperor's quarrel to the pope's own doorstep. Francis I's attack on the imperialists in Italy had included that *sine qua non* for any French intervention in Italy, an attack on Naples. On this occasion the forlorn hope had been entrusted to the duke of Albany. Even before Pavia Albany had realized the futility of this attack and had withdrawn to rejoin the king in the north, accompanied by the pope's kinsmen and the French king's allies – the Orsini family with their armed retainers. On 2 March only a few miles outside Rome they were surprised by the Colonna, whose numbers had been swollen by the guard and servants of the Spanish ambassador at Rome, the duke of Sessa. When Albany and the Orsini fled into Rome they were pursued, and soon the whole city of Rome was engaged in a battle which the pope was powerless to prevent. The Piazza Giudea and Monte Giordano in particular were the scenes of bloody battles in which the Roman partisans of both sides showed no hesitation in joining. The pope was justifiably incensed that his authority should be flouted even in his own city. Even more was he perturbed by the activities of the imperialists in Siena.

For the little republic of Siena had become the first victim of imperial ambition after Pavia. Charles was not without justification in intervening in Sienese affairs, but then what prince in Europe could not have made out a justification, based on real or supposed rights in the little state? Throughout its proverbially chequered history Siena had fallen into the habit of calling in outside help from anyone willing to give it. Most frequently, Siena sought assistance from all those who pursued an anti-Florentine policy, for, from time immemorial, Siena had been at odds with Florence over border rights, disputed territories and the protection of exiles. Such minor conflicts symbolized a much deeper hostility; Siena had long played a commercial role far inferior to that of Florence but she was jealous of her independence, which she rightly feared was threatened by Florentine ambition. So the border between the two states was always disturbed, providing frequent opportunities for the intervention of external powers, while within the city rival factions contended for power, one of the dominant parties having links with the Orsini, the Medici and the French, and one with the Colonna and the imperialists.

In 1521 the French had helped to instal Alessandro Bichi as head of the republic of Siena, and for four years he had ruled, trying, with some success, to break down the divisions which existed in this faction-rent city. Three months after Pavia he was murdered by supporters of the emperor in the city, who overthrew the government and set up an alternative régime which encouraged Charles V to think of the Sienese as 'inhabitants of Valladolid or of any other town in Spain'.[12]

Reflecting gloomily on the aftermath of Pavia, the Italians became convinced that the emperor not only regarded the inhabitants of Siena in this light, but regarded the whole of Italy as a subject province. They seemed helpless in the face of his victorious armies. And yet, desperate as affairs appeared to the Italians, and to the French, prostrated by the shocking news from Italy, they looked little brighter to the emperor's servants and generals in Italy. They had achieved the unthinkable – they had captured the French king in open battle, they had destroyed his army, and they had captured Milan. But they could not solve two elementary problems: how they were to supply and how they were to pay their army. On the very day that Pavia was fought the imperial army's arrears of pay already amounted to 600,000 ducats and there was still no indication as to how this sum was to be raised. In fact, there was not a ruler in Europe who had solved this logistical problem, for the truth was that no state was financially strong enough to support armies of the size that were now commonly deployed in Italian campaigns. That was one reason why Charles and Francis preferred to fight in Italy; they knew it to be wealthy and hoped that their armies would support themselves by conquest and pillage. In this way war could be made to pay for itself, but at a terrible cost. The soldiers became demoralized by constant looting, and their attention was fixed more on making profits from war than on successful war-making. It meant, too, that every government's bargaining position was weakened by the inevitable need to provide somehow, anyhow, for the maintenance of armies that could not be financed in any normal way.

So it was after Pavia. The imperialists should have been in a position of overwhelming strength in Italy. They should have been able to negotiate a position of such security as to put an end to all further fighting. This did not happen. The imperialists entered into negotiations but not for a political settlement. Their aim was to extract money from the Italian powers who were prepared to buy a breathing-space in the war.

The Italians proved surprisingly stubborn when it came to paying out hard cash in this way. The pope was particularly difficult, and it was decided to apply a little pressure and relieve supply difficulties by sending part of the imperial army to occupy the area around Piacenza. At the same time the Colonna embarked on a series of raids on Orsini territory. In the face of this dual threat Clement VII capitulated, and an agreement was hurriedly signed on 1 April 1525. It was an agreement which would benefit both parties if either observed it. There were important financial clauses; Florence was bullied into agreeing to pay 100,000 ducats, and the pope promised to pay the imperialists a further 100,000 if Lannoy, the viceroy of Naples, could persuade the duke of Ferrara to give him back Reggio and Rubiera. As this was recognized as being an extremely unlikely eventuality the pope extracted additional concessions: the imperialists promised to maintain the ineffectual Francesco Sforza in his duchy of Milan, to withdraw their troops from the pope's territory, and to maintain the pope's rights in Naples. Charles V was to ratify the treaty within four months.

On the same financial basis the imperialists made peace with other Italian states. Lucca paid 10,000 ducats for the dubious privilege of being placed under imperial protection, and Montferrat and Siena paid 15,000 ducats for the same privilege. Since all three were within striking distance of the imperial army they were in no position to forgo its proffered protection. Francesco Sforza, whose state was actually occupied by the army, had similarly little choice and promised to pay the emperor 600,000 ducats if Charles gave him the investiture of Milan.

The agreements were as worthless as the paper on which they had been written.

CHAPTER III

MORONE'S CONSPIRACY AND THE LEAGUE OF COGNAC

. . . although the enemy spread abroad hopes of peace – yet so great is their desire to destroy Italy and successfully establish the Monarchy that, forgetting more important matters, while they attempt to lull our suspicions with gentle words, they are on the other hand making every possible effort to effect the opposite.

Guicciardini

THE Italians were always to claim that if Charles V had observed the agreements made in 1525 general peace would have come to Italy, that general peace which was to escape the emperor for another five years. Certainly those were right who asserted that the imperialists never intended to observe the agreements in question. When Lannoy wrote to the emperor to inform him of the arrangements he had made in Italy he advised the emperor never to ratify the treaties, and Charles acted on this advice. In the following months when he wrote to his lieutenants in Italy he did not speak of peace but of punishment and chastisement, particularly of the fickle pope, of the proud and obstinate Venetian republic, and of francophile Florence. Lannoy made no move to urge the duke of Ferrara to surrender Reggio and Rubiera as agreed; and he left his troops quartered in the Church State. Clement put the worst possible construction on the behaviour of Lannoy and Pescara, for spies had already told him of the contempt in which the Italians were held at the imperial court. He knew that those servants of the emperor in Italy with whom he had but recently signed an agreement were writing to Spain urging Charles V to give papal Modena to the duke of Ferrara, to restore the exiled family of the Bentivoglii to their former ruling position in the papal city of Bologna, and to take over direct rule of Florence, Siena and Lucca.[1]

On the other hand, Italian arguments that they intended peace in 1525 cannot be accepted at their face value. Only twenty days after

Pavia a league was projected between Venice, the papacy, Florence, Siena, Lucca, Mantua and Milan. Such a league would not be easy to achieve nor would its purpose be easy to fulfil. As the Venetians, the moving spirits in these negotiations, argued, no league would be strong enough to resist the emperor unless it contained both the papacy and Ferrara. But how could such a league be created while the duke of Ferrara and the pope continued to quarrel about their disputed claim to Modena and Reggio?

This quarrel was the despair of all Italy where it had bedevilled diplomatic activity for more than a century. Ferrara owed its existence to its location on the commercial route between Bologna and Venice, to its value as a market town and, particularly with changing methods of warfare, to its strategic position: permanently protected by the Po, it was a natural fortress. The legal position in relation to Ferrara and the papacy was peculiarly difficult. Supposedly included in the territory given to the papacy by Pepin III and Charlemagne, Ferrara had again been conveyed to the Church by the Countess Matilda in 1107. The commune of Ferrara had seen no objection to formally acknowledging papal overlordship as long as it could continue to govern itself, which it had done quite successfully until, in the thirteenth century, it fell under the control of the Este family. From the point of view of the future history of the duchy it was unfortunate that through their hereditary lands, situated some forty miles north of Ferrara, the Estensi happened to be imperial subjects. From 1208 the Estensi ruled Ferrara, technically as vassals of the papacy, but practically as independent lords, their power reaching its greatest extent under Duke Niccolò III, who at the beginning of the fourteenth century ruled not only Ferrara but also Rovigo, Modena, Reggio, Parma and, briefly, Milan. Herein lay the seeds of future dissension with the papacy for, in the sixteenth century, it was over Modena and Reggio that successive popes quarrelled with the dukes of Ferrara. The Este family held these two towns by imperial investiture until they were captured by Julius II. Almost immediately they were ceded by Julius to the Emperor Maximilian, who later sold them to Leo X. And Leo had complicated the issue by promising to return them to Duke Alfonso d'Este after the battle of Marignano in 1515, and then failing to do so. By 1525 the quarrel between Este and the papacy over Modena and Reggio had reached such a pitch that they could not work together, even to keep the ultra-montane powers out of Italy.

If Ferrara was not to be part of an Italian League, it was essential to compensate for its absence by the inclusion of some non-Italian power, in the traditional Italian manner of setting a thief to catch a thief. The most obvious candidate was France – whose king was now hailed publicly as the saviour of Italy, despite his temporary sojourn in a Spanish prison.

By the summer of 1525 conditions were ripe for the formation of a league against the emperor. The motives of those wishing to join the League differed considerably. It is true, nonetheless, that Clement VII and Venice were united in their belief that Milan should be secured from all foreign interference. Indeed, Clement VII professed to believe that the only motive for entering the League must be to support the Sforza in Milan.

Clement's policies on Milan were remarkably consistent throughout his life. During the pontificate of Leo X when, as Cardinal Giulio de' Medici, he had played a substantial part in framing papal policy, Clement had held exactly the same views. Milan must be ruled, neither by France nor by Spain, but by its own native dukes. This was the policy which, from the first days of his pontificate, Clement had pressed on the emperor. But it is impossible to believe that Francis I shared the pope's beliefs. The French had fought almost continuously for a quarter-century in order to take Milan for themselves, and French adherence to a league, ostensibly directed towards establishing an independent Milanese state, cannot have represented the abandonment of French claims to the duchy. Rather, for Francis I, it is clear that the League offered an opportunity to continue his struggle with Charles V, largely at Italian expense. The Italian League came into existence and survived as a loose military alliance of states who for many different reasons were opposing the armies of Charles V in Italy. French interests lay in Genoa, Naples and the eventual restoration of French power in Milan. Clement VII feared that the Church State would be isolated between a Spanish Milan and a Spanish Naples; that Charles V as emperor would make a reality of his territorial pretensions in Lombardy, central Italy and Tuscany, in particular in Siena, Ferrara, Modena and Reggio; and that he would come in person to Italy and summon the general council which Clement personally dreaded. Venice was apprehensive about the dangers of invasion from the north. Her constant preoccupation was that the Archduke Ferdinand might replace Sforza as duke of Milan thus leaving Venice open to constant invasion from the north and the erosion of her northern and western boundaries. Scarcely a generation earlier the Emperor Maximilian had made a series of erratic forays into northern Italy to re-establish his rights in the Veneto, and those forays had been expensive and dangerous to the Venetian state. In southern Italy also, the emperor and Venice had conflicting interests. As for Sforza, it was fear of Charles V's designs that alone drove him into the league. Sforza respected and admired Clement VII, indeed he was unique among his contemporaries in the hero-worship he accorded the pope, but equally he respected Charles V. He trusted neither France nor Venice, which he suspected of having designs on Cremona, nor Ferrara nor Mantua, while he heartily despised and cordially disliked the duke of Urbino. His only aim was survival.

All in all these various powers did not represent encouraging material from which to forge a national Italian League, but it was all the material that was available. At first things moved very slowly. For the greater part of 1525 France played little part in the negotiations. The country was exhausted, politically, economically and militarily, and such diplomatic effort as could be made by France had to be directed towards securing the release of her king from his Spanish prison. The pope, too, was initially slow to enter into the negotiations. It was a period of acute financial crisis in the Church State, and Clement VII was preoccupied by the Ottoman advance on Hungary and Austria. While he believed that Christendom was threatened by the Ottomans Clement could not be happy about negotiating with Venice, whose relationships with Constantinople at this time were extremely cordial. But by June 1525 Clement was so angry with Charles V that he was even prepared to forgive the friendship of Venice with the infidel. Despite the terms of his agreement with the pope, the emperor had failed to force Este to make restoration of Reggio or Rubiera, or to make satisfactory arrangements about the purchase of salt for the duchy of Milan. By July the pope had embarked on an overtly anti-imperial policy, and on 22 August the Venetian ambassador Domenico Venier was able to inform his government that the pope was very enthusiastic about any projected league, particularly one of which France would be a member.[2]

The imperialists were unable to obtain any direct information about these negotiations but they observed that communication between Rome, Venice and Milan was very frequent; that Giberti's influence with the pope was increasing; and that Venice was putting her state on a war-footing. Charles still seemed unable to believe that Clement might have sound political reasons for acting against him and attributed the pope's participation in the League entirely to Giberti's influence. 'Can God allow the pope always to listen to that cowardly traitor?' he demanded of the papal nuncio.

Nevertheless, immediate attempts were made from the imperial side to prevent an open breach between pope and emperor. Sessa, the imperial ambassador, was instructed to tell Clement that a satisfactory answer to all his demands was imminent.[3] Yet the imperialists had acted prematurely. The Italians were not strong enough, even united, to take on the might of the Spanish empire alone, so they needed the assistance of France, and it was not in fact until 1 September that the French ambassadors first spoke of a league to which France would contribute 40,000 ducats and which would guarantee Sforza in Milan. Naples was to be taken from Charles V, and Venice would retain the towns she held in Apulia. Venice was dubious about this scheme, believing that its eventual success would have to depend on papal adherence, and this was still uncertain. Despite considerable pressure from England and Venice, Clement was still afraid to act openly against the emperor.[4] Instead Clement had reverted to the world of intrigue and conspiracy which was fatally characteristic of Italy at this time.

Convinced that the emperor was totally opposed to all his interests, Clement lent an ear to suggestions of the possibility of persuading the marquess of Pescara to defect from the imperial cause. One of the first results of the battle of Pavia had been a major quarrel between the imperial commanders. Without consulting either Pescara or Bourbon, Lannoy spirited Francis I away to Spain, publicly claiming that he alone had been personally responsible for the imperial victory at Pavia. It was public knowledge in Italy that Pescara's many and great services to Charles V had always gone unrewarded, and it was on this knowledge, and in the belief that Pescara had quarrelled irrevocably with Lannoy, that the pope and the other Italian powers now prepared to gamble. Among his many personal friends Pescara counted Girolamo Morone, the High Chancellor of Milan, an Italian patriot whose one ambition was the liberation of Milan from all foreign control. It was through Morone that a great conspiracy against the imperialists was hatched. The Regent of France, Louise of Savoy, the mother of Francis I, had promised assistance to the pope if he acted against the emperor in Italy, and, relying on this promise, Clement approached Morone. The pope urged the necessity of a general Italian league against the emperor, to include Venice and the figurehead duke, Francesco Sforza. These allies promised to make Pescara king of Naples if he, in his turn, would undertake the military management of their plans which were nothing less than to drive all foreign troops out of Italy. The temptation for Pescara must have been great, and for a time he may even have succumbed; but the conspirators basically misread his character. Pescara was among the most hispanicised of Italians: 'In all his habits he imitated the Spaniards, delighting in their language to such an extent that even with Italians and with his own wife, Vittoria, he always spoke Spanish.'[5] And he was a man of great personal honour. He revealed to Charles the entire plot of the Italian powers; on 15 October arrested the miserable Morone; and, although already a dying man, marched his army into Milan on 2 November.

The titular head of the state Duke Francesco Sforza fled into his impregnable fortress, but for the bulk of his citizens the imperial occupation of Milan at first made little difference. Ten years before the commune of Milan had wrested virtual autonomy from its duke. The citizens were accustomed to self-government and were therefore no more willing to be bullied by the imperialists than by the French or by their native Sforza dukes. The occupying forces found themselves at a considerable disadvantage for the city remained obstinately, if politely, anti-imperial. It had been assumed that taxes on Milan would pay the arrears of the army, but once in occupation of the city the imperialists found that money could only be raised after protracted arguments, negotiations and threats. Nothing was given except under duress. It was obvious that the first task of the army must be to lay siege to the citadel, but labourers would be needed for the works and labourers could not be found. It was only when the army threatened to sack all the small towns around the capital that labourers were miraculously produced. The Milanese officials were instructed that henceforth their business must be conducted in the emperor's name. The Milanese declined to exercise their business in the name of anyone other than duke Francesco. The duke, they pointed out, had not yet been tried for his part in the conspiracy; they had been exhorted by the imperialists to preserve justice, and it seemed a strange way to begin by denying justice to their own ruler. The commune continued to honour loans which had been made against the treasury of the duchy although the imperialists wanted to appropriate the money, and at the beginning of January the city government informed the imperialists that they would swear no oath of allegiance to Charles V for as long as the city was occupied by his troops.

These were brave words but no more than words. The imperialists had superior force at their command and it could only be a matter of time before the city gave way. After some judicious billeting of unruly troops in the most recalcitrant areas of the city, and some desultory sacking of the suburbs by the Spanish troops, the commune capitulated. The officials who held their office in Sforza's name were removed and were replaced by imperial nominees at the end of February. On the 24 February the population of Milan signified its acceptance of the imperialists as *de facto* masters of Milan by taking an oath of fidelity to these new officials. In doing so the commune ensured that the attention of all Europe would be centred on their city and on the Sforza duchy of Milan.

For Milan was one of the areas of greatest significance in Europe. Once it had been a prosperous industrial and agricultural state, but a quarter-century of warfare had squandered its resources. During these twenty-five years the Venetians, the Swiss, the French and the Spaniards had frequently intervened in the affairs of Milan. But the Swiss were no longer strong enough to play an active part although they were concerned that Lombardy should not fall into imperial hands; and the Venetians, too, had ceased to threaten the independence of Milan in recent years. But neither France nor Spain could abandon Milan to the other. Charles V could not permit Francis I to hold the duchy for, if he did, communication between Austria and Spain by the most direct route was impossible, Genoa would be lost for ever, and Naples would be directly threatened. On the other hand, Francis I knew that if Charles V held Milan he could contain Venice, maintain an imperialist-minded government in Genoa, and dominate Italy.[6] As for the Italian powers, they were prepared to accept the Spanish right to rule Naples, Sicily and Sardinia, but not one of them welcomed the Spanish presence in Milan.

All eyes turned to Spain to see what course the emperor would follow. Gattinara had always advised Charles well on Italian affairs. Doubtless now Charles reflected on his chancellor's advice given to him some years before. 'Sir,' Gattinara had implored then, '. . . neither in jest nor in earnest, do you make it known before your coming to Italy that you intend to take personal possession of Milan. Do not hand over the citadel to the Spaniards or take the town from the duke. Such things must not be spoken of, be it never so secretly, for walls have ears and servants tongues.'[7] As Charles read over his correspondence from Italy he may have reflected on the unerring accuracy of Gattinara's political judgement. True, the emperor's military advisers were urging him to get rid of the Sforza family once and for all and to take over direct control of the duchy of Milan, but they could not know what a hornet's nest the mere suggestion of such a move could stir up.

In December the pope, while sheltering behind the polite fiction that the emperor's agents in Milan had acted without his know-ledge, expressed his deep displeasure at what had happened: 'The duchy has been seized from the duke of Milan and he has been besieged in his castle. The citizens of his state have had to transfer their allegiance to Caesar, which deprives everyone of the hope of there ever being peace.' Clement urged Charles to restore Sforza as this would be the only sure road to peace in Italy. He warned the emperor that his delay in ratifying his agreements with the Italian powers, coupled with the behaviour of the imperialists over Milan, 'has caused any number of suspicions; although the Pope, because of the high regard he has for your Highness, cannot really believe them; but he cannot deny that being the Pope, and an Italian to those other Italians who implore him not to abandon Italy, that he is the universal father of all'.

But the pope assured the emperor, through his legate, that no desire was nearer his heart than that of being allied with Charles V, 'since he conceded that the emperor does not want everything for himself, but only looks for a universal peace'. Charles replied courteously enough; such had indeed always been his desire, 'and he did not believe that he had ever done anything to give anyone a contrary opinion. He did not want everything for himself, indeed it seemed that he had too many states already.'[8]

Yet the emperor had said nothing which could calm Italian suspicions. The Venetians, Charles learned, were determined that the duchy of Milan should go neither to him nor to his brother the Archduke Ferdinand. This was a timely reminder from Venice, vulnerable as ever on her virtually indefensible northern border. It was well known that the archduke had been campaigning vigorously to be given Milan, and in January he dispatched his most trusted adviser, Salamanca, to ask the emperor for the duchy.

The emperor's brother was not the only person to put forward claims to Milan. In fact, considering it was one of the most war-prone areas of Europe it was surprising how many people were prepared to contemplate taking it on. There was one man at the court of Charles V who was convinced he had a moral claim to the duchy which should override all other considerations. This was the exiled and dispossessed Charles, duke of Bourbon.

In the spring of 1521 Charles of Bourbon, the hereditary constable of France, had lost his wife Suzanna, daughter of Pierre and Anne of Beaujeu. As she left no children, in her will Suzanna designated her husband as her heir, but her estates were claimed both by the duchess of Angoulême and by Francis I. Angered by the king's failure to defend his rights the Constable began to negotiate with the enemies of Francis I and, when threatened by exposure and arrest in 1523, fled to Burgundy and the service of Charles V. Thereafter he served with the Italian armies of the emperor. An inevitable consequence of his treachery had been the forfeiture of Bourbon's French lands, and Charles V had originally appeared willing to compensate the ex-Constable by granting him the hand of his sister the queen-dowager of Portugal. Now Bourbon was to lose her, too, to his former overlord, for the queen through marriage to Francis I was to be the guarantee of the peace Charles was proposing with France.

Since this form of compensation for his lost territories was denied him, Bourbon now demanded another. He asked the emperor for the duchy of Milan. The supposition that Charles might agree was not entirely groundless. There were sound reasons for giving it to Bourbon, who, if not exactly of royal blood, was closely related to it, and had long had ambitions to rule an independent state. Indeed, that ambition underlay his quarrel with the king of France. And Bourbon had strong allies in Wolsey and Henry VIII, who were attempting to convince the pope that he ought to accept Bourbon as duke of Milan. This would be the price of peace in Italy. But Charles knew that, even if the English managed to convince the pope, the French and the Venetians would not accept Bourbon as duke of Milan. At the same time Charles was reluctant to offend Bourbon. So, for a while, he did nothing.

In December the pope intervened with another suggestion. Sforza was unacceptable to the emperor, who believed he had been implicated in Morone's conspiracy. What, then, of Federico Gonzaga, the marquess of Mantua, who could give up his marquessate to Bourbon, who was a Gonzaga descendant through his mother? At the same time Clement rather tactlessly offered the crown of Naples to Federico Gonzaga, but this, at least, the marquess had the sense to decline. The emperor, who had doubtless been surprised to learn that his kingdom of Naples, which he had no intention of surrendering, was being hawked around Europe behind his back responded by vetoing the whole project.[9]

At the imperial court Morone's conspiracy was regarded by many as a heaven-sent opportunity to 'conquer the whole of Italy, and give these people the punishment they so richly deserve for their treacherous acts'.[10] From the Italian point of view the discovery of the conspiracy ended all hope of keeping the negotiation of an Italian League secret, since in his confession Morone gave an only too full account of the negotiations as far as they had progressed. The discovery of the conspiracy and the imperial occupation of Milan ended Clement's period of hesitation. He was wedded to the idea of an independent, Italian, Milan, and it was now a question merely of means rather than ends. The pope's attitude was already bellicose. On 13 November the Venetian ambassador reported to him that there was a real danger of the citadel of Milan falling to the imperialists, and Clement spoke then of raising 3000 infantry, of fortifying Piacenza and of employing the Swiss.[11]

Yet before he could finally commit himself Clement had to overcome a natural suspicion of the French. At the moment they were asking for control of Genoa and a 100,000-ducat pension from the kingdom of Naples. The pope appears to have felt, naturally enough, that to accede to these demands would merely be to exchange one foreign threat for another. While objecting to these French conditions, Clement did sign a defensive league with Venice, both on behalf of Florence and on behalf of the papacy, on 10 December, although he asked that this be kept secret and continued to negotiate with the imperialists.[12] The pope had hoped that the negotiations with the emperor in Spain might result in Sforza being restored to his duchy, and on this basis Clement was prepared to come to an agreement, but by 20 December he knew that Charles would not withdraw from the duchy of Milan.[13]

In their negotiations up until the New Year of 1526 the French had been hampered by the fact that Francis I was still a prisoner in Spain, and that nothing could be allowed to jeopardize the arrangements for his release. On 14 January 1526, by the Treaty of Madrid, the king of France bought his freedom on extremely harsh terms: the surrender of Burgundy, of his two eldest sons as hostages, and the restoration of Bourbon to his estates. News of the treaty reached Brescia on 2 February, where it took the Venetians completely by surprise, and Rome eighteen days later.[14] At the papal court it was assumed that Francis I would never observe such stringent terms and could not, in reason, be bound by them. Clement therefore dispatched Paolo Vettori, the general of the papal galleys, to await the return of Francis I to his native land. Vettori's public commission was to congratulate the king on his release, but privately and circumspectly he was to sound out Francis I on the subject of the projected league. Above everything else he was to avoid giving any indication, before Francis declared himself, that the pope was considering breaking with the emperor. Vettori's instructions, which had been drafted by Guicciardini, were couched in such terms as to make it clear that Clement's real concern was the fate of the duchy of Milan. At the last minute an unexpected hitch occurred in the negotiations, for Vettori died on his journey to France and his place had to be hurriedly filled by

Capino da Capo of Mantua. In the meantime the pope had dispatched the protonotary, Uberto da Gambara, to England to induce Henry VIII to enter the League and to prevent Francis observing the Treaty of Madrid. Venice also was pressing both France and England to join the League.

It was not until the end of March that Francis I could be persuaded to make any positive move. Then he promised Capino that at the very least he would pay the Swiss to attack the imperialists in Milan; he was enthusiastic about the projected league but he would be much happier if he knew that Henry VIII, who overnight, despite years of rivalry, had become his dearest royal ally, were protector of any such alliance. The Italians were not deceived by this display of reluctance, and by the beginning of April it was clear that Francis did not have the slightest intention of observing the Treaty of Madrid and that he did have every intention of joining the Italian League.[15]

It was so vital that France should contribute to the League that the attention of all Europe was now centred on the French court, where Charles V was trying to exert pressure, equal to that of the Italians, to prevent Francis sending them assistance. In Italy there could be nothing but grave concern, for it was clear that Francesco Sforza could not hold out in the *castello* of Milan much longer. It had already been decided that papal and Venetian troops alone would have to try to relieve the fortress, for were it to fall to the imperialists the chances of saving the duchy of Milan were immeasurably reduced.

Francis had at last made up his mind. On 10 May the papal and Venetian ambassadors to his court received full mandates from their governments to conclude an agreement with him. In council on the same date, in the presence of the imperial envoy Lannoy, Francis gave the first public indication that he had repudiated the terms of the Treaty of Madrid by announcing that he would not cede Burgundy to Charles V.[16] By 17 May all of the difficulties between France and the Italian powers had been overcome and on 22 May 1526 the League of Cognac was agreed. Ostensibly it was a league for the defence of Italy and the emperor was to be invited to join it, if he agreed both to the repatriation of the French princes for a reasonable ransom, to the restoration of Sforza to Milan, and to the payment of outstanding imperial debts to Henry VIII. A large army, to which France, Venice, the pope and, eventually, Milan were to contribute, was to be put into the field 'for the preservation of Italy and the States of the allies'. A navy was also to be provided. Since the core of the French infantry would, as ever, have to be Swiss, it was agreed that the support of the Swiss cantons must be purchased, and the Swiss were guaranteed all the rights and pensions which they had previously held in Milan. As no overt statement against the emperor could be made as long as the pious hope remained that he would join a league obviously directed against him, the agreements had to be rather vague about objectives: Sforza was to keep Milan and was to be given a royal bride in the hope of providing a direct heir but, should no such happy event transpire, the duchy was to revert to Massimiliano Sforza, who was still languishing in his French prison. Asti was to go to France, Alberto Pio was to be restored to his estates, the Medici were to be protected in Florence, and the French interest maintained in Genoa. In other words it was hoped to revert to the situation extant in Italy before the battle of Pavia.

On 13 June the Sacred College of Cardinals unanimously approved the League of Cognac. The treaty had already been ratified by the pope and the Venetians, and the pope's envoy was galloping furiously to France with the good news. But Clement VII had been so eager to enter into hostilities that he had not waited for the completion of these negotiations before beginning his preparations for war. And the Venetians had been as enthusiastic. It is a strange fact that at its beginning this was one of the most popular of all wars. There was something new in the air – something exciting. The Italians had consciously chosen to go to war for 'liberty' – first for the 'liberty of Milan' and then for the 'liberty of Italy'. Even if the Italian nation did not yet exist, what was in question was an Italian aspiration. Italy should be freed from the domination of any ultramontane power and left to pursue her own disunity in peace. All these disunited Italian states – Venice, Florence, the Church State, Ferrara and Mantua – were being pushed by events into a new national consciousness, a redefinition of the meaning of the word *Italia*. Before this date Italy had meant little more than a geographical location whose inhabitants had shared to a greater degree than elsewhere the benefits of romanization. However dubious these benefits may have appeared at the time, the descendants of those first victims of Roman imperialism were convinced that in consequence they were a race apart. But that did not make them a nation. The events of 1525 nearly did so. The Italians saw that they could not hope to stand against either the great power-complex of Charles V or that of Francis I unless they pooled their resources. This, in the first spring of enthusiasm for the Italian League, they seemed prepared to do. In a certain sense the armies now being raised under the terms of the League of Cognac were the first Italian army.[17]

There was, then, that summer in Italy a new note of optimism in the air, a sense that somehow political life had taken on a new purpose. Yet to the outsider, to a hardened professional like Gattinara or Charles V or even Francis I, this attempt under the terms of the League of Cognac to dislodge the imperialists from Italy had the air of a foolhardy, albeit inevitable, exercise. This was no enterprise to be embarked on lightly nor with gay hearts. At this period it was only in very exceptional circumstances that armies were risked in full-scale battle. Whatever else had resulted from Pavia, that battle had reinforced generals in their conviction that too much was at stake in warfare for the issue to be decided on the open field. In such circumstances the advantage lay with the occupying power, which could only be defeated if it had not had time to fortify the principal stragegic positions, or if it proved unable to endure protracted sieges, starvation or disease. Although Charles V still lacked control of the sea-routes in the western Mediterranean, his position in Naples was very strong. All of the duchy of Milan, save the citadels of Cremona and Milan, was in imperial hands and guarded by a veteran Spanish army. Genoa also was in imperial hands; there was a pro-imperial government in Siena and in Ferrara; Mantua was terrorized to the extent of being unable to declare against Charles V; and even the Lucchesi were paying the emperor vast sums of money and refusing to declare for or against him.

CHAPTER IV

CHAPTER IV

POPE, EMPEROR AND ROME

*When the pope was Cardinal de' Medici he was pope, and now that he is
pope he wants another to be pope in his stead.*

Charles V

IN the great Italian enterprise which was now under way, none,
at first, was more enthusiastic than Clement VII. His preparations for war dated back to February 1526 when he had arranged
for the refortification of the twin papal towns of Parma and
Piacenza. In May, even before the ratification of the agreements
with France, Clement had appointed Francesco Guicciardini, the
famous Florentine writer, political thinker, historian and administrator, as lieutenant-general of his army, although Guicciardini lacked military experience. The pope had taken into his pay
the great mercenary leaders, his kinsman, Giovanni de' Medici of
the Black Bands, and Vitello Vitelli, and had ordered Guido
Rangoni to raise 6000 soldiers for the garrison at Piacenza. Clement
planned to bring down 5000 Swiss infantry to relieve the be-
leaguered duke of Milan; had announced that he was prepared to
suspend operations against Ferrara for ten months; and had
arranged for the Orsini to raise troops as a defence against any
possible attack on Rome by the Colonna. In theory, therefore, the
pope had arranged a satisfactory defence of his own territories
and was poised for an attack on the emperor's forces in Milan.

Even as Guicciardini sped northwards from Rome to join the
papal army at Piacenza, he encountered on the road an imperial
envoy to the pope, Don Hugo da Moncada, one of the emperor's
greatest Italian servants, a prince of the kingdom of Naples and a
famous soldier in his own right. Moncada was on his way to dissuade the pope from taking up arms against the emperor. Guicciardini did not know and could not guess that Moncada had been
given a wide brief by Charles V to offer substantial concessions to
Clement. As far as peace between Charles and France was concerned, Moncada was instructed to say that the emperor would
accept from Francis I a ransom of two million ducats in lieu of

Burgundy. If Clement were to object that this was too large a sum, 'rather than breaking with His Holiness, on whose alliance the success of all other negotiations depends', Moncada might reduce the sum by half a million ducats. Moncada was to promise, on condition, naturally enough, that Clement paid for imperial neutrality, that Charles would not assist the duke of Ferrara if the pope attacked his territories. The emperor was also prepared to make substantial concessions about provisions to benefices and ecclesiastical taxation in the kingdom of Naples, and, most important of all, he was prepared to countenance the restoration of Sforza to Milan, preferably with some compensation to Bourbon, although even this was not to be insisted upon. Yet Charles was clearly aware that the past history of his relations with Clement was such that even the promise of all these concessions might still not be enough to win the pope over. And if this did prove to be the case then Moncada had been provided with an alternative brief – one designed to put pressure of a different kind on the pope.

In the previous six months the Colonna had continued to build up their power in Rome and were now talking openly of attacking the pope in his own capital. In Milan people were reporting that Pompeio Colonna had laid siege to the pope in Castel Sant'Angelo, and although affairs had not yet in fact reached such a pass Cardinal Colonna's power was on the increase and his hostility to Clement was more marked than ever. It was to Pompeio Colonna that Moncada had been instructed to turn if Clement refused to see reason. Together they were to raise rebellion against the pope in Florence, Rome and the Church State, seeking the support of Ferrara for their enterprise.[1]

Moncada rode into Rome on 16 June and on the following day had his first audience with the pope. He found Clement in a most uncompromising mood; the pope declared categorically that he would not lay down his arms until the 'Emperor left Italy free, restored the French king's sons on fair conditions, and paid what he owed to the king of England',[2] and he refused even to consider the possibility of an agreement with the emperor unless his friends in the League were included. On 18 June Moncada returned to Clement and this time offered on the emperor's behalf to do whatever Clement wished both with regard to the duchy of Milan and to resolving the emperor's differences with Venice. Charles

Francis I, by Titian

Rout of the French army by the imperialists at the Battle of Pavia, 1525, from a tapestry at Capodimonte, Naples

would also agree to the departure of the imperial army from Italy provided Clement and other Italian powers made up its arrears of pay.

After three days of unsuccessful talks with the pope, Moncada and Sessa, the imperial ambassador, at last realized that their representations would be unsuccessful. This they might have inferred from an explicit declaration made to Sessa by Clement as far back as 9 June. The pope refused to abandon his allies in order to come to terms with the emperor. Both Moncada and Sessa were clearly very angry when they left the pope's presence for the last time. Sessa had with him his court-fool, whose grimaces and mockery expressed the ambassador's feelings to perfection and delighted the Roman populace. In accordance with the emperor's instructions the Spanish envoys immediately began to lay plans for a rebellion in Rome against the pope.

Material was not wanting for such a scheme. Clement was acutely unpopular in Rome, where the relations of the citizens with the papacy were frequently strained. The economic prosperity of the vast majority of Roman citizens, of whatever nationality, was dependent on the fortunes of the papacy. Rome was neither a major industrial nor a commercial town. It was not even a port; the Tiber, shallow, narrow and swift-flowing, was not accessible to ships of a deep draught, for the river is not tidal and its constant windings made navigation difficult and slow. Many of the Romans were employed directly by the papacy, the cardinals or the Roman nobility. The only significant industry in Rome was the hotel industry, dependent on pilgrims, embassies and legal visitors. Their importance had long been recognized by the papacy, and constant efforts had been made to provide for the safety of such visitors to the Holy City. A desire to extend this safety to the roads leading to Rome had been a significant factor in the extension of papal authority throughout the Church State. Julius II and Leo X both made considerable efforts, despite the open defiance of the Roman barons, to rid the pilgrim-routes of bandits, and their constructive edicts were reinforced by Clement in the bull *In Sancta*, of 12 June 1524, which also tried to ensure the safety of pilgrims inside Rome.[3]

Connected with this vast religious tourist trade, and yet apart from it, and equally dependent on the largely celibate church in

Rome, was the world of the Roman courtesans, a world which was at its peak of sophistication in these years. As much as three per cent of the population of Rome at this time lived by prostitution, but prostitution of a highly sophisticated nature. The great courtesans of Rome were true products of the Renaissance, priding themselves on their intellectual abilities, on their learning and their artistic talents. They were courted as much for attractions of their minds as for the beauty of their bodies; they included women such as the famous Camilla of Pisa, the correspondent of gentlemen and princes throughout Europe and authoress of a book, corrected by Francesco del Nero, and Imperia, the most famous of all, protected by and beloved of Agostino Chigi, whose daughter and heiress was brought up in the nunnery of Santa Maria in Campo Marzio, the most aristocratic nunnery in Rome. They included, too, the beautiful and cultured Clarice Matrema-non-Vuole, the beloved of Giovanni of the Black Bands, who had managed to commit to memory and recite, for the benefit of her admirers and patrons, all of Petrarch and Boccaccio and much of Virgil, Horace and Ovid. The world of these women was one of great luxury and elegance, supporting much of the culture of High Renaissance Rome and employing a whole host of relatives, dependent servants, and hangers-on; but it was still a world which depended directly on the prosperity of the Church in Rome.

It was indeed in service industries of one kind and another that the majority of Rome's citizens were employed; as cobblers, bakers, watermen, washerwomen, barbers, provision merchants, and clothiers. Few practised any craft; a pottery industry, dominated by immigrants from Bergamo, was centred in Regola, and there were some weavers, principally in Trastevere and in the area around Camp Marzio. A luxury craft, largely dependent on ecclesiastical demands, was that of the jewellers and the goldsmiths in Parione. Some builders and masons resided in the city, though considerably fewer than the amount of new building in Rome must have needed. Those who did live in the city were concentrated in the region of Campo Marzio.[4]

Rome, therefore, depended for its prosperity on the papacy, and yet, during the pontificate of Clement VII, anti-papalism in the city was so marked that it could be turned to imperial advantage at will. Of course anti-papalism was endemic at Rome, and theocratic government was always seen as an intrusion, a usurpation and even as a tyranny; nevertheless, there were peculiar circumstances which made Clement, with the possible exception of Adrian VI, the most hated of all sixteenth-century popes. He had, it is true, a genius for being misunderstood. From the beginning of his pontificate he appeared to show surprising weakness. His inability to pursue a firm and fixed course of action or even to maintain consistent good government in Rome, the Church State and Florence was frequently commented on. Yet Clement laboured under difficulties which were not of his own making. Despite the mounting pressure of business, which had been growing throughout the preceding 200 years, the papacy had failed to develop effective institutions of government. No pope, however conscientious, could hope to deal alone with all the increased business accruing to Rome. It was only in the course of the sixteenth century, and, for the most part, after the death of Clement, that institutions such as the congregations – commissions composed of cardinals and of specialists charged with making policy decisions – began to relieve the papacy of some of its burdens. For all his undoubted ability Clement was unable to deal effectively with any of the problems which beset him simply because there were too many: foreign policy, the spread of Lutheranism and other forms of religious dissent, reform of the Church, the Turkish advance, piracy in the Mediterranean, the government of Florence, and, most immediately, brigandage and lawlessness in the Campagna, unrest in Rome and a severe economic crisis which brought the papacy to the verge of bankruptcy and, for a while, absorbed all other problems in itself.

The hatred felt in Rome for Clement was not the result of a lack of concern on his part for the city. Clement seems to have convinced himself that the wars and diseases of recent years were a divine punishment for the disrepair into which many of the Roman churches had fallen and for a failure to observe canonical hours. From the beginning of his pontificate he, therefore, showed considerable interest in the government and development of Rome, and in the improvement of existing amenities. Although little new building can be attributed to his pontificate and not a single new church was built during it, a special visitation of bishops was ordered in 1524 to arrange for the repair, rebuilding and proper use of every church in Rome.[5] The roads and streets of Rome received special attention from Clement. New roads were built, existing regulations about the old ones were rigidly enforced and a special work-force was created to keep all the thoroughfares of Rome clean.

In the government of Rome the power of the papacy was now unchallenged, although the city continued to be administered by two different sets of officials – those of the papacy and those of the commune. The papal officials consisted of the prefect, a purely nominal office by this date, the castellan of Sant'Angelo, the captain of the papal guard, and the governor of Rome. The governor, the most important administrator in Rome, was head of papal justice in the city; he had authority over two prisons, the Corta Savelli and the Tor di Nona, and was charged with keeping order in the city. For this purpose he had a corps of police at his disposal. The commune of Rome retained its own councils – the Secret or Ordinary Council, which was made up of different municipal magistrates; and the Great Council, which contained the same personnel with the addition of the Roman nobility. Liaison between the commune and the papacy was provided by the conservators of the city. There were three of these and they were replaced once a quarter. Nearly always members of the old Roman nobility, they controlled prices, maintained the water-supply, presided over the councils and supervised the senator, who presided over the Capitol law-court. One other purely honorific office survived, that of *gonfaloniere* (standard-bearer) of the Roman people, which had become an hereditary title in the Cesarini family. The policing of the city was largely the responsibility of the thirteen *rioni* and their elected civic leaders, who selected constables to maintain law and order within their own districts.[6]

Since the government of Rome was now under papal control and the old spirit of the Roman commune was all but extinguished, conflict over the city government was not the real source of friction in Rome, and it is elsewhere that reasons for Clement's unpopularity must be sought. Some unrest was certainly occasioned by the predominance of Florentines in Roman life and in the administration of the Church State. It is possible that by 1527 more than thirteen per cent of the Roman populace was of Tuscan origin. Even under the Borgia popes Rome never suffered an

invasion of immigrants comparable to that during the pontificates of the two Medici. The first depositor-general of Leo X was
his relative, Filippo Strozzi, and the treasury and datariat were held
by Tuscans throughout his pontificate. The banking system of
Rome had also become dominated by Florentine financiers. By
1527 there were at least thirty Florentine bankers in Rione Ponte.
In 1520 the alum mines of Tolfa had passed to Florentine control,
and in 1524 Florentines replaced the Fugger as papal bankers.
Filippo Strozzi was deeply involved in every commercial enterprise at Rome, and with the Sienese, Agostino Chigi, could control the entire financial life of the city. So dominant were Florentines at Rome that Tuscan became the official language of the
papal court.[7] Although the responsibility for this influx of Florentines was as much that of Leo X as of Clement VII, the latter
suffered by comparison with his Medici predecessor. The liberality
of Leo X had endeared him to the Romans, who did not care by
what inexpedient financial measures this liberality was financed,
and Leo was lucky in that his pontificate coincided with a period in
which plague, death and warfare were unknown at Rome. On the
contrary, the city profited from the disorders in the rest of Italy by
an influx of wealthy refugees. With the populace as a whole Leo
further ingratiated himself by the mistaken policy of creating
Roman cardinals. Leo's popularity at Rome was such that he was
the first pope to whom a statue was erected in the Campidoglio.

Clement's main difficulties were, from the beginning, occasioned
by his financial problems, and this applied as much to his relations
with the city of Rome as to the wider field of papal affairs.[8] The
vacillation for which contemporaries blamed Clement VII was in
the main caused by a constant financial problem, hand-to-mouth
expedients, and a complete failure to achieve a permanent solution
to the papacy's economic difficulties. By 1527 the papacy was
bankrupt.

As far as the Italian League was concerned, the financial embarrassment of the papacy was critical. Clement was imprisoned
by his own financial need at a time when it was politically, morally
and militarily imperative that he should act promptly and vigorously. Yet very few contemporaries believed in papal poverty. On
the contrary, there were many popular misconceptions about papal
wealth. The Venetians, for instance, had clearly been misled by

the optimistic report of Domenico Trevisano on the finances of Julius II, who was described as having 'ways of getting as much money as he wants'.[9]

In fact, Clement inherited a crippling financial burden. Despite personal parsimony and political retrenchment, Adrian VI left no more than 2000 ducats in the papal treasury. The ordinary revenues were still mortgaged, an arrangement entered into by Leo X, who was said to have spent the income of three pontificates, his own, Julius II's and Clement's.[10] To his credit, Clement was to begin the great work of reorganizing the papal finances, often to his own disadvantage. Had it not been for political pressure he would clearly have preferred to impoverish the Church and to begin a thorough reform of the administration, a labour for which his talents were admirably suited.[11] Although circumstances conspired to make Clement play a continued part in the Italian wars, he did what he could to improve the administration of the papacy. From the beginning he set his face against the increasing venality of papal government.[12] By 1525 the only means he had of raising ready cash was to create more cardinals, but this, on principle, he refused to do, despite the advice of all those close to him.

Cardinal Armellino, Clement's principal financial adviser, had also assisted Leo X. Although, during the pontificate of Leo X, he had been unable to prevent the pope squandering the fortune left by Julius II, in the pontificate of Clement VII, whose own financial understanding was by no means negligible, he utilized and developed some sound financial devices. The appropriation of income towards specific ends, first initiated by Julius II, was continued; in 1524 a special college of forty curial officials was set up to oversee the rebuilding of St Peter's and to make sure that money destined for this purpose was not misappropriated.[13] In 1526 Armellino was partially instrumental in setting up the Monte della Fede, the first public debt of the papacy, which at $12\frac{1}{2}$ per cent represented a more economical method of borrowing than hand-to-mouth loans raised with individual bankers who often charged an interest rate of 40 per cent. A real effort was made to exploit the alum mines at Tolfa for the benefit of the papacy.

Yet, although economically necessary, many of Armellino's measures were politically disastrous. At a time when the papacy was making real progress in establishing effective government throughout the Church State, Armellino subjected this previously immune area to harsh fiscal extractions. Taxes were imposed on cereals, meat, shops and immigrants. In 1516 Armellino advised the imposition of a salt-tax which, although it would have benefited the papacy by 25,000 ducats, aroused such strong opposition in the Romagna that Leo X was forced to abandon the project. In 1519 his fiscal policy resulted in actual rebellion in the Church State at Fabriano, which, after the sack of that city by the Spaniards, was unable to meet Armellino's fresh impositions.

It was in Rome, however, that Armellino's policies had the most damaging effect. The Roman clergy were heavily taxed, and absenteeism among the clerics was punished by fines. The tariffs of the customs duties were almost doubled. The *macinato*, a tax on flour, was introduced, and in 1524 Clement imposed a heavy tax on artisans and tradesmen. While the heavy tax on all Roman wines caused particular annoyance to the general populace of the city, other measures were acutely mistimed.[14] Taxes on merchants were imposed at a time when they had already suffered substantial losses in the war and were waiting for a return on some of their enterprises.[15] Some measures were merely mismanaged; during a period of shortage Clement had corn imported from Sicily, only to find that by the time the supplies arrived the crisis was over and, in order to sell the imported grain without loss, the price of corn had to be artificially raised.[16] In fact, throughout his pontificate the whole question of price-fixing and rationing of wheat caused friction between Clement and Rome. The kind of profit that could be made is indicated by the Spaniard, Perez, who in January 1527 reported that the pope was proposing to sell corn for 5½ ducats the *ruggio*, which he had imported at a price of 1½ ducats the *ruggio*.[17] The sale of food monopolies artificially elevated the prices of vital commodities at a time when they were in any case high and were rising steadily.[18]

Even with this increased income Clement was still forced into other expedients to save money. As early as January 1525 Armellino was cutting the salaries and allowances of papal ambassadors, and by June 1526 the diplomatic service was even denied the necessary cash to send dispatches by post, the quickest means of communication. For several months the Roman officials and the professors at the University received no salaries. The Swiss guard also went unpaid and resorted to dubious means of their own to support themselves.[19]

For a variety of reasons, therefore, Clement was acutely unpopular in Rome, so unpopular that over a long period of time the imperialists were able to create disturbances at will in the pope's own city. In all resistance to papal government and in anti-papal riots the imperialists were clearly implicated. In the last week of June 1526 Armellino imposed a fresh tax on butchers throughout Rome. Coming on top of other high taxes, this drove the butchers into open revolt. Threatened with arrest, they took refuge with Sessa in the Spanish embassy; the papal police were forced to withdraw and Clement had to repeal the offending tax.

This episode was but the culminating offence of the Spanish official representatives in Clement's eyes. In alliance with the Colonna, Sessa had for months been subverting Rome, producing an unfortunate background to the negotiations with Clement. Clearly Sessa and Moncada had now provoked an open breach with the pope, who was shamed and humiliated by the incident at the embassy, and there was little point in the Spaniards remaining in Rome. On 26 June Moncada left the city and was straightaway followed by Sessa, who was going on to Naples to collect money and troops. Moncada travelled to the Colonna property at Genezzano and there revealed letters from Charles V which authorized an attack on Rome. The Spanish alliance with the Colonna was at last an open secret. From the safety of their fortresses, Ascanio and Vespasiano Colonna were boasting openly of raising a rebellion in Rome, of bringing troops from Naples and with these, the peasants from their estates, and the troops they were even now hiring 'they will one day enter Rome'.[20] Hearing of these preparations, Clement did not make the mistake of supposing that he was dealing with a purely local rebellion, but responded on an international level. Sanga was authorized to go to France to ask the French king to assist him by immediate military diversions in Flanders and the Pyrenees. In Rome the pope began to raise infantry, which he placed under the over-all command of the Orsini count of Anguillara.

The pope had already entered into an open contest with the emperor. Clement recalled from Spain his legate, Salviati, who had been sent to negotiate the ratification of the articles agreed with

Lannoy, and in a brief of 23 June 1526 Clement justified a resort to arms against the emperor. In the brief Clement recalled that, following the battle of Pavia, he had paid the imperialists 100,000 ducats on condition that the confederation between pope and emperor was ratified and that the imperial forces would not enter Milan; neither condition had been fulfilled. The brief described the entire relationship between pope and emperor since the beginning of Clement's pontificate and was remarkably consistent in the attitude which Clement adopted over the duchy of Milan. The pope claimed that, although he had always been a loyal friend to imperial interests, he was not obliged to follow the emperor without question into error, and it was Charles V's hostile attitude to the duke of Milan which had obliged him to join the Italian League for the common defence of Italy.[21]

This brief was not received by Charles V until 20 August at a time when the 'anti-Italian' Lannoy was in great favour and a week after the emperor had already announced that the aggression of the pope, France and other Italian powers had forced him to take up arms. Nevertheless, the papal brief, which even the Venetian ambassador, Navagero, thought was unnecessarily strong in its wording, was bitterly resented by Charles V. The emperor's wrath was carefully fanned by Gattinara and was encouraged by the whole atmosphere in Spain, where an unusual note of anti-clericalism is distinguishable throughout the political world in these months.[22] The emperor's first reaction was to talk vaguely and wildly to all the league ambassadors to Spain about a general council and a universal peace. In particular, Charles reminded the French ambassador that if his master had kept his promises all would yet be well, and warned that he would not return the French princes, 'even if compelled by force to abandon all his realms'.[23] He instructed the more prominent theologians in the country to spend the summer compiling detailed answers to such questions as: To what limits was an emperor obliged to obey the pope? Whether it was always obligatory to pay annates? Whether provocation justified war with a pope?[24] Clement countered the emperor's veiled threats by setting on foot research in the Vatican archives that led to the 'discovery' of the papal bulls which forbade an emperor to hold the kingdom of Naples, Lombardy or Tuscany.[25]

The papal envoy to Spain at this time was the famous Baldassare

Castiglione, who, unlike so many of his scholarly friends, strongly favoured Spain and all things Spanish. In his *Courtier*, the prescribed manual of polished behaviour for all aspiring young Italian gentlemen, he had specifically urged his courtier to learn Spanish as well as French and had welcomed the introduction into spoken Italian of Spanish words and phrases.[26] He had long been a devoted admirer of Charles V and was bewitched by the imperial presence. In consequence he was now deeply distressed by the conflict between pope and emperor. Moreover, to Castiglione had fallen the unpleasant duty of delivering the papal brief of 23 June. At the beginning of September he was still trying to justify the pope's actions to the emperor, unaware that Charles had already authorized the Colonna to take offensive action against Clement VII. The emperor had scarcely a good word to say for the pope and declared that Clement had been hostile to him ever since his election. On 17 September Castiglione saw the emperor in the company of the French and Venetian ambassadors. Together, they urged Charles to restore the French princes to their father, who was represented as pining away in the absence of his children, although those same children were, in actual fact, having a splendid holiday in Spain at Charles's expense. The ambassadors urged Charles to join the League of Cognac, but the emperor, instead, chose to use the occasion to sow dissension among the allies. In an obvious attempt to discredit the French with the pope and the Venetians, Charles began to reminisce about the days of Francis's captivity in Spain, 'when the French king urged me to go to Italy and told me that he would help me to make myself lord of all, that we would depose the pope and make him our chaplain. I told him that this was not my intention and that I thought of nothing except war against the Turk.'[27] For the future goodwill of the League it was probably fortunate that most of the Italians had already been offered a version of the same conversation by Francis I, although Francis, naturally, had been at pains to explain that it was *Charles* who had suggested the conquest and division of Italy between the two of them.

Just as in the streets of Rome, so at the imperial court there was constant gossip about the possibility of Charles calling a general council in order to judge Clement. Such gossip could do nothing but harm, for 'there is nothing that popes hate, suspect or fear more than the word "council" '.[28] In a private audience of 18 September, Castiglione complained to Charles that the pope was being bullied by threats of such a council.

Charles, who was often at his most conciliatory in his discussions with Castiglione, did not attempt to disguise how much he had been hurt by the papal brief. He complained that, since the pope maligned him, a general council of the Church was his only recourse, but he maintained that he had no intention of offending the pope or any other Italian power, and that his only concern was to defend his territories against the Turk. Castiglione was told that Charles had already ordered the drafting of a reply to the papal brief, that in it he could not fail to mention the possibility of calling a general council, 'but it will be done so modestly and with such conditions that His Holiness will have nothing to complain of'.[29]

In fact, the document to which Charles referred was as subjective in its interpretation of recent history as any that had emanated from Rome. Assuming from the start that he himself was without blame, Charles asked whether Clement considered his current behaviour was in keeping with his pastoral office; whether he really considered that he should have drawn the sword which Christ had ordered Peter to replace in its scabbard. Yet there is little evidence to suggest that Charles himself believed the pope was wrong to exercise temporal power. Indeed, the arguments used make it plain that what Charles objected to was not that the pope had a sword but that he had unsheathed it against rather than for imperial interests. It is abundantly evident that Charles regarded Clement as his creature and had been angered by the pope's failure to support him. Clement's conduct, so Charles's argument ran, had not protected the safety of Italy or Christendom, or even of the Holy See, which in any case stood in no need of weapons and troops as no one was threatening to attack it. Considering that Moncada had already opened negotiations with the Colonna for an attack on Rome, this argument of the emperor's can only be regarded as less than honest.

This Spanish State Paper, which was formally handed to Castiglione on 18 September 1526, was of the greatest importance. Obviously emanating from the imperial chancery, where the Erasmian humanist Alfonso de Valdés was still the predominant influence, it was couched in terms of which even Luther might not have been ashamed. It represented most accurately the feelings of the emperor towards the pope and became the inflexible basis of all future negotiations between the two. It was dispatched to Rome, together with a letter for the cardinals which, drafted separately on 6 October, went some way towards stirring up an anti-papal movement within the Sacred College itself. The letter to the cardinals contained the suggestion that if the pope refused to summon a general council it was the responsibility and duty of the cardinals to do so, without his consent. Thus the emperor had more or less committed himself to overt war with the papacy, for any pope, and not just Clement VII, would have found it difficult to accept two such clear threats to his own authority within and over the Church.

CHAPTER V

THE LEAGUE AT WAR

*Captains in these days have often had greater difficulty in maintaining
discipline among their troops than in conquering enemies in dangerous
undertakings or doubtful battles. . . .*

Paolo Giovio

O N receiving the news of the signing of the League of
Cognac the Venetian Senate had written to Clement urging
him to begin a war of liberation in Italy. For some time the
Venetian army of 10,000 infantry, 900 lances and 800 light cavalry,
which had recently been re-formed by the duke of Urbino, the
Venetian captain-general, and to which Pesaro had been appointed
proveditor, had been ready for war. It had transferred to the Bres-
ciano to await the arrival of the papal and Swiss troops.

This arrival was somewhat delayed. Clement's original contribution to the Italian League was restricted to negotiating for Swiss
infantry with the castellan of Mus, a proverbially unreliable ally
whose only policy was to sell the impregnable position of his
fortress, dominating Lake Como, to the highest bidder. It was unfortunate that the castellan was the traditional enemy of the Grisons, the most easterly of the cantons of the Swiss confederation,
for the support of the inhabitants of this area was essential to any
eventual league success; they controlled the mountain passes, and
in particular the Valtellina which linked Lombardy with Austria
and Germany. On 28 May, after protracted negotiations with all
the parties concerned, Clement felt able to inform Venice that the
castellan and the Grisons would hold these passes against an anticipated invasion of German lansquenets and that the papal
treasury had forwarded money to Bologna in order to raise
infantry. The Venetians were dubious about trying to raise troops
through the offices of the castellan and the inefficient Veroli, bishop
of Lodi, but when the Venetian ambassador questioned Clement
on 2 June he was assured that the pope was making every effort to
ensure the speedy arrival of the Swiss.[1]

Speed was essential to the success of the enterprise, for, temporarily, the imperialists in Lombardy were in a very weak position. Their army was small and badly paid, while the whole of the local population was ready to rise as soon as a liberating force approached. In June the Venetian cavalry was already able to prevent the imperialists using any mill outside Milan, thus causing an acute shortage of flour within the city.[2] An attack on Lombardy became, therefore, the first part of an elaborate plan of campaign, drawn up by the confederates, which bore all the hall-marks of Italian ingenuity. The attack was to be made by the Venetians and papal forces aided by French mercenaries and subsidies and assisted by a promised Anglo–French invasion of Flanders or Spain. Simultaneous attacks were to be made on Genoa, on Siena, using the exiles from that state, on Naples, using the Orsini, and on the coastal parts of southern Italy, using the League's fleet. Unfortunately, this excellent plan failed to take account of the French king's inability to fulfil his rasher promises, of the English king's lack of real interest, or of probable imperial counter-manœuvres: threats against Rome from the south or against Florence from the north. As it was, political instability in Florence, a protracted quarrel with Ferrara and threats by the Colonna had already combined to delay the pope's preparations. At the end of June the papal army was still at Piacenza and the agreement with the Swiss had not been concluded. Since the imperialists, the pope and Venice, which traditionally recruited from the Val di Lamone, Umbria, Urbino and the March of Ancona, were all raising troops in the same area, progress in making up units was necessarily slow.[3]

The league campaign was weakened by the lack of over-all command. The duke of Urbino, in terms of military theory one of the best generals then alive in Europe, was nothing more than captain-general of the Venetians, but since none in the papal army was his equal in age, rank or experience he imagined that he had a natural right to take all the decisions. On the papal side there was no captain-general to counterbalance Urbino's claims, and the papal lieutenant-general, Guicciardini, was despised by the duke as a civilian who had no right to an opinion on military matters. Guicciardini got little more respect from his own subordinates in the papal army. His ignorance of military customs infuriated them and his efficiency was even more unpopular with men who customarily operated a system of acknowledged corruption. But these same papal commanders got on no better with Urbino than they did with Guicciardini, for the duke believed them to have an inadequate grasp of the theory of war. The natural consequence of this state of affairs was a constant bickering between all the commanders about strategy, with Urbino consistently refusing to have anything other than the final word. On the evening of 21 June all the league ambassadors in Venice were suddenly summoned to the Senate to resolve one of these frequent quarrels between the commanders. Urbino, who valued numerical superiority above all other considerations, had asked the papal captains to cross the Po to join up with him and make an advance on Milan from the east. The papal commanders, on the other hand, wanted to cross the Po higher upstream and to approach Milan from the opposite direction. Since it took at least eight days for messages to be sent to Rome and Venice and for replies to be received, much valuable time was wasted contacting the pope and the Venetians in order to obtain consent for Urbino's plan.[4]

For the sake of peace, and exhausted by representations from the pope that his lieutenant was not being properly treated by Urbino, the Venetian Senate finally ordered Urbino to keep Guicciardini abreast of all military developments. But although a *modus vivendi* was finally worked out between the Venetian captain-general and the papal lieutenant-general, they maintained a hearty dislike for each other. Nor was mutual trust a noticeable quality in the league armies; at every turn Urbino found himself hampered by a host of spies sent to his camp both by his own masters and by the pope to see that he was doing his job efficiently.

The refusal of the papal captains and, above all, of Guicciardini to agree implicitly to any plan that Urbino might put forward had political repercussions. The Venetians were convinced that Clement was deliberately hindering the progress of the campaign and suspected him of negotiating secretly with the imperialists, while Clement, for his part, suspected that the Venetians cared for nothing but the protection of their own borders. Moreover, both Venice and the pope were already irritated by the failure of Francis I to do more than make expansive promises. There was still no sign of the expected French troops, 'of which we have need, for Caesar is not sleeping . . .'.[5]

Despite these arguments, by using the time-honoured method of treachery from within rather than siege and attack according to the 'rules of war', on 24 June Urbino, having crossed the Adda, scored a notable success by taking Lodi, a town which the imperialists maintained was vital to the defence of the city of Milan. Indeed, in the imperial canon of strategy it was of such value that it was one of the few cities worth defending to the last man,[6] and its capture, facilitated by the ill-treatment the city had suffered at the hands of the occupying imperial troops, was therefore a great triumph for the Italian League. The capture of Lodi opened the way for an immediate advance on Milan and Pavia, guarded by Lodovico, Count of Lodron, with no more than 1000 lansquenets, 'because these cities, situated as in a triangle, are no more than twenty miles one from the other'.[7] Most important of all, this success ended all arguments about the joining of the two armies; on the same day that Lodi fell, the papal army crossed the Po and took Sant'Angelo. On 26 June Guicciardini joined with Urbino, and the two armies lodged near old Lodi, intending to move on Milan with all speed. Guicciardini always remained convinced that if an attack had now been made the league army would have gone on to total victory. Giberti, in Rome, was of the same opinion; he already saw the country of his birth freed from the imperialists, but his rejoicing was premature. His hopes foundered on the not entirely misplaced, and very fashionable, judgement of Urbino, reinforced by his experience of the imperial troops at Lodi, that Italian infantry alone, without Swiss or German reinforcements, could be considered useless for the purpose of attacking a well-defended city. He refused even to consider an attack on Milan before the arrival of the expected Swiss troops. Advance was, therefore, painfully slow; on 28 June the army reached Marignano, but here again there was a delay until, on 3 July, the army advanced on San Donato, half-way between Milan and Marignano. The following day it was at San Martino, only three miles from Milan, when at last the first 500 Swiss arrived. The delay had already given the Constable of Bourbon, who had disembarked at Genoa, time to bring money and men from Spain to the assistance of the imperialists in Milan.

It was not until 7 July that an assault was finally made on the suburbs of Milan. In numerous skirmishes the league forces, in particular the 'Black Bands', the crack troops of Giovanni de'

Medici, had the better of the enemy and it was assumed that on the following day an attempt would be made to relieve the fortress of Milan, but at five in the evening Urbino announced to Guicciardini his intention of retreating. He had no wish to risk the Venetian army so far from the borders of the Venetian state before all of the Swiss had arrived. The papal commanders disagreed with Urbino, for they were certain that Milan could be taken, and as soon as Guicciardini was apprised of the duke's decision he asked for a discussion before any order was given. Urbino's mind, however, was made up, and there was nothing Guicciardini could do. Strong words were exchanged and the argument grew even more heated when, on reaching San Martino, where the duke had said he would stop, the papal lieutenant-general saw the ranks of men continuing to retreat. Urbino then informed him, calmly enough, that he thought lodgings at Marignano would be both safer and more comfortable. When Guicciardini tried to insist at least on staying at San Martino, Urbino finally lost his temper and declared: 'When my masters want the leadership of his expedition to be in other hands than mine, I shall be very pleased and I shall obey everybody very gladly, but until they give it to someone else I wish to control all the movements of the war myself. . . . If I am in command, I want us to go to Marignano.'[8]

The papal lieutenant-general comforted himself with the conviction that perfidious Venice had ordered Urbino to withdraw, but, in fact, the Venetian Senate was appalled by the duke's failure to press the attack and Urbino found that he was being asked to justify his decision to his own masters as well as the papal representative.

It was perhaps fortunate that neither Guicciardini nor the Senate knew quite how great an opportunity had been lost. The situation of the imperialists in Milan was desperate and chaotic. When Bourbon arrived in the city he was horrified. From the first he quarrelled with del Guasto and da Leyva who were only too ready to hand over the responsibility for everything to him. Bourbon was equally anxious to avoid taking on the responsibility of the city's defence, for he was frankly unimpressed by the quality of the imperial soldiery in Milan. It was his frequently – if somewhat tactlessly – expressed opinion that they had been badly led. Discipline had been relaxed to such an extent that he seemed to be dealing with a rabble rather than an army. He found that the army absolutely refused to leave Milan unless its arrears of pay, dating back since before Pavia in some cases, were made up. There were daily threats that the army would demand Milan to sack in lieu of payment, and Bourbon realized that he would be unable to leave the city until he had somehow paid his troops.

Despite constant pressure, Urbino refused to attack Milan again. The only success for the League in these depressing days was the capture on 22 July of Monza and its fortress.[9] Urbino's strategy was still dependent on the arrival of the Swiss, for when they arrived he planned to divide the army in two in order to blockade Milan. Following the fall of Monza the duke removed from Marignano to Casaretto on the Lambro where he set up a strongly fortified camp. Here he held a council of war. News had come from Milan that Sforza was on the point of surrendering to the imperialists and it was clear, even to Urbino, that some action should be taken to prevent such a disaster. Yet it was with difficulty that the papal captains managed to persuade him to agree to an attack on Milan on the following night. He was terrified that any assault by the league troops would be rebuffed and that the imperialists would then force a pitched battle. As far as Urbino was concerned the only possible issue to such a dreaded event was another Pavia.[10]

The issue never came to trial, for on the following day news came that the garrison of the citadel, reduced to starvation and despairing of assistance, had surrendered on the best terms possible. Almost simultaneously it was learned that the Grisons were so annoyed by the League's employment of the castellan of Mus that they would only agree to hold the passes against the expected lansquenets for a fortnight, unless their differences with the castellan were settled and a fresh agreement was negotiated.

Victory which had seemed temptingly close had been snatched away. The Swiss had still not arrived, and the condition of the remainder of the papal army left a great deal to be desired; the officers were often incompetent; there was need of a first-class captain of artillery; and a review of the troops, officiously conducted by Guicciardini, revealed that not a single company was up to full strength. The highest proportion of vacancies was among the troops of Guido Rangoni, who was an indulgent officer, but neither Vitelli nor even the famous Giovanni de' Medici could be totally absolved from blame; 'the excuses are many and everyone offers them in his own manner'.[11] Rangoni and Medici quarrelled so frequently and so publicly that Guicciardini begged Giberti to dispatch Paolo d'Arezzo, in whom Medici had great confidence, in order to compose their differences.[12] Even the arrival of the castellan of Mus with the long-awaited Swiss brought fresh problems, for the pay of the Swiss fell due immediately, Guicciardini had no money with which to pay them and it was well known that the Swiss would brook no delay, for they were troops whom 'one does not pay with words'.[13] Guicciardini was extremely irritated when he discovered that, on top of all this, the Swiss had been hired at an extortionately high rate. The normal rate of pay for the infantry was $3\frac{1}{2}$ ducats a month, usually payable monthly, although this could be a matter for negotiation – the Venetians, for instance, paid their troops every thirty-six days. But the Swiss and the lansquenets always tended to be more expensive, particularly when they were employed by the pope, with the result that there was a long-term tendency for the Venetian infantry to defect to the papal army. This did not make for good relations between the allies in the League, and they would have been well advised to standardize the payment of their mercenaries.[14] But it seems probable that no piecemeal reform of this nature could have solved the problem which every contemporary observer recognized – on the whole, mercenary infantry forces did not make good troops. Their reputation was low and men of breeding or ability preferred to serve, as they had traditionally done, in the cavalry, or if they were particularly enterprising, like Pedro Navarro, they studied the new science of ballistics and became captains of the artillery, or experts on fortification, like Federigo Gonzaga da Bozzoli,

> with the result that the infantry is made up of the worst and lowest of men. . . . And where is that captain-general, albeit of divine virtue, who can fight a war reasonably, given that the soldiers, on receiving their pay often go over to the enemy camp, refuse to put up with the fortunes of war, steal from the supplies, cannot bear that wine or fresh victuals should be lacking in camp, and, finally, are not ashamed in battle, when the trumpet sounds and the enemy starts advancing, to demand their pay before fighting ?[15]

Only an officer with no previous experience of the Italian wars in 1525 could have claimed that he had not met with all these problems at one time or another, and if he had fought regularly with the Swiss they were problems to which he would have become inured through habit.

To Guicciardini, however, whose experience of warfare was still limited, the problems were sufficiently novel for him to make efforts to resolve them. But while he was in the midst of trying to sort out problems over the pay of the Swiss he was approached by the castellan of Mus, demanding 3000 ducats which he claimed he had already spent on the League's behalf. To ensure that there would be no question about this demand for expenses he had arranged for the arrest of two Venetian ambassadors who were attempting to cross Lake Como into France and whom he was now offering to ransom. 'There never was', according to Guicciardini, 'a worse suggestion than that of placing affairs in the hands of a man of this nature; the results of doing so have been the worst possible.'[16] Within a day or so the castellan's demand for expenses had more than doubled and by the beginning of September he was threatening to ally with the imperialists.[17]

The failure of Francis I to display any real interest in Italian affairs continued to perturb the other members of the League. Guicciardini and Giberti continually urged Acciauoli, papal envoy to the French king, to spur Francis into action. They suspected that Francis was hoping to achieve his ends through diplomatic channels, relying on the activity of the Italians to put sufficient pressure on the emperor, for although the French king had dispatched du Bellay to raise Swiss infantry he had not sent sufficient funds to pay them. At the beginning of August there was no sign in Italy of a single French soldier, of the French fleet, nor of the promised French diversion in Flanders. The Grisons, convinced that the French were indifferent to Italian affairs, indicated the possibility that they might transfer their allegiance to the imperialists, just as the first rumours began to spread of the emperor's intention of dispatching a fresh army of lansquenets to Italy.[18]

Meanwhile, in Tuscany, the League had been no more successful than in Lombardy. An attack on Siena and especially on its Ghibelline government had always been an integral part of the League's plan of campaign, just as the maintenance of a favourable or sympathetic government there had become an integral part of the imperial defence system. It was probably unwise to risk an attack on Siena since it exposed the papacy on two fronts and broadened the theatre of the war. On the other hand, the imperialists there appeared most vulnerable; an attack would at least divert some of the imperial resources from Lombardy, while pleasing Florence, and, like all exiles, those from Siena were extremely optimistic about the chances of success.

Although the imperialists had been surprisingly conciliatory over the whole subject of the restoration of the Sienese exiles,[19] the hostility of both the pope and Florence to the new régime was very marked. The Orsini, Clement's allies, were in open conflict with Siena over the county of Pitigliano which Siena claimed was part of her territory, held unjustly by the Orsini. Apart from protecting the exiles, Clement had spent considerable sums in purchasing support inside Siena, had banned all visitors to Rome from passing through Sienese territory, and had done nothing to prevent Florentine raids over the border.

At an early date Siena became aware that the pope was planning war. At least two conspiracies to overthrow the government were discovered in the city, and, acting under instruction from the magistrates, Giovanni Battista Palmieri, who held a *condotta* of 100 infantry from Siena, had approached the pope pretending that he would hand over one of the city-gates to an invading army. Since Clement VII continued to believe in his good faith, Palmieri was able to keep the government of Siena informed about all the preparations being made by the League against the city.

These preparations were extensive. The troops to be used, in addition to the inevitable, numerous exiles, anxious to return home, were all provided by the pope and were captained by five Italians, Virginio Orsini, the Count of Pitigliano and his son, Gentile Baglione and Giovanni da Sassatello. The army was sizeable: 600 cavalry, 8000 infantry, for the most part Florentine, and 9 pieces of artillery. The attack began early in July with a simultaneous advance from five quarters; Pitigliano from the Maremma, Virginio Orsini through the Val d'Orcia, some Florentines through the Val d'Arbia, and the remainder through the Val dell'Elsa. The seaports were to be attacked by Doria, who succeeded in taking Talamone, a small port which had been purchased by Siena in

1303, and Port'Ercole, the only other port in Sienese territory, and a town whose possession was constantly disputed by Siena and Florence. A plan which was once again theoretically sound proved to be weak in detail. No attempt was made to set up a supply line as the league troops advanced on Siena, and these forces were quite insufficient to besiege Siena if it were not taken by fraud. The pope depended completely on the good faith of Palmieri. Altogether the expedition was to turn out to be nothing more than an expensive fiasco. It brought great discredit upon the League and earned Clement hostility in Florence that he could ill afford at this juncture. Having failed to capture Montalcino and Monteroni, an essential prerequisite for success in an attack on Siena, the papal army took up an insecure position outside the city at Porta Camollia. There was no rising in Siena and the exiles began to quarrel among themselves. Siena, although only garrisoned by some 400 troops, under the command of Giulio Colonna, was stoutly defended; civilian morale being raised in the classical Tuscan fashion by summoning the populace to arms, public prayers, vigils and fasts. The keys of the city were ceremoniously handed over to the Virgin, traditional guardian of Sienese liberty. The papal troops settled down into a desultory siege, finally abandoned on 25 July. The affair ended with a disgraceful rout of the papal forces by the Sienese. The net result of the campaign had been to ensure the total hostility of Siena to the Italian League.[20]

Despite these depressing results in the campaigns in Lombardy and Tuscany, the League retained one advantage – domination of the sea. The league fleets denied the imperialists much needed supplies, particularly in Lombardy, threatened Genoa, impeded communication and gave to the league troops an essential mobility which had some effect on military operations in Italy.

At the beginning of the war Venice chose Luigi Armero as *proveditor* of the fleet and dispatched him to Corfu to join Giovanni Moro, who was anchored there with the full Venetian naval forces. From these Armero detached thirteen galleys and sailed for Civitàvecchia where he was to unite with the French and the papal fleets, the whole league navy having been placed under the command of the experienced veteran Pedro Navarro. Armero united with Andrea Doria, who had entered papal service under a *condotta* of eight galleys, at Terracina on 28 August. From Terracina they sailed to Leghorn where they were joined by Navarro and the sixteen French galleys, and then to Portovenere, a town devoted to the Doria family, which, together with La Spezia and Monaco, surrendered immediately to the allies. The fleets now separated, the Venetians and Doria going to Portofino and Navarro to Savona which was also taken over by the League.[21]

The capture of Genoa was obviously the object of greatest moment, for Genoa would be a key element in any eventual success. The history of the previous forty years made it abundantly clear that 'who holds Genoa will also hold Milan. Genoa is the key to the whole of Lombardy; it is she who feeds the State of Milan, and if Genoa is taken Milan cannot be held.'[22] Control of Genoa was vital for any power wishing to control Italy: 'He who is not lord of Genoa and master of the sea can hardly expect to rule Italy.'[23]

Control of Genoa, however, was no easy matter. In the Middle Ages it had been divided as even no other Italian state was divided, torn by the strife between her leading families – the Ghibelline (White) Spinola and Doria, and the Guelf (Black) Fieschi and Grimaldi – and by the struggles between the noble and popular parties in government. During these years Genoa had gradually fallen under French domination and it was this connexion which made Genoa the object of general attention in the early sixteenth century. Despite the loss of her colonial empire in the fifteenth century, Genoa remained a commercial, banking, shipbuilding and trading centre of the first importance. One of the main objects of the Holy League, and in particular of Julius II, who had allied with the exiled Gian Fregosi, had been to end French influence in the city. After the French defeat of 1513, Genoa, under the Fregosi, returned to an autonomous government, but with a new French expedition the Fregosi were once more expelled.

As the Italian wars developed into the distinctive struggle between Hapsburg and Valois, Spain naturally began to play a more prominent part in Genoese affairs. Yet, aside from the political rationale for this interest, there were strong economic links between Spain and Genoa. These links originated first through Sicily where, by the end of the fifteenth century, Genoa dominated the field of maritime assurance, and through Naples, where the entire economy was dominated by foreigners and the Genoese were gradually ousting the Florentines from their established position. The export trade in foodstuffs and silk and in grain was based on a group of determined Genoese families who, in the absence of a Neapolitan mercantile marine, tended to monopolize Neapolitan commerce. At Genoa, too, were based the emperor's principal shipbuilders, the Doria, the Sauli, the Negroni, the Imperiali and the de Mari. And, if Spain was dependent on Genoa, conversely Genoa was dependent on Spain and increasingly so as the years passed. The fortunes of Genoa were founded on, and maintained by, the silk trade. At first most of the raw silk for these manufacturies came from the east, but even by the end of the fourteenth century Genoa was experiencing difficulty in obtaining silk from Asia and was looking elsewhere for supplies. In 1525 the source of these supplies was Spanish; by 1460 Genoa was regularly importing silk from Calabria, and by the beginning of the sixteenth century almost all the raw silk coming to Genoa came from Spain or the Spanish dependencies of Sicily and the kingdom of Naples. These dependencies also fed Genoa – the principal source of Genoese grain was Sicily, where it was purchased in Palermo. So great was the volume of this trade that the Genoese merchant marine was too small to maintain it, and use had to be made of Portuguese and Spanish ships. Without these auxiliary fleets Genoa would have starved.[24]

Thus the community of interest between Spain and Genoa was great enough to explain increasing Genoese tolerance of Spanish interference in the political life of the state. After the battle of Novara (1513) it was with Spanish help and approval that Ottaviano Fregosi was appointed doge. Ottaviano, however, was himself under pressure from Gian Fregosi, who had gained control of Savona and was threatening Genoa with the Adorni and Fieschi families. Afraid both of Gian and of the imperial aspirations of Duke Massimiliano Sforza of Milan, Ottaviano made a secret agreement with the French and, after the battle of Marignano, ceded Genoa to Francis I, driving the Adorni into alliance with the Spanish.

On 30 May 1522 with the change of fortunes following the battle of Bicocca, Genoa was occupied by an army of Spaniards led by Prospero Colonna and Pescara, and subjected to a terrible sack. Ottaviano Fregosi was taken prisoner to Naples and was replaced as doge by Antonietto Adorno, who ruled under strict imperial surveillance. In 1526 that surveillance was still active, and Charles V did not hesitate to warn the Genoese as the league fleets approached their coast that if the city surrendered, 'without being taken by force', all Genoese property would be seized throughout the imperial dominions.[25] The threat was taken very seriously, and Genoa prepared itself to suffer a long siege.

Pedro Navarro's plan was to take the city by a combined use of sea and land forces. By August 1526 he had succeeded in blockading the port completely, and many vessels, loaded with valuable war supplies, were captured by the League. The commanders of the fleet were buoyant and expected Genoa to fall any day, for they already had fifty-six vessels engaged in the blockade, were arming two of the large ships captured from the enemy, and were expecting another eleven galleons from the shipyards at Marseilles where they were being fitted out. It was a constant frustration to Navarro that Urbino would not send a land-force, for he had secret intelligence that Genoa would surrender should such a force appear, and he knew that an imperial fleet was expected from Spain which he would have to pursue once it appeared in Italian waters, thus breaking the blockade.[26]

Thus it was that the League in Lombardy was being pulled in two directions – towards Cremona, where the city-fortress still held out for Sforza, and towards Genoa. Both cities could be taken but each would require the total resources at the command of the league commanders and there were strong political reasons for concentrating first on Cremona. Its capture would satisfy Venice, who felt that her western border was very vulnerable, and would ensure that Sforza would not try to make a separate peace with the imperialists. But there were, of course, equally strong arguments in favour of throwing all the League's resources into the capture of Genoa, the sole major northern Italian port available for imperial use. Although the fleet continued to be successful before Genoa, its commanders did not feel strong enough to launch an attack on the city without a supporting land army. Urbino was perfectly ready to promise such assistance once Cremona had fallen or the marquess of Saluzzo had arrived with the promised French troops but would not release a single soldier before then.[27]

The siege of Cremona, gallantly defended by the able and courageous Spanish captain Corradino, was proving to be not only tedious but expensive, and with each day that passed the operations there took on a more massive scale. On 1 September Pesaro wrote home to Venice to explain that the chief papal engineer needed at least 1000 new sappers and more gunpowder in order to complete his mines and, the following day, demanded more money, 'because I don't have a penny here'.[28] Pesaro was also perturbed by the dubious activities of Federico Gonzaga, marquess of Mantua, whose little state adjoined the scene of operations and who was in an excellent position to give succour to the enemy.

Sympathetic as one may be to the problems of Federico Gonzaga, torn between the conflicting sides by a dual allegiance, he is not an attractive character. Throughout the Italian wars he had shown a marked reluctance to back either side in any conflict for fear that it might prove the loser and he was not above adulterating urine samples, provided for his doctors, with pig's blood, in order to obtain an 'authentic' medical excuse for not appearing in support of either France or pope or emperor. His relationships with all the great powers were by now so complicated as to defy disentanglement as he struggled for political survival. In the pontificate of Leo X Mantua had earned the displeasure of the pope by harbouring the dispossessed della Rovere family, but Leo, like Clement after him, was always anxious to detach Mantua from France and Spain and to make the marquess 'a good Italian'. The price for this detachment was high; Gonzaga wanted Leo to make him captain-general of the Church with a highly valuable *condotta* which might help to restore the shaky finances of his little state. Thus, in an agreement made in December 1520 Federico Gonzaga became the pope's captain-general and agreed to take service against anyone, including the emperor, his legitimate sovereign, from whom he held the marquessate of Mantua in fee. In August 1523, Federico was confirmed in his title with a *condotta* of 10,000 ducats for three years.

Clearly the time had now come when the captain-general of the Church might be expected to appear in the field, but there had been many indications in the preceding months that in any conflict Gonzaga would have a tendency to lean towards the emperor. In June there had been talk of renewing his *condotta* and of sending him to join the league army, but then it was found impossible to produce the original document in which the marquess had agreed to take service against the emperor. Subsequent investigations revealed that Mantuan agents had stolen the document from the papal archives and that it had been destroyed.

Now not only was the marquess refusing absolutely to give assistance to the League but it was quite clear that the imperialists in Cremona were receiving assistance which originated on Mantuan territory although the marquess blandly denied that he was in any way implicated. He did not succeed in deceiving Pesaro or Guicciardini. Four Mantuans had been caught red-handed smuggling desperately needed gunpowder into Cremona, and the explanation given by the marquess that gunpowder was readily available for sporting purposes in this season was unimpressive. The league commanders had to fall back on deterrence rather than rely on Mantua's word that such incidents would not occur again; all those who attempted to assist the imperialists were executed.[29]

Disturbing rumours were reaching the league camp from all quarters; that Charles had written to his brother, the Archduke Ferdinand, asking him to come to Italy with an army of lansquenets; that Charles himself was coming to Italy, to call a council, reform the Church and scotch the Lutherans; that Charles had invested the duke of Ferrara with the pope's temporal possessions.[30] On 4 September, therefore, Pesaro again wrote home to Venice asking for money to be sent immediately and reported that work on the mines at Cremona was being slowed up since he had been unable to hire any sappers from Piacenza. Although Cremona was defended by no more than 1500 men, in the middle of September 13,000 infantry, 300 lances, 400 light cavalry and 2000 sappers were engaged in the siege of the city, inching slowly forward over the approaches. Their every move was watched by hostile peasants, who promptly reported it to the imperialists. The League of Cognac might be an Italian league but the league army had singularly failed to recommend itself to the population of Lombardy. The country was being systematically looted for miles around Cremona, and the only crumb of comfort for the Venetians was that their troops had behaved marginally better than those of the pope.

As the league army settled into the long siege of Cremona a

mood of despair seemed to creep over Italy. The time of year favourable to military operations was already past, with little to show to the League's advantage. The news of the failure of the attack on Siena and that of the surrender of the citadel of Milan had plunged the pope into a mood of blackest despair. Letters reaching Acciauoli, in attendance on the French court, were almost uniformly depressing: 'Letters from Rome', he reported to Gambara in England,

> are full of fears because they are worried about the imperial fleet, which is to leave soon and land between eight and ten thousand infantry in the kingdom of Naples. It will arrive and find the pope without money, men or leaders, and with little reputation because the affairs of the League are in a depressed state . . . and it seems that at Rome they expect . . . great disaster. When the Spanish arrive it is doubtful whether the pope will be able to remain in Rome.[31]

Clement was complaining bitterly about the Venetians, about Urbino and, above all, about Francis I. Still the Italians waited on succour from their French allies and still they were disappointed. By the beginning of September Saluzzo had advanced no further than Asti and was not expected in the league camp for another three weeks. England, too, from whom so much had been hoped, remained coldly aloof. The Italians and the pope were isolated. On 1 August the secretary of the French embassy described the condition to which Clement had been reduced. His letter faithfully portrays the pope's disillusion and the decline from that optimistic spring in which the League of Cognac had been signed:

> I was with his Holiness yesterday, and do not think that I ever before saw a man so distracted, depressed and careworn as he was. He is half-ill with disappointment, and said to me several times that he had never thought he could have been treated in such a way. You have no idea what things are said about us by persons of high standing in the Curia, on account of our delays and our behaviour hitherto. The language is so frightful that I dare not write it. The ministers of His Holiness are more dead than alive. You can picture to yourself that the enemy will make use of the situation.[32]

CHAPTER VI

THE COLONNA RAID

Pontifex privavit Columnam et Columna privabit Pontificem.
Letters and Papers . . . of the Reign of Henry VIII,
vol. IV, pt 2, p. 1210

THE moment for which Pompeio Colonna had plotted and waited through so many long months seemed to have come at last. Now he could take his revenge on the Medici pope who had consistently frustrated his ambitions. With Moncada he plotted to lull the pope into security, and so bring about the disarmament of the papal troops around Rome; the capture and murder of the defenceless pontiff would follow. Then, at last, Colonna believed he would see the path clear for his own ascent to St Peter's chair.

Throughout July 1526 the Colonna remained quiet within the confines of their own territories, hoping to allay the pope's suspicions. Meanwhile, Sessa, in order to keep in touch with the progress of events at Rome, asked for a safe-conduct to return there for medical treatment. Certainly he had need of such treatment for he died soon after his return to Rome on 18 August, but not before he had passed on to Moncada and the Colonna information about the desperate state of the papal finances. A new envoy, Guillaume Du Bellay, Sire de Langey, had arrived from France, but he had come empty-handed. He brought nothing more than general professions of goodwill and fresh claims on behalf of France; a tenth of the revenues of the Church in France for his sovereign and a cardinal's hat for the Chancellor Du Prat.

Now was the propitious moment for the Colonna to enter into negotiations, and the occasion was seized. Vespasiano Colonna, whom alone among the Colonna Clement had favoured, at least to the extent of trying to arrange a marriage for him with the wealthy Giulia Gonzaga, was chosen as mediator. On 22 August he arrived in Rome to negotiate a truce between the Colonna on one side, the pope and the Orsini on the other. The terms were not unfavourable to the Colonna. At least one intelligent provision was included: the Colonna would not take up arms against the Church except on behalf of the emperor, in which case they would surrender their possessions in the Church State. This was the only logical way in which the dual alliance of the Colonna could be resolved. It was also reasonable to specify that Clement would not attack the Colonna estates, nor permit the Orsini to do so, for, had this provision been observed, the outbreak of any major incident through Orsini–Colonna rivalry might have been prevented. It was agreed that the Colonna should retire to the Kingdom of Naples and should remove all troops from their lands within the Church State. In return Clement gave the Colonna permission to serve the emperor against anyone who attacked Naples and granted a full pardon to the entire faction.

The pope immediately disbanded his troops, thereby facilitating Pompeio's plans for the capture of Rome. Colonna had never intended to keep the truce which had been made with the express intention of disarming Clement. As soon as Pompeio was sure that Clement was indeed standing down his forces, he dispatched his light cavalry to attack Anagni, where Clement had a garrison of 300 troops, aiming to cut all the communication-routes with Rome.[1] Pompeio's next task was overcoming the moral scruples of Vespasiano Colonna, who had at least some doubts about breaking an agreement he had just helped to make. Together Moncada and Pompeio Colonna rode to Vespasiano Colonna at Fondi and 'corrupted him, demonstrating that in the service of the emperor, their overlord, any breach of faith was permissible . . . as long as it led to victory'.[2]

Writing on 14 September from the Colonna territories Moncada informed the emperor of all that happened and outlined the current Colonna plan. He had persuaded the council of Naples to supply troops, on the pretext that they were to be used to relieve Siena, 'but our intention is to enter Rome'. Of the troops raised, 800 cavalry and 2000 infantry were supplied and paid by the council of Naples, 1000 were tenants of the Colonna and 2000 had been recruited secretly in the Abruzzi. Another 1000 infantry were to be transported to Ostia by galleys of the Neapolitan fleet. Two days later Moncada informed the council of Naples of his real intentions, but by this time it was too late for them to stop him.[3]

Communications between Rome and Naples had been as suc-

cessfully interrupted as Pompeio had intended and no news of the
Colonna reached Rome until the late evening of 19 September.
When news arrived of the Colonna movements Clement hurriedly
summoned the Venetian ambassador and poured out to him his
misery on the subject of that perfidious family. He still knew of
little more than the attack on Anagni but this in itself he regarded
as a wicked breach of faith. 'Holy father,' the ambassador reminded
him, 'you have now seen their faithlessness on at least two occasions, first over Siena and the second in this agreement which they
have broken.' However, although he was prepared to agree that
the Colonna were altogether a faithless bunch of rascals, the
Venetian was unwilling to admit that Clement should immediately
withdraw his troops from Lombardy.

For a man not cast in the heroic mould, and that Clement certainly was not, this must have been a terrible day. He had a genuine
affection for Vespasiano Colonna and was personally hurt that he
had broken his solemn word. But news of the hostile movements
of the Colonna, although the most immediately important, was not
the most terrible news to reach Rome on 19 September. Reports
had come, too, from far-distant Hungary of the battle of Mohácz,
in which the armies of Sulaiman the Magnificent had destroyed the
Hungarian forces and killed the young king Lewis, last of the
Jagielleon kings of Bohemia and Hungary. Clement, who always
had the inclination, if he did not always have the time, to be a
conscientious father of Christendom, was horrified, and summoned every foreign ambassador in Rome to announce the terrible
news, 'offering to ride in person against the Turk; and as vicar of
Christ to sacrifice his life'.[4] For a brief time every other consideration paled and Clement spoke again, as he had often spoken before,
of going to the emperor himself in order to arrange a general peace
of all the Christian powers. There is little doubt that Clement
recognized in Mohácz a divine judgement on the warring nations
of Christendom, and acknowledged how great was his own guilt
in the matter. Nevertheless, the only practical action which the
pope took that night was to order that the city-gates should be
closed against the Colonna and that troops should be raised in the
morning.

These measures were already too late. The Colonna, led by
Moncada, Mario Orsini and their Roman ally Cesare de' Sabbatini,

marched all through the beautiful moonlit night, covering sixty miles in twenty-four hours and reaching Rome at dawn. The entry of the Colonna forces into the city took place in its least densely populated area, on its eastern boundary. At least two gates, Porta San Giovanni in Lateran and Porta San Paolo, and possibly a third, were captured in the early hours of the morning when they were opened to let out the mules and the beasts of burden which brought wood into the city each day. Within the city the first intimation that anything was amiss was the sight of an army pouring into Rome through Porta San Giovanni, as far as Sant'Apostoli, where the soldiers retired into Palazzo Colonna, one of the oldest of the Roman palaces, to rest and refresh themselves.[5]

Clement was desperate. His soldiers were disbanded and the papal treasury was empty. As soon as he heard that the Colonna had entered Rome he threw himself on the mercy of the Roman populace. Cardinals Campeggio, Cesarini and Jacobacci were sent to the Capitol to ask the people of Rome to take up arms on the pope's behalf. As an ally of the Colonna, Jacobacci might have been expected to carry some weight with the Romans but, in fact, the representatives of the people declared themselves unwilling to provide either arms or money for the pope's defence. The Colonna had for so long been undermining the pope's position in Rome that the passage of their army through the city quickly took on the character of a triumphal procession. 'The artisans, like men who have no fear, without even closing their shops, spread out along the banks of the Tiber to watch the Colonna pass under the Janiculum.'[6] Pompeio Colonna sent his own herald through the city to tell the citizens there was nothing to dread and to urge them to rise in his support, 'because they had not come to harm this city, which was their home also, but for the liberty of Rome'.[7] It seemed that the hour had come in which the events of 1511 would be repeated, with victory this time going to the Colonna and not to the pope.

In the morning, still unmolested by any papal troops, the Colonna forces gathered at the church of Saints Cosmas and Damian. Pompeio Colonna, who as a cardinal of the Church possibly felt the incongruity of his appearing in person in this attack on the pope, remained in Palazzo Colonna. Crossing the bridges of the Isola Tiberina into Trastevere, the Colonna progressed up the Lungara past the new palace of Agostino Chigi, towards the Borgo. The first resistance which they encountered was at Porta San Spirito. Although, at the pope's request, the Swiss Guard had retired with their artillery into the fortress of Sant'Angelo, Stefano Colonna, Ettore Romano and Francesco Salamone with little more than a hundred infantry held the gate for about an hour.[8] When it became clear that it would be impossible to take the gate without heavy losses on the part of the attackers, the commanders on the Colonna side resorted to a diversion, and finally circumvented Porta San Spirito by passing over a part of the city wall which had been broken down and then advancing through the vineyards of Cardinal Armellino.[9] The Colonna, who now had the slight advantage of fighting downhill, were able to thrust back the defenders and move up the Borgo Vecchio to the Vatican and St Peter's where Clement who, like Pompeio Colonna, appears to have been well read in thirteenth-century history, 'abandoned by all, intended to die on his throne'. It was only the urgent entreaties of the cardinals, Filippo Strozzi and the Venetian ambassador that induced him to flee along the covered passage to Castel Sant'Angelo at about five o'clock in the afternoon, carrying with him the most important of the papal jewels and ornaments.[10]

The main purpose of the attack, the capture of Clement, had therefore failed, owing to the delay in making an attack on the Borgo. Deprived of their prey, the soldiers resorted to plundering the Leonine city, or at least such parts of it as were beyond the reach of the guns of Castel Sant'Angelo. It was not a sack which was motivated entirely by gain, however. There was a strong political complexion to it as well. Francesco Berni, the poet, had moved to Rome from his native Florence in 1517, and by 1523 he had entered the service of Giberti, to whom he was devoted. Now the Colonna made immediately for his apartments in the Vatican, rifled his correspondence and were about to carry off such letters of the datary as were to be found there when they were interrupted by a sudden alarm.[11] Since the only possible motive for the theft of this correspondence was political – to discover more about the Italian League and papal commitments to foreign powers – and since this correspondence could only be of real value to the imperial government, it may be safely concluded that servants of Charles V were prominent in this looting of the Borgo.

In all, about one-third of the Leonine city was sacked; the area stretching as far as Palazzo Ancona.

> The papal palace was almost completely stripped even to the bedroom and wardrobe of the pope. The great and the private sacristy of St Peter's, that of the palace, the apartments of prelates and members of the household, even the horse-stalls were emptied, their doors and windows shattered; chalices, crosses, pastoral staffs, ornaments of great value, all that fell into their hands, was carried off as plunder by this rabble; persons of distinction were taken prisoners. The dwelling and stable of Monsignor Sadoleto were plundered; he himself had taken refuge in Sant'Angelo. Almost all the apartments in the corridors were treated in like manner except those of Campeggio, which were defended by some Spaniards. Ridolfi lost everything; Giberti had removed some articles of value, but lost not a few. Among other damage, his porcelain, worth 600 ducats, was broken in pieces. Messer Paolo Giovio, in his History, will be able to recall misfortunes like those of Thucydides, although he, with a presentiment of harm, had concealed the best of his belongings in the city some days before.[12]

Losses subsequently reckoned at about 300,000 ducats occurred before the looting was brought to an end by a sally from the castle in which some property was recovered and about sixty prisoners, including Mario Orsini, taken. The Leonine city had been denuded of much of its wealth; even the tapestries of Raphael had been taken from the Sistine Chapel. To add to the general confusion, all the prisoners in the Borgo escaped and proceeded to plunder of their own accord.[13]

In normal circumstances the pope should have been able to withstand a siege in Castel Sant'Angelo indefinitely, but the retrenchment policy of the administration, and the inefficiency of the castellan, Giulio de' Medici, had together ensured that the fortress was completely unsupplied. Through the medium of the Portuguese ambassador Clement opened negotiations with Moncada and the Colonna. Niccolò Ridolfi and Innocenzo Cybo were sent by the pope as hostages while Moncada came to Castel Sant'Angelo to parley. On this first visit Moncada was full of fair speeches. To the disgust of the Colonna, who had thought of besieging the pope in Sant'Angelo, Moncada restored to Clement the silver pastoral staff and the papal tiara which had been stolen during the raid. He assured the pope that Charles V had never sought supremacy in Italy, 'although he might, by right, aspire to it'.[14] On Clement's part the reception of Moncada seems to have been frigid. He spoke little, but with bitterness, on the subject of Cardinal Pompeio Colonna.

On the following morning Moncada returned to the pope, and had a long interview with him while the cardinals waited in an adjoining room. Talks went on all day but Moncada insisted that before agreement could be reached Castel Sant'Angelo must be surrendered to the emperor. Since Clement felt that no clearer evidence of the emperor's determination to control central Italy could have been offered, the request was refused. All that could be agreed upon was a truce until three o'clock on the following afternoon. Moncada then reopened the talks, warning that he would bombard the castle and even ordering heavy guns into position. Colonna, meanwhile, kept his troops drawn up in battle order in the Baths of Diocletian, where they remained for some three weeks.

After consultation with his cardinals, on 22 September Clement again summoned Moncada and continued the negotiations, 'His Holiness continuing to scheme and draw things out in order to better our condition and to come to an agreement on the most advantageous and least shameful terms possible'.[15] The cardinals, on the whole, were opposed to an agreement, but they were over-ruled by Clement, who saw that the only course open to him at this time was to make a virtue of necessity.

The truce finally arranged displeased Pompeio Colonna, for although it granted his family and adherents plenary absolution it achieved none of his original aims and even made provision that he and the Colonna army should retire to the Regno. However, from the imperial point of view, it was ideal; it provided for a cessation of hostilities for four months in the duchy of Milan, the kingdom of Naples, Genoa, Florence, Ferrara and Siena, while Clement promised to withdraw his troops within the confines of the Church State. In return, Moncada agreed to withdraw his troops from papal territory. Clement was forced to give two hostages, Filippo Strozzi and a son of Jacopo Salviati. Yet this was all less than Moncada had expected. On 22 September he confessed to the Ferrarese ambassador that he had been forced to come to an agreement because the Colonna had misled him into believing that there would be an armed uprising in his favour inside Rome and because he had lost control of his troops once looting had begun in the Borgo.[16]

It was, in fact, already apparent that the attack, having failed, had been a grave political error. Public opinion in Italy swung sharply against the imperial cause. Realizing this, Moncada warned the emperor to express to Clement, through Castiglione, his great grief at what had happened. The Colonna had few, if any, Italian sympathizers. Isabella d'Este, who had been resident in Rome during the attack was profoundly shocked and peculiarly displeased that Vespasiano Colonna, whose marriage with Giulia Gonzaga she had previously sponsored, had taken part in the raid. She subsequently refused to take part in the marriage festivities of the couple. The Colonna openly asserted that, in sacking the holy places of Rome, they had acted under explicit instruction from the emperor,[17] and the raid provoked an anti-imperial backlash and a temporary resurgence of papal popularity at Rome that had not entirely evaporated by the following May. During the night of 3–4 October an alarm was raised that the Colonna were planning to return to Rome to sack it. All of Rome rose to the defence of Clement and there were shouts of 'For the Church' and 'Long live Pope Clement', uncommon enough cries in Rome at this time.[18] It was suggested by contemporaries that Clement himself had raised the alarm in order to test Roman reaction. If he did so, he must have been well satisfied. The city remained in arms and in a posture of defence throughout the night. At the end of December the Romans were still prepared to provide for the defence of the city against the Colonna.[19] More significant perhaps were the popular, fearful speculations on the possible consequences of the Colonna raid. It was thought highly probable that the Colonna attempt would encourage the emperor to more ambitious projects, 'since he sees that it is so easy to attack Rome and deprive the pope of his own'.[20]

The fact that the Colonna made no immediate move towards withdrawing to the kingdom of Naples but continued to occupy their own properties in the environs of Rome lent credence to such suggestions. Clement appeared to be keeping his side of the bargain. He withdrew a few troops from the league army in Lombardy; on 2 October the whole city of Rome was able to witness the arrival of Vitelli with 400 lances and a band of Swiss infantry. With these Clement fortified Porta San Spirito, the hills of San Onofrio and the Sistine bridge.[21] In fact, although this was not generally known, Clement had asked for the dispatch of these troops before the Colonna raid, on 19 September, and Guicciardini had already begun to plan for their departure, when news of the raid, along with a further request for the urgent dispatch of troops from Lombardy, arrived.[22] It was clear, however, that the pope did not intend to do more than observe the truce nominally, for the request for the dispatch of troops was coupled with a second letter from Giberti, ordering that their departure be delayed until after the fall of Cremona.[23] Clement's original intention was to leave all his troops in Lombardy at the League's disposal, ostensibly under the French flag, but paid from Rome.

The pope was determined to continue his alliance with the Italian League, for there were signs that the defence of Cremona was at last weakening, and Clement had heard of this even before the Colonna raid. A proposal for a negotiated surrender was tendered by the imperialist defenders of Cremona as early as 22 September, but its terms were so liberal to the imperialists that they were flatly rejected. On the following day the defence virtually admitted defeat, and agreed to a cease-fire for a month on condition that if help had not come to them within this period Cremona would be surrendered.[24]

Vitelli, therefore, cannot be said to have damaged the League cause in Lombardy by leaving for Rome. Clement, however, had already found that his demands on the Lombard armies would have to be substantially greater than he had at first intended. He had heard that the long-expected Spanish fleet had arrived in Italian waters and feared that it threatened Rome. Hurriedly he instructed Guicciardini to withdraw with 5000 infantry south of the Po in order to guard the northern Church State. When Guicciardini announced to the Venetians that they would be left in Lombardy with only 4000 papal infantry under the command of Giovanni de' Medici, they were understandably enraged by this apparent defection at the very moment of victory. They were not convinced by Guicciardini's argument that the position was inevitable, given the events at Rome: the arrival of the Spanish fleet, imminent papal bankruptcy and the refusal of Florence to spend a further ducat on the war. Like many contemporaries, the Venetians never realized that the war had to be won in the south as well as in Lombardy and always failed to take account of the real dangers the pope faced from the Campagna and Naples.

Yet that those dangers were real the Colonna raid had clearly demonstrated. Clement was vulnerable on every border and at every front, and the emperor, in alliance with the Colonna, had been able to exploit that vulnerability. In doing so the Colonna had exposed every other weakness of Clement: his financial straits, his unpopularity in Rome, the lack of support from his allies, and fundamental strategic weaknesses in the defences of Rome. Lessons had been learned that would not be forgotten. Although the Colonna were temporarily bruised and hostile, believing that they had been tricked by Moncada and abandoned by the imperialists, they now represented a continual danger to the pope, lying as they were within striking distance of the city of Rome itself.

CHAPTER VII

THE WAR AGAINST THE COLONNA

The state of the Colonna was dismembered in such a way that, if it had not been remade through our misery in the sack of Rome, the Holy See would . . . have completely subjected them.
Marcello Alberini, in D. Orano, *Sacco di Roma*, p. 227

THE pope's position after the Colonna raid was very difficult. If law and order were to be upheld in the Church State, he could not afford to ignore so overt an affront to papal authority as he had just experienced. Yet the Venetians were opposed to any punitive expedition against the offenders, and Clement also knew that while the Colonna remained in alliance with the emperor any attack would worsen papal relations with the imperialists in Naples and that the threat from that direction might be intensified at any moment by the long-awaited arrival of the viceroy and the Spanish fleet.[1] The pope, nevertheless, acted with uncharacteristic vigour; a permanent committee of five cardinals for war and another of five for the public treasury were named. By 12 October 1526 the pope had a total force of some 7–8000 troops in Rome, and, as far as the populace of Rome was concerned, Clement's intentions against the Colonna became an open secret on 28 October when seven pieces of artillery were seen being dragged towards Porta San Giovanni. These, the Romans learned, were to be used against the castles of Pompeio Colonna. On 7 November Clement made his first public statement, declaring his intention of punishing the Colonna both temporally and spiritually, and it was clear that the matter of most immediate importance to the pope was that Pompeio Colonna should be deprived of the cardinal dignities he had betrayed.[2]

The public charges made against Pompeio Colonna ranged back to the first weeks of Clement's pontificate; little was forgotten and nothing forgiven.[3] Colonna was given nine days to present himself in court and answer the charges but failed to appear. Instead he countered the pope's attack by yet another appeal to a general council. Proceedings against Colonna began on 16 November, and on 21 November he was sentenced to the deprivation of all his benefices and dignities. On 14 November a similar citation summoned Ascanio, Vespasiano and Giovanni Colonna, Pietro Francesco Macello and Jacobo da Zambeccarii.[4] They also failed to appear, were excommunicated, and with all members of the Colonna family were deprived of their properties in the Church State.[5]

Meanwhile, on 1 November, the pope's mercenary captain, Vitello Vitelli with the captains Luca Antonio da Terni and Battista Corso, 9000 infantry and 1000 cavalry opened a military campaign against the Colonna with an attack on Grottaferrata and Marino. By 10 November Vitelli had taken Marino, Grottaferrata, Frascati, Montefucino, Valmontone, Genezzano, Cave, Giuliano di Roma and Roccapriora.[6] In the general confusion the opportunity was seized for unauthorized private expeditions: papal supporters from Priverno attacked Sonnino, Giuliano, San Stefano, San Lorenzo and Vallecorso.[7] The inhabitants of Velletri who, since 1505, had been quarrelling with the Colonna over the boundaries of Nemi, destroyed Marino completely.[8] Rocca di Papa, which had been sold to the Colonna by the Annibaldi in 1425, was likewise destroyed by Vitelli, although the fortress was not taken and remained standing among the surrounding ruins and rubble.[9] Ceccano, Supino and Rocca San Stefano were all razed to the ground as was Subiaco, the favourite residence of Pompeio Colonna and one of the earliest centres of printing in Italy.[10]

Thus the Colonna lost all their property in the Church State except the fortresses of Rocca di Papa, Montefortino and Paliano, but in order to achieve this Clement had to put into the field an army which, including the cost of the troops in Lombardy, drained the papal treasury of 60,000 ducats a month. At the same time the Colonna had been driven into even closer alliance with the emperor, for their only hope of recovering their property was now through imperial support. They increased their pressure on the duke of Bourbon, urging him to march south. In the second week of November the council of Naples dispatched its own envoy, Musscetola, to the pope to try to persuade him to desist from his punishment of the Colonna, and Moncada warned Clement that any action against the Colonna would be construed as an attack on the emperor.[11]

Desperately short of money and hard-pressed by the imperialists in the south, Clement was anxious for good news from Lombardy. But from this source came little news, save of dissension between the commanders, of inactivity and other problems. The mercenary troops were still proving troublesome. From the opening of the campaign the Swiss and the Grisons, despite the faith placed in them by Urbino, had proved as much of a liability as an asset. Late in arriving, they clamoured constantly for money, threatening to desert whenever they were not immediately satisfied; but, since the Swiss and the Grisons were an important buffer against the imperialists in the north, it was too dangerous to risk offending them. At the beginning of every month a fresh agreement had to be made with the Swiss to prevent them leaving the League's service, and on 25 November a thousand of them, having asked in vain for a supplement to their wages in order to buy winter clothing, deserted – the first of many who would leave during the coming winter. The Venetians, in particular, were suffering heavily by desertion, since they were finding it difficult to pay their troops. Often forty or fifty days elapsed between payments, and the Swiss troops bore delay in their wages with ill grace.

The camp on the Lambro, whither the bulk of the army had retired, was proving unsatisfactory, but every attempt to move was thwarted by the weather. The project of taking Genoa had to be abandoned, for news was coming through of Frundsberg's imminent descent into Italy. In order to come to the assistance of the imperialists in Italy, George von Frundsberg, the famous leader of the lansquenets had pawned his towns and possessions in the south Tyrol, even his beloved castle of Mindelheim, together with the personal ornaments and jewels of his wife. Convinced that the pope was oppressing the emperor and the House of Colonna, and believing that it was God's will that the pope, the instigator of the war, and the emperor's greatest enemy, should be punished and hanged, Frundsberg had been gathering troops throughout the summer, preparatory to a descent into Italy. For the enterprise he was joined by such famous German captains as Schertlin von Burtenbach and Conrad von Bemelberg.

The Italians had long been aware that this great host was gathering, and certain news of their arrival at Trent now paralysed all League activity. The entire spy-service of the Venetians was devoted to discovering the route which the lansquenets would take. While France attempted to bribe the Grisons to hold their passes, particularly the Valtellina, against the lansquenets, Venice, convinced that Frundsberg intended to invade the Veneto, used her resources to fortify its northern boundary.[12] Inevitably this had an effect on the army in Lombardy, from which some companies of cavalry were withdrawn, and for which less money could now be spared, for Venice was feeling the expense of the war. On 5 October the state had to launch a Public Loan to raise money; on 8 November Saluzzo asked Venice for a loan of 10,000 ducats which she was unable to raise; the castellan of Mus had also to be purchased by the payment of 5000 ducats, half by the pope and half by Venice, nominally a ransom for the Venetian ambassadors who were still in the castellan's hands, and by a *condotta* of 400 infantry with which he was to guard Lake Como.

Since there was not time to close all the passes the defence of Venice was at first centred on Bassano, for it was believed Frundsberg would attack down the Valsugana. Accordingly, the Brenta was blocked, the bridge at Cismondi Grappa was cut, and the road rendered impassable. Rumours continued to multiply about the lansquenets. With the Valsugana closed, their most likely passage was down the Adige to Verona. Venetian troops were, therefore, transferred into the Veronese, and when Frundsberg, guided by his brother-in-law Count Lodovico of Lodron, moved down the western route into the Mantovano the Venetians were hurriedly shipped across Lake Garda to Salò. By 19 November the lansquenets had reached the environs of Brescia, and on 22 November they were within the confines of the state of Mantua, in the Serraglio, a fortress, half-formed by nature and half-built by man, bounded on the west by ditches and a wall, on the south by the Po and on the east by the Mincio. Here the lansquenets appeared to be preparing to cross the Po, 'into the Bolognese, in order to come, so they say among themselves, to attack the Church State, and to enter Tuscany, where, if they find no resistance, they will have the road clear to Rome'.[13] The future plans of the lansquenets might still be unclear, but what was certain was that Federico Gonzaga, the marquess of Mantua, was supplying Frundsberg with food and equipment. Even Gonzaga's enemies had to admit that in this he had little choice, for Frundsberg had warned him that if supplies were not forthcoming the whole territory of Mantua would be burnt and pillaged; but this aid to the imperialists did not endear Gonzaga to the league commanders, whose one aim was to prevent Frundsberg crossing the Po.

The Venetians now learned that Frundsberg had at least 16,000 men in his army, more even than had been feared. However, apart from those provided by an exile from Cremona, Niccolò Varolo, who had joined them with 200 first-class cavalry, they had few horses and no artillery.[14] Yet it was ominous that such horses as were accompanying the lansquenets were artillery horses, for this could only mean that they would be supplied with some of the valuable artillery of Alfonso d'Este, duke of Ferrara, who, it was rumoured, was about to open hostilities against the League by attacking Modena.

Pressure both from the pope and from Venice had forced the duke of Urbino to take some action against Frundsberg, although this meant entering into a campaign with weakened troops at the worst season of the year, when under normal circumstances the armies should have been resting and preparing for the spring campaign. As they were not strong enough to risk a battle, Urbino and Giovanni de' Medici hoped simply to prevent a conjunction between Bourbon, who was still in Milan, and Frundsberg. On 23 November Frundsberg's troops began to leave the Serraglio, making for the fortress of Governolo, with its important bridge across the Po. On the following morning Frundsberg's men were attacked by Urbino and Medici but were able to repulse the assault and to reach Governolo in safety. Harried though they were, and despite heavy snowfalls, by 27 November all of the lansquenets had crossed the Po, were within the confines of the Church State and appeared to be advancing on Modena. For the League it had been a peculiarly fruitless and tragic campaign, for, in the fighting at Governolo, Giovanni de' Medici had suffered a fatal wound. Predatory as his troops, the 'Black Bands', might be, the twenty-eight-year-old Giovanni de' Medici was one of the few Italian military commanders of genius still alive and fighting for the League. His 'Black Bands', 4000 of those Italian infantry so despised by the duke of Urbino, owed much of their *esprit de corps* to Giovanni's superlative training and leadership, and, as they had proved during the assault on Milan, were the best troops at the

League's disposal. Giovanni's death was universally mourned, not least by his kinsman the pope, now left without a military spokesman of authority in the league camp to counterbalance Urbino, who had been confirmed in his customary prudence by the events at Governolo.

Shortly after Medici's death, Frundsberg, in heavy rain and without the supplies he had anticipated from Bourbon, made his way upstream into the Piacentino. Here, in appalling conditions, he lodged his men for four months between Castel San Giovanni and Fidenza.[15] Medici's death and Frundsberg's arrival, the Colonna raid, heavy desertions, particularly among the Swiss, and approaching winter, all combined to end the League's offensive. All its troops were now engaged in purely defensive operations. Saluzzo took up quarters at Parma, Urbino at Casalmaggiore and Guido Rangoni, now the leading papal commander, at Piacenza.

Already serious weaknesses had become apparent in the military operations of the League: the incompetence of its generals, particularly Urbino and Saluzzo, the lack of money and supplies, the division of political command, and the need to garrison so many towns and fortresses that the resources of the armies were constantly depleted. Saluzzo was, by all accounts, incompetent and incapable of maintaining discipline. His French aristocratic background and training told against him, and although he was personally courageous he had little idea of strategy or tactics. To make matters worse, owing to the inefficiencies of his home government, Saluzzo was very rarely in a position to pay his troops. The majority of these were able, well-trained men, but many of the officers were Italian adventurers whose only aim was to make a profit from the war.[16] In consequence there was a regrettable tendency for discipline to break down among Saluzzo's troops, and there was much unauthorized pillaging and robbing, particularly within the Church State.

Urbino had proved already that he was more often a liability than an asset. He was not, strictly speaking, an incompetent general; indeed, on questions of discipline and supply he was a master and he had played a prominent part in the reorganization of the Venetian army. He was courteous in council and prepared to listen to advice, though less ready to take it when it was given. An independent Venetian observer spoke highly of his skill and knowledge, and of his relationship with his troops.[17] Yet he did not shine when it came to matters of strategy; his ideas were dominated by the remembrance of the battle of Agnadello in 1509 and of the loss of the entire Venetian mainland territory on that one day; he was unimaginative about everything except supposed plots against his person, and was incapable of planning a successful offensive campaign. His natural caution and belief in the desirability of limited objectives made him an excellent servant of Venice, never noted for rash policies, but a poor servant of the League. Urbino's attitude to the Medici and to Florence was unrepentantly, if excusably, hostile – an attitude which was generally reciprocated – and it was popularly believed that Urbino would use his position in the league armies to recover the district of Montefeltre, the mountainous region between the Marecchia and the Foglia, and the town of San Leo, which he had lost to Florence during the War of Urbino in the pontificate of Leo X. It is difficult to avoid being prejudiced against Urbino by contemporary Florentine historians and commentators who never had a good word to say for the duke. Yet, surprisingly, Charles V thought highly of his abilities – or so he said. A friend of Duke Alfonso of Ferrara, as duke of Sora a Neapolitan subject and, traditionally, the enemy of Sforza, Urbino would have made a natural ally for Charles V had the situation not been complicated by claims of Ascanio Colonna to the duchy of Urbino.

Guicciardini and Urbino were temperamentally unsuited to working together, not least because Guicciardini regarded everything in terms of the need to defend the Church State, an almost impossible proposition. The defence of the northern Church State was based on strategic fortresses, guarding the main routes to the south. There were many of these, and to defend them all adequately required so much manpower that it was unrealistic to consider keeping a large field army as well. Guicciardini and Rangoni did their best, but they could not avoid withdrawing troops into the towns of the Church State at moments of crisis. So on 28 November Guicciardini demanded 1000 infantry from the league camp for this purpose. Urbino would only release 500 men but had to send 500 ducats so that Guicciardini could try to make up the number from other sources.[18]

Politically, the League was also running into difficulties. Clement had been racked by doubts, uncertainties and fears for months. The arrival of the lansquenets, and the imminent arrival of the Spanish fleet, together with the Colonna raid, had long since cured him of any remaining illusions about the goodwill of Charles V. The lansquenets and the Spanish fleet had been sent 'to hedge us in, and to force us to accept the yoke patiently, and to give him the monarchy' of Italy.[19] Hard upon the news of the death of Giovanni de' Medici came further adverse political tidings. Definite advices reached Clement concerning an alliance between Alfonso d'Este, duke of Ferrara, and the emperor. There had long been rumours that negotiations for such an alliance were afoot. As Clement's relations with Charles V had worsened so Alfonso d'Este had become more inclined to an imperial alliance. This was uncharacteristic, for Ferrara, despite the dual allegiance of her dukes to pope and emperor, had traditionally been a French ally, protected by Louis XII against Julius II, and at the time of the imperial election Alfonso d'Este was still allied to France. By his agreement with Leo X of 8 May 1521, Charles V promised to assist the pope in recovering Ferrara for the Church State. It was only after the French defeat at Bicocca in 1522 that Este would even receive the imperial ambassador, although he brought with him from the emperor the investiture to the state of Este and a promise of the restoration of Modena and Reggio.

Charles, however, was prepared to bid high in order to have Ferrara on his side. It was with good reason that Alfonso d'Este had chosen as his heraldic emblem a bombshell, symbolizing concealed power propitiously released. In the opinion of Charles V the duke of Ferrara was outstanding among the Italian princes for his skill both in civic administration and in diplomacy. For the duke, therefore, the emperor already had a certain sympathy as of one professional with another. Moreover, the briefest glance at a map revealed that Este's lands, which bordered the Veneto and the Church State, constituted an important buffer-state, and that the duke would be a dangerous enemy to have on the borders of Milan where he could permanently tie down even the most efficient army. He was reputed to be wealthy and certainly had the best artillery in Italy in his possession. He even had substantial propaganda value. There had been reports from Spain in August 1526 of discussions by theologians seeking to justify war with Clement VII

on the grounds that successive popes had unjustly made war on
Ferrara. It was clear that the emperor should go to considerable
lengths to win Este as an ally. Indeed, in September 1526 Moncada
went so far as to advise Charles that the whole success of the
imperial cause in Italy depended on a declaration by Ferrara for
Charles V.[20]

On the other hand, until September Ferrara was by no means
totally committed to the emperor, for Charles and his advisers had
displayed an annoying tendency to abandon Este in pursuit of
higher objects. Ferrara's aims were limited: the possession of
Reggio, Rubiera, Modena and Carpi. Towards this end he would
negotiate with both sides, indefinitely if possible, although he was
anxious to prevent his talks with the other Italian powers from
coming to the attention of the emperor.

Within Italy the duke of Ferrara had consistent advocates in the
Venetians, with whom he had been friendly for some time and
whose relations with the papacy were not infrequently as strained
as his own. It was thus a natural result of the renewed friendliness
between the pope and the Venetians in 1526 that Venice should
press Clement VII to enter into negotiation with Ferrara. Although
Clement already suspected Este of leaning towards the imperial
cause, he had agreed to talks and asked Venice to arrange a five-
month truce with the duke. Este opened the discussions by asking
for a suspension of any negotiations concerning Reggio and
Modena, but to this Clement would not agree; it was only reluctantly, under extreme pressure from France and Venice, that the
pope relented slightly – 'he doesn't so much favour a suspension
but rather to arrange things with the duke in such a way that they
will always go smoothly and to make such a union with him that
he will always be allied with the Pope'.[21]

But Este was more interested in immediate and tangible objects,
and when he insisted on retaining Reggio and Rubiera, Clement
broke off the negotiations. In May the pope suggested a new basis
for agreement: Este was to surrender all the territory he had
occupied during the two previous vacancies of the papacy and, in
return, would be granted lands to an equivalent value in the
Romagna. This was a plan sponsored by Guicciardini, long an
advocate of papal accommodation with Ferrara, for he had had
bitter personal experience of the difficulties of the existing

situation. He was convinced that some agreement might be reached on the basis of the surrender of Modena and Reggio in return for Ravenna – Modena and Reggio being indispensable to the papal defence system.

As soon as he joined the league armies in Lombardy Guicciardini realized how urgent it was that the pope should satisfy Este. Duke Alfonso had long been making serious military preparations, and on 27 September Guicciardini learned that he was gathering troops around Carpi preparatory to an attack on Modena. The fact that this threatened attack was planned at a date so close to the Colonna raid on Rome indicated a high degree of collaboration between Colonna and Este, although neither had yet declared himself openly for the emperor. Este certainly had strong links with the Colonna, for in the pontificate of Julius II they had assisted in thwarting that pope's attempt to arrest Este.[22]

An unexpected result of the Colonna raid was Clement's sudden readiness to adopt a more realistic attitude to the problem of Ferrara. The pope now declared that he was ready to cede Modena and Reggio on payment of 200,000 ducats, but the duke, whose negotiations with the emperor on the same subject were prospering, maintained that the sum must be considerably reduced. In Spain his ambassador had negotiated a treaty with Charles V giving him the investiture of Modena, Reggio and Rubiera and the grant of all the confiscated property of Alberto Pio da Carpi. Este was to be created imperial captain-general in Italy, and his eldest son Ercole was to marry the emperor's illegitimate daughter.[23] On 3 October 1526, the Ferrarese ambassador to Spain received the investiture.

In his ignorance, Clement continued to negotiate, and Francis I, in a fit of temporary enthusiasm for the League, sent Ugo da Peppoli to facilitate the talks. On 13 November Guicciardini received a papal brief, giving him full authority to conclude a treaty with Este, and on 17 November the lieutenant-general, optimistic about the possible outcome of the negotiations, sent an envoy to prepare conversations with the duke and to ascertain whether a personal visit by Guicciardini to Ferrara would be worth while. Three days later the envoy was back with many kind messages from the duke, who claimed that he desired a treaty above all things. Perhaps he did, but he was now too deeply involved with the imperialists to be able to withdraw. On 22 November rumours reached the league command of his agreement with the emperor. Guicciardini had already left for Ferrara, but on 25 November, riding just beyond Cento, he was waylaid by the duke's councillor, Iacopo Alvarotto, who warned him that it was useless to go on. The Venetians learned of the treaty on 27 November when Este's ambassador to Venice showed them letters which told of the proposed agreement with Charles V.[24] The news seems to have reached the pope on the following day when the city of Rome was already disturbed by high taxation, plague and famine.

Almost at the same time the alarming intelligence arrived that Charles de Lannoy, the viceroy of Naples, with the imperial fleet, was approaching the coasts of Italy. The pope was by now desperate. Politically and militarily out-manœuvred, with an empty treasury and fearing a Florentine rebellion, he was convinced that he had been deserted by France and England, in his hour of greatest need. 'The pope', Giberti reported, 'sees nothing ahead but ruin, not just his own, which he cares for little, but that of the Apostolic See, of Rome, of his own country, and of the whole of Italy, and that there is no means to prevent it. Not only has he expended all his own money, but all that of his friends and his servants. Expended, too, is all our reputation. . . .'[25] On 28 November the Milanese envoy, Landriano, commented on the pope's reception of the news of the defection of Ferrara. 'The Pope seemed struck dead. All the attempts of the ambassadors of France, England and Venice to restore him were in vain. Unless something unexpected takes place he will make a peace or some day take flight. He looks to me like a sick man the doctors have given up. From France nothing is heard, and this drives everyone to desperation.' A few days later the same envoy wrote that neither gold nor news came from France, save that the king was amusing himself well with dancing, 'and we are more dead than alive. . . . The extreme necessity of the hour will force us to an agreement with the enemy.' Even the Secretary of the French embassy admitted that without speedy help from France the pope could make no further resistance nor stay longer in Rome.[26] At the beginning of December, Acciauoli complained to Francis I that the pope and Florence had already contributed more to the League than they had been obliged to and asked Francis what he proposed to do about Frundsberg's army. In his reply Francis skilfully avoided making any concrete promises about additional help to the League, but five days later Acciauoli asked specifically for the dispatch of money to Clement and for 8–10,000 Swiss with which to counterbalance Frundsberg's lansquenets. Failing all else the League tried to persuade Francis to move to Lyons so as to be close to Italy. But the French king continued to show a notable lack of concern. In despair, Acciauoli reported to Giberti and Salviati on 22 January that, despite the urgent needs of Italy, he had been unable to talk to Francis, who had been absent for twelve days' hunting. In fact, Francis was engaged in delicate negotiations with Henry VIII over the possibility of a marriage between his second son and Princess Mary and a joint attack on Flanders – negotiations which he was afraid Italian importunity would jeopardize.[27]

In December Pompeio Colonna again appealed to a general council of the Church which was to be summoned at Spiers in Germany. He was now claiming that, as Clement had given away all his benefices to the cardinals on assuming the papacy, he had been guilty of simony, and that Julius II had issued a bull permitting the cardinals to summon a simoniacal pope before a general council.[28] Colonna's actions and statements pushed Clement into extending hostilities in southern Italy, even to the point of attacking Naples in the person of the viceroy, Charles de Lannoy. Lannoy, having put in at San Stefano, reached Gaeta at the end of November. Clement immediately dispatched Alvarode Quiñones, the General of the Franciscan Observants, who was much beloved by the emperor, to consult with Lannoy over the possibility of a truce. Lannoy asked that a papal ambassador with a mandate to make peace be sent to him.[29] There seemed to be little hope that the viceroy was sincere in expressing a desire for peace. Letters from Lannoy to the council of Naples, which were intercepted by papal spies, had already announced his intention of capturing Rome. Since Clement refused to pardon the Colonna and since every proposal of peace made by the viceroy included the provision that the Colonna be pardoned, it did not look as though negotiations could come to any satisfactory conclusion.[30] The pope began to make renewed efforts in the field; an order was issued for an extra 3,000 infantry to be raised and Cardinal Trivulzio was dispatched as legate to the army of the south, which he joined on 10 December.

The twelfth of December was a day of great importance at Rome, representing a significant widening in the breach between pope and emperor. Clement was as yet unaware of the exact imperial attitude towards him, for he had received no official reply to the brief of 23 June. Nevertheless, it was clear that open war between the pope and the kingdom of Naples could not be delayed for much longer. With this in mind, on 12 December Clement published a monition against all invaders of the Holy See.[31] On the same day Quiñones returned from Naples and informed Clement of the viceroy's terms; a truce for six months, the surrender of Parma, Piacenza and Ostia or Civitàvecchia and the payment of a large sum of money. Alberto Pio was insistent that Clement should not accept these terms, which amounted to a virtual abolition of the temporal possessions of the Holy See, and warned Clement that if he did accept them he would free the imperialists for an attack on Florence or Rome.[32] Giberti also disapproved but recognized the realities of the situation: 'We are forced to accept not conditions for agreement, but laws for slavery.'[33] The majority of the cardinals was also in favour of an early peace, and this was being discussed in Consistory when the bombshell burst.

The imperial reply to the papal brief of 23 June had been received by Perez on 9 December but he had kept it a close secret for four days. On 12 December he appeared unexpectedly at the Consistory with a Spanish notary and Spanish witnesses and delivered both his State Paper and the letter from Charles to the cardinals. Immediately after leaving the hall, he had his notary draw up an act to notify the delivery of the documents, with the result that, very shortly, the streets of Rome were resounding with the news that the emperor had demanded a general council of the Church, even in defiance of papal wishes. To the imperialists at Rome this news was cause for open rejoicing, and the rejoicing was redoubled when at the beginning of January it was learned that the duke of Bourbon had left Milan and was advancing on the Church State, having made up his mind 'to join the lansquenets and march on Bologna, Florence and even Rome if need be'.[34]

CHAPTER VIII

THE ADVANCE OF BOURBON

They already see Florence and Rome thrown down, and Rome pillaged.
Federico Gonzaga, marquess of Mantua

IT was not the sacrifice of Giovanni de' Medici's life at Governolo which, through all these months, had kept Bourbon in
Milan. The imperial commander-in-chief had always been
anxious to join forces with Frundsberg, but his army flatly refused to leave Milan unless it was paid, and money was the one
thing Bourbon was unable to obtain. When the duke first arrived
in Milan he was treated as an object of contempt by the Spanish
troops; more than once his life had been threatened by mutinous
soldiers, and he became accustomed to being branded 'traitor' by
everyone with whom he came in contact, friend and foe alike.[1] It
was only slowly that he began to assert his authority, and until the
first week of December 1526 he was largely occupied in using what
influence he possessed with the troops in preventing their sacking
Milan. At this point, still quite unable to make the army obey
orders and march out of the city, he summoned the Spanish captains, harangued them on the need to perform their duty, only to
learn that they in their turn were powerless to control their own
men. Next came news of the arrival of Frundsberg and at once the
financial pressures on the imperial leaders increased, for Frundsberg was no more able to pay his soldiers than Bourbon was to
pay his; both had been promised money from Spain – neither had
received any. Bourbon's hand was thus finally forced; in lieu of
paying his men, he had to countenance the looting of monasteries
and shops that began in Milan on 15 December. Forced loans
were raised from the Milanese aristocrats, and silver from the
churches was seized and melted down to be minted into coinage.
By such dubious methods some 40,000 ducats were raised. Another 20,000 were paid as a ransom by Morone, a sum extracted by
the simple expedient of threatening immediate execution if he
failed to find it. However, given that Bourbon was also responsible for Frundsberg's troops and their pay, these sums were still

totally inadequate; before the Spaniards would even leave Milan, they insisted on two months of their back-pay, a sum which amounted to over 62,000 ducats. It was at a suggestion of da Leyva that additional cash was raised by a forced loan from officers in the imperial army; Bourbon contributed 3000 ducats out of his own pocket, and da Leyva and del Guasto pawned all their jewels in order to meet their obligations.[2] Thus, on 2 January 1526, the Spaniards were finally persuaded to leave Milan, where da Leyva, with 10,000 infantry, was to remain as governor.[3]

Bourbon was now free to turn his attention to the problem of Frundsberg's army, which the emperor had unleashed on Italy without any clear instructions as to how it was to be paid. Already over two months had passed and the lansquenets had not received a single pay; their estimated arrears amounted to 93,000 ducats. They lacked even the most basic essentials of life – food and clothing. They were cold and wet and hungry. It was no wonder that there were daily alarms about mutinous lansquenets threatening to descend on Milan to remain there until they were paid. Secretly the imperial commanders were resigned to this possibility and, indeed, in the worst days of January it seemed the only solution. Nothing had been heard from Spain, although bills of exchange were anxiously looked for every day, communications within Italy were completely disrupted and Bourbon could not make contact with the viceroy for, after Moncada's truce expired in January, Giberti began refusing passports to imperial couriers who wanted to travel between Milan and Naples through the Church State. In the middle of January Bourbon quelled an incipient mutiny of the lansquenets by sending word that he would pay them a florin and a ducat each which would not be deducted from their arrears, and then found himself in the embarrassing position of not being able to raise even this small sum. Disaster was only averted by the Prince of Orange and del Guasto beating down the demands of the lansquenets to the minimum of a ducat and a pair of shoes per head, 18,000 pairs of shoes having been fortuitously seized in Milan only the week before. Temporarily the imperial commanders could breathe a sigh of relief – all of them, that is, except del Guasto who remained as a hostage with the lansquenets, and Orange who rode back to keep him company.[4] But the respite was, indeed, temporary. When Bourbon

first met Frundsberg in council with the other imperial commanders on 14 January, none could have foreseen an end to their
current hand-to-mouth existence and none could have been in
either a pleasant or an optimistic frame of mind.

At Rome, however, the difficulties of the northern imperial
armies were less apparent than the threat which these great forces
presented to the Church State. The necessity for negotiation with
the imperialists seemed more urgent than ever. As a prelude to
peace overtures Clement pushed forward with vigorous measures
for the defence of his territories. On 1 January he paid tribute to
the military capabilities of Orazio Baglione by releasing him from
imprisonment in Castel Sant'Angelo and instructing him to co-
operate with Renzo da Ceri and Camillo Orsini in organizing the
defences of Rome. Cardinals Orsini and Cesarini were given
special responsibility for the government of the city and con-
trived to infuse it with some degree of martial spirit. A survey of
all available men, arms and supplies in Rome was made; the
Roman people promised to raise 4000 infantry at the expense of
the commune and turned up in surprisingly large numbers at
musters of the militia from each *rione*, 'making a pretty good show
of military array'.[5] Nor did the cardinals ignore the fifth column
within their midst; imperial subjects living in Rome were excluded
from the muster, and plans were made to confiscate their weapons
and to remove the doors from their houses. Arrangements were
also made for barricading the streets in the event of an attack, and
for the rationing of food. So remote had Rome been from the
disasters of former Italian wars that there was an air of novelty
and excitement about all these arrangements, and in some cases
the Roman citizens entered into the spirit of the thing as if it were
a game; but for all that Rome was a city of alarming rumours.
Already it was being whispered abroad that Lannoy had told his
soldiers to expect no other pay than the sack of Rome and Florence.

Against a background of such rumours and fears, negotiations
with the imperialists continued. On 11 January Quiñones returned
to the viceroy, reaching his quarters at Coprano on 5 January. If an
accommodation had been possible Clement would have made it,
but Lannoy put forward no peace proposals that were remotely
acceptable. He was now asking for all the fortresses he had originally mentioned as well as Pisa and Leghorn and would speak

only of a peace settlement. A truce was out of the question. Inevitably, the viceroy demanded the restoration of the Colonna as a first condition. Clement, who was determined never to restore the Colonna, now relied on the arrival of Renzo da Ceri with the 20,000 ducats he was expected to bring from France; but to the pope's bitter disappointment Renzo arrived empty-handed. Simultaneously, Clement heard of Lannoy's new financial demands: the pope was to provide 200,000 ducats with which to pay Frundsberg's lansquenets and a further 200,000 to pay the Spanish troops in Lombardy. Clement considered that 200,000 ducats for the Spaniards was excessive but he was prepared to pay a portion of that sum and even offered to restore their property to the Colonna provided they remained exiled from the Church State. To the restoration of Pompeio Colonna's cardinal dignities he swore he would never agree.[6]

Meanwhile, Lannoy was having his own, unexpected, difficulties. The council of Naples declared its reluctance to embark on a costly war with the pope. Clement, they feared, might use the war as an excuse to summon the French and the Anjou claimant of Naples, Vaudémont, into the kingdom, where there was still a strong Angevin party, and so they pressed Lannoy to continue negotiations. They pointed out that, officially, Moncada's truce was still in operation and Clement had made no attack on Neapolitan territory. Indeed, throughout the subsequent campaign, Moncada refused to take part on the grounds that he did not wish to violate his own truce.[7] Members of the council of Naples were well aware that Clement was extremely reluctant to commit himself openly against the viceroy and that he had turned down a French-inspired proposal of Renzo da Ceri for a Neapolitan campaign. The furthest Clement would go was to include the viceroy in a general excommunication of all the barons of the kingdom of Naples, a move which was forced on him by a temporary resurgence of Colonna power. With Lannoy's assistance, the Colonna had captured Coprano and Pontecorvo, 'the keys of the Campagna',[8] and had attempted to seize Anagni.[9]

Lannoy shared none of the scruples of the more responsible of the Neapolitan barons. Advancing from Coprano with 1600 lansquenets, 4000 Spaniards and 10,000 Italian mercenaries, without waiting for the expiration of Moncada's truce, he laid siege to the papal town of Frosinone, 'the principal town in the Campagna'.[10] Under the generalship of Renzo da Ceri the bulk of the papal troops had been positioned in Ferentino, about five miles to the north of Frosinone, which was garrisoned with 1500 of the 'Black Bands' and 100 cavalry of Alessandro Vitelli.[11]

Although Frosinone was not a fortified town, its location on a steep hill provided a perfect natural defensive position, and Lannoy was unable to bring his artillery within range of the town. On 2 February Stefano Colonna tried to relieve Frosinone by force. He was attacked by four bands of imperial troops against whom he scored so notable a victory that, in the early hours of the morning, dragging their most valuable pieces of artillery by hand, the imperialists were forced to retreat to Coprano, pursued by the papal light cavalry. 'Since God has chosen to give us this victory', Cardinal Trivulzio wrote enthusiastically to Clement, 'we have decided to follow it up, even if your Holiness sends us a thousand briefs and letters forbidding us to.'[12] At Coprano the imperialists hurriedly began to throw up fresh fortifications and began to construct a bridge across the Liri.[13] Clement saw in the whole affair the hand of God and hoped that it would bring an agreement nearer, 'which, because of the pride of the viceroy, had formerly been impossible'.[14]

The viceroy and the Colonna were equally unsuccessful in their attempt to use Napoleone Orsini, the abbot of Farfa, against the pope. Farfa had been induced to defect from the papal side 'against the honour of his family' by the promise of pay in the imperial service and the daughter of Vespasiano Colonna with a dowry of 30,000 ducats. In return Farfa agreed to give free passage through his territory to the troops of Charles V and to procure the opening of one of the city gates of Rome. At the same time, the abbot was to assemble his troops and appear with them in the Borgo, under the pretext of protecting the pope; in reality intending to murder him and eight of the anti-imperial cardinals. It was by the sheerest good fortune that Farfa took into his confidence one of the few Roman barons loyal to the pope, the count of Anguillara, who promptly informed Clement of the plot. The pope was therefore able to forestall Farfa, capturing him at Bracciano, then incarcerating him in Castel Sant'Angelo, where he made a full confession.[15]

The papal army at Frosinone and Ferentino waited for the heavy artillery and reinforcements to arrive before launching an attack on the kingdom of Naples. The viceroy was compelled to fall back on Gaeta, while the whole of Rome rejoiced at this success against the imperialists under Lannoy, 'the greatest enemy of the Holy See'.[16]

Such rejoicing was tragically premature; the true danger to Rome lay not in the south but in the north. Bourbon's army having joined with Frundsberg's lansquenets in the third week of February, the two imperial commanders were already preparing for a great campaign into central Italy. It was supposed that the campaign would open with an attack on Piacenza, a key town in the papal defence system, long contested between empire and papacy, and the gateway to the Via Emilia, but the duke of Ferrara dissuaded Bourbon from an attack. This was doubtless for reasons advanced by del Guasto; the city, defended by Guido Rangoni, was strongly fortified with a garrison of 6000 men.[17]

There had long been talk of the danger to Rome from the army in Lombardy. In November 1526 Federico Gonzaga, the marquess of Mantua, warned his mother, Isabella d'Este, to leave Rome, whither she had retreated in protest against her son's immoral life. Although he and his mother were at cross-purposes over this particular matter and Gonzaga had no desire to have her back in Mantua, he was also unwilling to leave Isabella exposed to danger and reluctantly wrote to warn her about the imperial troops: 'They already see Florence and Rome thrown down, and Rome pillaged,'[18] he said of the lansquenets. Similar warnings had also frequently been made by prominent imperialists like Vives who, in December, had warned the pope that he would lose Rome. Throughout his entire stay in Rome as ambassador, the duke of Sessa never tired of threatening Clement with the imperial forces in Italy.[19]

It is clear, therefore, that from the very beginning of this campaign an attack on papal rather than on Venetian territory was contemplated, and it is almost certain that some of the imperial commanders intended an attack on Rome from the moment they left Milan. Rome, it was mistakenly believed, could provide cash to pay the troops, and an attack there might force Clement to abandon the League even if he were not actually captured. An assault on Florence might also have served both these objects, but a march on Rome stood a better chance of military success since it could be combined with an attack from Naples.

Much as Lannoy and Bourbon disliked each other, they were able to subordinate their antagonism to the overriding needs of the imperial cause in Italy and co-ordinated a plan for a dual attack on the papacy: Lannoy and the Colonna would advance from the south while Bourbon would attack from the north, campaigning through the Church State.[20] Bourbon at first intended his progress to be leisurely; on 20 December he told the Mantuan representative with his army, Sigismondo della Torre, that he was intending to attack Parma and Piacenza, but if there were any difficulties he would move slowly to Bologna, 'and that there he wanted money, and then to Florence, and in the end to Rome. . . . And that from the other direction the Viceroy would move against the Pope.'[21] It was only when Lannoy was defeated at Frosinone and began to retreat that the need for a swift attack on Rome from the north became apparent to Bourbon.

The possibility of a revolution in Florence under the imperial aegis was also still being considered. The idea of Florence as the point at which to attack Clement VII had always been in the commanders' minds and they were certainly using the promise of the sack of Florence to encourage the army to advance. Yet, as late as 18 February, the army council was still debating whether or not they should take Bologna, 'or go to Florence which is the thing the soldiers desire most'.[22] It was already known that the Colonna and the viceroy would be making an attack on Rome, but Bourbon continued to negotiate with exiles from Florence. Then, in the second week of March, Bourbon received letters from Lannoy urging him to advance on Rome from the north, and simultaneously promising an attack from Naples; these letters, closely followed by news of the disastrous turn of events in the Neapolitan war, seem to have influenced Bourbon's decision to march immediately on Rome.[23]

The imperial army which Bourbon had now assembled was an impressive war-machine. Even by sixteenth-century standards the army was large; it already consisted of 700 lances (about 3500 men), 800 light cavalry, 10,000 lansquenets, 5000 Spanish and 3000 Italian troops.[24] At the end of the first week in March the army was joined by a troop of horsemen from Carpi but it was still weak in cavalry, essential both for foraging and scouting. Throughout the campaign of the following months the imperialists were short of horses of all types: for haulage, transport, scouting and fighting – a major problem for an army whose declared intention was to live off the country. Bourbon had let it be known that any locality which refused supplies would be plundered but that those which gave voluntarily would not be molested. Special officials were created to see that these dispositions were obeyed, and the army was thus protected from complete starvation. Supplies came from Mantua and Ferrara almost daily; in February bread came from Fidenza; and in the same month fourteen cartloads of supplies, including some hay for the horses, veal, chickens, wine and cheese came from Reggio.[25] But often there were not enough horses to collect food when it was available; and those there were suffered constantly from lack of fodder, for the weather was so bad that the animals could not sustain themselves by grazing.[26]

As Bourbon's army began to move south, it was, inevitably, joined from time to time by Italian adventurers, anxious to profit from imperial successes. But, nevertheless, the hard core of his army was made up of professional troops, who were well trained and seasoned, brave, accustomed to victory, and campaigning away from home in an alien country where their only loyalty was to their comrades. Despite great hardships, the lansquenets and the Spaniards developed and retained an *esprit de corps* never shared by any of the Italian troops in either the imperial or the league armies, with the possible exception of the 'Black Bands'. Frundsberg's lansquenets were some of the best infantry to have been seen in Italy, at a time when, following the battles of Marignano and Pavia, the reputation of the Swiss was already declining. Discipline in these early months was first class; there were no serious outbreaks of looting, mainly because Frundsberg went out of his way to ensure that his troops were well supplied. Everyone who came in contact with the lansquenets was impressed; della Torre was full of praise for them, particularly the cavalry who were prepared to fight on foot when necessary and did not believe that in doing so they lost face, while Federico Gonzaga described them as 'a brave band which will cut to pieces all resistance', and even Guicciardini admired their constancy, resilience and bravery.[27] These new German soldiers had not yet acquired that unenviable reputation for brutality which was subsequently to make them a by-word throughout Italy.

The lansquenets were organized in regiments made up of colonel, lieutenant-colonel and regimental staff, with a varying number of companies commanded by captains and their subalterns, the lieutenants and ensigns. A company or 'colour' numbered usually about 200 men. The captains were famous for their concern for the welfare of their men and always took pains to ensure that they were regularly paid. Pay fell due every thirty days, and it is noteworthy that while the pay of the Spaniards and Italians was falling into arrears the demands of the lansquenets serving in Milan were regularly met until December 1525. Amongst the more notable features of the lansquenets were their disciplinary code, which admitted the right of the rank and file to judge matters which touched the honour of the whole company, and the women who marched with the regiments and had a definite place in the army's corporate life.

Camp-followers were also of importance in the Spanish army. It fell to the women to bake the bread which fed the armies, and they also ran mobile stores, supplying necessaries to the soldiers while on campaign. Both armies also had their share of camp-boys, military apprentices who learned their trade while performing such services as burnishing armour for the true soldiers. But this vast additional army, although useful, brought with it its own problems as far as lodgings and supplies were concerned, and could seriously hinder a campaign when speed was essential.

From Pavia to the battle of Rocroi (1648) the Spanish army was held to be the finest in Europe, with a reputation for invincibility. Its success stemmed from the reforms which had been initiated during the Neapolitan campaigns of 1503. The most important change had been the abolition of a system by which commands over numerous companies, most of them feudal levies of varying size, were only temporary, existing no longer than the day of battle. The Spanish army was now professionalized, formed into battalions of infantry under colonels who retained their command after a battle. Every battalion was divided into 5 companies of about 200 men each. Adopting the best points of the Swiss system, the Spanish infantry fought with a combination of pike and musket and were among the first troops to make skilled use of artillery on the battlefield. In addition, the Spaniards serving under Bourbon were, for the most part, Pescara's veterans; many had served in Italy since 1509 and were used to hardship and the vigorous discipline for which Pescara was famous.

Bourbon divided the command of his armies between the Prince of Orange, Frundsberg, Gian d'Urbina and del Guasto. Orange was entrusted with the vanguard, the command of the lances and the light cavalry, del Guasto and later Gian d'Urbina with the Spanish infantry, while Frundsberg remained responsible for his own lansquenets. These leaders were all men of outstanding ability. Harsh words have been written about the duke of Bourbon, not least by his contemporaries who accused him of treachery, double-dealing and self-interest. Certainly he *was* avaricious and unscrupulous, and in his relations with Francis I he showed a marked inability to come to terms with reality; but for all this he was capable of loyalty to, and of considerable sacrifice in, the imperial service. In time of war he was distinguished by his, 'liberality, astuteness and courage' and by his military abilities.[28] Like Giovanni de' Medici, Bourbon was never backward in courting danger and thus earned the admiration of his soldiers. With them he was always popular. As a leader in battle he was impressive, dressed all in silver and white, with his beard cut in the Spanish fashion as a compliment to his adopted country, and his yellow, black and white standard with its motto of 'Espérance, Espérance'.[29]

Frundsberg had long been famous as a soldier. A man renowned for his great height and strength, he had been one of the principal creators of the lansquenets, had experience of warfare in Italy dating back to 1499 and, a Lutheran of conviction,[30] was trusted, feared and obeyed by his men in the most adverse circumstances. In these early months Frundsberg alone was responsible for the high morale of the German troops. He proved to be an utterly loyal and devoted servant of the emperor and a capable and chivalrous soldier. He lost one son during the sack of Rome and saw another succumb to wounds and disease in the campaign in Lombardy. But, for all his loyalty to the imperial cause, Frundsberg must bear a heavy responsibility for the element of brutality and gratuitous cruelty so commonly found among his soldiers. Nor was he the ideal subordinate; from the time of his arrival in Italy Frundsberg believed he had been cheated by Bourbon from whom he had been expecting supplies. But, whatever difficulties Frundsberg made, because he was one of the few men alive who could control an army of lansquenets, Bourbon could no more dispense with him than he could with Gian d'Urbina, whose influence with the Spaniards was phenomenal. Within Italy Urbina had the most sinister of reputations as the man who, in defiance of Pescara's expressed intentions and wishes, and possibly even in defiance of orders, had led the mutinous Spanish soldiers in a brutal pillage of Como in 1521. Certainly Urbina was often cruel and always arrogant, but he was a brilliant soldier, a great favourite with Charles V, and the Spanish soldiers loved and genuinely respected him. Del Guasto was a Neapolitan, a cousin of Pescara, entrusted with the command of the imperial troops in Italy from the death of Pescara until the arrival of Bourbon. In this capacity he proved himself a loyal servant of the emperor, selling two of his best estates in the kingdom of Naples in order to keep the troops contented in the absence of regular pay from Spain, and giving one of his castles to Urbina when that commander threatened to desert the imperial cause. But honourable and loyal though del Guasto was, he suffers by comparison with Frundsberg and Urbina, for, although much loved in the army, he was never able to maintain discipline. Orange, who subsequently became famous for his liberality towards, and concern for, his men, had influence over the Spaniards, although the lansquenets always found him unsympathetic. Tall, fair-haired, blue-eyed and known for his incurable love of gaming, in 1527 Orange was still only in his twenty-fifth year and appeared to have a brilliant career ahead of him. Like Bourbon, he had been alienated by Francis I, who had impolitic, if understandable, designs on his territories, and he had been imprisoned when trying to escape from France. Released under the terms of the Treaty of Madrid, Orange hastened immediately to join Bourbon in Italy. He was brave, although impatient, and took a personal part in every engagement; nonetheless, he was capable of taking advice from fellow officers and of restraining his natural impulse towards action.[31] But what most distinguishes Orange among the imperial commanders is his highly developed sense of responsibility and his faithful service in the imperial cause.

Not the least of Bourbon's difficulties was that his force was made up of two, if not three, different armies and suffered greatly from internal stresses and eruptions of jealousy. The difficulties faced by Charles V, in ruling a multi-national empire, are nowhere seen more clearly than in this army, made up of Spanish, German and Italian troops, all essentially loyal to the emperor but representing quite different traditions. With each nation different problems arose, and different settlements had to be made. What satisfied the Spaniards almost certainly would never please the lansquenets, while the lansquenets could only be obliged at the risk of provoking mutiny among the Spanish. In the Spanish army the most prominent captains were Alonso de Gayoso, Rodrigo da Ripalda, Vergara, Corradino, who had conducted the defence of Cremona so ably and who had served previously as a captain of the lansquenets in Milan, and Giovanni Bartolomeo Gattinara, subsequently to become commissar-general to the imperial army. The Italian troops were led by Fabrizio Maramaldo, Caiazzo, Federico Carafa, Marc Antonio Colonna, Luigi Culla, and Ferrante Gonzaga who joined the army on 28 February.[32] The last was an excellent officer; a son of Isabella d'Este, he had been educated in Spain and his obvious talents led to a steady rise in his career, until he finally succeeded Orange as captain-general of the imperial army.

On 22 February, by-passing Piacenza, the imperial army reached Firenzuola and Fidenza. Both places suffered at the hands of the soldiers, particularly the anti-clerical lansquenets, who were seizing every opportunity for gratuitous sacrilege.[33] Thereafter the army made rapid progress – at a rate of about ten miles a day. No delays were made for bridges to be thrown across rivers; they were all forded.[34] On the morning of 1 March the army reached Ponte di Reno and, in the evening, Marsaglia, where Bourbon sent to ask the duke of Ferrara to build a bridge of boats over the Panaro at Finale. Up till now the armies had suffered no serious supply problems, although there was a chronic shortage of bread, but it was generally accepted that Bourbon's real problems would only begin once he left the vicinity of Ferrara.[35] The weather on the following day, however, was terrible and completely disorganized the armies. Many of the carts had to be abandoned in the mud. By the evening the troops had hardly advanced beyond the River Secchia and had to be most unsatisfactorily lodged.[36] Bourbon, nevertheless, despite continuing bad weather, pressed on to Bastiglia and on 5–6 March the armies crossed the Panaro, the old river-boundary of the Church State, by bridges which had been prepared, as requested, by the duke of Ferrara.[37] The crossing of the Panaro was the last major operation of the army for some time. From 5 until 8 March it was encamped at Buonporto and on 9 March halted at San Giovanni, a Bolognese fortress twelve miles from Bologna. The halt was called because heavy rain and unseasonable snow made further progress impossible.[38]

Naturally enough the Italian League did not remain unmoved by Bourbon's threatening advance. Response came both on a military and a diplomatic level. At Urbino's camp at Casal-maggiore December and January had been spent in constructing bridges by which the Venetian army could cross the Po, once per-mission arrived from Venice. In Rome Clement pleaded with the Venetian ambassador to secure permission for the papal and Vene-tian armies to join together, while from Modena, Guicciardini bombarded Averoldi, the papal nuncio to Venice, with anxious letters asking that orders to Urbino to cross the Po be dispatched with all speed. Clement, now engaged in full-scale conflict in the south,[39] was anxious to protect his northern frontier, but Venice still feared an imperial attack on Bergamo, where refortification was incomplete, Brescia and Verona, and would not authorize Urbino to leave Lombardy. Urbino was making his own idio-syncratic difficulties; he had managed to convince himself that the pope and emperor were plotting to give his duchy to Ferrara and he asked Venice to take his state under her protection. If this were refused, he threatened to give up his employment.[40]

Not surprisingly, the papal commanders Guicciardini and Guido Rangoni were in despair. Aware as they were of the political vulnerability of Florence, should the imperialists elect to march into Tuscany, and of the pope's financial straits, they knew that only a miracle could prevent Clement VII being forced to come to terms with the imperialists.

By the middle of January Venetian intelligence was assured that the imperial armies would march into Tuscany and Venice promised Guicciardini that, provided there were no possibility of a surprise attack on the Veneto, Urbino would be sent to the aid of Florence and the pope.[41] But Urbino proved, as usual, to be dilatory, and it was not until 1 February that he would agree to the crossing of the Po, in an attempt to dislodge Frundsberg from the environs of Piacenza. Urbino proposed that, once Bourbon had moved, the papal army should provide for the protection of Modena and Parma and then fall back on Bologna, while he, with the Venetian troops, would follow Bourbon at a distance of about twenty-five miles. His plan suited Venice, which would still be protected by Urbino's army, but not the pope, who saw that the road into Tuscany and Rome would be left open to Bourbon.

In the event of an advance into Tuscany the bulk of the defence would fall on the papal and French troops who, it seemed, would be forced to concentrate on the defence of the major cities, breaking up their field armies and reducing their mobility. A compromise was reached by providing skeleton garrisons in all towns which were to be reinforced if threatened by imperial troops.[42] To reduce the importance of manpower considerable work was done on the fortifications of all the papal towns. At Piacenza in February 6000 sappers were at work on the defences.[43] At Modena completely new fortifications, approved by Guido Rangoni and Federigo da Bozzoli, were being constructed throughout February; the old castellated city-wall was replaced by a new wall with four permanent bastions.[44] This organization of the papal defences was as efficient as could be expected and extremely effective. In the event Bourbon was not able to risk an attack on any town in the northern part of the Church State. In the Po valley Guicciardini so organized his troops as to make the best use of the material available; a fleet of boats had been built in January by which the commanders were able to move their troops swiftly between Piacenza, Parma, Reggio, Modena and Bologna, the key fortress-towns of the papal defence system. These arrangements had not been easy; there was constant friction between the papal towns and the league army which increased the difficulties of Guicciardini, Rangoni and Saluzzo. Bologna proved particularly difficult. Despite genuine efforts on Saluzzo's part to discipline his army and to prevent any plundering, the populace refused to have any troops billeted in private houses.[45] However, by mid-February, the papal defence system was completely organized;[46] on 20 February Federigo da Bozzoli declared that the towns of the Romagna were now well provided for, and on this basis Guicciardini released him from this task and sent him to Florence to organize the defences there. Meanwhile, Saluzzo and the papal troops, having established that the Venetians would guard Parma, made for Bologna, while Guido Rangoni moved his troops from Piacenza to Modena.[47]

As instructed by Venice, Urbino had crossed the Po on 5 March in order to reach Parma, but there remained immobile, pleading sickness as an excuse for inactivity. On 14 March the duke's mysterious illness was diagnosed as gout, but he still maintained that he could not move as he had no litter for transport. In fact, Urbino seemed to be losing control not only over himself but over the whole campaign; three days later a Venetian observer arrived and was appalled at the degeneration of his army. There was no discipline or order, no supplies were reaching the camp, and the commanders were spending their time blaming each other for the selection of the site. Heavy snow added to supply problems since the horses could not be put out to graze and had to be supplied with corn which was badly needed for making bread. On 18 March Urbino arrived to make his apologies, 'as was his wont, promising the Venetians when he was miles away from danger that victory was certain, not of course because of any virtue in the armies of the allies but because of the difficulties of their enemies'. It was not until the end of the month that Urbino could even summon up the energy to abandon his inadequate lodgings. Then, at last, he moved to Reggio, only ten miles from the imperial camp.[48]

Already, however, the whole military situation had been complicated by the first defection from the Italian League. News had arrived that the pope, in desperation, had come to an agreement with Lannoy and the council of Naples.

CHAPTER IX

LANNOY'S TRUCE

Even Attila respected bishops.
Giberti, 26 April 1527

DESPITE the surprising papal victory at Frosinone, the outcome of the war in Naples remained uncertain. The papal commander, Renzo da Ceri, advanced very slowly into the kingdom of Naples, supported by the navies of Venice, France and Clement VII. Renzo da Ceri met little resistance, for the Neapolitan provinces had not been supplied or prepared for an invasion and the local populations failed to rally to the imperial cause. Nevertheless, the league fleet, lacking adequate reinforcements, could do little more than hold the coastal towns it had already captured. The weather was terrible and the land-army could not be supplied.

Inevitably, peace talks continued, for although Clement had received three gifts of 30,000 ducats from Venice, England and France the financial pressure of the war was appalling.[1] Clement was terrified that Bourbon would attack Florence and did not believe the Medici régime could survive there if Bourbon entered Tuscany; 'He says if he is the cause of bringing an army into Tuscany all his relatives will be banished.'[2] The pope had been bitterly disillusioned by the failure of any of the league powers to react to the Colonna raid. He reasoned that if this insult to the papacy could not provoke assistance there was little to be hoped for from them.[3] In particular, Clement despaired of Francis I, whose repeated fair words had produced very little practical assistance. As Sir Gregory Casale commented, French contributions to the League to date were 'to our necessity as a fly to an elephant'.[4] Thus the pope willingly lent an ear to the suggestions of Giberti that agreement be made now when, in the face of defeat, Lannoy might be expected to be more reasonable.[5]

The existence of the war in Naples had diminished neither the quantity of negotiations nor the number of official and unofficial envoys that passed between the pope and the viceroy. The English ambassadors, Sir Gregory Casale and Sir John Russell, were particularly active. Russell had recently arrived from England with the gift of 30,000 ducats for the pope and had been instructed by Henry VIII to proceed to the viceroy to request him to desist from hostilities and to make a truce for which Clement should not be financially responsible. It would have flattered Henry VIII and Wolsey had they been able to play an effective role in bringing peace to Italy, and Clement had expressed a desire that Henry should act as arbiter between himself and the emperor.[6] But the English, like all the other negotiators, found one fundamental stumbling-block: Lannoy was unwilling to consider peace unless Pompeio Colonna was reinstated, and Clement would not even consider the possibility of such a reinstatement – 'which seems to His Holiness more harsh than any other condition: to see before him the man who tried to take his life. Even if His Holiness could forgive his private injuries, he could not, without endangering his soul, permit such a pernicious example, for the sake of the Church.'[7]

At the end of January 1527, Lannoy dispatched Cesare Ferramosca, a Neapolitan subject of the emperor, to the pope with fresh imperial demands. Ferramosca reached Rome on 25 January.[8] Lannoy's previous demand for the surrender of papal fortresses had not changed but, in addition, he was now demanding that the pope pay 150,000 ducats, restore the Colonna, accept Bourbon as duke of Milan, and furnish the emperor with an army for use in Italy.[9] When these proposals were set before the Sacred College the cardinals agreed that a truce was desirable but rejected Lannoy's terms. The most they would do was agree to a suspension of hostilities for a week while a messenger was sent to Venice to seek the agreement of that state, agreement which the cardinals could be fairly certain would not be forthcoming.[10] Events proved the cardinals right in their judgement; in an effort to divert the pope from his pacific aims, Venice offered a gift of a further 30,000 ducats and sent an urgent warning to France that Clement was on the point of making peace. In consequence, on 16 February Clement's Florentine representative to Francis I, Acciauoli, had a most embarrassing interview with the French king. Although his own conduct would have been difficult to justify, Francis still felt able to criticize that of the pope: 'It seems very strange to us that His Holiness is prepared to put his faith in

Caesar, given that the emperor wants to turn him into a simple priest.'[11] It seemed incredible to Francis that Clement should be considering a truce now that the League had, at last, started to win battles. Francis maintained that neither he nor Venice would ever sign a truce with the emperor, even were the pope to become 'Caesar's servant'.[12]

But Clement was not to be moved, either by Venetian promises, or by French sarcasm, or by his own military success. It was in the north that the pope hoped to see substantial gains. Like Guicciardini, he knew that, 'on this occasion, he who wins Lombardy takes all'.[13] And those gains were not forthcoming. On the contrary, the entire weight of papal and Florentine diplomacy had to be spent in persuading the Venetian government even to order Urbino to cross the Po. Financially, every day weighed heavier and heavier on the pope, who was already paying for the war with the English, French and Venetian subsidies alone. Acciauoli warned Francis I that it would only be a short time before the pope went begging for his own food.[14]

On 21 February Russell and Ferramosca brought more reasonable proposals from the viceroy. Lannoy, it appeared, was ready to agree to a truce either for one year or for three. Although Russell was opposed to the proposal unless Venice also agreed, Clement warned that he would have to accept the terms if Venice and France did not support him financially.[15] Speculation about the possibility of a truce thus became the main burden of letters to Venice from Rome in the first week of March. Venice reacted immediately, attempting to accommodate Clement over the defence of Florence; 3000 Venetian troops were ordered there without delay, and Urbino was exhorted to do his best to unite with the papal and French troops.[16] The attitude of Venice was consistent: 'The truce is not only inopportune, but extremely injurious to all Italy',[17] the doge maintained.

Initial successes of the papal army in the kingdom of Naples were not sustained. For over a month, while negotiations continued with Lannoy, the pope's troops remained inactive at Popoli. Supply-lines were bad and hunger within the army so general that more than half of the infantry deserted before the army moved to the coastal towns. Inefficiency and dishonesty were rife among the commanders, who consistently demanded full pay for companies they knew were not even up to half-strength, 'nor has His Holiness been able to invent enough honours and titles to satisfy the ambition of many of the captains, and when they don't get immediately what they ask for they threaten to go over to the other side.'[18]

Clement and Giberti continued to meet in secret with Ferramosca, who returned on 11 March from Lannoy, to discuss the possibility of a truce. On the previous day Guillaume Du Bellay had arrived to represent French interests with the pope: 'The one and the other are working to completely opposite ends with the pope; we shall see which is the stronger. . . .'[19] For four days in the Belvedere of the Vatican, Clement continued discussions with Capua, Ferramosca and Giberti and finally at some time during the night of 15–16 March Clement agreed to accept Lannoy's latest offer.[20] On 25 March, the viceroy, with an escort of cavalry, rode into Rome to ratify the truce; he was received by the pope with great honour, and lodged in the Vatican.[21] Nevertheless, Clement found it difficult to join whole-heartedly in the enthusiastic celebrations of the truce which the imperialists felt bound to provide in Rome. As he had remarked gloomily to the Venetians a few days earlier: 'I know it is a bad thing to make a truce, and it is also a bad thing to make war; but to make the truce seems the lesser evil.'[22]

Clement had specified that in the capitulations there should be no mention of a payment to be made by the pope, for both he and Giberti were acutely conscious that other members of the League might well wonder how the pope could afford to pay for a truce when he could not afford to pay for a war. However, by a secret agreement, Clement did agree to pay 60,000 ducats to Frundsberg's lansquenets. The imperial army would then evacuate the Church State. It was hoped that if the agreement ever became public the papal agents would be able to suggest that the money was for the ransom of Filippo Strozzi and Giacomo Salviati, who were still being held hostage in Naples as a guarantee of Moncada's truce, although subsequent developments had done much to make that truce obsolete.[23]

Lannoy's truce could have been a disaster for the Colonna. Had it been observed, they would have been ruined. It recognized the *status quo* at a time when the papal armies had had a considerable

success. Although Clement promised to reinstate Pompeio
Colonna and to absolve other members of his house from ecclesiastical censures, the Colonna were otherwise exempted from the
benefits of the agreement. They were permitted only to retain
such property as they still controlled in the Church State on
15 March 1527, and Lannoy had to guarantee that they would
make no more attacks on papal or Orsini property. For the
Colonna, therefore, survival depended on Lannoy's truce being
deliberately broken by the imperialists. Thus their attention
shifted once more to the north, to the duke of Bourbon and his
troops, to see whether they also would be halted by this putative
agreement between pope and viceroy.

Ever since the first week in March Bourbon's army had remained stationary at San Giovanni, while important talks took
place between Bourbon and Alfonso d'Este on the border between Modena and Ferrara. In these weeks Este proved of invaluable assistance to the imperialists, providing Bourbon with
supplies, money and even with medicines to heal the sick, almost
daily. At the beginning of March the duke had promised to give
Bourbon at least six pieces of heavy artillery and the necessary
powder and ammunition, flour, provisions and transport to go
with them. Within a week eight cannon with ammunition and
twelve boat-loads of bread were ready for dispatch to the imperialists. In addition Este promised to provide back-pay for the
Spanish garrison at Carpi when he took it over, under the terms of
his agreement with the emperor, thus releasing those troops for
service with Bourbon.[24] Again, at the end of the month, Este gave
the army 1000 sacks of wheat, as many again of flour, 20,000
pounds of gunpowder, 1000 pounds of saltpetre, and 30 horses
with equipment for the field artillery, with an additional 15,000
ducats. In recompense for all this assistance, on 7 March the abbot
of Najera, Charles V's direct civil representative in Lombardy, had
handed over Carpi to the duke, who installed his own governor
and garrison.[25]

In the meantime, without overtly commencing hostilities against
the pope, Este had been making as many difficulties as possible for
the papal governors in the Romagna. Grain, intended for Modena,
where there was a severe shortage, was confiscated in transit across
Ferrarese territory, nominally in retaliation for a confiscation

by the Modenese of supplies which had been bound for Carpi's Spanish garrison.[26] The occupation of Carpi by Este presented novel problems of defence for the papal commanders, whose resources were now stretched to their limits, for in the hills around Carpi were many small castles and villages, dependent on the jurisdiction of that town, which Clement had undertaken to defend on behalf of the dispossessed prince, Alberto Pio. Instructions were now sent from Rome that these places must be defended as Este was threatening to occupy them. From Bologna a commissioner was sent to the area to supervise the defence, and the companies of troops were dispatched from those remaining at Modena. This was unfortunate, for it soon became clear that it would only be a matter of time before Modena itself was attacked, and Nerli, papal governor at Modena, was certain that his resources would be insufficient to meet such an attack. At this crucial point in the general war he was therefore inundating Salviati, Guicciardini and Giberti with requests for assistance for Modena.[27]

Without the benefit of a truce, yet unmolested by the league forces and well supplied from Ferrara, the imperial troops were able to put this breathing-space to good use. The imperial army was completely reorganized in preparation for a swift march over the Apennines. Among the major problems was that of the camp-followers, whose numbers had grown out of all proportion to the size of the army. There were said to be at least 25,000 already, 'which is something to astound the world, to see the infinite number of women and other hangers-on'.[28] Now most of this vast additional army was ruthlessly sent away, although each company was allowed to keep three prostitutes. Seventy wounded men were abandoned at Ferrara and in preparation for the coming march every five infantrymen were issued with a horse which was to carry five days' supplies for them.[29]

The only major problem which had not been overcome was the payment of the army. On 13 March the abbot of Najera finally managed to borrow 15,000 ducats from Ferrarese bankers, and this sum was distributed among Frundsberg's lansquenets, who would not let any part of it go to the Spaniards. This insult, coupled with rumours of an impending peace, which would deprive them of all hope of recouping their losses by a profitable sack, and the heavy downfalls of snow and rain which were turning the camp into a swamp, goaded the Spaniards at last into mutiny. They flung themselves in fury on Bourbon's lodgings in the fortress of San Giovanni, demanding payment in full of all their arrears. Bourbon himself was forced to take refuge in a horse-stall in Frundsberg's quarters;[30] one of his gentlemen was murdered; a rich bed, originally a present to Bourbon from the emperor's sister, was destroyed, tables were broken to pieces and all the money which could be found, though it amounted to little more than 400 ducats, was seized. Within the imperial army mutiny was an infectious disease and the Germans quickly followed the Spaniards shouting 'Pay, pay' and refusing to quieten down unless they were paid their arrears in full. Since it was apparent that order would not be restored in the army except by cash, the officers exerted themselves in trying to get as good terms as possible. Gian d'Urbina managed to persuade the Spanish troops to accept one ducat per head, but the lansquenets would accept no less than one half-month's pay. Najera and del Guasto were therefore dispatched once more to Ferrara where they managed to raise a further loan of 12,000 ducats.[31] They were back in camp on 15 March, and the money was divided equally throughout the armies. But the sum was insufficient to satisfy the lansquenets; on 16 March they mutinied again and presented their own terms to their officers. The spokesman declared that they would not move unless Bourbon would promise more money on account when the army was within sight of Florence and would pay all their arrears, a sum which would amount to about 15,000 ducats, on 21 April. Knowing that there was little chance that he would ever be able to fulfil any such engagement, Bourbon refused to enter into it. Instead he required of Frundsberg that he pacify his mutinous lansquenets. The German leader called his men together and addressed them with great earnestness. But all his representations were useless. 'Pay, pay,' shouted his furious soldiers as they turned their pikes against their captains. So hard did Frundsberg labour to pacify them that he was struck by a fit and fell speechless on a drum. It was rumoured that he would not be able to march any further with the army; either he would die or be forced to remain at Ferrara. And if this were to happen, Najera reported, 'we shall not know how to deal with these Germans, he being the only man who has any influence over them'.[32] These same Germans were now only pacified by their commanders' promise that the army might enjoy the 'law of Mahomet' – the right to recoup their losses by plunder and sack.[33]

The council of war had decided, in the light of the impregnability of Bologna and the proximity of the Venetian forces, that an advance should be made towards Florence by way of Sasso. Bourbon addressed his men and informed them of this decision, emphasizing still that an attack would be made on Florence.

The agreement reached by Lannoy and Clement VII on 15 March should have halted Bourbon's advance; but the truth was that the pope had been deceived by the viceroy and Bourbon acting in collusion.[34] Trusting Lannoy, despite the viceroy's unenviable European reputation for treachery and double-dealing, Clement had already carried out his treaty obligations in the most conscientious manner, withdrawing his forces from the Neapolitan war and reducing the number of troops available for the defence of Rome. Lannoy, meanwhile, dispatched Ferramosca with 60,000 ducats provided by the pope, the Florentines and his own purse, to inform Bourbon of the truce and to make a public demand that his troops retreat. Although apparently unconvinced that Lannoy meant this truce to be observed any more faithfully than the last, Ferramosca dutifully sped north to Bourbon's army.

The reception given to this messenger of peace by Bourbon's army was peculiarly hostile:

> the captains having called the men together, urged them to accept the truce; their reply and the tumult were such that [Ferramosca] could not see any possibility of agreement. Also they twice tried to kill him and he was so afraid that he went into hiding outside the camp. [He said] that not being able to do anything more he would return and throw himself on the mercy of the pope, so that His Holiness might assure himself that he at least proceeded in this sincerely.

The whole affair represented an outcome which, in fact, the Venetians had clearly foreseen.[35]

The incident raised in its most serious form one of the recurrent questions which troubled imperial servants in Italy; where, in fact, did authority lie? The difficulty of operating without the physical, unifying presence of Charles V was a problem endemic to the whole empire, but which in Italy had now become acute. Here the emperor had many agents operating – Bourbon, da Leyva in Milan, the Colonna, Lannoy, the Neapolitan council and Este, but there was no one, central, co-ordinating authority. Thus, although a plan might exist for an over-all military strategy in Italy, it could founder on the weakness of individual links and on the difficulty of communication. Questions about authority were always being raised – was the viceroy the representative of the emperor's person throughout Italy or did his authority merely extend to Naples? This question, as a result of Ferramosca's arrival, was now being openly discussed in the streets of Ferrara where it was argued on Bourbon's behalf 'that the viceroy cannot command him throughout Italy, for if the one is viceroy at Naples the other is vice-emperor in Italy'.[36] To overcome this difficulty it had been hoped to create Alfonso d'Este lieutenant-general of the imperial troops so that he might co-ordinate the campaigns of Lannoy and Bourbon. But Este, an exceedingly crafty and far-sighted man, steadfastly refused the appointment; Bourbon was offended that the offer had ever been made and questions were once more asked about his authority even within the highest ranks of his own army. Privately Charles V had already authorized Bourbon to do whatever he liked in Italy, and, in particular, authorized an attack on Rome if the duke felt 'strong enough for the undertaking'.[37] In his own mind Bourbon was clear enough about the position – 'anyone who says that I do not have more authority than the viceroy, granted me by the emperor, is a liar'[38] – but unfortunately this authority had never been made public. Thus, as Bourbon seemed to be about to reject the truce, apparently deliberately disobeying Lannoy, many of the Neapolitan officers of his army now found themselves in a very delicate position. Indeed del Guasto and other captains refused to continue in service with the army, 'lest they should disobey the imperial mandates respecting the obedience of the truce'.[39] The position over ultimate authority was never made clear because Charles did not want it to be clear; he deliberately misled the pope by telling him that Bourbon was to be instructed to obey the viceroy in all things.[40] But if there were political advantage to be gained in this way there were corresponding disadvantages; as Clement himself complained, it was so

difficult to know with whom he was supposed to treat that it
scarcely seemed worth negotiating at all.[41]

On Monday, 25 March, the day of the Annunciation, Bourbon
called a council of war to discuss with his officers what should be
done about the viceroy's peace. Ferramosca was ordered by the
duke

> to repeat all that I had said to him in the presence of his cap-
> tains. This I refused to do because I saw perfectly well that he
> had evil intentions, and that he did not want to accept this truce;
> but as he pressed me very hard I had to do it. For more than an
> hour I was occupied in representing their necessities, the diffi-
> culties that they would have to endure, and the provisions the
> enemy were taking for the defence of Florence and of many
> other towns, while devastating the countryside.[42]

Discussions then began among the commanders, and it soon became apparent that a majority of the officers was in favour of an
advance, with the result that del Guasto and the other Neapolitans
withdrew from the discussions. Meanwhile Ferramosca laboured,
again at some personal risk, to persuade the men to accept the truce,
but first 'the captains of the Spanish infantry replied . . . that many
of their men, and indeed almost all, were in a state of mortal sin
and wanted to go to Rome to gain absolution; and that for such an
expedition they had not asked and would not ask for a penny in
pay'.[43] Mocked by the Spanish infantry, Ferramosca turned next
to the cavalry, but with little more success, and to the lansquenets,
who said that they were indifferent whether they advanced or not,
but that they intended to have all their arrears paid in full. To the
lansquenets it was as clear as it was to the Spaniards that 'their
common interest lies in an advance upon the Roman territory, as
otherwise they will never be paid'.[44] From the beginning Ferramosca's task had been hopeless, for Bourbon was, at that very
moment, suborning his captains to arrange for another mutiny and
a demand for an additional 90,000 ducats. Lannoy and Bourbon
had long realized that a truce with the pope was the one certain
remaining way to raise money;[45] they had planned on this basis,
and it proved in the event that they had planned most profitably.
Bourbon went out of his way to ensure that Clement was informed

in detail about this last mutiny,[46] with the result that Florence offered, on the pope's behalf, an immediate payment of 80,000 ducats with the promise of an additional 70,000 in May.[47]

The behaviour of Lannoy and Bourbon contrasts strongly with that of the members of the council of Naples who hampered the activities of the imperial commanders and forced them to disguise their real intentions. The council utterly refused to countenance any breach of the truce with the pope and explicitly instructed Lannoy not to use the Neapolitan army in any undertaking against Clement. In his Italian policy the emperor was coming into conflict with some of his most prominent Italian servants, who found that their role as Italians interfered with their expected duties as imperial citizens. However, Charles V had clearly decided to dispense with Neapolitan advice, for evidence from Spain reveals that Bourbon and Lannoy had total imperial support. On 12 May Navagero was to report that the truce was disapproved of by the emperor and his court; 'they censure the viceroy to the utmost, and praise the duke of Bourbon to the skies, solely because they think he will not keep it'. Charles took care to warn the ambassador that Bourbon would not observe the truce, 'a proof that he wishes him thus to do. The emperor's confessor also says so much about this and speaks so strongly against the pope, as to render it very evident that the truce and the peace desired by the imperialists, so long as they have no hope of obtaining their ends, is to admit of no equals, choosing everybody to be subject to them and themselves masters of Italy and the world.'[48]

By 28 March the die was cast. Bourbon consulted his astrologers, who assured him that all the omens were now in his favour, 'That today is the last day of privations and disasters and that in the future he will be happy and content.'[49] Since even Bourbon had not had a square meal for weeks few predictions can ever have been more welcome. Everything was in favour of advance. On Saturday, 30 March Ferramosca left the armies and returned to Rome, and on Sunday, in a letter written from San Giovanni, Bourbon politely explained to the pope that it was quite impossible to halt his army but that he hoped Clement, for his part, would observe the truce. On the very same day del Guasto wrote to the pope to congratulate him on the truce and to suggest that Clement might care to divert his forces in a crusade against the infidel.[50] But

Clement showed not the slightest indication of any readiness to accept the suggestions of either Bourbon or del Guasto: 'I have trusted to the viceroy,' he complained, 'given the emperor the investiture of Naples, and disarmed my own army. I well deserve any calamity that may befall me.'[51]

Clement's hopes now rested once more with the Italian League, but these hopes did not initially appear to have much foundation. The other members of the League had, naturally enough, been extremely displeased that the pope had seen fit to come to an agreement with Lannoy. The truce had threatened the alliance at its most vulnerable point. It was no longer possible to co-ordinate the papal, French and Venetian troops. The Venetian senate, angered by the pope's action and afraid that Bourbon might accept the truce and attack the Veneto, ordered Urbino to unite immediately with Saluzzo and to restrict his activities to protecting the Venetian state. On no account was he to risk an attack on Bourbon.[52]

When news of the truce arrived in France the wrath of Francis I knew no bounds. He railed against the pope and warned Acciauoli that Charles would depose Clement and make him once more a simple priest. In defending the pope Acciauoli emphasized again and again that the truce had been made purely for financial reasons, but this was an excuse which Francis I found he could easily dismiss. The French king was particularly annoyed because he had now definitely decided on an attack on the Regno. After a month of complaints and reproaches, Francis spoke to Acciauoli about his intention of sending enough troops both to conquer the Regno and to recover Lombardy. To this Acciauoli, whose patience was wearing thin, replied: 'It would have been far better to do in the past that which you say you want to do now; because if you had done it you would by now have been victorious, and the pope would have had no reason to make an agreement.'[53]

It was at least clear that, despite the papal defection, Venice, with some support from England and France, would fight on, and it was hoped that Ferrara might now be induced to join the League. Venice even suggested to France the terms of a new confederation; a further 30,000 infantry would be raised, the cost to be borne equally by the two countries. Francis was prepared to agree, on condition that Venice would bear half the cost of a Neapolitan expedition. Each country would provide sixteen galleys for the purpose.[54] Thus, at a time when the League was significantly weakened by the defection of one of its members, its aims and objectives suffered a considerable extension which the resources of the main participants could scarcely sustain. Nevertheless, provision for an immediate invasion of the kingdom of Naples became henceforward an integral part of the League's programme and was the price of continued French participation.

At Venice, on 25 March, the contrite legate of the pope, together with the Florentine ambassador to the republic, appeared before the Senate to beg for help. They had received letters from Guicciardini which announced that if the Venetians withdrew their forces beyond the Po the whole 'enterprise of Italy would be ruined, and that it would be as well to wait and see what Bourbon will do. He does not want to accept the truce unless his men get seven pays and he is given Cremona and Lodi for himself. And that even if the viceroy is content Bourbon says that he is Caesar's lieutenant in Italy, and that he does not want to accept it and will go with his army to Florence. And that he, Guicciardini, had written to Ferramosca to tell him that if agreement is not reached by the twenty-fifth he will understand that war has broken out again, writing that, above everything else, our army must remain on that bank of the Po. The doge replied to the legate, "This pope will be the ruin of all Italy." '[55]

It was understandable that the Venetians should be irritated, but clear that Guicciardini was right. Bourbon was not going to accept the truce, and Clement would have to be aided. Guicciardini could only express reluctant admiration when, on 31 March, the imperial army began its advance. Heavy snow and rain had turned all the roads to mud but, with the assistance of army-carts dragged by oxen, which had been dispatched from Ferrara, Bourbon covered the seven miles from San Giovanni to the bridge over the Reno at the western boundary of Bologna. An unsuccessful attempt was made by the papal troops to prevent the imperialists crossing the bridge, and Bourbon lodged for the night on the hill of San Luca, overlooking the city.[56] The weather did not improve, and it was impossible to march either by Sasso or Prato or by the direct route to Florence over the Futa pass which was still blocked by snow. Bourbon, therefore, took the easiest route down the Via

Emilia into the Romagna where supplies were plentiful. In the Bolognese *contado* he left a wake of destruction; trees were cut down and more than 2000 houses burnt.[57]

Guicciardini and Saluzzo had known since the middle of March that, despite the truce, Bourbon would enter the Romagna, but this knowledge was of little use since, as usual, pay was owing to the Swiss, who would not leave Bologna without it. In the end their pay had to be guaranteed by a personal loan from Guicciardini. On 1 April, Saluzzo and Guicciardini, with the French and the Swiss, left Bologna for Imola, in pursuit of Bourbon.[58]

They reached Imola before Bourbon, who was therefore forced to by-pass the city, setting up camp on the Via Emilia a little beyond the city. Leaving a trail of burning hamlets behind it, the imperial army fanned out into the countryside in search of supplies. From Imola Bourbon turned due north as if to attack the Veneto and on 7 April he lodged at Castel Guelfo di Bologna. Bourbon had intended to advance from here, to cross the Lamone and to attack Villafranca, a dependent town of Forlì, but found the rivers which here intersect the terrain too swollen by the recent rains. And so he turned his attention to Cortignola, a well-fortified papal town, which had enraged the soldiers by first promising supplies and then refusing them. After a brief assault Cortignola surrendered by agreement, but the terms of the agreement were not kept and the castle was ransacked, although many of the defenders, fearing reprisals from Urbino, deserted to the imperial service.[59] The imperialists, in fact, found less food than they had anticipated in Cortignola, but what they did find was distributed freely through the army. Russi and Granarola were taken by force, while the army remained based on Cortignola. Thereafter the army's pace quickened; since Siena had promised to supply whatever artillery was needed, the heavy guns were left with a Spanish governor and garrison at Cortignola, and Bourbon turned south. Crossing the Via Emilia, he brought the army to Meldola, a castle of Alberto Pio, close to Forlì, intending to cross the Apennines by the Val di Bagno. The damage done by the army was already estimated at 500,000 ducats;[60] Meldola was taken and ravaged to such an extent that signs of this sack were still visible twenty years later.[61] Civitella di Romagna, the next settlement up the valley, 'a small,

weak castle of the Church', was taken by agreement but still ransacked.[62] Continuing to climb through the Apennines the army
passed through Galatea, Santa Sofia, a Florentine town, reached on
16 April, and San Pietro in Bagno (17 April), ransacking and burning them all.

On 18 April Bourbon's army was before Pieve San Stefano,
situated only a few miles to the south of the point where the Tiber
rises, and the first fortress to make any effective opposition to
Bourbon. Although it had been scantily provisioned and contained
only fifty pounds of gunpowder, the town managed to repulse the
lansquenets four times.[63]

While encamped outside the town, Bourbon was joined by
Lannoy, who had suffered an eventful journey to the camp. He left
Florence on 15 April and four days later was attacked by the inhabitants of Santa Sofia, who forced him to take refuge in the
abbey of the Camaldoli, Santa Maria in Cosmedin. Thence he was
smuggled to the safety of the imperial camp. He brought with him
from the pope and Florence the promise of 150,000 ducats in
addition to what had already been paid, but the financial demands
of the army had already risen to 240,000 ducats and would soon
reach 300,000. Promising to obtain it from the pope, Lannoy
retired to Siena on 25 April.

Bourbon now advanced on Arezzo and did great damage in the
countryside around that town before his army left, after a halt of
one night, for Florence. The imperial army was apparently exhausted: 'I have heard that for many days they ate nothing but
grass and vile meat, even the meat of their donkeys, never tasting
bread or wine, which is no wonder, considering the barrenness of
these regions.'[64] In fact, the problem was less that there was no
wine available than that sporadically there was too much; these hill
regions were famous for their good but extremely strong wine,
and many of the lansquenets drank too heavily, often sickening and
dying in consequence.[65]

It was therefore probably fortunate for Bourbon that he met no
opposition as his army crossed the plain of Arezzo through Mon-
tedoglio, Anghiari, Castiglione, Tabocchi and Tirina to Montevarchi. The passage through these towns was ominous to all
members of the Italian League; it was at last obvious that Bourbon
was about to threaten Florence; beyond that his intentions were

unknown but no doubt terrible. In Rome Giberti was beside himself with anxiety, the soldiers, he wrote, 'do not come solely to prey on Italy but to destroy and ruin her, they come to overthrow the Church and the faith of Christ. . . . Bourbon would regard it as the pinnacle of glory to deprive the pope of his throne.'[66]

CHAPTER X

FROM FLORENCE TO ROME

. . . the dissatisfaction of these people of Florence, who in these days have shown themselves to be of the most evil disposition.
Vatican Library ASV MS. Fondo Pio n.54 f.41

FOR most of the period between 1512 and 1527 Florence had little freedom of action, being ruled more or less directly by the Medici, under the cloak of a republican form of government. So well, indeed, did the Medici manage the city that in 1526 Clement was described as 'absolute master of Florence'.[1] To control Florence as the Medici controlled it was no easy task for, as a contemporary remarked, 'it is very difficult to know how to maintain power in this city, and whoever would rule it needs to be a man of great intelligence, born and bred in it; and even then he will scarcely succeed . . .'.[2] By 1526 Clement's system of management was breaking down; at Florence, as at Rome, he suffered in comparison with Leo X, whose pontificate had fortuitously corresponded with a period of relative prosperity in Florence that was not repeated during Clement's pontificate. Leo was equally fortunate in that his political intrigues benefited Florence. He, who spoke of the city as 'the light of his eyes',[3] had granted the whole state of Montefeltre and San Leo to Florence in recompense for the city's expenditure during the War of Urbino (1516–17), and from Lucca Florence recovered Pietrasanta which she had lost in 1494. In contrast, Clement's intrigues against Siena, which should have benefited Florence, were an expensive fiasco, the brunt of the cost being born by Florence.

Clement himself governed Florence justly and well for Leo X, 'humane, in his deeds, and most patient in giving audience'.[4] He brought order into the administration of the treasury and limited expenditure. He took constructive measures to prevent the flooding of the Arno and went some way towards modernizing the city's defence system, 'increasing its greatness and its dignity and in no way diminishing its beauty'.[5] He restored the appearance of liberty and a measure of the reality. It was a good record and one that did not go unappreciated, 'for everyone in Florence said that the city had never been governed by the Medici . . . with a greater appearance of liberty'.[6]

Nevertheless, throughout these years, an opposition to the Medici flourished among the aristocratic families who were related to the Soderini, an opposition which was carefully fostered by Cardinal Pompeio Colonna. The origins of the connexion between the Colonna and the Soderini can be traced back to the fifteenth century and, specifically, to the brief period of Piero Soderini's rule as *gonfaloniere* in Florence, after the exile of the Medici in 1494. At that time the alliance was based on the common antipathy of the Colonna and the Soderini to the Medici–Orsini family.[7] In 1512 the Medici returned to Florence and the Soderini were exiled, but the penalties against them were extremely mild and Cardinal Soderini even acted as papal legate in Rome for Leo X. However, during the conclave of Adrian VI, the old antagonisms of the Soderini and the Medici came to the fore, as Soderini raised the question of Giulio de' Medici's legitimatization, questioned its legality and suggested that it barred Medici from canonical election. This argument was later to be one of the main weapons in Pompeio Colonna's attack on Clement VII. The voicing of similiar doubts by Soderini in 1521 created a deadlock in conclave. Pressure had to be put on Medici elsewhere, and this was done in Florence where the Soderini staged a revolt which, although unsuccessful, convinced Medici that the conclave must be brought to a speedy end. Throughout the subsequent pontificate of Adrian VI the Soderini maintained their attack on the Medici and their supporters, in particular Cardinal Armellino, whom they accused of financial corruption.[8]

Cardinal Soderini and Cardinal Colonna were able to collaborate through the medium of Piero Soderini, the ex-*gonfaloniere*. Summoned to Rome in 1512, for the next ten years he was assiduously courted by the Colonna and took up residence on their territory. In 1516 he was joined by Cardinal Soderini, who had been implicated in a conspiracy against the pope and had been compelled to flee from Rome. Visitors to the Soderini in these years included many friends and relatives from Florence, and there can be little doubt that the anti-Medici party flourished under the protection of

Pompeio Colonna, who continued to protect the Soderini even after Piero's death in 1522.[9]

After 1524 the leadership of the Soderini clan devolved upon Gian Battista Soderini who, throughout the winter of 1526–7, urged Bourbon to use his army to change the government of Florence, joining his voice to similar pleas by Pompeio Colonna.[10] Through the Soderini and the Colonna, then, an uprising in Florence was planned to coincide with Bourbon's arrival outside the city-walls. As early as January 1527 Perez confidently reported that 'long before the lansquenets reach Florence a deputation is to go out and meet them with offers of money and conditions of peace'.[11] In February the Venetian ambassador to Florence warned that a rebellion was certain if the imperial army passed that way.[12] The danger had certainly existed for many months; the Medici were always weakest when they began to lose support from within their own party since their control over elections to government posts, on which their power was based, became inadequate when the *palleschi*[13] were split, and even in the early months of Clement's pontificate it had been obvious than an opposition party was forming from some of the *palleschi* and other aristocrats who had distrusted the Medici ever since the restoration of 1512.[14] A dozen picked Medici supporters were summoned to Rome to discuss the future government of Florence, but, of these, three strenuously opposed sending the young Ippolito de' Medici to govern Florence under the tutelage of Cardinal Cortona, as Clement planned, 'showing that it was neither honourable nor useful for our city that the government should be in the hands of a cardinal – a cardinal moreover, who came from one of the subject-towns of Florence'.[15] Apart from such aristocratic and anti-clerical prejudice there were solid objections to the choice of Cortona as governor of Florence. Bornin Cortona and educated at Rome, he had no real understanding of the complicated world of Florentine politics and intrigue. His concern was to please Clement and to serve Rome and he was careless that he appeared indifferent to Florentine interests; 'to him it seemed that ruling the state consisted in making everyone obey him, and in preventing the magistrates doing anything without his instructions. He thought that in Florence there was a large number of citizens who would always have to follow the fortune of the Medici whatever happened, and that he could treat them as he liked.'[16]

The Medici supporters had always supposed that the benefits which accrued to Florence at the hands of Leo X would be renewed under Clement VII, but in this they were disappointed. There were many among them also, who, while favouring the Medici in general, were not happy to see their power becoming more autocratic; but it is clear that the aristocrats as a whole, although often opposed to the Medici over many issues, had no alternative policy, programme or form of government to offer. Basically they remained, as always in Florence, the most powerful single element in the city, but their lack of constructive policies, their inexperience and inadequate financial backing, prevented them exercising their power to the full.

In 1526 and the early months of 1527 the likelihood of rebellion in Florence increased. Apart from the unsettling effects of the news of the death of Giovanni de' Medici, a kind of Florentine folk-hero, and of Bourbon's advance in the face of which Cortona seemed to be taking no action, plague, scarcity of provisions and shortage of work came at a time when Florence was being blatantly used as a bank by the League, which appeared to be doing little in return to protect Florence.[17] Apart from direct subsidies to the League, Florence was also committed to heavy expenditure both on her own defences and on those of her subject-towns, where she had to provide for internal security. The expense of the refortification of Florence was considerable. The whole system was modernized under the direction of Antonio da Sangallo, Federigo Gonzaga da Bozzoli and Pedro Navarro who, in defiance of Florentine opinion, ordered that, 'all the towers, which like a garland crowned the walls of Florence round about' be 'ruined and torn down' in order to make room for gun emplacements.[18] In addition, in the early months of 1527 Clement demanded further sacrifices from the Florentine state; the subject-towns were to be refortified, as the whole Florentine state was to be put on a war-footing.

In December 1526 Florence declared her reluctance to spend more on the war, and the city was described as being in total confusion. Many of the major Florentine families had already left for Venice or Pisa. Clement had no illusions about Florentine loyalty. In various ways he deliberately tried to strengthen his position in the city. In the last days of 1526 he dispatched cardinals Ridolfi and Cybo to assist Cortona in the government of Florence; but this proved to be a grave mistake, for Ridolfi was himself a Florentine aristocrat and had ties of blood, sympathy and obligation with the opposition to Clement VII, while Cybo was both a stranger and a foreigner.

In January the pope had urged Venice to use her influence with the Florentines, particularly with the Florentine community resident in Venice, who, it was hoped, might put pressure on the government at home to offer more enthusiastic support for the League. Clement had little hope that any measure would influence events in Florence and frequently expressed the opinion that Florence would make a separate agreement with the emperor. Already Florence was urging him to accept any terms for peace proposed by the imperialists and warned him that if he did not Florence would. In February Clement showed Domenico Venier, the Venetian ambassador, letters from Florence which threatened that, were the imperial army to approach Tuscany and 'ask for 100,000 ducats, the Florentines will pay 200,000 rather than risk the danger of sack' and which revealed many other signs of acute discontent in the city.[19] The Venetians had complied with Clement's request for assistance in managing the Florentines and dispatched their ambassador, Foscari, to Florence where he urged on the city the virtues of a vigorous defence. Ippolito de' Medici, aware of his tottering position in the city government, begged Foscari to make a declaration in favour of the Medici, but this was no part of Venetian policy, which would have been content with support for the League from any régime in Florence. However, Foscari could give his own government little hope and warned that unless some drastic action were taken Florence would certainly seek a separate peace with the imperialists.

This was the situation when news arrived of the pope's truce with Lannoy, for a moment offering hope to Florence, which had heard with increasing panic both of Bourbon's advance and of Urbino's inactivity. These hopes were immediately dashed, for it was learned that Bourbon would not keep the truce and was continuing his advance. And everyone who loved Florence was aware that Bourbon's soldiers habitually swore to sack that city.

For once fortune smiled upon Florence. Warnings of the danger to the city were not without effect. Even the Venetians finally realized that only the intervention of Urbino would hold Florence for the League and they ordered him to advance, while Guicciardini, the papal lieutenant, ignoring the official conditions of the truce, was already speeding to the city with the few troops remaining at his disposal.

Guicciardini reached the city on 23 April and found it practically in revolt. In a full report which he wrote to Rome on the day after his arrival, the papal lieutenant prophesied that the Medici state would be ruined if nothing were done and warned that any delay would prove dangerous. The revolt, however, was avoided for only two more days.

Since the city was full of troops the young men of the opposition were demanding arms to defend it against friend and enemy, and on the morning of 26 April the Piazza de' Signori was full of these young men and their agitation. Actual rebellion was sparked off by a dispute between a soldier and a tradesman of the city that caused an uproar throughout Florence. Fuel was added to the fire when it was learned that cardinals Cybo, Cortona and Ridolfi, together with Guicciardini and the two young Medici, had left the city. Although they had in fact left for the sole purpose of meeting Urbino outside the city-walls, it was only too easy to interpret the action as flight from a threatened city. The moment was seized by the opposition. The young men armed themselves with whatever weapons came to hand and, with the old cry of 'People and Liberty', rushed on the Palace of the Signori, where many of the more moderate Florentine aristocrats, among them Luigi Guicciardini, the *gonfaloniere*, were already gathered. It was only too easy for the young men to capture the palace, for 'it was scarcely guarded',[20] and to hold it for several hours while the more mature members of the anti-Medici party were consulting on what course of action they should follow. Eventually the Signoria agreed to declare the Medici banished, and to restore the government as it had been in the time of the Soderini.

It was characteristic of Cortona that, as soon as news was brought to him of the rebellion in the city, he should have panicked, even though a clear assessment of the situation would have shown him that the legal government was temporarily in a position of overwhelming military superiority. He immediately ordered his troops to place themselves on a military alert. More sensible of the situation than Cortona, the Medici, the duke of Urbino, Ridolfi, Cybo and Francesco Guicciardini advanced purposefully on the Piazza de' Signori. Here they discovered that the young men had barricaded themselves into the palace, and had begun firing on Cortona's troops. Urbino was quite prepared to take the palace by force, and was already beginning to set up his artillery for the purpose when 'Cardinal Ridolfi and messer Francesco Guicciardini for love of their country . . . begged Federigo Gonzaga da Bozzoli to go to the Palace to discuss terms'.[21] Bozzoli returned from what appeared to be a fruitless errand and had a hurried consultation with Guicciardini in which he informed him of the obstinacy of the defenders in the palace. Guicciardini, who was convinced that it was fear rather than courage which was causing the deadlock, was able to persuade Bozzoli to represent the case to Cortona as being less black than it actually appeared, and was able to persuade Cortona to promise a general pardon to the insurgents. Bozzoli and Guicciardini returned once more to the rebels – among whom were numbered even Guicciardini's brother the *gonfaloniere* – and, on these terms of a general pardon for all, managed to quell the tumult without further bloodshed.

In this way the rebellion which became known to Florentine history as the 'Friday Riot' was put down. It was an attempted *coup* which was carefully planned and in which both Bourbon and Pompeio Colonna were implicated. If things had gone according to plan, this rebellion in Florence would have opened the gates to the imperial army. Urbino's timely arrival had preserved Florence, but it was clear that were anything to upset affairs in Rome the days of the Medici in Florence would be numbered. During the uprising the Medici had failed to register any kind of support in Florence; only Baccio Valori and some half-a-dozen of his supporters had remained loyal to the régime during the crisis. Defections from the Medici party were significant; apart from Salviati, whose antipathy to the régime was already notorious, Niccolò Capponi, a moderate and a member of one of the most illustrious Florentine families, the Alemanni, the Strozzi, Clement's close relatives, and the Martelli were involved in the rebellion. The Strozzi and the Capponi were bound as closely to the Medici as any family in Florence. They had played a prominent part in the restoration of 1512, and, although absent from Florence, Filippo Strozzi was at this time one of the papal-nominated ruling body, the Eight of War.

For the moment, however, Florence was safe both for the Medici and from the imperialists. With Urbino's arrival Bourbon had to abandon all hope of taking Florence, and on the day after the 'Friday Riot' he turned aside to fulfil instead the second part of the imperial plan, the capture of Rome. At first Bourbon had some difficulty in deflecting the Spanish troops from all hope of sacking Florence, but Gian d'Urbina quelled their incipient mutiny and, crossing the Arno, the army passed down the Val d'Ombra into the state of Siena. Here Bourbon abandoned the carriages, heavy baggage, light artillery and camp-followers.

News of Bourbon's steady advance and constantly increasing demands for money had finally convinced Clement that he had been fooled by the imperialists, that Rome was really in serious danger, and that his only hope of salvation lay with the Italian League. On 25 April he rejoined the League he had so precipitately abandoned. To Urbino he wrote imploring help of any kind and to the ambassadors of the League then present in Rome he promised miracles if their masters would only succour him. Three days later Florence finally entered the League.[22]

However, any assistance to the pope from the League had now come too late. Although there was constant heavy rain throughout this week, it scarcely hampered Bourbon's advance on Rome down the old Via Cassia. From 27 April the pace of the advance quickened and the soldiers travelled with incredible speed, averaging between twenty and forty miles a day, 'by such strange paths in such perverse weather that everything which we had had to endure which had seemed extreme to us at the time, seemed nothing . . . in weather so bad that it was impossible to ride'.[23] The roads within the Church State were normally bad and in this cruel spring had deteriorated into muddy water-courses. But no natural obstacle was allowed to delay progress; the River Paglia, swollen by late snowfalls and the heavy rain, was forded, the soldiers clinging together in groups of thirty or fifty or onto the horses' tails, and by 1 May Bourbon had reached Aquapendente. On the previous day the viceroy had received intelligence from the Colonna which he immediately passed on to Bourbon that the Colonna had decided 'to come to Rome on 10 May . . . and that at the sixth hour of the night twenty to twenty-five armed men would go towards Monte Cavallo and at Campo Marzio they will try to rouse people to arms, and at this moment all their party will cry "Colonna" and immediately approach Rome. They also let it be known that they have two nephews in Rome to arrange all this.' The Colonna then promised to open Porta del Popolo to the army and advised Bourbon that Cardinal dal Monte had agreed to assist them.[24]

Secure in the knowledge that he was expected at Rome Bourbon advanced through Bolsena to Montefiascone, which, on denying the imperialists entrance, was taken and sacked. But the capture of the city had delayed the advance and was the kind of impediment which Bourbon, intent now on reaching Rome as swiftly as possible, was anxious to avoid. Orange was therefore sent ahead to Viterbo, then held in fee from the pope by the Knights of Jerusalem, in order to arrange a night's lodgings for the army. Despite their obligations to their feudal superior the Knights were ready to accede to Orange's request, and on 3 May the imperial army lodged in the greatest comfort it had known for months.

It was on 4 May that the imperialists made their first appearance in the Roman Campagna. A few cavalry sent out from Rome to reconnoitre surprised some of Bourbon's light cavalry in the vanguard and took about ten prisoners. That night Bourbon's army lodged at Isola Farnese, only seven miles from Rome.[25] Bourbon had now to decide whether or not to launch an immediate attack; he was aware that the Colonna, who could open the city to him or provide artillery, would not reach Rome for another five days. Without the Colonna the possibility of a successful attack on Rome seemed unlikely, but Bourbon had neither the money nor the supplies to permit him to wait long and he feared the advancing league army. His plan up until now had been to capture the pope without destroying Rome, so that he could get money from Clement with which to pay his army, 'However, he said to me', Gattinara recorded, 'that we should not be afraid of harming the enemy, nor give them time to provide for their defence.'[26] Thus the fate of the imperial armies, of the imperial cause in Italy, of the papacy and of Rome hung in the balance as Bourbon meditated on what course of action he should pursue.

CHAPTER XI

THE SACK OF ROME

The ruin of this most forlorn city.
Sanuto

O N Holy Thursday, 18 April 1527, a devout multitude was assembled in the square in front of St Peter's. According to an ancient custom of the Church a prelate read aloud the bull *In Coena Domini* before Clement raised his hand to pronounce the pontifical blessing. At that very moment a semi-naked man, whose wild red hair fell streaming to his shoulders, adorned with a halter round his neck, a crucifix in one hand and a death's-head in the other, who had managed to clamber up onto the statue of St Paul, shouted to the pope: 'Thou bastard of Sodom, for thy sins Rome shall be destroyed. Repent and turn thee! If thou wilt not believe me, in fourteen days thou shalt see it.' In this somewhat flamboyant way, the Sienese fanatic Brandano announced his arrival in Rome. His fame had, no doubt, preceded him, for he had already had a long career as a popular prophet and supposed worker of miracles. For years he had wandered through Italy attacking the general iniquity of men and threatening the wrath of God in the shape of war, plague and other terrible visitations. In those troubled days in Italy his vague prophecies had only too often been fulfilled. Now, with cries of woe, he announced to Rome the certain downfall of its priests, the death of the pope, the destruction of the city and the renewal of the Church.

On Easter Eve 1527 Brandano surpassed himself. Passing from Campodi Fiore to Castel Sant'Angelo he cried out in a loud voice, 'Rome, do penance! They shall deal with thee as God dealt with Sodom and Gomorrah.' Then he said more quietly, as if to himself, 'He has robbed the Mother of God to adorn his harlot, or rather his friend.' Although Clement promptly ordered his imprisonment, Brandano from the shelter of his gaol continued to prophesy the imminent doom of Rome.[1]

Without a doubt these preachings had an effect. For those who believed in Divine Providence or in the capricious activities of the goddess Fortuna it had long been apparent that disaster was threatening Rome. Ever since 1524 the astrologers had been making consistently gloomy prognostications, partially borne out by the bad flooding of the Tiber in 1526 and the plague which had visited the city; from February until July 1524 a severe epidemic had raged which broke out again between September 1525 and January 1526, when many of the papal household were among the victims.[2] Further ominous portents had not been lacking; a mule was said to have given birth in the Cancellaria; a part of the covered way between Castel Sant'Angelo and the Vatican fell down; a statue broke spontaneously; and the host, reserved in the papal chapel on Good Friday 1526, was found the following morning on the ground.[3]

Many were credulous but many more were prepared to ignore portents, always notoriously difficult to interpret before the event; such were 'hardened in their hearts after the ways of the Scribes and the Pharisees . . . and too lost in lust, avarice and ambition to be moved by such divine demonstrations'.[4] Plain common sense also seemed to recommend calm in the face of the imperial threat. Although the Spanish envoy Perez believed that Rome would not be able to withstand an assault, his confidence was not shared by Bourbon's army.[5] It was rare for a town to be taken by assault at this date. At Rome, it is true, the situation was unusual; the defences of the city were out of date and the city-wall was too long to be defended by the artillery of the papal armoury or to be adequately manned with such forces as were available. Yet, on this occasion, the enemy could only approach from the north bank of the Tiber, the breaching of a city-wall was an uncommon feat, and Bourbon had deliberately abandoned his artillery while the Colonna had not arrived to reinforce him with their guns. No one even considered breaching the wall without artillery; Bourbon planned to gain access to Rome by scaling it, always a risky venture. If the city were not taken immediately a siege would be out of the question, for the imperial army was so ill-supplied that it could not have lasted two days without replenishment, and in two days the league army would be at Rome. Bourbon knew that in the unlikely event of his army breaking into the Borgo and Trastevere the city-bridges could be cut and the rest of Rome saved. Even if all the possible defences were broken through Bourbon must have been aware of one other overriding consideration; in the circumstances he would find it impossible to forbid the sack of a city which he had been promising his troops for months. But in the sixteenth century a sack meant the certain disintegration of any army, and all experienced military commanders therefore went to extraordinary lengths to prevent their soldiers embarking on the systematic sacking of towns.[6]

Among the prominent Romans few believed that Rome could be taken, though some of the prudent, such as Cardinal Como, Sadoleto and Filippo Strozzi, left the city before Bourbon reached it. Clement, who had refused to accept a suggestion made by Cardinal Farnese in January that he should leave Rome,[7] publicly declared his belief that Rome was inviolable and posted guards at the city-gates to prevent a mass exodus. Some private citizens had already shipped goods to Ancona for safe-keeping, but Clement now forbade any merchant to transfer goods from Rome.[8] The average Roman citizen did not panic but assumed that, in the unlikely event of Rome being captured, the situation would not differ from that during the Colonna raid. Common rumour in the city argued that if the imperialists did take Rome it would not be a disaster, for then the emperor would take up residence there and the Romans 'would prosper and have the same advantages and honours as they had had under the dominion of priests'.[9]

For about a week before Bourbon's arrival in the Campagna the pope had been in consultation with the city of Rome. On 26 April he sent Cardinals Farnese, Orsini and Cesarini to ask for a gift of 60,000 ducats from the commune and threatened to leave Rome if it were not forthcoming. Within three days the Roman citizens had agreed to the gift but only on condition that their 60,000 ducats should be regarded as a third, the other two-thirds being made up by the prelates and courtiers. It is doubtful whether there was time for all of this to be collected although, of the courtiers, some at least made their contribution; Casale pawned his boat and all his jewels to pay it. As a last desperate measure, on 3 May Clement agreed to the simoniacal creation of six new cardinals.[10]

Probably on the same day, although the meeting may have taken place as late as 4 May, Clement summoned the Great Council of Rome. As an unusually large number chose to attend, the meeting took place in the church of Santa Maria d'Aracoeli, which adjoined the Capitol, and which had long represented the political centre of Rome.[11] At this meeting, Clement, through the medium of four of the cardinals, urged the people of Rome to defend themselves. It would only be necessary to maintain the defence for three days at the most, since the league army was so close. As a proof of his good intentions, Clement offered to leave the Borgo and the protection offered by Castel Sant'Angelo and to take up residence in Palazzo Venezia.[12]

From this meeting the Roman people seem to have gone away determined to assist Renzo da Ceri in his preparations for the defence of Rome. Renzo da Ceri, although not a distinguished offensive soldier, lacked neither competence nor courage and had made a considerable name for himself in Europe in defensive warfare. He cannot be blamed for failing to cut the bridges over the Tiber, for the Romans prevented him from doing so. All that he was able to do in the time available to him was to reinforce the weaker parts of the Leonine wall and to erect defensive works actually within the Vatican in the great court of the Belvedere.[13] Throughout, he was hampered in his work by the Roman populace, who not only had their own ideas about the conduct of operations but were engaged in trying to come to a private agreement with Bourbon. They elected two sets of three ambassadors to negotiate with the duke. The first group was prevented by Renzo from leaving the city and the second never even got a chance to leave as it had not reached Trastevere when the imperialists broke into Rome.[14]

According to the ancient ordinances of the city and more recent instructions, in a time of crisis every *caporione* should have sounded the drum for an assembly of all able-bodied men. There should, therefore, have been thirteen companies ready for action with more to follow. In fact, only six made any appearance at all, and the quality of these left much to be desired. They were well below the numerical strength Renzo had expected, and, since the services of the more able had already been purchased by the owners of the great palaces, they represented the dregs of Roman society. Renzo was forced to raid the cardinal-palaces and to impress artisans in order to make up his numbers. For the core of his defence he had to rely on 4000 regular infantry, 2000 of the Swiss Guard and 2000 of the 'Black Bands', who had somehow survived in Rome during the past two months since they had been technically disbanded. Although their *esprit de corps* was as strong as ever, they had in many cases been forced to sell their armour in order to support themselves. Since relations between the Swiss Guard and the 'Black Bands', for professional reasons, were so bad that in the past weeks they had had an armed affray in which twenty people were killed, Renzo must have had some difficulty in persuading them to act together as a combined fighting force.[15]

The aristocracy, the merchants and the cardinals meanwhile continued to compete with Renzo for troops of their own to guard their palaces. The Florentine merchant, Alessandro del Bene, raised 50, among them Benvenuto Cellini; Cardinal Cesarini raised 200 and Cardinal Piccolomini 150.[16] Since an attack by the Colonna was still expected, Renzo believed it was essential to man the entire length of the city-wall and posted along it a motley collection of Roman citizens, monks and priests, although he warned the pope not to expect too much from this improvised army. Subsequently he brought round his professionals to instruct the new recruits in the art of defence but many of them had already wandered away and abandoned their posts, either to show off the scrappy military equipment which Renzo had been able to issue to them or because they were hungry and no one had brought them food.[17]

In the disposition of his troops, given that he believed he had to defend the whole city-wall, Renzo made the best of a difficult situation. His artillery was concentrated where it would be most effective and the troops were well distributed, the best being retained to defend the Borgo. The command of the wall was distributed in the following manner: at Belvedere were Simone Tibaldi, a brave young Roman, and a Bolognese soldier named Gianbattista; between Porta San Spirito and Porta Posterula was Captain Lucantonio Tomassoni, who had been a lieutenant and favoured pupil of Giovanni de' Medici, and who now commanded the 'Black Bands', with Captain Giulio Ferrara in charge of the artillery and Sergeant Salvaloglio directing the battery. The two sculptors Lorenzotto and Raffaello da Montelupo acted as bombardiers. Also in command here were a Florentine, Niccolò, and Giovanlione de Fano, *caporione* of Ponte, 'a valiant warrior'.[18] As reinforcements there were 1000 men from Rione Parione under Camillo Orsini and the Ensign Cristoforo Bufalo. The Swiss were drawn up towards

Porta Pertosa. In Trastevere, at Porta Aurelia, under Valerio and Gian Paolo Orsini were the captains, Romano da Corso, Mario Napoletano, Niccolò, Count of Tolentino, and some *caporioni*. At Porta Settimania were some *caporioni* with their troops and 200 gentlemen cavalry. Orazio Baglione had been given command of the defence of Trastevere but also had responsbility for the area between Ponte Milvio and Campo Marzio with Antonio Santacroce and some *caporioni*. Some artillery in the Vatican was put in the charge of Stefano Colonna, whose infantry was to defend the papal palace; other guns were placed on Monte San Spirito, the Via Giulia, the Sistine bridge and at San Pietro in Montorio. Together with the heavy artillery of Castel Sant'Angelo it was thus possible to cover the entire area of San Spirito. It is clear that, far from being negligent in his provisions for the defence, Renzo da Ceri had made a realistic assessment of the deficiencies at San Spirito, discovered by the Colonna in September, and was making reasonable efforts to prevent the enemy exploiting this tactical weakness.[19]

On 5 May Bourbon lodged his armies in the fields on Monte Mario, the highest of the Janiculum hills, just north of the city-wall; the officers in Villa Madama, with the army encamped in the fields about. Orange with his light cavalry and some infantry was lodged at Ponte Milvio, but it was impossible to cross the Tiber, for the bridge was securely defended and when some of the lansquenets tried to cross by boat their vessel was sunk by Orazio Baglione. Protocol demanded that the first step of a commander whose forces appeared before a town was to send a formal summons for its surrender, and Bourbon therefore dispatched a herald to Renzo da Ceri, demanding free passage through Rome to Naples and a ransom for the city of 300,000 ducats. But the dispatch of this herald was a mere formality since Bourbon had decided on an immediate assault. It was only after one or two skirmishes in which the imperialists suffered heavy losses from the artillery fire of Castel Sant'Angelo that Bourbon was persuaded by his captains to defer the attack until the following day.[20]

Accordingly, at about midnight, Bourbon inspected the walls of the Borgo and Trastevere, and drew up his army to give them the customary harangue, by which sixteenth-century commanders inspired their troops before a battle. 'He had not even reached the

end of his oration before a joyful and excited murmur began to fill
the camp, from which it could be guessed that for that multitude
every hour to be endured before the assault would seem like a
century.'[21] The captains issued their battle orders and the troops
began to construct wooden scaling-ladders to use on the morrow.
Bourbon spent the rest of the night reviewing his troops. The
army was impressive in size but badly equipped. There was no
artillery, and no supplies of any kind. Most of the men were
clothed, or rather half-clothed, in rags, and all were desperate;
deprived of the necessities of life, in an empty and barren country
with an enemy in their rear, Bourbon's soldiers now saw that their
only means of deliverance was the capture of Rome.[22] Within
Rome itself the night was spent in terror, the defenders springing
to the alert at every sound, for the possibility that the city might
be taken by treachery was uppermost in everyone's mind. All
through the night the great bell of the Capitol rang the tocsin,
calling the defenders to their posts.[23]

On Monday morning, 6 May, at about four o'clock the attack
began. Dressed in white, Bourbon rode out in front of his troops
to encourage them to attack. To each he promised glory of a kind,
'and told the Spaniards, the Germans and the Milanese that it was
now needful that they show for the third time that virtue and
ferocity which he had found in them in the past'.[24] To the Italians
he offered the obvious inducement that if they failed in the attack
they would be punished with death by the pope's troops, and the
Lutherans he urged on by the joyful anticipation of murdering
priests.

Battle commenced with a duel of arquebus fire from both sides,
lasting for about an hour, while the imperialists tried to place
ladders against the walls. Sciarra Colonna, with one division of
light cavalry and two squadrons of Italian infantry invested Ponte
Milvio. An assault, under the over-all command of Melchior
Frundsberg, George von Frundsberg's son, was ordered at three
points; the Belvedere, Porta Pertosa, and between Porta Torrione
and Porta San Spirito. The assault at the first two points was
merely a feint to draw away the defenders from what was, in effect,
the weakest point of the wall. As the Colonna had discovered in
September, at Porta San Spirito, behind the vineyards of Cardinal
Armellino, the walls were lower and the slight elevation of the

ground was to the advantage of an attacker. There was an additional weakness; part of the wall just here was formed by a small private house which, although camouflaged, had not been adequately strengthened. A gun-port of slightly larger diameter than usual served as a window. It was at this point that the imperialists pressed their attack, with spears, pistols, and ladders hastily constructed from garden railings.[25]

Making as little noise as possible the Spaniards, as was usual in the imperial army, led the assault, but the brunt of the main attack at San Spirito was borne by the lansquenets and 300 lances under the command of Orange and Gonzaga. Here, as at the Belvedere, the lansquenets were vigorously repelled. Old and frail as he was, Cardinal Pucci remained constantly in the forefront encouraging the defence, 'and injuring the enemy with words'.[26] The imperialists were within range of the guns of Castel Sant'Angelo and the Swiss Guard made up the core of the defence. It was here that Captain Niccolò was killed by an arquebus shot. Immediately his sergeant, Salvaloglio, summoned aid and was joined by Giovanlione da Fermo. In the fighting which followed, the papal troops managed to capture five imperial banners which were sent immediately to the Vatican, and the imperialists suffered considerable losses.[27]

Nevertheless, the numerical superiority of the imperialists was beginning to tell, and Salvaloglio went in search of Renzo da Ceri, who came himself to direct operations at San Spirito. He directed Salvaloglio to go in search of reinforcements. When the sergeant returned it was to report that none were available. Renzo therefore ordered him to instruct the gunners at Monte San Spirito to open fire on the imperial flank. But already such a move had been rendered futile by the thick fog which rose from the marshes and which crippled the defence. From the imperial point of view the one disadvantage of an attack on San Spirito was that it was within range of the heavy guns of Castel Sant'Angelo. Effectively these were now silenced, along with all the field-artillery. The defenders were reduced to hurling rocks from the walls onto the imperialists and shouting abuse. 'Jews, infidels, half-castes . . . Lutherans' were but some of the epithets flung at them.[28]

A lull in the fighting occurred while the attackers went in search of implements with which to pull down the city-wall of

Rome. Then the fighting was renewed with even greater ferocity; Fabrizio Maramaldo is said to have killed imperial deserters with his own hand. Immediately there followed the first disaster of the day. Many years before an old man with the gift of second sight had prophesied that Bourbon would die at the very moment of capturing a great city.[29] That moment had now come; Bourbon's death occurred suddenly while he was leading forward the lansquenets and urging them to scale the wall. He was holding a ladder when he was shot down by an arquebus. His death became immediately known both to the defenders, many of whom abandoned their posts and rushed through the Borgo crying 'Victory, victory', and to the imperialists among whom the news caused widespread panic. It was only with considerable difficulty that Ferrante Gonzaga was able to quell this panic and to turn the thoughts of the imperialists to revenge for the death of their leader. When the fighting was resumed both sides fought bravely for an hour, but the imperialists now benefited from their numerical superiority. As each attacking party tired, it was relieved, and the pressure of the assault never slackened. The numbers involved were so great that the imperialists were able to tear down the wall with their bare hands. On the papal side, for the first time, it began to seem that Rome might be lost.[30]

Between six and seven o'clock, just as the fog was beginning to lift, the imperialists broke into Rome. Entry was made, almost simultaneously, at the three points of the original attack.[31] To all intents and purposes the defence collapsed as soon as the wall was breached. Although Renzo da Ceri and Orazio Baglione tried to kill all deserters from the wall, the Roman populace immediately rushed to barricade their own homes, the majority crossing over the Sistine bridge and abandoning the Borgo. Many tried to escape by boat and were drowned. Some of the regular papal troops joined the enemy, for in the confusion that prevailed there was no way to distinguish between friend and foe. It was only the Swiss Guard and some of the Roman militia who fought heroically against the fearful odds. Not ten of the company of Lucantonio Tomassoni survived the fighting, and he himself was twice wounded before being captured by Luigi Gonzaga. An inscription near the Church of San Spirito still commemorates another member of the Roman militia, the papal goldsmith, Bernardino Passeri, who fell there in defence of Rome, having slain many of the enemy and captured one of their standards. Giulio Ferrara was killed, with all his company, and the company of Antonio da Santa Croce was also annihilated. Giuliano dei Massimi, son of one of the wealthiest men in Rome, was mortally wounded; his more fortunate brother, Luca, having seen Giuliano fall, took refuge in the Hospital of San Spirito and, having hidden all his marks of rank and wealth, took to one of the beds. He subsequently persuaded some of the first Spanish soldiers who broke into San Spirito to ransom him for 200 ducats, a sum of money which his father was only too willing to disburse. Of the young students from Collegio Capranica who had rushed to the walls to assist in the defence, not one survived. The Swiss had taken up their position near the obelisk, then still standing near the Campo Santo, and there they were cut to pieces. Their captain, Röust, was carried, gravely wounded, into his own house and laid gently on his own bed, where, a few minutes later, he was slaughtered before the eyes of his wife by soldiers who had broken into the house.

Renzo da Ceri had rushed immediately to the Campidoglio in a vain attempt to organize the defence of the city of Rome and to persuade the Romans, at last, to cut the bridges across the Tiber. Meanwhile, a few of the Guelf barons were defending the Sistine bridge, where, under the protection of the guns of Sant'Angelo and with only 200 men, they were able to prevent the imperialists from crossing into Rome until they were put to flight by Orange and forced to retreat into the fortress, 'cursing the pope and his faith in the viceroy and lamenting their own ill-fortune'.[32] The palace of Montegiordano, the Orsini stronghold, built by Giordano Orsini in the fifteenth century, and Montefiore, had already been fired by the Spaniards and the flames could be seen all over Rome.[33]

Clement, meanwhile, had been attending mass and praying in the Vatican whence he was hustled as the enemy made their entry into the city: 'So narrow was the pope's escape that had he tarried for three creeds more he would have been taken prisoner within his own palace.'[34] While he fled along the covered way into Castel Sant'Angelo, accompanied by Cardinal Farnese, who was so infirm that he had to be carried, and by Paolo Giovio, the historian, Clement could see the battle raging below and was even fired at by

Spanish troops. Castel Sant'Angelo was virtually unsupplied and had to be rapidly provisioned from near-by shops while the battle was going on. Crowds of people were trying to make their way into the fortress which was already crowded with refugees and soldiers, milling around together. It was with difficulty that the drawbridge of the castle was raised and, even so, many continued to press forward and fell into the moat.[35]

In a city taken by storm, according to the laws of war, no quarter was given, and almost any licence was condoned, although churches and churchmen were technically secure. Now the imperialists, led by Gian d'Urbina, enraged by a wound which he had sustained in the face from a Swiss pike, swept through the Leonine city and killed all who crossed their path; 'every person, even if unarmed, was cut to pieces in those places which formerly Attila and Genseric, although the cruellest of men, had treated with religious respect'.[36] Almost all the inmates of the Hospital of San Spirito were killed, many of them being thrown into the Tiber alive; the orphans of the Pietà were all slaughtered. In the general confusion all those held prisoner in the Borgo, including the impossible abbot of Farfa, were freed, to contribute to the murder and looting that was going on around them.[37] This plundering was, in fact, quite contrary to the strict orders given by the imperial commanders, who had issued instructions that the army should refrain from plunder until the city was completely taken. The soldiers had been commanded to slaughter all beasts of burden found in the Leonine city in order to prevent the transport of booty.

The imperialists had captured some twenty pieces of artillery in the Borgo but they could not hope to occupy their position for long since the fog had lifted and the guns of Sant'Angelo were still trained on their troops. A council of war was hurriedly called in the palace of Cardinal Cornaro, where it was decided that the attack must be transferred to Trastevere. The abbot of Najera was, therefore, dispatched to Trastevere in order to try to negotiate a surrender and ransom. On his return without a satisfactory answer, it was decided to effect an entry by force. Porta Aurelia was battered down while the Italian infantry, under Luigi Gonzaga, made their way through the vineyards to Porta Settimania. They broke through the wall, opened the gates and, having rejoined the rest of

the troops, advanced on the Sistine bridge. A party of arquebusiers was sent ahead, but excessive precautions were unneces-
sary since the bridge had been more or less abandoned. Between
eleven o'clock and midnight the imperialists entered Rome.[38]

The imperialists reached Campo di Fiori without incident.
Although some plundering had begun, the army remained under
reasonable control and took up position; the lansquenets on
Campo di Fiori and the Spaniards on Piazza Navona. The latter
were the first to break away for booty but they were swiftly followed by the lansquenets, 'some going here, some there, wherever
seemed the most likely place for gain'.[39]

The sack that followed was one of the most horrible in recorded
history: 'Hell itself was a more beautiful sight to behold.'[40] To
begin with there was no end to the slaughter; every individual encountered by the imperial troops was murdered. It was only the
consideration that by killing the Romans they were depriving
themselves of potential ransom money and information about
hidden treasure that eventually caused the Spaniards to put an
end to the carnage. Then they began to take prisoners, and their
example was swiftly followed by the lansquenets.

The Romans had assumed that the sack would be directed
specifically against the French, the Guelfs and the Orsini, and that
imperial supporters would be safe. It was for this reason that, as
soon as the imperialists had broken into Rome, Gian Paolo Orsini,
at some personal risk, rode through the city to the nunnery of
San Cosimato in Mica Aurea where his sister was a nun. His intention was to take her away to safety, 'because the enemy was, in
particular, the capital enemy of all of the Orsini blood'.[41]

In fact, fidelity to the emperor was to count for nothing. The
lucky ones were those who had relatives or friends among the
command of the imperial army. Such a one was the humanist poet,
Tranquillo Mosso of Casalmaggiore, the former tutor of Pierluigi Farnese. Farnese used some of his own mercenary troops to
protect his mentor's house, although he had already had to spare
a quarter of his company to prevent the sack of his own palace,
which was used as a store for booty. But Mosso was peculiarly
fortunate; apart from the Spanish church of Santiago and the
home of the imperial ambassador, where some 200 persons had
taken refuge and which was ransomed for 2000 ducats, there was

scarcely a single church, palace or major house in Rome that was not pillaged. And, as Perez was at pains to inform the emperor, it was only by the greatest good fortune that he had been able to save the imperial embassy itself. Since his own salary, like the salary of every other imperial official in Italy, was months in arrears, he had been forced to raise ransom money by borrowing from good friends on his own personal security.[42]

Giovanni Battista Alberini, a life-long opponent of the temporal government of the papacy, which he regarded as the source of all misery, and related through his wife to the Pichi, a client family of the Colonna, was convinced there was nothing to fear from the imperialists, but for greater security took refuge in the Cancellaria with all his family. From the *loggia* of the palace they watched the fighting in and around the Borgo until the imperialists began to cross into Rome. Technically the Alberini should have been secure in the Cancellaria, for it was a house of Pompeio Colonna and was the home of Bernardo da Rieti, the consistorial advocate and servant of the Colonna. But at the time of the imperial attack Rieti was in prison in Castel Sant'Angelo, and in the general confusion his servants forgot to hang out the Colonna and imperial standards which should have saved the palace.[43] It received the same treatment as all the other palaces of Rome, for it was taken and ransacked, and all those found within the walls were taken prisoner, and held for ransom.

Some merchants and bankers did preserve their property intact, for their businesses were deliberately spared by the troops to serve as houses where people might raise money with which to pay their ransoms. The German bankers were especially protected in this way. Other buildings were ransomed, but protection could not be guaranteed and was never complete. Thus, almost all the major palaces were sacked. The Cancellaria was the first, but it was quickly followed by the cardinal-palaces on Campo di Fiori, among them the imperialist Cardinal dal Monte's palace, which was razed to the ground. Some of the troops had made immediately for the Portuguese ambassador's palace, the strongest fortress in Rome, where a number of merchants had stored property in the hope that it would be saved. Two Spanish captains offered to set up their headquarters there and defend the palace under the imperial flag, in return for a heavy ransom. A minor diplomatic battle was waged as the ambassador heroically proclaimed that he needed no other protection than the flag of the king of Portugal. He refused to pay off the troops he had defending the palace, 'saying that in such a deed there would be dishonour to the king his master'.[44] The Spaniards promptly brought up reinforcements and broke through the defence into the palace which was completely ransacked. The ambassador was captured, stripped of all that he possessed, left without coat or shirt and only with breeches and jacket on, and his life was only spared through the good offices of Gian d'Urbina. Within the palace the imperialists seized property worth upwards of 500,000 ducats, 'because that had been thought the most secure palace in Rome, and there were almost all the silver, money, gems and pearls of the Roman nobility, money and fine goods belonging to merchants, and all the valuables of the Jews'.[45]

For about a week the palaces of the Ghibelline cardinals, Siena, dal Valle, Enkevoirt and Cesarini, situated in Rione San Eustachio, stood untouched. But many had taken refuge there or deposited goods for safe-keeping and the temptation was too much for the imperial troops.[46] In the first days of the sack all the cardinals had paid heavily for protection, and Spanish captains were taken in to prevent an attack. Having observed the value of the property stored in each palace, the Spanish captains clearly decided that they would be fools not to capitalize on the situation and demanded ransoms from the inmates of each palace. At first they asked for 100,000 ducats from each palace, but in the end, apart from separate compositions made by refugees within the palaces, Cesarini's was ransomed for 45,000 ducats, dal Valle's for 35,000, Enkevoirt's (Palazzo dell'Anima) for 40,000 and Siena's for 35,000. These sums had to be paid in ducats to the full amount; all other coins and precious stones were rejected. The ransoms were therefore paid by those within the palaces who were in a position to advance ready cash, the obligation to refund it being divided among the wealthiest refugees. Two hundred and two persons contributed at dal Valle's palace, the cardinal himself making the largest contribution of 7000 ducats.[47]

Even these ransoms proved useless, since the lansquenets now demanded an equal sum, which the cardinals could not raise. Finally the Spaniards had to announce that they could no longer guarantee protection. The lansquenets fell first on the palace of Siena and after four hours' fight captured it and put it to sack. Siena, Cardinal Piccolomini, renowned throughout Europe for his goodness and his legal learning, was led out into the Borgo, where he was ransomed for 5000 ducats. Thence he fled to the protection of Pompeio Colonna. His brother, too, was seized in the palace and was ordered to pay 5000 ducats for his release. 'Then they tied him up in a stable and threatened to cut off his head if he did not pay yet another 5000 ducats; and because he had no money he was forced to give them a bank-note.'[48]

In consequence of what had happened to Siena, cardinals Cesarini, dal Valle and Enkevoirt, the friend and companion of Adrian VI, also fled to Palazzo Colonna. They had scarcely left their own palaces before the looting began. Every person found there was taken and ransomed. The loss of goods from the palaces of dal Valle and Cesarini amounted to 200,000 ducats apiece, and that from Enkevoirt's and Siena's 150,000 ducats apiece. Cardinals Cajetan and Ponzetti were also dragged through the streets in fetters and subjected to ridicule and torture. Ponzetti, a life-long imperialist 'more than eighty years old, and more dead than alive'[49] had to pay a ransom of 20,000 ducats and died in consequence of the injuries he received.

For some time it seemed that the palace of Sant'Apostoli would be spared, for it was, temporarily, the residence of Isabella Gonzaga, mother of the imperial commander, Ferrante Gonzaga. In her compassion, she had given refuge to more than 1200 ladies and 1000 citizens, including Sanga and his family.[50] The palace had been turned into a small fortress and the doorways strengthened with freshly flung-up bastions. From its security the inmates had been able to watch events all through the long first day of the sack before they had any certain news of their fate. It was not until dusk that Isabella's nephew, Alessandro Gonzaga, was seen making his way to the palace gates. He was shortly joined by the Spaniard, Don Alonso da Cordova, who told Isabella that, before his death, Bourbon[51] had ordered him to protect Sant' Apostoli. Finally, about ten o'clock that night, Ferrante Gonzaga himself arrived, having finally been released from his post at the bridge of Sant'Angelo. It was a strange reunion for a mother and son who had not seen each other for two years, and must have brought Isabella little comfort. The greed of Cordova was no less insatiable than that of his fellows in the imperial army, and on seeing the wealth accumulated in Sant'Apostoli he demanded a ransom of 100,000 ducats from the refugees who had been gathered there. Bargaining over the exact sum went on for two days, until separate amounts of 40,000 and 12,000 ducats were agreed to. Of this, 20,000 went to Alessandro Gonzaga, 20,000 to Cordova, 2000 went to pay off four of the lansquenets, while a rumour current at the time claimed that 10,000 went to Isabella's son, Ferrante. If it did, he enjoyed little benefit from it, for Ferrante Gonzaga, like the majority of the imperial commanders, made no personal gain from the sack. Such money as he obtained was immediately handed out again in loans and gifts to enable the many friends he had in Rome to pay their ransoms to the common soldiers.

On the morning of 6 May, the Venetian ambassador, Domenico Venier, had been peacefully strolling back to his palace, with the ambassador of the duke of Urbino, Gieronimo Lippomano, and his personal secretaries, secure in his belief that Rome could not be captured, when refugees running through the streets told them that the city had been taken. With no more possessions, therefore, than the clothes they stood up in, they had taken refuge with Isabella Gonzaga in Sant'Apostoli. Despite a plea by Venier for diplomatic immunity, Cordova and Alessandro Gonzaga insisted that he must be ransomed for 5000 ducats. As he had lost everything he possessed during the sack and could not raise the money immediately, he was left in the hands of Isabella Gonzaga while he appealed to the Venetian Senate to send him money. Even Venier's secretaries had to pay a ransom of 150 ducats, and 10,000 ducats were demanded from his compatriot Magnifico Marcantonio Justinian, 'who was trying to get himself made cardinal'[52] at the time he took refuge with Isabella. Even after all these compositions, Sant'Apostoli was constantly threatened by the lansquenets, and on two occasions Ferrante Gonzaga was forced to fetch Orange to use his authority to prevent the storming of the palace. As it was, as soon as Isabella left for Ostia on 18 May, the palace was sacked.

Torture was common, being used, on the whole, to gain information about supposed buried treasure. Many died as a result or committed suicide. One of the proposed new cardinals, de Cuppis, who had changed 20,000 ducats into gold in order to purchase his elevation, was forced, under torture, to reveal the money to the Spaniards. A peculiarly touching letter, written by Giorgio Borassi to his brothers in Venice, records how the Spaniards originally placed a ransom of 1000 ducats on his head. After torturing him to no effect, they realistically reduced their demand to 140 ducats, which he begged his brothers to send quickly, 'for I have lost everything, though I care little for it. But I do not want to die so young.'[53]

For a large number of the imperial soldiers the sack was an opportunity for a religious vendetta. Luther had long predicted the destruction of Rome, and he was not alone in doing so. It was a prediction which had become part of the standard stock of all prophets of doom. The Lutheran captains in the army had constantly reminded their troops of these prophecies during the long march to Rome and the final assault on the city. In Frundsberg's army there was a very large Lutheran element, among them the German veteran Grunwald, who had often proclaimed his intention of eviscerating the pope that Luther might be justified and Clement punished for clouding the word of God with falsehood. Before the capture of Rome, Clement spoke optimistically of the fate awaiting these soldiers, 'God, in his mysterious way, having brought them to the principal seat of his Holy Religion, in order to make a notable example of them by having them all cut to pieces'.[54] How hollow those words must have sounded in recollection as the very Lutherans he had spoken of rushed through Rome, destroying everyone and everything they came across. The host was trampled underfoot; nunneries were violated, 'nuns of the most holy and virtuous that there were in Rome, being sold in the streets of Rome for a *giulio* each';[55] monasteries, such as the Minerva, were plundered.[56] At the monastery of San Pietro in Vincula damage to the extent of 30,000 ducats was recorded. Churches, attractive to the looters because of their easily accessible and wealthy furnishings, and monasteries, where many had taken refuge or left goods for protection, suffered particularly. At St Peter's, 'even on the high altar more than 500 men were slaughtered, holy relics were burned or destroyed. . . .'[57] The tombs in the church were violated, including that of Julius II. The head of

St Andrew was thrown on the ground, the napkin of St Veronica was stolen and offered for sale in the Roman inns. A lansquenet fixed the Holy Lance, the spear that pierced the side of Christ, to his own lance and rode through the Borgo with it. The actual tomb of St Peter was left uninjured, but the chapel of Sancta Sanctorum, the most holy place in Rome, to which no woman was ever admitted, was plundered, although the special treasure of the chapel was preserved by its huge iron enclosure. When the plundering was over, the most famous church in Europe was turned into a stable for the imperial cavalry.

The new church of the Florentines, but recently completed, became a barracks. At the nunnery of San Cosimato the oratory was used as a shambles, and the cloister housed the animals before they were slaughtered. The soldiers who took over this building found it already deserted, for the seventy nuns, who had the good fortune to be ruled over by Sister Julia, an abbess of great courage and ability, who believed that she had been specially chosen by God to confront this awful moment with dignity, had been shepherded across Rome to the comparative safety of the nunnery of San Lorenzo. They abandoned practically everything to the marauding soldiers, their dearly loved and richly decorated image of the madonna, their new red velvet altar-cloth, which had recently become an object of the greatest pride, and the riches of their sacristy. At San Lorenzo the nuns could scarcely be welcome guests, for nearly 200 people were crowded into living-quarters which had formerly housed half that number. There was a terrible shortage of food and of water, and the nuns lived in constant fear. They had originally arranged to ransom themselves and their nunnery and had it guarded by a captain of the imperial soldiery, but they soon found that this gave them little protection. Almost every day bands of drunken soldiers attempted to break in, until at last one night they found it impossible to resist any longer and were forced to open their doors to a plundering mob: 'The ravening wolves came in and by a divine miracle failed to see the sisters, the brides of Christ who were prostrate in the choir, praying to their bridegroom with tears to deliver them from so great and manifest danger.'[58] From rape and murder, at least, these nuns were preserved, but not from the loss of their property; despite the ransom they had paid, their nunnery was as effectively pillaged as any other in Rome. Like every other consecrated place, San Lorenzo lost its relics, for their rich mountings and cases made them an obvious attraction for imperial greed or Lutheran hatred. Some of the most holy of the relics of Rome, which for centuries had drawn pilgrims to the city, were used as targets by Lutheran arquebusiers and many would have been lost for ever had it not been for the piety of individual Romans; the head of St John the Baptist from Saint Sylvester in Capite, for instance, was preserved by an old nun.[59]

On one occasion the Lutherans vented their hatred on an old priest whom they killed when he refused to communicate an ass. On another they turned their attention to their captive, Cardinal Aracoeli; 'a large group of them carried him in a coffin, as if he were dead, through all the streets of Rome, singing his obsequies continually'. A halt was called for the preaching of a mock funeral oration, 'and instead of his praises they repeated many lies and filth'.[60] Rome had for so long been the accepted centre of the Christian world that contemporaries were appalled by the irreligious silence which fell on the city where, for more than a month, no mass was said, where indeed not one chalice survived with which to say mass, and where every bell and clock in the church towers was silenced. 'Those men, though heretics rather than Christians, have done deeds which one has never even heard were done by the Turks in any place.'[61]

As the lansquenets and the Spaniards began to quarrel among themselves so the horrors of the sack increased. Ten Spanish soldiers in a pillaging party were overjoyed to discover what they took to be a sack of gold crowns, but were in fact valueless tokens. When they refused to share their booty with a party of lansquenets, the Germans promptly burned down the shop with all inside it. Within a week the Spaniards and the lansquenets were attacking one another's lodgings in order to take plunder from each other. Since it had proved impossible to come to any agreement about profit-sharing, many people had to pay their ransoms twice over; once to the lansquenets, once to the Spaniards, or once to the soldiers and a second time to their commanders. The wealthy Florentine, Bernardo Bracci, was captured by a party of Spaniards who agreed to ransom him for 7000 ducats, but while they were dragging him off to the bank of a German merchant from whom he hoped to raise the sum they were met on the Sistine bridge by the marquess de la Motte, soon to be selected as a suitable governor for Rome. Motte's response was no doubt characteristic: 'This is a very small ransom. If he won't pay another 5000 ducats to my account, I order you to throw him into the Tiber immediately.'[62]

Whenever there was the remotest possibility of gain, ransoms were placed on every individual aged three years or more. In every case they were extremely high. Five thousand ducats seems to have been the normal market rate for a high-placed ecclesiastic, but more was extorted whenever it could be obtained. While the wealthier members of the community do not appear to have had too much difficulty in raising money, for the middle-ranking Romans the effect could be ruinous. Before the sack Giovanni Battista Alberini, a prominent Roman citizen, had been a tolerably wealthy man and had been offered 2000 ducats for a house he owned in Rione San Eustachio. On that occasion he had refused to sell it, but when the imperialists placed a ransom of 400 ducats on his head he decided to realize his asset. The same house sold to his sister-in-law, Camilla de' Mattei, now fetched no more than 200 ducats. This kind of malpractice, forced on people in the strained days following the sack, was extremely common and led to considerable administrative confusion in subsequent years, for Clement later issued permission for contracts made during the sack to be rescinded.[63] There was, in fact, a general collapse of personal morality. By too many the sack was regarded as a glorious excuse for wiping the slate clean of all old debts. In October Master Borardino, a shoemaker who kept a shop in the Borgo, was still trying to get payment of debts incurred before the sack of Rome, but, although many of his debtors were deeply devout, he could get only one, a certain Caterina, to admit that she owed him money, and none at all to pay him.[64]

A market in benefices and offices sprang up under the pressure to raise ransom money. The *scriptoria*, with a usual market price of 3000 ducats, sold for 700. So depressed did the market in offices become that, of the 300,000 ducats' worth which fell into papal hands through deaths during the sack, none could be realized.

Those who could not pay their ransoms suffered horribly. Christopher Macellio, a Venetian resident in Rome, was captured and all his movable property was taken. Having nothing left with which to pay his ransom he was tied by the Spaniards to a tree-trunk, and had a finger-nail pulled out each day until he eventually collapsed and died, worn out by pain, hunger and shock.

By 9 May the imperial commanders were making efforts to regain control of their troops. The league army was within a day's march and it was reasonable to assume that it would attack Rome, even after all due allowance had been made for the chronic caution of the duke of Urbino. Orange had never been entirely without authority; he was able to prevent the sack of Sant'Apostoli and of the Vatican Library. After five days he was able to mount a heavy guard on Castel Sant'Angelo and to lodge the troops with some semblance of order, the lansquenets in the Borgo and the Spani-ards in the Banchi, although on 12 May there was still no guard on the city-gates and on 19 May Gattinara could write that each man in the army was his own master.[65] Certainly Orange's task was not made any the easier by the inevitable pillagers who had fol-lowed his army to prey on the ruins of Rome. Whatever the army had left they ransacked, most disastrously of all, since plague was already spreading, the spiceshops, 'breaking and throwing the containers to the ground so that one cannot buy even an ounce of spices in Rome, not for ten ducats the ounce'.[66]

The first relief to the Roman populace came with the arrival of Ascanio, Vespasiano and Pompeio Colonna with 8000 men, on 10 May. As soon as they entered Rome, it was perhaps inevitable that the Colonna troops should join in the pillaging, but, at the earliest opportunity, Pompeio Colonna put a stop to it. There could be no doubt that Cardinal Colonna rode to Rome in triumph. His hostility towards Clement did not seem to have abated. He had the papal vineyards at Ponte Milvio burned, an action which Clement interpreted as a repayment for the burning of the Colonna castles in the Campagna. Colonna, too, was re-sponsible for the burning of Villa Madama, which Clement had built on Monte Mario while he was still a cardinal. 'In his heart he rejoiced at the great damage and the danger of the pope.' But the sight of Rome moved even Colonna to tears of pity, 'and all the more because he saw that his *patria* had been ruined without the ruin of the pope, who had escaped, contrary to his desires. Accor-ding to his way of thinking, it seemed that he who had caused this disaster should suffer for it, not the miserable, innocent Roman

The Duke of Bourbon conducting the attack on Rome, an artist's conventionalised view

Bourbon is slain by an arquebus shot at the moment of victory

The Sack of Rome, attributed to Pieter Brueghel the Elder, with
the places identified by the artist. It is based on earlier maps

The Pope besieged in Castel Sant' Angelo, as
pictured by an imperial artist

Pope and emperor
ride through
Bologna after the
imperial coronation
in San Petronio, a
symbolic portrait.
Soldiers and
cardinals form the
procession

CLEMENS VII PONT MAX IMP CAES CAROLVS V P F AVG

Clement VII and
Charles V, by Vasari

people.'[67] Pompeio opened his palace to refugees, and among those who fled there were the imperial cardinals, many nuns and Marcello Alberini and his mother. He paid ransoms for many people, even for those from the families of his political enemies. Among his first actions was that of recommending Giovanni Battista Alberini to the imperial troops, with the result that Alberini was transferred from the open into the relative comfort of confinement in Palazzo Cybo. In the end Colonna was even moved by the plight of the pope and began to work for Clement's release, realizing that this must be the first step towards freeing Rome of the imperial soldiery.[68]

It is impossible to tell how many died in the sack.[69] A Spanish sapper, captured by the League, claimed that on the north bank of the Tiber alone he had buried nearly 10,000 corpses and that he had thrown another 2000 into the river. Ecclesiastics, curial officials and lawyers suffered proportionately high losses. Starvation and plague were to add to the toll. Whole families were decimated. Giovanni Battista Alberini lost his three daughters, Lucia, Ascania and Laura, and one of his two sons as a result of their sufferings in the sack, while he himself was taken prisoner and nearly died of starvation.[70] The final departure of the imperial army was to bring further loss of population and investment. Since they feared reprisals from the Roman populace many of the German and Spanish nations left the city for ever. By the following January the population of Rome had been halved.

The cultural life of Rome had been immeasurably harmed. Beautiful palaces like those of the Massimi or Cardinal Como were completely destroyed. Artistic monuments were attacked, either for their religious significance or their pecuniary value. Paintings and church ornaments suffered particularly. Whole libraries were lost; Gieronimo Negro lost all his work, Accolti's famous collection was destroyed in its entirety as were those of Giraldi and Giles of Viterbo, the famous Augustinian preacher, who lost the manuscript of his *Historia xx saeculorum*. The library of Angelo Colucci, so rich in Greek, Latin and Hebrew works, was dispersed.[71] The Paduan scholar and professor of the Sapienza, Augusto Valdo, saw his precious books and his work on Pliny used to light kitchen fires and never forgave the emperor. Giovio's tale, on the other hand, that much of his work was lost in the sack of Rome was pure invention, so that his work might logically be compared with that of Livy.[72]

The records of the apostolic chamber were ransacked and considerable damage was done there. Since the reign of Sixtus IV the archives had been located on the ground floor of the Vatican in the Secret Library of the popes. Here were kept the records of the chamber, the papal registers and the most valuable books of the papal collection. The value of these was well known to Roman pillagers, and many were stolen during the sack. The imperialists took all books with valuable covers or else tore the books from their bindings. Among volumes to suffer in this way was Henry VIII's richly bound *Assertio*, the pamphlet attacking Luther which had earned for the English king the title of Defender of the Faith. Twenty years later the Vatican library was still repurchasing volumes lost in the sack. In the end the majority of the books was recovered but in the archives much was totally destroyed, in particular, financial documents, object of the fury of the Roman populace, who had been angered by Armellino's fiscal measures, and of that of the Lutheran soldiers who hated the papal tax to which they were subjected in their own country and which was known as 'Peter's Pence'.[73] Clement, himself, who subsequently testified to the losses, referred to documents which were deliberately stolen from the papal archives and which, he claimed, would have cleared him of imperial calumnies.[74] The search and sack would have extended even further into the Vatican Library had not Orange commissioned the building for his wardrobe. It was extended, however, to the private archives of the bankers. In the Banchi all the records were emptied into the street, 'and from Castel Sant'Angelo we could see the street of the bankers as far as the mint covered with writings. It looked as though it were dappled with sunlight. . . .'[75]

The Sapienza, Rome's famous university, was completely ruined. Under the patronage of the Gonzaga family, Lodovico Boccadiferro had been lecturing there on Aristotle. Now he escaped from Rome and returned to his native city of Bologna. This was a typical loss for Rome; Boccadiferro was acknowledged to be one of the greatest living Italian philosophers, and subsequently became so renowned that he was offered a salary that can only be described as fabulous to teach at the University of Pisa.[76]

Many other members of artistic and intellectual circles were for ever lost to Rome. Benvenuto Cellini and Raffaelo da Montelupo[77] found employment as gunners in Castel Sant'Angelo, and Baldassare Peruzzi, architect of the Farnesina, escaped death at the hands of the lansquenets by painting a portrait of Bourbon, but these were peculiarly lucky. The school of Raphael, famous throughout Europe, was completely broken up; the spirits of Vicenzio di San Gimignano and of his companion, Schizzone, were completely broken, the former returned to his native town and the latter died shortly afterwards. Fabio Calvo, who had translated the work of Vitruvius for Raphael, died in the sack. Polidoro fled from Rome, and his friend and colleague, the painter Maturino, died of plague, while Perino del Vaga and Giulio Clivio were tortured and robbed of all that they possessed. The Florentine painter, Gianbattista Rosso, was captured by the lansquenets and despoiled of all his possessions, being used by them as a beast of burden until he managed to escape to Perugia. The painter, Parmigiano, saved his life by executing drawings for the imperial soldiers and then left Rome for Bologna. Paolo Bombace, the eminent Greek scholar, master of Erasmus, friend of Aldus and secretary of Cardinal Pucci, was fleeing with his master to Castel Sant'Angelo as the imperialists broke into Rome and he was overtaken and killed. Mariano Castellani, man of letters and intimate friend of Bembo, died heroically, fighting against the enemy. Agostino Foglietta, one of the closest and most esteemed of the papal advisers, had been killed by an arquebus shot during the capture of Rome. The new and swiftly developing arts of engraving and *intaglio* suffered many losses; among those who lost everything in the sack was Raphael's Bolognese engraver, Marcantonio Rainaudi, who fled, empty-handed, to his native city.[78]

Rome was denuded of almost all movable wealth for, since there had been no fear of the city being captured, nothing had been properly hidden. Some hurried efforts had been made to conceal valuables in sewers or wells or to transfer them to churches, monasteries, cardinal-palaces or the houses of Spaniards or Germans living in Rome. But Pesaro reckoned that even property which had been hidden had generally been discovered. It was true that most of the big houses and palaces had secret hiding-places within them, but the majority of these had only been installed during the panic following the Colonna raid. There were too many servants, carpenters and builders who were willing to trade their knowledge of such secrets for their own life, liberty or money. Treasure which had not been hidden had often been entrusted to friars for safe-keeping, but all of their houses were sacked. Contemporaries reckoned that between seven million and twelve million gold ducats were lost to the city.[79]

Hardly a house in Rome was left undamaged, and the longer the occupation went on the worse the damage became. Large parts of the city were burnt down and many houses completely destroyed. The Vatican was almost gutted and in many places badly burnt. In the months that followed, such houses as had survived the sack, both in Rome and in the surrounding countryside, were frequently ransacked and every combustible fitting, including beds and mattresses, was seized to feed the fires that became so necessary, not only for cooking, but for warmth as the autumn approached.[80]

Trade had been brought to a standstill. Shops were emptied of their stocks which, frequently, were merely trampled underfoot. The only shops to survive the sack were the few apothecaries which the imperial commanders had had shut up before the sack began. These were subsequently ransomed by their owners, who inevitably made a great profit[81] since of more than a hundred apothecaries and herbalists in Rome only three survived. All those who owned cattle, horses, sheep, goats or deer in Rome lost them, and this meant a loss of livelihood for the many herdsmen and shepherds who had been employed in the city.

As the smell of gun-smoke evaporated, to be replaced by the stench of open drains and decaying bodies; as the shouts of the soldiers, the screams of their victims, the clash of steel on steel was gradually replaced by the unearthly silence which enveloped Rome after the sack, the Romans took stock of the disaster which had befallen them. They saw the sack, justly, in terms of loss, of livelihood, of life, of home and of honour within Rome. What they did not yet see, and who can blame them for not doing so, was the wider implication in an Italian context of the fall and destruction of their city. But the fall and sack of Rome was to be of the utmost consequence in determining the ultimate fate of the rest of Italy and its relations with Charles V.

CHAPTER XII

ROME AFTER THE SACK

His Imperial Majesty ought not to trust too much to his lucky star, for it is not every day that God works miracles.

Lope de Soria, 21 July 1527

FOR a fortnight after the capture of Rome there was no effective government in the city, but gradually some form of *de facto* organization began to evolve, although almost everything remained in total confusion. The army was now officially lodged, Fabrizio Maramaldo and Luigi Gonzaga having command of their Italian forces in Trastevere, the lansquenets in occupation of the Borgo, and the Spaniards on the other side of the Tiber around Campo di Fiori. The armies were broken up in this way in order to prevent them fighting with each other. The Colonna family also played an important part in guarding the city, and with their troops, who were considerably better controlled than those in the imperial army, maintained a defence at the bridge of Sant'Angelo and in the adjacent quarter of the city as well as at Ponte Milvio. The command of the imperial army had, inevitably, been weakened by the death of Bourbon. In the absence of any other obvious successor, Orange had automatically assumed the over-all command, but he was still very young and inexperienced and liable to make mistakes; the first was to appear to favour the lansquenets at the expense of the Spaniards. Under Orange, the supreme executive authority of the army was vested in the army council, which at the end of May consisted of Hesse, Captain Corradino – the veteran of Cremona – Ferrante Gonzaga, Najera, the German-born Lodovic, Count of Lodron, Gian d'Urbina, Pompeio and Vespasiano Colonna, Girolamo Morone, and Giovanni Bartolommeo da Gattinara. As it was feared that all civil officials would leave Rome, the council elected the marquess de la Motte de Noyers as civil governor of the city and on 16 May lodged him in Como's old palace on Campo di Fiori. Since the governor of Rome was made officially responsible for the maintenance of law and order in the city, and was competent to deal with all criminal cases, it is clear that the army-council was anxious, above all else, to reimpose discipline both civil and military within Rome. At the same time the council created an imperial *auditore di camera*, a legal office whose continuing existence was essential if the administration of the city were to operate at all.[1]

Yet the imperial commanders were working in the dark, for they desperately required instructions from Spain in order to know how to proceed. On 19 May Gattinara wrote to Charles seeking enlightenment, 'to know how your Majesty intends to govern this city of Rome, and whether or not any kind of apostolic see is to be retained in it'. Personally Gattinara advised the emperor against any concessions to the papacy, 'which must be kept so low that your Majesty will always be able to dispose of it and command it as you will'.[2] However, he admitted that the troops were still undisciplined; 'If your Majesty does not come,' Gattinara warned, 'all Italy will be destroyed, especially because this army thinks of nothing but sacking and destroying everything.'[3]

Despite all these efforts by the imperial commanders, the civil government of Rome was not to recover for more than a year. In most of the public records of Rome for this period there is at least a nine-month lacuna. The responsibility for this breakdown in government was clearly that of the imperialists, since their suggestions for a permanent government of the city by the Colonna were, in the circumstances, bizarre. They were manifestly unacceptable to the pope who, on being asked to appoint Pompeio Colonna papal legate in the city, replied, with some feeling, that 'the imperial army can do as they please, since they are the masters; he himself will neither authorize nor consent to such an arrangement'.[4]

Rome had become an occupied city with no corporate life, no valid administration and no recognized justice. The pope, normally the head of the civic administration, was totally cut off from the city, incarcerated in the fortress of Castel Sant'Angelo. He had been accompanied into this refuge by many distinguished refugees. Of the cardinals then present in Rome, all but dal Valle, Aracoeli, Cesarini, Minerva, Trani and Enkevoirt had fled into the castle. Cardinal Pucci, who had been running from San Spirito to the fortress as the imperialists invaded the Borgo, was trampled underfoot by the crowd and had to be hauled up into the castle through a window. Cardinal Armellino, who had been burying the most important of the papal jewels in his garden, had also to be hauled up in a basket. Giovan Tommaso Manfredi and Camillo Orsini had scaled the wall into the fortress, but Camillo subsequently escaped through the Belvedere and made his way to Spoleto. Among other notables of importance who took refuge with the pope were Jacopo Salviati, Giberti, with his secretary Francesco Berne, Orazio Baglione, Schomberg, and the most famous displaced person of the sixteenth century – Alberto Pio da Carpi. But, as far as possible, the number afforded shelter had been restricted, for supplies in the castle were very limited. Accommodation was found for 950, including the garrison of 350 soldiers. There were supplies of grain and wine sufficient for a month, and these could be supplemented by some salt-meat, horse- and donkey-meat, and cheese, but living-quarters were extremely crowded and uncomfortable. The Venetians, who did not have a change of clothes between them, slept eight to a room with Cardinal Pisano, taking it in turns to do guard-duty.

The castle had always been well provided with artillery, and all the guns were still operational. There was, at first, a shortage of fine powder for the arquebuses but this deficiency was soon made good in an improvised factory, and as there was no lack of spirit among the picked troops who, under the joint command of Orazio Baglione and Renzo da Ceri, were incarcerated with the papal court there were daily sallies from the castle. By the end of May sharp-shooters within the castle had succeeded in wounding both Orange and Gattinara, and Orange for the rest of his life bore a scar on his handsome cheek as a reminder. The heavy guns, commanded by Antonio da Santacroce, also maintained a constant fire, keeping the imperialists out of at least a third of the Borgo. The cannon could also cover the bridge of Sant'Angelo and effectively prevented its use by the imperialists, who had to replace it by a bridge of boats out of range of the artillery.

Some compensation for the discomfort and tedium of life in the fortress was provided by the military and spiritual exercises in which all the inmates of Castel Sant'Angelo participated. Francesco Pesaro remarked that his stay in the fortress reminded him of a sojourn in a religious house; 'in the castle psalms were sung daily, litanies were said, and, through all the hours of day and night, two people read from the scripture'.[5]

On the imperial side, the siege of the castle had been entrusted to the capable hands of Gian d'Urbina and his Spaniards. The siege-works, which were begun within a week of the capture of Rome, had to be built by the soldiers themselves since there were no engineers in the imperial camp and no money with which to hire any.

The imperial captains in Rome were worried by the proximity of the league army, whose numbers approached 40,000, but for all the apparent activity in which this army indulged they might have spared themselves the trouble, since it was rendered ineffectual by internal disagreements. Guicciardini, no longer protected by the authority of the pope, found that his strictness, arrogance and civilian manners, which had inspired hatred in the papal captains, were now being repaid. He experienced open insolence and insubordination. His relations with the duke of Urbino had deteriorated after the disaster which had befallen the pope, but in this he was not alone, since most of the commanders frankly disagreed with Urbino's dilatory tactics, and those who could exercise individual initiative did so.

Urbino had prepared to leave Florence as soon as he was certain that Bourbon had left Florentine territory. On 25 April Guido Rangoni, with his own cavalry, that of Caiazzo, and 5000 papal and Florentine infantry, set out immediately for Rome. They were to be followed on 1 May by the rest of the army, and it was hoped that Bourbon would be overtaken before he reached Rome. Even if he were not, it was reasonable to suppose that Rangoni would reach the city before it was captured. The plan was nearly successful; Rangoni and his light cavalry did reach Rome on the same day as the imperialists but, believing that they could do nothing against so vast an army, they retired to Otricoli. Meanwhile the bulk of the league army left Florence two days late, reached Arezzo that evening, and was still advancing south as the imperialists broke into Rome. Urbino might yet have brought much needed assistance to the pope if he had not been tempted away from the direct route to Rome. The news of the fall of Rome encouraged the duke to waste precious time ridding Perugia of a régime which he believed to be hostile to his own little state of Urbino. So, while Rome was being sacked and the pope was at the mercy of the imperialists, Urbino was negotiating with the city of Perugia, into whose territory he marched his army between 8 and 10 May. Urbino's declared price for the removal of his rapacious army from Perugian territory – which it was systematically devastating – was the departure of Gentile Baglione, papal governor of Perugia. It was not, therefore, until 13 May, when Gentile and his adherents left Perugia for exile, that Urbino advanced towards Orvieto and Viterbo in order to threaten the imperialists in Rome.

Already Urbino had been faced by insubordination and disruption within his army. Stefano Colonna had escaped from Rome to the league camp and was imploring Urbino to come to the assistance of Rome, while a pathetic letter addressed to Guido Rangoni from Castel Sant'Angelo, begging for relief and help, reached the league camp on 12 May. This letter expressed despair that no news of the league army had reached the besieged and it urged an immediate advance on Rome, 'where if you come you will find these men in Rome . . . completely occupied with their booty, which they can neither leave, nor send away, nor guard . . . so that from this evil may yet come our salvation. If you do not want to attack Rome, you could lodge close by and use the cavalry to rescue us.'[6] Distressed by this appeal, Federigo Gonzaga da Bozzoli revolted against Urbino's caution and, in open disagreement with his commander, declared in a council of war of the league army that with only 150 lances and cavalry he was prepared to attempt the liberation of the pope and the cardinals. Since Urbino could not prevent an attempt which was universally approved by every other commander of rank, and since he was already under pressure from Venice to rescue the pope before the imperialists could complete their siege-works around Sant'Angelo, it was agreed that Bozzoli and Saluzzo might make the attempt. They left on the same day, and because the whole success of the enterprise was dependent on secrecy the two commanders took different routes; Bozzoli was to pass through Narni, Città Castellana and Nepi, while Saluzzo took the Orvieto–Viterbo road, meeting up with Bozzoli between Sutri and Monterosi. It is scarcely surprising, given the hasty and inadequate planning of the enterprise, that it should prove unsuccessful. By 17 May Bozzoli was back in camp, blaming his failure on the fall of a horse.

Thus another five days had been wasted, during which the imperialists strengthened their fortifications. With no firm plan in his mind, but knowing that he must do something, Urbino ordered an advance to Casale. Constantly speaking of the need to rescue the pope, but delaying the attempt from day to day, on 22 May Urbino authorized the league army to move to Isola Farnese. Here, however, it was learnt that the imperial siege-works around Castel Sant'Angelo were nearly complete, and Urbino declared that no further advance would be either reasonable or safe. For Guicciardini it seemed the end of the world. 'We are here,' he wrote, 'waiting from hour to hour for the ruin of all things; not only the overthrow of dominions and states, but to see cities put to the sack, without respect of the honour of women, or religion, or of the holy sacraments . . . in fact, we are completely ruined, and without any remedy, unless help comes to us soon.'[7] Yet the moment when assistance could have made any difference was already past; within Rome the Spanish troops at work on the siege-fortifications had laboured day and night, assisted by a few professionals supplied by the Colonna, and by 27 May Castel Sant'Angelo was completely invested, the fortifications stretching from San Spirito to the Tiber. Six attempts were made to mine the castle. Although only two of these ever had any chance of succeeding, and, of these, one was ruined by a countermine, they still caused consternation and fear. 'Oh God!' prayed a correspondent of the duchess of Urbino, 'What a century this is! Has it come to pass that we are to see a pope and a whole flock of cardinals blown into the air by fire?'[8]

Those within Castel Sant'Angelo found that their isolation made fears multiply. The imperialists placed a very strict guard over the siege-works, and not even the most innocent-looking person was allowed to cross them and live. Even an old woman carrying a gift of lettuces to the pope was arrested and strangled in full view of watchers from the castle battlements. It was only at the greatest risk to those who carried them that messages were passed out of the citadel to the league camp every night. Yet messengers *were* found, for the pathetic plight of the pope evoked in many men feelings of loyalty which had so often in the past been conspicuously lacking. Sanga escaped from Rome in the entourage of Isabella d'Este on 18 May and could easily have travelled on to safety. Instead he wandered through the Roman Campagna from hill-town to hill-town, and finally to Civitàvecchia, trying to devise ways of getting back into Rome and joining the pope in Castel Sant'Angelo, 'for I would far rather be a prisoner with him than free elsewhere'.[9]

Urbino and his troops were still at Isola Farnese, and refugees from Rome, among them Lucantonio Tomassoni, daily straggled into his camp. However, despite eloquent speeches by Guicciardini and the urgent appeals from Castel Sant'Angelo, it was clear that Urbino had no intention of attacking the imperialists. Once more lamenting the lack of good pikemen in his army, the duke declared that he would not attack Rome unless he had 16,000 more Swiss, 10,000 Italians, 3000 sappers and a large artillery force.[10]

Urbino's troops were suffering considerably from bad weather, shortages of supplies, and general deprivation: 'Everyone in this army suffers from lack of food.'[11] The soldiers were so hungry that they could not be prevented from pillaging the surrounding castles and villages. Heavy rains continued almost daily. Since all the troops were undernourished it was inevitable that plague should invade the army; on 24 May the first five men died, and orders were given for the soldiers to sleep out in the open, in order to reduce the spread of infection. But this could only bring temporary relief; as a result of hunger and plague the league army was being rapidly enervated. On 1 June the army began to retreat to Viterbo, having abandoned all hope of rescuing the pope.

Although Rome was now finally given up to the imperialists and it seemed likely that before long the pope, too, would be in their hands, still the imperial captains had hoped for a better issue to events. Many questions remained unanswered: the army was still unpaid and even more out of control than it had been at any time in the previous two years; Colonna's desires were unsatisfied; in August Genoa, so vital to communications with Spain, fell to the League; while the mind and will of the emperor far away in Spain were as unclear as ever. It was already apparent that the capture of the pope would, in fact, be a positive embarrassment, for it was difficult to see what could be done with him. Were he to be removed from Castel Sant'Angelo, either voluntarily or by force, the problem of the imperialists would really begin, for if the pope left Rome as less than a free agent a schism of the Church would almost certainly ensue.

Just as the commanders had feared, the sack of Rome weakened the imperial army. As an army it was now virtually useless, thinking of nothing but sack and destruction. For the succeeding months the commanders were involved in finding a solution which would both re-impose some control over their troops and satisfy Clement VII. Pillaging was still going on in a desultory fashion and the soldiers were becoming even more rapacious over ransoms. While going about his own business, Marcello Alberini was captured in the streets of Rome and taken off to Velletri to be held as a prisoner. His mother, now the sole surviving member of a family of seven, in order to ransom him, had to borrow 100 ducats at an interest-rate of 7 per cent for two months, and to offer this sum with her only other remaining assets, a pair of shoes, a dress and a gold ring.[12]

The officers of the imperial army, when they exercised authority at all, did so only with difficulty and were hampered by the refusal of the armies to acknowledge one single commander as a successor to Bourbon. At the end of May the lansquenets were refusing to acknowledge the viceroy's authority, while the Spaniards would take orders from none but Urbina. As the months passed and the troops remained unpaid, problems over discipline increased. The officers were soon so terrified of their own troops that they refused to share their quarters. Anxiously the imperial leaders waited for the army to break up, as stragglers made off to the kingdom of Naples with their newly acquired wealth.

The sack of Rome had merely accentuated every problem of organization with which the imperial commanders had had to contend since the occupation of Milan. Supplies and finance were still wanting. There was an acute shortage of food in Rome, and, despite some imports of grain from Naples, famine soon threatened. There was no wine to be had, and water had to be rationed.[13] There had been a shortage of grain in Rome ever since April, when it already cost ten ducats the *ruggio*,[14] and the sack had totally dislocated the economic life of the city; every baker and artisan had been taken prisoner or had disappeared. Since all communications within the Church State were disrupted, and the French still controlled the sea, normal imports of wheat were interrupted, and its price in Rome rose to between thirty and forty ducats the *ruggio*. Bread cost a ducat a loaf; fowls, when they could be found, two ducats each. The cavalry horses had to be fed on grass and green corn, and their condition deteriorated. While the imperial soldiers debated the question of driving the remainder of the Roman population out of the city, in order to relieve the situation, they sacked houses once more in search of food and wine. People were so desperate that they resorted to hiding bread inside the mattresses of the beds on which people sick with plague were lying. In this struggle for existence the previous payment of a ransom was no guarantee against further ransacking. By the beginning of June the poor were dying of hunger in the streets and they continued to die in this terrible way for as long as the imperialists remained in the city.

When the soldiers went hungry it was inevitable that they should vent their rage in pillaging and looting. There was virtually nothing the imperial commanders could do to prevent it. Their own war-chest was empty, the treasury of Naples was exhausted, and Alarçon and Orange had no greater success than Bourbon when it came to extracting hard cash from Charles V. The army was overweighted with too high a proportion of officers to men, and the senior officers lacked adequate imperial authority. The number of irregular profiteers who joined the army inevitably increased after the sack. Alarçon stressed all these problems in writing to the emperor and urged him to attempt to solve at least some of them. He suggested that Charles should give both the viceroyalty of Naples and command of the army to the same person, and that he should reduce the number of captains in the army. The lances should be reformed and their captains prevented from handing over their command to civilians. The numbers of the Italian infantry should be frozen 'because, although the Spaniards are destructive enough, experience shows that 4000 Italians waste more and destroy more in two months than 10,000 of any other nation in four'. Finally Alarçon expressed himself with an almost religious intensity on the subject of arrears of pay, the subject which was now dearest to the hearts of all the imperial commanders. If money were not sent, the daily murders, violence and plunder of Rome would continue, and 'God will not permit that the emperor's greatness and power be maintained by such wicked means, nor is it just that Christendom, having the remedy in its hands, tolerate it for any length of time.'[15]

Alarçon was in many ways the most sympathetic of the imperial commanders. He was peculiarly sensitive to the sufferings of the populace of Rome. He disliked the injustices involved in billeting troops on the civilian population of the ravaged city, for he realized the degree of hardship this entailed. When, in September 1527, four soldiers were allocated to the Alberini household, the master of the house had to sell the remaining stock of family wine, his sole asset, in order to feed them.[16] More and more houses were deserted as citizens left Rome rather than act as unwilling hosts to the imperial soldiery. In September Alarçon experimented with a system of issuing the infantry with petty cash so that they might support themselves, but anything done in this line could only be a stop-gap measure. The most pressing need was to get the army out of Rome.

An even more impressive argument was the rapid spread of plague in the city that resulted directly from the administrative chaos into which Rome had been plunged at the time of the sack. Practically no sanitary arrangements were made in a city which had always suffered a chronic shortage in the supply of good water: the stench in the streets was unbearable; bodies lay about the streets unburied, heaped so high in places that they obstructed the road; cellars were full of corpses, graves had been opened in search of hidden treasure; drains and sewers lay uncovered as the hottest season of the year approached. Among the first victims of the plague was Antonio Gambara; by 23 May four members of Bourbon's household were dead, and by the beginning of June an epidemic was raging. Everyone was convinced that the imperialists must leave Rome, 'which the majority of the soldiers desire, for the stench of the city is so fearful that one cannot set foot in the streets, without holding one's nose'.[17]

Thus the pressure mounted on the pope and the imperialists to come to some kind of an agreement. From the pope's point of view, the principal difficulty was that he was operating in isolation, with an uncertain knowledge of what was happening beyond the narrow, limited world of Castel Sant'Angelo and the desolation which was all that observers in the fortress could discern in any direction. And such information as did percolate through the imperial defences to reach Clement was almost uniformly depressing; he learned that throughout the territories of the Church all was in confusion. With brutal abruptness the sack of Rome had interrupted a process by which good government had been slowly developing in the Church State.

CHAPTER XIII

THE LOSS OF THE CHURCH STATE

The Italian League want me to make the emperor master of Italy and I will do so.

Clement VII

IT had been traditional papal policy, ever since the days of Cesare Borgia, to reform and develop the government of the Church State; indeed, it could even be said that reform dated back to the pontificate of Martin V in the early fifteenth century. The improvement in the government came not so much from centralizing institutions as from the introduction of constitutions enjoying papal protection and the replacement of bad governors by good. As the old tyrants and vicars were removed, they were replaced by papal nominees, but these men were often in fact as powerful within their own area as the tyrants they replaced. Papal legates and governors received princely salaries; the presidents of the six legations (Bologna, the March, Romagna, Patrimony, Perugia, Campagna) each received a salary of 1200 ducats a year, and, as governor of Modena alone, Guicciardini received the same salary. Theoretically the district representatives of the papacy, the papal governors in the towns of the Church State were in fact subjected to no law or control and they had total power over the life and death of their subjects:

> The pope being far off and occupied with much greater affairs, his subjects can only have recourse to him at great expense and with great difficulty, and very little likelihood of success, so they think it a lesser evil to bear the injuries done them by their governors than to seek a remedy, losing time and money and further provoking those who are in a position to damage them. Hence the governor both is and seems the master of the city.[1]

In such a situation it is clear that the quality of local government depended on the quality of papal representatives in the context of peculiar local conditions. Certainly, throughout his pontificate,

Clement was aware of the need to reduce the Church State to uniform standards of justice and order, and he made sporadic efforts towards this end. In contrast to Leo X and Alexander VI, Clement consciously and publicly renounced a policy of aggrandizing his family at the expense of the territorial rights of the Church. In the north Guicciardini was active, imposing new standards of papal justice and attempting to eradicate the worst examples of factionalism and particularism. At Viterbo in 1524 Clement imposed a new constitution and in the same year intervened decisively in the affairs of Perugia, overthrowing the faction of Orazio Baglione. In the south the hostility of Clement to the pretensions of the Roman barons was consistent. That it was also creative is suggested by the spread of good government throughout his state – a development identifiable as a surprising dividend of church reform. The corruption and venality in Rome during former pontificates often led to a situation in which the pope was forced to depend on corrupt administrators. Alexander VI, for instance, recognized the need for administrative reform in the Church State, but had few good servants among his cardinals. The high quality both of the Sacred College and of the pope's personal friends, servants and advisers, during Clement's pontificate, led to the better government of the Church's temporal possessions.

Yet, even before the sack of Rome, there was considerable popular discontent within the Church State where, particularly in the north, the burden of the war lay very heavily; Piacenza, Parma, Modena and the surrounding areas had suffered terribly during the imperial occupation of 1525–6 and from the presence of the imperial army in the spring of 1527.[2] Subsequently, allied troops had been billeted in the northern cities for months on end and had caused widespread damage. Simultaneously there had been heavy taxation in the Church State, which had previously been an immune area. Since the pontificate of Leo X the Church State had suffered from the savage fiscal policy of Armellino. In 1516 the Romagna had been brought almost to the point of rebellion, and Leo X had been forced to abandon a proposed new tax; in 1519 Fabriano had actually rebelled. In December 1526 Piacenza had been asked by the pope for a loan of 25,000 ducats, a normal year's income of the city treasury, and did give 6000.[3] Novel systems of fortification were introduced throughout the area, which were always very

expensive, and often involved the destruction of famous landmarks or private property, 'and the throwing-down of certain
beautiful buildings which were outside Piacenza; that is, the
Church of the Nazareth, the Misericordia, St Anthony's, St Lazarus
and every other building within two miles of the city'.[4]

In the Church State and in Tuscany the league army was very
unpopular. At Bologna and Imola incidents occurred which provoked outright opposition to the League. Every attempt made by
the League to raise a loan at Bologna had been frustrated, and the
populace finally armed itself to keep the troops out by force. With
the possible exception of Saluzzo, not one of the league commanders made any attempt to observe customary regulations about
billeting, and the soldiers became notorious for cruelty. The
presence of these troops in the city meant little more to the citizens
than a dearth of provisions and fresh water. The city aqueducts
were deliberately destroyed in an attempt to flood the imperial
camp. 'To be in Bologna', at that time, 'was like being in purga-
tory.'[5] Word of the atrocities committed by league troops spread
rapidly; on 10 April 1527 Imola refused entry to Vettori, who
reported that all over the Romagna towns were denying the League
admittance, and, indeed, on the following day, Faenza closed its
gates to Guido Rangoni and Ugo da Peppoli.[6]

Since opposition to papal government was often so marked, it
is scarcely surprising that after the sack of Rome it looked initially
as though the Church State would break up completely. The provinces were virtually without government; none of the papal
administrators could get letters of exchange honoured or raise cash
for their day-to-day administration; at Rimini the treasurer abandoned his office in despair and fled to Venice. Bologna expelled the
papal governor and all other papal officials and showed signs of
recalling her exiled ruling family, the Bentivoglii. When Casale
reached the city in June he found it in upheaval; preparations were
being made to surrender the city to the imperialists. At Viterbo, the
Ghibelline faction assaulted the Guelfs and virtually destroyed the
ruling party. Papal officials throughout the Church State had no
instructions about how they were to act and were left in isolation
to make the best of a very difficult situation.[7]

A forlorn attempt was made by a group of pro-League cardinals
to govern in the papal name, as during a vacancy, the only possible

precedent. Centred at Parma, they tried to salvage as much of the papal dignity as possible. French-supported, despite the predicament of Clement, they remained staunchly anti-imperialist and instructed the Romagnol towns not to surrender to the emperor even if expressly ordered to do so by the pope.[8] As soon as the terms of the papal–imperial agreement became known, Cybo and Cortona moved to Parma and Piacenza to prevent their surrender to the imperialists.[9] At the end of November this group of cardinals included Farnese, Cortona, Cybo, Ridolfi and Gonzaga. Of this group Farnese was the most experienced, but the most active was Cardinal Cybo, who thwarted a move by the French to get the cardinals to move to Avignon, a move which would have led inevitably to schism in the Church; and it was also Cybo who negotiated an alliance with the duke of Ferrara.[10] These cardinals gradually made contact with other high-ranking ecclesiastics who had been absent from Rome or who had subsequently escaped. Clement, for instance, succeeded in persuading Sanga not to cross the imperial lines into Castel Sant'Angelo, and convinced him that he could be more usefully employed in watching over the pope's affairs from Civitàvecchia, Verona or Vicenza.[11] It was in this way that the nucleus of a party was formed, a party which was gradually becoming strong enough to reassert papal independence. There is, after all, some sense in the traditional *dictum* that the pope is never so powerful as when in captivity, and, from the first, Clement had been careful to preserve all the papal dignities intact. A bull of 1527 referred to the possibility that the pope might die while in prison, and empowered the cardinals in this eventuality to meet in Bologna, Perugia or Ancona for the election of a new pope; or, if these cities were under interdict or in open rebellion against the Church, at Florence, Turin or Mantua.[12]

Where resident papal legates were already active they continued to represent papal authority and were sometimes even granted additional powers by Clement; Wolsey was granted full papal powers in England for the duration of the pope's captivity.[13] Elsewhere the continuity of papal government was maintained by bishops who retired from Rome to their sees, which in some cases they were visiting for the first time. Accolti, for example, fled to Ancona where he was able to exercise a considerable influence in civic affairs and attained an unusual importance.[14] But confusion in the running of the Church was inevitable; within a month of the sack of Rome so many problems had arisen about provisions to benefices that Clement was urged to delegate this part of his authority to special officials.[15]

Other forms of confusion mounted throughout the Church State. At Modena there had been disturbances and trouble since February when the Guelf Tassoni returned to the city, quarrelled with the Rangoni, led a movement which refused to accept the billeting of league soldiers within the city, and renewed their quarrel with the Foiani. The population had assisted in financing and in building new fortifications to strengthen the city defences but, although it was said to be ready to defend itself against attack by the imperialists, it is clear that only the presence of a substantial papal garrison kept Modena loyal to Clement.[16] After the sack of Rome, the papal troops, whose pay had fallen due on 5 May and could not be met, began to drift away by the beginning of June; and Lodovico Rangoni, who had been left in military command of the city, was unable to hold it with the 900 troops left to him. When the duke of Ferrara, ignoring Venetian advice, threatened to devastate the harvest, the Estensi party inside Modena offered the city to him and he took possession on 6 June.[17]

Duke Alfonso may well have reflected that the behaviour of Venice in the Romagna negated well-meaning advice that he should do nothing to antagonize the pope. From the first the Italian League had been both a highly sophisticated and an artificial creation which carried within itself the seeds of its own destruction. The allies were pursuing totally incompatible policies with disastrous consequences. Thus, none saw more clearly than Venice that the destruction of the papacy as an independent power was a threat to Italy as a whole, and peculiarly a threat to the Venetian state. When on 11 May news reached the republic of the sack of Rome, terror struck the city, 'not with regard to the pope, whom I know they would be glad to see reduced to worse straits, but in case all Italy should fall to the emperor'.[18] The news was met by a vigorous determination that Clement should be rescued if this could be done without endangering the league army. On 15 May the Senate instructed Pisano 'to combine with the captain-general and to go with the army towards Rome, because if the pope is not aided one can say that all Italy is lost'.[19] Venice saw immediately that only an overwhelming league victory at this point could ensure the freedom of Italy from imperial control. Even before the end of May news arrived from Vicenza and Trent that the Archduke Ferdinand was coming to Italy with an army of 20,000 men, 'and when those letters had been read everyone remained stupified, seeing things go so badly'.[20] Arrangements were made to lend the duke of Milan 6000 ducats to enable him to fight on, and letters were sent to Francis I optimistically urging him to dispatch 10,000 Swiss, 'and to do more, because if it is not done quickly the imperialists will be masters of Italy'.[21]

It is possible that without swift diplomatic action on the part of Venice the Italian League would have collapsed at this time. For once, the Venetians managed to impress a sense of urgency on Francis I, who was stung into swift action. News of the disaster at Rome did not reach the French court until 22 May, but on 4 June Francis I was already able to speak in detail of his plan to send Lautrec to Italy, and by the end of the month a new alliance had been arranged between France, Venice, Florence and Milan.[22]

In the military sphere Venice maintained all her obligations to the League and even went beyond them, trying to make up for the failings of one ally or another. On 2 June Venice dispatched 50,000 ducats to the league camp, of which only 15,000 were on her own behalf; 30,000 were sent on behalf of Francis I, who had failed to send any money. The other 5000 ducats almost certainly represented either payments to the remaining papal troops in the league army or a contribution on behalf of the eternally impecunious Sforza.[23] As the papacy had effectively ceased to be an ally, and as Francis I was so dilatory in providing assistance, Venice came to be the most important member of the League, for which her support remained whole-hearted. Before the advent of Lautrec and the first effective Florentine assistance, she carried the burden of the defence against the imperialists virtually alone. However, demands were being made on the Venetian republic at a time when she could least afford them. The upkeep of the navy and defences against Mediterranean pirates were costing more each year and were naturally inflated in a period of general warfare; the harvest of 1527 was as disastrous in the Veneto as elsewhere in Italy, and this made it impossible to provision the troops adequately save at terrible expense. Had the imperialists launched an attack on Venice immediately after the sack of Rome, or in the autumn or winter of 1527, the mainland power of the republic might have been permanently destroyed.

Despite all this, and despite the fact that Venice was the ally of the pope and genuinely concerned that he should be rescued, it was impossible for her to resist acting on a different and incompatible political level. Since time immemorial Venice and the papacy had been at odds over Ravenna, Cervia, the Romagna and over questions concerning provisions to benefices within the Venetian state. Such issues were part of the wider struggle between Venice and the papacy for predominance among the Italian powers. Now Clement was helpless in Rome and the whole administration of the Church State seemed to be crumbling. Continuing in the old pattern of Italian politics and ignoring the ideals on which the Italian League was supposedly founded, Venice was tempted into using the situation as she would have used any period of *interregnum* in the Church.

Initially Venetian interference in the affairs of Ravenna and Cervia was caused by fear that those two cities would fall to the imperialists. Although Venetian motives for intervention were undoubtedly mixed, the Republic had the approval of the League in preserving Ravenna against a peculiarly dangerous combination of the Rasponi, the exiled ruling family, and Guido Rangoni. In the early years of his pontificate Clement had dealt summarily with the Rasponi, who, under the leadership of Ostasio Rasponi, had dominated the government of Ravenna throughout the pontificate of Adrian VI to the perversion of all justice and good administration. Clement had exiled the Rasponi to Ancona and had encouraged all those who had fled from their tyranny to return to Ravenna.

During the early months of 1527 the Rasponi moved to Ferrara, a haven for all refugees from Medici rule, where they negotiated both with the duke and the imperial army. They gained a promise of support from the garrison left by Bourbon at Cortignola, and, after the sack of Rome, began a career of terrorism in the countryside around Faenza and Ravenna and of piracy at sea from hideouts in the Comacchio which represented a serious threat to Venetian shipping. As early as 24 May the inhabitants of Ravenna were soliciting aid from Venice. Then, in the first week of June, Guido

Rangoni arrived with his own personal army of 400 cavalry and 1000 infantry, and demanded entrance to Ravenna. Since the papal representative at Ravenna was totally without resources to meet the threat and Ravenna was determined to keep out the Rasponi, assistance was again sought from Venice. The republic dispatched first her constable, Marc Antonio of Faenza, with 200 infantry and 2 galleys, and, on a second request by the chancellor of Ravenna, who informed the Venetian senate that Ravenna wished to renounce her allegiance to the pope, Alessandro Gavardo was sent. Gavardo brought with him 600 ducats, with which to raise troops to be handed over to the papal governor and the commune, and two small fighting galleys to help combat the Rasponi at sea. The Rasponi had already corrupted the castellan of Ravenna, and on 15 June made their expected attack, assisted by Rangoni and the Spaniards from Cortignola. Venice was forced to pour in further reinforcements; and when the castellan, whose plot had been discovered, bought his way to safety Venetian troops occupied the citadel of Ravenna. In the absence of effective papal authorities, the city government of Ravenna was in chaos. There were faction fights; the property of the Rasponi in the city was sacked; there were disagreements between the citizens and the Venetian troops; and there was no money in the city treasury. It was, therefore, inevitable, with the Venetians in a commanding military position, that the commune should have asked them to take over the formal government of the city. At Cervia events followed a similar course. Of the two towns Cervia was probably the more valuable and the greater loss to Clement. Cervia's *contado* was particularly fertile, and its salt-pans were one of the largest single sources of papal income. The seizure of both these towns by Venice virtually ensured that Clement would never rejoin the Italian League, even were he to regain his freedom.[24]

Closely linked with events at Ravenna and Cervia were those at Rimini. Although lacking any genuine popular support, Sigismondo Malatesta, son of the tyrant Pandolfo, had already returned to the city in 1525, whence in the following year he was driven out by Clement. As soon as news arrived of the sack of Rome, the principal families fled from Rimini, taking with them all the food, money and valuables they could carry. With them went the city treasurer, leaving behind troops whose services had only been purchased for a month and a papal administrator who had no means of raising funds in order to keep the soldiers' loyalty. With the assistance of Duke Alfonso d'Este, it was inevitable that Sigismondo Malatesta should repossess himself of his father's city.[25]

Perugia was the largest and the richest of the Umbrian towns and was of the greatest importance to the papacy to whom a *census* of 4000 ducats was paid each year. More than 100 castles fell within the boundaries of Perugian jurisdiction and, counting all the small villages, more than 200 places altogether. The income of the city each year was in the region of 38,000 ducats. After more than a century of faction fights, surpassed only by those of Siena, Perugia was in May 1527 ruled by a papal nominee, Gentile Baglione, who had been appointed by Clement in order to put an end to civil discord. He was never popular in the city, and in January 1527 there was public rejoicing in Perugia at the news of the release of his rival, Orazio Baglione, from Castel Sant'Angelo. Inevitably, therefore, the sack of Rome brought about a palace revolution at Perugia. A brave attempt on the part of the commune to direct its own affairs was frustrated by the intrusion of the Baglioni into city politics. On 13 May the commune drove out Gentile Baglione and, in the resulting vacuum, attempted to revive the old government of the commune. On 25 June a new constitution was approved, but it proved to be a short-lived experiment, for Orazio Baglione, who had escaped from Rome, had already returned to the city and was resolved to seize power himself. Within two weeks of having sworn a solemn peace, at the command of the commune, with Gentile Baglione, Orazio, in one of those internecine feuds to which the Baglioni were peculiarly addicted, had had him murdered along with two of his own nephews and his cousin, and had seized power in Perugia.[26]

The loss of those towns, and the apparent collapse of the administration in the Church State, were crushing blows, yet, undoubtedly, the news which Clement found hardest to bear was the far more grievous loss of his own native city of Florence, which had used the opportunity of the papacy's worst hour to rebel against her Medici master.

The sack of Rome had a profound effect at Florence. Economi-

cally it was disastrous. In terms of trade alone, Florence lost weekly
8000 ducats in Rome and 3000 ducats in Naples. 'Rome was the
marrow and heart of this city', the Florentine government reported to Venice, '... lacking which we remain like a dead body'.[27]
Florentines in Rome had been among that city's wealthiest inhabitants and suffered proportionately in the sack. They lost more
than a million ducats. Offices in the Curia, bought by Florentines
to an estimated value of 350,000 ducats, could also be written off
as a loss. When Bourbon's army advanced on Florence, many had
sent valuables to Rome for safe-keeping, among them Jacopo
Gherardi, who lost practically everything he possessed in the sack
and subsequently had to beg his daughter's dowry from Clement.
Human nature being what it is, it was perhaps inevitable that every
Florentine who had lost anything by the sack of Rome should tend
to blame Clement personally. Nothing of this kind, after all, had
happened in the great days of Leo X.[28]

News of the sack reached Florence on 11 May[29] and became
generally known on the following day. It was not difficult to
guess the consequences. The sophisticated world of Florentine
politics is not always easy for the modern reader to grasp,[30] but
contemporaries had no difficulty in reading the signs of the times.
Many of the traditional Medici supporters guessed correctly[31] that
a disaster of this nature must produce a revolution in government
and left immediately for Venice or Lucca. Niccolò Capponi was
already publicly inciting the populace to rebel; and, although urged
to do so, Cortona hesitated to arrest so influential an aristocrat.
The city was still full of papal troops, but these had seen their ultimate guarantee of pay cut off by the sack of Rome. Their commander did go to Cortona and offered to put down the republican
movement in the city if Cortona would give him 20,000 ducats;
but the cardinal, unused to making major decisions without
reference to Rome, delayed his reply. This delay proved fatal, for
on 16 May Filippo Strozzi reached Florence from Rome and induced Francesco del Nero, the treasurer, over whom he had a
business hold, to send the funds in his charge to the house of
Strozzi's brother. The moment at which Cortona could have acted
had passed, and the initiative was in the hands of the opposition.
The defection of Filippo Strozzi from the Medici party was of the
greatest importance, not only because of his own position but

because of those he brought with him into the opposition camp, above all Francesco Vettori and Matteo Strozzi. Through his friendship with Gianfrancesco Ridolfi, Strozzi was also able to neutralize Cardinal Ridolfi, who did nothing to assist Cortona at this vital moment although he had been sent to Florence specifically to strengthen Cortona's hand.[32]

By the following evening the first stage of a revolution was peacefully over. In the morning Strozzi persuaded Cortona that the only way to avoid bloodshed was for the Medici to leave Florence without delay. In the late afternoon they left the city, accompanied by Filippo Strozzi, who was to escort them as far as Lucca and take over the citadels of Pisa and Leghorn which the Medici had agreed to consign to the popular régime in return for their safe departure.[33] It is some measure of the extent to which support for the Medici had declined in Florence that, apart from Pietro Onofrio, no one thought it necessary to leave Florence with them. With the departure of the Medici, effective power in the city passed to the Signoria – that is, to the Eight Priors of Liberty and their president the Gonfaloniere of Justice, Francesco Antonio Nori, the titular head of the state. The Eight, whose constitutional position was that of an aristocratic advisory committee, responsible for justice and internal administration, ordered all soldiers to keep to their quarters for two days until it had been decided what action to take.[34]

Basically, government remained at this moment in the hands of a very restricted oligarchy, effective power having passed to the traditional opposition party within that oligarchy. Ever since the fifteenth century the aristocrats had aimed to maintain their position of supremacy within the constitution and had, normally, accepted Medici predominance because it facilitated this. Their initial impulse was to do nothing, and concessions to popular feeling were limited. Such changes as were projected were conservative and unimaginative, in tune with the doubts of the city's greatest political thinker, 'whether in a corrupt state it is possible to maintain a free government'.[35] Under the Medician system the core of government lay in the Eight and in the other two great aristocratic advisory bodies, the Twelve Goodmen and the Sixteen Gonfaloniers (*Sedici*). Even under the Medici, all legislative authority technically resided in the ancient Council of the People and the Commune, but ever since the ascendancy of Cosimo de' Medici in the fifteenth century these had been supplemented and eventually supplanted by a small council of one hundred, nominated by the Sixteen and so more amenable to control. The principal work of administration was carried out by the Council of Seventy, an institution of Lorenzo the Magnificent, and the central pivot of Medician supremacy. Its members were 'elected' from among supporters of the régime, and served in turn as the Twelve Procurators, responsible for drafting legislative decrees, and the Eight of War (*Otto di Pratica*) who attended to all diplomatic and military questions.

This elaborate constitutional framework was managed by the Medici by a series of sophisticated election-controls, which, when they worked effectively, permitted the Medici to nominate officials from their own supporters for every office in the city. The great strength of the Medici lay in the fact that, normally, the aristocrats were perpetually under attack from the less privileged members of the Florentine world, and would, therefore, support the Medici rather than abandon their own privileged positions. Similarly the great weakness of the Medici was that when they lost this aristocratic support their whole system of control over the constitution was liable to crumble. Now such a situation had occurred, and the aristocrats were faced with an upsurge of republican and popular feeling to which some concessions had to be made.[36]

Within the ancient Florentine republican myth, the key element was the ancient Council of the People and the Commune, commonly known as the Great Council, which was believed to be the form of government in existence at the time of the foundation of the city and which had been the supposed heart of the republican régime between 1494 and 1512. It was, therefore, virtually unavoidable that a promise should be made that the Great Council would be restored, but the arrangements for its meeting were deliberately delayed. In the meantime the Signoria, the chief aristocratic executive body,[37] was to be controlled by a council of 120 which was to have a life-span of four months and which would replace the old Medici councils of the Seventy and the Hundred.[38] The new council would elect a committee which would organize and control the Great Council. For this every male citizen over the age of twenty-four was eligible. Once the Great Council had met, the old republican Ten of War and Peace was to replace the Eight, and the Council of Eighty was to be resurrected, 'as it used to be before the return of the Medici'.[39]

In the following days, however, it became obvious that the oligarchy was under pressure from those who were still excluded from the government and who, under the leadership of Antonfrancesco degli Albizzi, 'a noble man and brave enough, but proud, inconstant and blown up by ambition',[40] united with the popular element in the city. They had few illusions about the group now in power who, they believed, aimed at perpetuating a government by the few in the traditional Florentine manner, 'which they call by a Greek name, thinking that we do not understand it, aristocracy; that lot did not throw out the Medici in order to free us, but only for their own self-aggrandizement'.[41] Various factors encouraged a mistrust of the new government; Clarice Strozzi, Filippo's wife, returned to live in the Medici palace, taking the Little Duchess (Duchessina) Catherine, daughter of Duke Lorenzo of Urbino, with her: and Cardinal Ridolfi and Ottaviano de' Medici returned to the city. Disorders and unrest continued, fostered by fears of a Medici return, until the more prominent citizens realized that some concession must be made to popular feeling. Accordingly, the Great Council was summoned a whole month earlier than was originally intended. Preceded by a solemn mass in the Palazzo della Signoria it met on 21 May, and more than 2500 persons attended. Opposition to the original creators of the revolution had increased with the failure of Filippo Strozzi to recover the two citadels of Pisa and Leghorn, of vital importance to Florence as they controlled her outlet to the sea. When Strozzi reported his failure to recover them from their papal captains, his whole policy of reconciliation with the Medici party was discredited.

Sharing some of Strozzi's discredit, the old Signoria was forced from office on 28 May and the fifty-three-year-old Niccolò Capponi was elected Gonfaloniere of Justice. In some respects Capponi was a strange choice; he was closely related to the Medici, having married a sister of Filippo Strozzi. It is also clear that, although, like Vettori and Guicciardini, Capponi preferred a republican régime to the rule of the Medici, he was convinced that such a régime could only function effectively if the aristocrats had a decisive share in the government.[42] But certain factors operated overwhelmingly in Capponi's favour; he was clearly a man of very considerable personal charm, with a gift for inspiring a devoted personal following, and from a republican point of view he had an impeccable political past. While still only in his teens he had been sent to work in his uncle's bank at Lyons and had subsequently visited the French court with his father, an ambassador from Florence. Such a record was bound to make Capponi popular with the francophile republicans, and it was also general knowledge that ever since the Medici return of 1512 Capponi had been a prominent opponent of their autocratic rule, and had been among the most outspoken of the aristocrats in attacks on Cortona.

The new Gonfaloniere was essentially a moderate man, and it was certainly contrary to his wishes that full rein was given to the anti-Medici hysteria now gaining ground in the city. It had long been a Florentine custom to display, in the church of the Annunziata, wax images of prominent Florentines. Among others hung portraits of Leo X and Clement VII which the powerful pressure-group of the 'angry ones' or the 'young men' now destroyed. The arms of the Medici were blotted out throughout the city, even in the churches which owed most to the patronage of that family, like San Lorenzo and San Marco. Demands were also made for the erasure of the famous epitaph of Cosimo de' Medici, 'Pater Patriae', on the grounds that he was not the father but the tyrant of his country; the epitaphs of Marsilio Ficino, the great Florentine humanist, and of Antonio Squarcialupi, the organist, were similarly denounced and deleted of phrasing which was held to be too complimentary. Michelangelo, an ardent believer in republican Florence, was even said to have suggested razing the Medici palace to the ground, creating on its site a piazza which was to be known as the 'Square of Mules' – a delicate Italian allusion to the pope's illegitimate birth. Much republican opposition centred round the Medici palace, which was eventually appropriated by the state and handed over to the Trustees of Minors, whose work, as a result of the plague, had been greatly increased.

The plague epidemic of that summer became the first consideration of every citizen of Florence and probably saved the great palaces of the exiled Medici supporters from sack by the 'angry ones'. The city of Florence had been an early victim of the pestilence which was first brought to the city by a traveller from Rome in 1522. From the summer of 1527 until the winter of 1528 the epidemic was at its worst with nearly fifty people dying from the disease every day. Industry and trade suffered so severely that Florence, which may have lost as much as a quarter of its population, never really recovered. The epidemic represented a terrifying problem for the new republican government, but one that was met bravely. Immediate measures were taken to combat the infection; those who were rich enough left Florence, although this soon proved to be an ineffective move as the infection spread to the countryside.⁴³ The rich retired to their villas and the poor flocked to the subject towns; Prato was crowded out with refugees. In Florence itself the shops were closed for the duration of the epidemic and all domestic animals were destroyed. A special magistracy was created to alleviate the sufferings of the sick and to endeavour to check the infection, but little more could be done than to insist that all business be conducted out of doors and to forbid access to the city to arrivals from other plague-centres in Italy. The other magistracies of the city functioned only with difficulty, for they had insufficient members to form a *quorum* and the total number necessary for the Great Council to sit had to be halved during the epidemic. When all other measures failed to alleviate the situation the Florentines had recourse at last to religion, and the city gave itself up to prayer, penitence and processions.⁴⁴

During this critical period, the Gonfaloniere became increasingly unpopular. His weakness in relation to the domestic politics of Florence derived from the fact that he was a political realist. The 'angry ones' had managed to foment a wave of anti-Medici feeling to which he was forced to conform, but he did not give up hope of reconciliation. He believed that it was negotiation not defiance that might, in the end, persuade Clement to accept the republic. Capponi, as a merchant, knew that some connexion with Rome was vital to Florence's trade and prosperity, to the very life of the city. In the first days of the republic, Florentines were forbidden to visit Rome, for fear they might fall under papal influence, but by 1528 Capponi had begun to grant licenses to business men to enable them to take up their affairs in the papal city once more.

However realistic, such a policy was bound to render Capponi unpopular. He could no longer consult with supposed Medici supporters, and certain ex-Medici servants, such as Francesco Vettori, Filippo Strozzi and Francesco Guicciardini in public, but he continued to listen to their counsel in private. They, at least, were able to reassure Capponi that the pope was only too aware of the dangers of unleashing an ultramontane army against so eminently sackable a town as Florence, which he sincerely loved, and that he was prepared to be conciliatory. So Capponi continued to look for a peaceful solution to the quarrel between the pope and Florence.

Such a policy did not attract the Soderini faction or the 'angry ones'. Their fury against the Medici continued to mount as they realized that, despite all that had happened, Clement VII did not regard Florence as lost. By the summer of 1528 they had succeeded in totally discrediting the aristocrats and isolating Capponi. His friends were gradually driven from Florence. One of the first to go was Filippo Strozzi, who had been a frequent visitor at the Gonfaloniere's house. This fact had not escaped the notice of the extreme republicans, and one of their number, Jacopo Alemanni, threatened to murder Strozzi in broad daylight if he continued his visits. Naturally enough, Strozzi objected to such threats and asked Capponi to punish Alemanni in the appropriate manner. But the Gonfaloniere's realism again stood him in good stead; he advised Strozzi to leave the city and not to resist the dictates of Fortune. So Strozzi left, to join the growing band of Florentine exiles at Lucca,[45] while Capponi remained more and more alone in a hostile and frightened city.

It was against the background of these events in Florence and the Church State that papal negotiations took place with the imperialists. Talks had, in fact, been initiated almost as soon as Rome had fallen. On 7 May Schomberg wrote from Castel Sant' Angelo, in the pope's name, requesting that either Bartolommeo Gattinara or Najera, accompanied by an officer from the imperial army, should go to the castle to treat. On the same day Gattinara visited Clement to make known to him the demands of the armies, and for the next four days he acted as a go-between. On the papal side negotiations were carried out by the pope and his immediate advisers and by representatives of the four classes incarcerated in Castel Sant'Angelo: Giberti on behalf of the prelates, Alberto Pio for the ambassadors, Casale, a Roman by birth, for the citizens, and Giuliano Leno for the merchants and artisans. Although the imperialists began by demanding that Clement and his court should go to Spain or to Naples, negotiations were principally financial. Since the imperial soldiers did not want Clement freed before their arrears of pay had been met, and since these arrears amounted to at least 300,000 ducats while the pope claimed that he could raise no more than 100,000 ducats, even by selling everything in Sant'Angelo, further discussion seemed likely to prove unprofitable. During the following weeks the substance of the imperial demand did not change; Clement must pay 300,000 ducats and go either to Naples or to Spain. Both sides were, in fact, waiting on events. Clement wished to see what the League would do on his behalf; the imperialists were waiting for instructions from Spain.

Agreement was approached on 17 May. Clement was to pay 100,000 ducats immediately, another 50,000 within twenty days and 50,000 more within a month. As security he was to hand over nine hostages and the vital fortresses of Piacenza, Parma, Modena, Civitàvecchia, Ostia and Castel Sant'Angelo. The money was to be raised on loans from the bankers against the security of a promised tax on the Church State. The lansquenets were induced to accept this agreement by Orange's promise that they would be paid the rest of their arrears within a month and that until they *were* paid they should hold Parma and Piacenza in pawn.

On 20 May Gattinara, Najera and Vespasiano Colonna went to Castel Sant'Angelo, hoping to have the capitulation signed, but as the pope still could not raise the necessary funds, four more days had to be spent negotiating and obtaining securities for the bankers. On 24 May, Clement, who had encouraging news of movement by the league armies, changed his mind about signing the agreement. With the consent of a majority of the cardinals – only Campeggio, de Cessis, Accolti and Rangoni dissenting – he asked for a six-day term within which he might not be bound to his agreement if help came to him. Although this type of agreement was very common the army-council refused Clement's request.

The pope had for some reason always put great faith in Lannoy; 'the Pope has always believed in the viceroy and trusted in him, as if he had been a god, and it was this which caused the ruin of . . . Rome'.[46] It was at Clement's request that Najera now summoned the viceroy to Rome in order to take part in the negotiations. Lannoy reached Rome on 28 May. Orange had been unwilling to accept this intervention, for he knew that the army distrusted Lannoy, and his arrival could not fail to raise the question of Orange's position and authority. During a stay of scarcely a week in Rome, Lannoy succeeded in making himself unpopular with everyone. He showed a marked reluctance to get embroiled with the soldiers or to assist their commanders. While expressing annoyance that Orange was exercising the powers of a commander-in-chief without authority from the emperor, he was quite unable to make any alternative suggestions about the command. His crowning triumph was to drive the Spaniards, usually the most tractable of the troops in the imperial army, to mutiny. He had told the lansquenets that the papal ransom would be used to pay their arrears without making any mention of the equally important Spanish arrears. News of this promise so enraged the Spanish troops that they fell on the lansquenets, killed one of their captains and three of their men, and drove Lannoy out of Rome.[47] The viceroy retired in high dudgeon to the Colonna castle of Città Lavinia, eighteen miles from Rome, whence he was continually pressed to return by Alarçon, Najera and Moncada.

In the event, assistance in completing the negotiations came to the pope from the most unlikely quarter. On 1 June Pompeio Colonna was invited to have an audience with the pope. It is not known what Clement expected from the meeting, but it achieved even more than he can have hoped. The two men, for so long enemies, but united in their sorrow over the fate of Rome, met with tears in their eyes, and Pompeio promised to do all in his power to work for the pope's deliverance. In subsequent months the pope recognized Colonna's assistance publicly, restoring him to his cardinal-dignities and showering privileges on the Colonna family. To Pompeio Colonna himself he promised the valuable Legation of the March of Ancona.

It was with Colonna's active assistance that a supposedly final agreement was reached on 5 June and signed by the imperial commanders on the following day. On 7 June the papal garrison left Castel Sant'Angelo, and Alarçon, with three companies of lansquenets and three of Spanish infantry commanded by Felipe Cervellion, whom Bourbon had selected as castellan of Sant' Angelo before the imperial army reached Rome, took possession. Among the lansquenets was Schertlin von Burtenbach, who described the sad plight of the pope and the cardinals who had retired into the keep of the fortress: 'They were making great lamentation and weeping bitterly; as for us, we all became rich.'[48] The households of the pope and the cardinals had been substantially reduced; Clement retained ten servants and the cardinals four amongst them all. The terms of the agreement were similar to those of 17 May; Castel Sant'Angelo with its armaments, Ostia, Civitàvecchia, Città Castellana, Piacenza, Parma and Modena were to be surrendered. Clement's ransom and that of all those in Castel Sant'Angelo with him was set at 400,000 ducats, 80,000 to be paid immediately, half in cash and half in plate, 20,000 within six days, 150,000 within twenty days, a sum to be raised from Genoese bankers against the security of the tithes of the kingdom of Naples, and the remainder to be collected with the assistance of the imperial army from the promised tax on the Church State excluding the Campagna. As a security for this vast sum Clement handed over hostages: Cardinal dal Monte, Cardinal Pucci, the archbishop of Pisa, Giberti, Jacopo Salviati, and Lorenzo Ridolfi and Simone da Ricasoli, who were probably chosen because of their relationships to wealthy Florentine financiers. Clement also agreed to restore the Colonna to their possessions, to reinstate Cardinal Colonna and to remove all ecclesiastical censures from the imperial armies.[49]

CHAPTER XIV

THE POPE ESCAPES

On the soil which the Spaniard has trodden no grass will grow.
Italian proverb

CLEMENT had seemingly secured his freedom by agreeing to a harsh treaty with the imperialists. But, in respect to the conditions of this treaty, serious difficulties immediately arose. The first problems concerned the payment of the pope's ransom. It was gradually borne in upon the imperialists that Clement had spoken nothing but the truth when he told Bourbon in April that to expect any additional payment, over and above the 100,000 ducats already disbursed, was as realistic as expecting heaven and earth to meet.[1] Every available papal asset was sacrificed to meet imperial demands. Of the papal tiaras only that of Julius II was spared; the rest, their precious jewels removed and concealed, were melted down by Benevenuto Cellini in a wind furnace constructed for the purpose on the top of Castel Sant' Angelo. Melted down, too, were all the remaining gold and silver ornaments in the fortress, and the famous treasure from Loreto. Church property was sold, and on 6 July the pope raised an expensive loan at 25 per cent from the Genoese banker Grimaldi and the Catalonian merchant Michael Girolamo Sanchez. Although Clement gave as securities for this loan the town of Benevento, the quit-rents and the tithes of the kingdom of Naples, as well as valuables worth 30,000 ducats, Grimaldi and Sanchez were to cause the pope considerable embarrassment over this loan. After the pope's flight from Castel Sant'Angelo the two bankers sued him in the Roman court, fearing that he would default on repayment. Their fears were scarcely exaggerated, for essentially the pope had been bankrupted by the sack of Rome. Clement did pay the first two instalments of his imperial ransom money; in September 1527 he paid an additional 100,000 ducats, but after 6 December and a payment of 145,000 ducats the imperialists received nothing more.

Other provisions of the agreement simply could not be fulfilled.

Of the fortresses promised as a security, the Spaniards held only Ostia which was delivered to them on 8 June. Città Castellana was held by the League; Doria was still holding Civitàvecchia and refused to surrender it until he was paid 15,000 ducats still owed by the pope on his *condotta*, and the garrisons of Parma and Piacenza would not surrender to the imperialists, having been secretly persuaded to resist by the pro-league cardinals.

Clement had provided hostages to ensure the fulfilment of his obligations, but even they did not prove to be the good risk that the imperialists anticipated. Simone da Ricasoli, for instance, who was already old and sick, was spared the indignity of prison and chains suffered by the other hostages, for his son paid a ransom for him, daily, in order that he might be nursed in his own house. But even this care could not prevent him dying of shock and despair.

Given these initial difficulties, it is scarcely surprising that the behaviour of the imperial troops showed no immediate improvement after Clement's capitulation; indeed, on the very evening the agreement was signed, the Spanish troops mutinied. The scarcity of foodstuffs at Rome was so great, Salazar reported to Gattinara, that wheat was costing anything up to forty ducats the *ruggio*, and,

had it not been for the grass, the green corn, and other herbs which men give their horses, barley would be at the same price as wheat or a little less. Fowls are not to be had even for sick people, and when procured cost two ducats. . . . Indeed, it may be asserted that as far as articles of food and dress are concerned the sack of Rome still continues, especially on the part of the lansquenets, who plunder everything they find and will not listen to reason on this score. Your lordship cannot imagine the atrocities that are committed daily and the number of people who are either slain, tortured, or otherwise ill-treated without any regard for rank, profession, or nationality. Every one of us is utterly ruined, for besides being plundered of our money, our clothes and other valuables, we have been taxed at sums which it is impossible for us to pay. Those who cannot pay are imprisoned, and then taken to the public market to be sold as so many slaves.[2]

It was, therefore, clear that the most imperative need was to get the imperial troops out of Rome. To this end, money was hastily coined from the plate which had been extracted from Castel Sant'Angelo as part of Clement's ransom. The original 80,000 ducats were paid by the pope and handed over to the lansquenets, but on 23 June Clement had still not produced the additional 20,000 which were to have been paid by 12 June, and which had also been promised to the Germans. The pope was desperately trying to coin money from such silver ornaments as still remained to him and had, in the meantime, dispatched Schomberg to Naples to try to borrow both this sum from anyone foolish enough to lend on the pope's rather dubious securities, and a further 50,000 ducats, now needed urgently to satisfy the Spanish troops, who had finally revolted at the favouritism shown to the more riotous lansquenets. The imperial commanders continued to hope that the emperor would send money to pay his troops. Charles, however, had managed to convince himself that his army could become self-financing, by extracting infinite amounts from the pope and from Florence, and sent only 100,000 ducats by bills of exchange, a sum which was totally inadequate in relation to the needs of the imperial army. It was at this period that 'money from Spain' acquired the same proverbial status in Italian as 'assistance to Pisa' had done a generation earlier. By 15 August Clement had been able to raise no more than the first instalment of his ransom, the imperial troops were restless, and their commanders were desperate.

Meanwhile, even for the hardened imperial soldier, the city of Rome had become uninhabitable. Hunger and pestilence had reached a terrible level, and men were dying in the streets in their hundreds. In such circumstances, burial of the dead was out of the question and the plague spread with more virulence than ever. In consequence, to the undisguised joy of the remaining Roman citizens, the imperial army left Rome on 10 July. Two thousand troops only remained to guard the city and Castel Sant'Angelo.

Orange with 150 of his cavalry went to Siena. Bemelberg and Schertlin von Burtenbach invaded Umbria with the lansquenets. The German troops were quite out of control; by the time they reached Orte they had already destroyed their general's tent during a mutiny. It was only by threatening to lay down his command that Bemelberg was able to bring the mutineers to their senses once more. Among the more beautiful hill-forts around Rome was Narni, once Roman Narnia, a papal town with Orsini connexions which stood on the fast-running River Nera. The inhabitants refused to admit this wild horde of marauders and made a desperate resistance before the town was captured. 'Then it was put to sword and fire by the imperial soldiery, who united with the inhabitants of Terni, implacable enemies of Narni, to make an example of the town through three months.'[3] For months after the visitation of the imperialists Narni remained uninhabited. All the small neighbouring villages were similarly burned or destroyed. Terni, Sutri and Vetralla were all sacked.[4]

In the Campagna, banditry had always been a way of life for some, but with the breakdown of civil government all curbs on it were removed. The less reputable members of the Orsini family overtly encouraged and participated in acts of violence. In December Cardinal dal Monte, Cardinal Pucci and the bishop of Salamanca were captured and robbed by Mario Orsini at Bracciano. The abbot of Farfa, presumably feeling that banditry on land was not yielding sufficient profit, took to piracy and, acquiring two armed vessels, seized all merchant vessels entering or leaving the Tiber. Those ships lucky enough to escape his depredations were subjected to arbitrary tolls or to seizure of goods by the Spanish garrison at Ostia. The Colonna also used the opportunity provided by the collapse of civil government to increase and consolidate their territorial control in the Campagna. In early January 1528 Ascanio and Sciarra Colonna captured three castles close to Orvieto. In April Sciarra, with 70 light cavalry and 700 infantry, was raiding the Campagna up to the very gates of Rome.

Cardinal Pompeio Colonna, meanwhile, was reputed to be spending much of his time with the lansquenets and to have promised to assist them in obtaining the rest of their arrears, 'in the hope that one of these days if not paid . . . they will mutiny and murder the pope'.[5] Hurriedly the imperial commanders planned what to do in the event of such a mutiny; the pope was to be permitted to escape down the Tiber to Ostia whence one of his galleys would transport him to the relative safety of the Neapolitan port of Gaeta.

By the beginning of October the imperial troops had exhausted

such possibilities for rape, pillage and arson as were provided in
the Campagna and were beginning to return to Rome. Their
activities, in combination with the antecedent war, famine and
plague,[6] had ruined the prosperity of the Campagna. In the following years land there changed hands for practically nothing. A
commission of cardinals, authorized by Clement, sold off thirty
holdings in the Campagna, including whole communes such as
Riano and Ronciglione, and were still able to raise only 192,855
scudi. The countryside for thirty to fifty miles around Rome had
been reduced to a wilderness.[7]

First the lansquenets and then the Spaniards turned their backs
on their handiwork and began to return to the holy city, 'demanding the pope and their pay. All Rome is fleeing before them.'
Morone and del Guasto hastened to intervene and engaged to give
the lansquenets two and a half months of their arrears. In consequence, the troops returned quietly enough to their former
lodgings in the city.[8] There was, of course, little else they could
do; Rome had been so completely ransacked that the worst form
of fresh damage done in these weeks was to doors, window-frames
and the timbers of houses, which were torn out for firewood. The
troops were on the whole subdued; the cavalry were always more
amenable to discipline than the infantry, and the lances were persuaded to retire from Rome to Nepi and Sutri.

The infantry continued to concentrate on extracting the maxi-
mum from Clement and their commanding officers. The imperial
army was by now in a terrible state. It had been drastically weakened by deaths and desertions: there were only 6500 lansquenets
and 2500 Spaniards in Rome. The Spaniards, in particular, were
deserting in large numbers to the kingdom of Naples where,
despite efforts to prevent their leaving Italy, they were taking ship
for Spain. As early as June the Venetians had captured a caravel
bound from Ancona with thirteen Spanish soldiers on board who
were leaving with their valuable booty.[9]

At the beginning of October, money sent from Naples, as del
Guasto and Morone had promised, paid two months' arrears of
the lansquenets. But the morale of the army remained low, and
discipline, particularly among the lansquenets, was practically
non-existent. Pompeio Colonna was now the only person of any
rank to retain any influence over them at all, and he busied

himself in the emperor's service. He promised the Germans another pay, saying that the cash for this would be raised by the pope from among his courtiers and servants, although Colonna knew full well that it was impossible for the pope to raise any more money at the moment. Still the imperial commanders hoped against hope that money would be forthcoming and that hard cash, together with the promise of comfortable quarters at Viterbo, where they could forage for themselves, would induce the troops to leave Rome. The need was great, for every day the abbot of Farfa was making more and more outrageous raids on Spanish personnel in the Campagna. On 19 October a council of war decided that a punitive expedition must be launched against Farfa without delay and that the imperial army would then go on to destroy the armies of the League.[10]

Alarçon, whose thankless task it had been for all these months to mediate between Clement and the common soldiers, was pessimistic and completely dispirited. On 22 October he decided to address his Spaniards. In a tone of deep moral indignation he urged them to come to some agreement about the pope's release and reminded them that, 'being Christians, how great an iniquity it was to keep a pope prisoner, being vassals of the emperor, how great a burden of guilt they brought on themselves, by holding him prisoner against the wishes and instruction of their lord, and that being soldiers of His Majesty, employed to defend his interests, how much they could be and had already been judged, losing time in this city'.[11] Alarçon further reminded his soldiers of the plague and the other disasters which had befallen the army, all of which he attributed to divine justice, a punishment for the sack of Rome. With the Spaniards – who agreed to take up lodgings outside the city on the Viterbo road after being paid a ducat per man – he had some success, although the lansquenets still refused to leave Rome. On 6 November the Spaniards began to leave:

> The infantry with their standards unfurled, were already assembled at Piazza Navona. Just as everything was in order to leave, men began to mutiny shouting, 'Paga! Paga!' most of them refusing to follow the standard-bearers of their respective companies who, attended by the drummers and by a few honest

and well-disposed soldiers, had already left Rome with the
Marquess del Guasto at their head. The rioters then went out by
another gate and took the road to Naples, but Gian d'Urbina
ran after them, and after a great deal of talk persuaded them to
return to Rome for the night.

The Germans had meanwhile taken over the abandoned lodgings
of the Spaniards and had begun plundering them, 'until their
colonel, being informed of the fact, had a certain proclamation,
threatening with death whomsoever should be found stealing,
read to them'.[12] Del Guasto, having realized that the Spanish
infantry were not after all following him out of Rome, returned
and found the affairs of the imperial army in chaos. By dint of
going from house to house, and imploring the men to return to
their duty, Gian d'Urbina had persuaded most of the Spanish to
return to their colours in the Borgo, but once they were assembled
together on Piazza San Pietro the rioting broke out again; the
troops broke away and rushed across the Sant'Angelo bridge into
Rome, firing their arquebuses wildly and crying once more for
their pay.

Gian d'Urbina continued to labour ceaselessly for the next two
days to bring the Spanish troops to their senses. Often he was in
danger of his life. On more than one occasion when he was up-
braiding his troops for their behaviour, attempts were made to
assassinate him, but he seemed to bear a charmed life, which was
as well for the imperial cause, since none but he could control the
Spaniards. Yet it was clear that imperial affairs were deteriorating
so rapidly that personality alone would not be enough to maintain
order. Money must be had to pay the imperial army and it must be
obtained quickly. The chief financial difficulty was the 250,000
ducats still owing on Clement's ransom. The bankers would lend
no more, and, although the soldiers were not prepared to free the
pope before it was paid, it was clear that there was little hope of
raising so vast a sum from the Church State unless Clement was
granted his liberty. The imperial commanders toyed with various
expedients for raising cash; a favoured suggestion was to
threaten Velletri with being designated as a billet for the imperial
troops, on the reasonable assumption that the inhabitants of the
little town would pay a heavy ransom to avoid such a privilege.

Clement himself was desperately unhappy. He had been forced to do what he had always set his face against doing – agree to the simoniacal creation of cardinals. He knew that his friends held as hostages were ill-treated by the lansquenets; and the news that he had of affairs beyond the narrow confines of Castel Sant'Angelo was uniformly depressing. The final insult came in discussion with the imperialists when they tried to force the pope to agree that those of the imperial troops who had taken houses or other property in Rome in lieu of ransom money should be allowed to retain possession of the property in perpetuity: 'I will not go on with this treaty,' Clement exclaimed, 'nor speak any more of my liberation.'[13]

In fact, of course, it was inevitable that negotiations should continue, and the pope had little choice but to agree to new capitulation terms on 26 November. These agreements, which had the authority of the emperor, freely admitted that while the captains of the imperial army were anxious to release Clement, their troops were not and would not do so until they had been paid all their arrears of pay. The emperor declared himself willing to have the pope restored to his full spiritual and temporal powers, and both parties expressed a desire for a general peace, to be followed by a council of the Church and a war against the Turk. Clement again engaged to hand over the security fortresses and to give fresh hostages to the lansquenets. He promised to pay 73,000 ducats in gold and 169,000 in silver within ten days, at the end of which period he would be released and Castel Sant'Angelo restored to him. He would then pay 35,000 ducats, and the army would leave Rome and never return. In order to raise the money, the pope undertook to sell one-tenth of the ecclesiastical property in the kingdom of Naples, the profits of the sale to be divided equally between pope and emperor. The imperialists were confirmed in all the property they had obtained since the sack, and it was guaranteed that no reprisals would be taken against them.[14] In the event, out of the sums mentioned in this agreement, Clement never paid more than 65,000 ducats.

In any case, the lansquenets quickly sensed that they were being done down by the agreement and still refused to leave Rome unless they were paid in full. On the very day after the signing of the capitulations they mutinied, imprisoned two of their own captains, whom they threatened to murder, shouting that they had been promised 9½ ducats each and were only to receive 3.[15] Even Cardinal Colonna went in fear of the lansquenets now; together with the German officers, he took refuge in the Alban hills. The furious lansquenets promptly invaded Colonna's palace, took out the papal hostages and led them through the streets to Campo di Fiore where they had erected a scaffold. It was clear that they really intended to hang the wretched hostages, and they only agreed to lead them back to prison in the Colonna palace when Cardinals Orsini and de Cessis promised that if they did so the lansquenets would be paid in full on the following day.[16]

Naturally enough, no money was forthcoming on 29 November but, luckily, Giberti and Jacopo Salviati, no doubt with the connivance of at least some of the imperialists, succeeded in making their warders drunk, and on 30 November escaped. Thereafter the behaviour of the lansquenets deteriorated even further, 'threatening the pope and saying that they wished to cut him to pieces'.[17] Fresh conferences with the pope were immediately initiated and yet another agreement was signed; within two weeks Clement would pay the lansquenets 110,000 ducats and the Spaniards 35,000. The two cardinals, Orsini and de Cessis, already in Pompeio Colonna's palace would remain there in his custody and a third would join them to take the place of Giberti and Jacopo Salviati, who had fled from Rome. Before being given back Castel Sant'Angelo, Clement was to place two more cardinals in the hands of Colonna and Alarçon.[18]

Although Cardinals Pisani, Trivulzio and Gaddi were duly handed over to Alarçon and subsequently taken to Naples to be imprisoned in Castelnuovo, the agreement ran into difficulties, for Clement was unable to find pledges and guarantees for the cash he still owed on the previous engagements. But, at last, on 6 December 1527, the imperialists left Castel Sant'Angelo, and the pope's captivity, which had lasted some seven months, came to an end. Clement, however, totally distrusted the imperial troops, knowing them to be still largely unsatisfied as far as their arrears of pay were concerned. With the connivance of Alarçon and other imperial commanders, but without the knowledge of the imperial soldiers, or of Moncada, on 7 December, two hours before day-break, the pope fled from Castel Sant'Angelo dressed in the clothes of his major-domo. Luigi Gonzaga was waiting for him with a troop of soldiers in the fields outside Rome, and the pope hastened under their protection to Montefiascone and Capranica, leaving Cardinal Campeggio as his legate in Rome. On 8 December the pope reached safety at the ancient stronghold of Orvieto.[19]

CHAPTER XV

THE POPE IN EXILE

Pope Clement VII, memorable for his ill-fortune.
Jacopo Nardi

ORVIETO was a perfect natural fortress on the boundary between Roman and Tuscan territory, 'the strongest possible site, being situated on a volcanic rock, with precipices and a steep fall around it, so that although in many places the city lacked a wall it was so high and sheer that no one could possibly climb up to it'.[1] It stood, in fact, at 315 metres above sealevel, dominating the surrounding countryside, with the result that in the Middle Ages it had been a Guelph stronghold and a frequent refuge for the popes. Here Clement was at least secure from the dreaded lansquenets. Nevertheless, on arrival at Orvieto he must have been tempted to despair. He had no money and no means of carrying on the ordinary government of the Church. He did not even have available a curial official with the necessary knowledge to write a papal brief. With the exception of his person and his ecclesiastical rank, Clement had apparently preserved nothing; he had lost his property, almost all his states, and the obedience of the majority of his subjects. He was not even able to keep his promise over the Legation of the March of Ancona for Pompeio Colonna, for the whole area of the March had revolted against papal authority. Once the pope had ruled over the greatest city in Christendom from a palace adorned with all the masterpieces of Western art. He now inhabited a small cramped bishop's palace, with an inadequate water-supply, in a small and obscure hill-town. Once he had ruled over the Sacred College of Cardinals, the proud and wealthy princes of the Church. Now these same cardinals, the pope's greatest friends and most reliable supporters, were prisoners in the hands of the imperialists. At the end of December there were still only four cardinals with the pope, although in January he summoned to him another three of those who were at liberty. But, of these seven, three were new appointments with little knowledge of the workings of the Sacred College.

In March, cardinals Orsini and de Cessis, who had been held as securities by the imperial army, were released and, little by little, things began to improve as numerous prelates made their way to Orvieto, where the normal business of the Curia was resumed. But poverty was common to all, not least to the pope. On 23 November Roberto Boschetti visited Clement, who told him, 'They have plundered me of all I possess; even the canopy above my bed is not mine, it is borrowed'.[2]

The English ambassador, Stephen Gardiner, arrived on a most delicate embassy from his monarch – to obtain from the pope a decretal commission to enable Henry VIII to have his matrimonial case tried in England and the matter finally settled there. Gardiner was scandalized by the pope's condition and horrified when he was received by Clement, sitting on a form which had been covered by an old coverlet, 'not worth 20*d*'.[3] The miserable condition of the pope did not enhance his prestige in the eyes of Henry VIII's ambassador. Good churchman though he was, Gardiner could not help comparing the papal court at Orvieto with the brillaint court at home, the weakness and poverty of the pope with the power and wealth of the English monarch. Venetian observers made even more unfavourable comments; of the cardinals, who had for the most part been forced to dismiss their personal servants, only Piero Gonzaga was able to live according to his rank; the rest were reduced to riding through the steep streets of Orvieto on mules, 'as if they were cardinals of the early Church', although the reform of their habits had not been accompanied by any reform in their morals, 'and they would sell Christ for a ducat'.[4]

There had been a complete revolution in personnel of the papal advisers. Armellino had died in October, while the pope was still captive in Sant'Angelo; Giberti was replaced as datary by Pier Paolo Crescentio, left the court and retired to his bishopric of Verona.[5] Giovan Matteo Giberti was still a comparatively young man; he was aged only twenty-nine in 1527, but he was totally disillusioned with politics and the world of the Curia. Like Clement he interpeted the sack of Rome as a divine judgement on the Church for its failure to initiate reform, and this conviction was to turn Giberti into one of the great model bishops of the Counter Reformation. The details which, even now, he was working out in the administration of his own diocese would eventually be incorporated in the decrees of the Council of Trent.[6] Schomberg's influence evaporated with the sack of Rome, for Clement no doubt now found his pronounced pro-imperialism distinctly irritating. The pope's closest advisers were his secretary, Sanga, the pro-French Jacopo Salviati, and Cardinal Alessandro Farnese, whom Clement was subsequently to select and train as his successor. As far as Florence was concerned, the greatest influence on the pope was his old friend Cardinal Pucci, but Pucci never allowed himself to show concern for any matters which did not directly involve Florence.

The pope's position was beset with difficulties of so manifold a nature that Jacopo Salviati remarked to Cardinal Campeggio that 'Clement is in such dire necessity that, like David, he must perforce eat the shewbread'.[7] It was impossible to see how the papal finances could ever recover; Clement was still burdened with enormous debts to the imperialists; the Church State was in total disorder, so devastated in parts that no taxation could be imposed, and the revenues of the valuable salt-pans at Cervia were in Venetian hands. The pope was also preoccupied by many other problems: Florence, the situation in Rome and the Church States, and his relations with the emperor. Against the background of the sack of Rome, Clement was gradually evolving new policies, while watching the progress of the Neapolitan expedition and the Lombardy campaigns. Not least, his mind was turning once more to the question of church reform. An unexpected and unwelcome visitor at Orvieto was Brandano, who arrived in March with his normal prophecies of disaster. He was now foretelling the continuation of Italian troubles until 1530 when the Turk would take captive the pope, the emperor and the French king and embrace Christianity, thus inaugurating a new era in the life of the Church. Clement continued to exercise exemplary patience for as long as Brandano restricted himself to commenting on the fact that Clement's election had been canonically void, since he was a bastard, and only arrested the prophet when Brandano tried to incite rebellion among the citizens of Orvieto. In many ways Brandano's insistence on the need for reform of the Church was paralleled by Clement's own belief; on Palm Sunday 1528 the pope addressed the cardinals and prelates of the Church on the need for reform of the Curia and spoke of the sack of Rome as just chastise-ment for the Church's sins.[8]

Although Clement's continued residence in Orvieto was strain-ing the resources of the little town, a return to Rome was out of the question. For months law and order had been totally ignored in the Campagna and all ordinary communications had been inter-rupted. On 26 March Perez reported to the emperor that, of twenty letters written to him from Orvieto, only one reached him; because of the insecurity of the roads, 'no Spaniard dares go thither or to Rome from fear of being assassinated on the road'.[9] Bitter as he may have felt towards the Spaniards himself, Clement had no wish to see his authority openly flouted in this way and posted armed forces along the route between Orvieto and Rome, but this was almost as far as his influence stretched. A situation now arose which showed the precise limits of the pope's authority.

Vespasiano Colonna, that same Vespasiano who had played so prominent a part in the Colonna raid, had now chosen this in-opportune moment to die (13 March 1528), leaving all his property to his only child, Isabella, and desiring that she should marry either Ippolito de' Medici or Luigi Gonzaga. Regarding with horror the prospect of a Medici entering into so substantial a Colonna property, Ascanio Colonna claimed Vespasiano's inheri-tance through the line of Prospero Colonna. Certainly the legal position was by no means clear, but Clement forestalled any action by Ascanio and occupied the disputed properties. To add insult to injury he effected this occupation with the assistance of the abbot of Farfa. The Colonna, the Savelli and Ottaviano Spirito im-mediately began to gather troops to use against Farfa, and in April attacked Paliano, which was guarded by Luigi Gonzaga for the pope. Gonzaga left the city to raise reinforcements, and Giulia Gonzaga, Vespasiano's widow, fled to take refuge in Rome. A long struggle ensued, with the Orsini being drawn in on the papal side – 'as usual,' Contarini remarked wearily. At the end of the first week in May Luigi Gonzaga forced his way back into Paliano, and recaptured many of its dependent villages. In September Sciarra Colonna captured and sacked Anagni, a papal town. On 22 September an attempt was made to capture Cardinal Orsini, who barely escaped with his life to Città Castellana. When Clement remonstrated with the Colonna about these latest outrages he was politely informed 'that in the estates of the Church they will show His Holiness every respect and reverence; but in overcoming their enemies they hope never to be found wanting and will do all that is in their power'.[10] It was not until October that this area was once more under papal control.

Meanwhile there had been a similar disturbance in Camerino. This town, second in importance of the towns of the March, with an income of about 10,000 ducats annually, and vital to communications between Ancona and Rome, had for more than two centuries been dominated by the Varano family. The ruling member of the family, Duke Giovanni Maria Varano, died in August 1527 leaving as his only heir a daughter, Giulia, whom Clement wished to succeed to Camerino, since the rival branch of the Varano family were exiles in Ferrara and had married into the Estensi and Colonna families. But, when the will of Giovanni Maria was read, it was unexpectedly revealed that he wished Giulia to marry into this rival branch of the family. This was a situation which, even in normal times, would have caused disturbance, and these times were hardly normal. Giulia immediately became the coveted bride of every enterprising adventurer in Italy, including Guidobaldo della Rovere, who was promised Giulia's hand by her mother, Caterina Cybo, against the wishes of the pope, the Sacred College and Orazio Baglione, who wished to marry her to his son. With the duke of Urbino's consent, Orazio set out now for Camerino, which had meanwhile been attacked by Sciarra Colonna, acting for his cousin Ridolfi Varano, the illegitimate son of Duke Giovanni Maria, and Ercole Varano of Ferrara. For over a year the duchy was to be devastated by the disputants until Ercole and Ridolfi were driven out by Guidobaldo della Rovere.[11]

Meanwhile the condition of the city of Rome itself remained one of extreme distress. Clement's flight from the city in December 1527 did nothing to alleviate the sufferings of the Romans. Indeed, the pope's escape was regarded by the imperial soldiery as an excuse for fresh outrages in the Campagna, and in the city of Rome itself which was 'being gradually destroyed so that in a very short time it will be a heap of ruins' – as Perez told the emperor. 'As most of the wealthy citizens desert their homes', he continued, 'for fear of having soldiers quartered upon then, it naturally follows that the moment the owners are gone the houses are gutted and pulled down for the sake of the timber, which is sold in the markets and public places as firewood, as cheap as if there were a large forest in the neighbourhood of Rome. If to this be added that bread and wine are so scarce and dear that none but wealthy people can procure them, and that many people, once rich and prosperous, are actually begging in the streets',[12] then Perez supposed that the emperor would be able to imagine the terrible condition of Rome. Between 22 and 24 December the Spanish troops ran riot through the Roman countryside and launched an attack on Velletri, to Clement's intense annoyance. He remonstrated with the imperial commanders in the strongest possible terms.[13]

On Christmas Eve the Spaniards returned to Rome, and both they and the Italian troops declared their willingness to obey their commanders. The imperial leaders were only too aware that the advance of a French expedition led by Lautrec made it imperative that the imperial army be withdrawn from Rome in order to defend the kingdom of Naples. Therefore, in an attempt to break the deadlock, on 3 January Cardinal Colonna offered to pay the lansquenets three months of their arrears and to give a bonus of thirteen gold ducats to each officer if they would leave Rome. Most of the day was spent by the Germans in council, discussing this proposal and the appointments of Orange as captain-general and del Guasto as commander of the infantry which had been announced on 1 January. No decision had been made when the council, which was held out of doors, was broken up by a bitter wind and heavy rain. Despite continued thunderstorms, the consultation was resumed on the following day but, again, nothing was decided. It was only on 5 January that the lansquenets agreed to accept Orange's appointment and the financial terms of Colonna's offer.[14]

This arrangement had been made on the assumption that Clement would be paying 50,000 ducats in the middle of the month, which would be added to 20,000 ducats which arrived from Naples on 10 January. The imperial commanders were, therefore, thunderstruck when Campeggio made it clear to them that Clement would not be able to meet this obligation. Pompeio Colonna, rightly foreseeing trouble, hurriedly left the city, while on 17 January the lansquenets met together in council.[15] Rome waited in terror for the sacking to begin again. Ambassadors from the lansquenets were sent to Orange, who disclaimed all responsibility for the promises of Colonna, which had been made without his authority. The lansquenets immediately began to mutiny, and it was not until 20 January that Orange once more had them under control. On 18 January he suggested that after paying each of the lansquenets two ducats he should go, with some of their representatives, to Naples to see whether money could be obtained there. For three days the offer was considered. The mood of the lansquenets was ugly and they were spending their time in looting the wine- and food-shops which had reopened on Piazza Giudea and Campo di Fiori. Many Romans began moving their goods into Castel Sant'Angelo for safe-keeping. Finally the lansquenets agreed to wait ten days. If they were not paid then they would return home. The following day they received their two ducats each, and on 29 January it was learned that Orange had managed to extract from the treasury of Naples an advance of 105,000 ducats and from private bankers the promise of an equivalent amount.[16]

Discipline, however, was still slack, and incidents were occurring daily in the Campagna, where, against the orders of their officers, the men were plundering for food. As soon as Orange left Rome for Naples to collect their pay, 'the lansquenets determined to pay a visit to certain farms and country houses' for plunder, a determination which was swiftly carried out, 'after which they went to Marino, a town belonging to Ascanio Colonna, four miles hence, where they committed the same atrocities, sacking the place and ill-treating the women'.[17] Altogether the picture remained an unhappy one. As Lope de Soria informed Gattinara on 8 February, the lansquenets were 'as mutinous and disorderly as ever, insisting on being paid all their arrears. Between them and the Spaniards there is by no means that conformity of opinion that ought to exist between soldiers serving the same master. The same may be said of the generals, the prince and the rest seldom agreeing as to what must be done in the present circumstances.'[18]

It was not until 11 February that the imperial commanders were able to persuade the troops that they must march out of Rome at once, and then they were largely convinced, not by argument, but by the payment of two months' arrears from the money brought by Orange and del Guasto from Naples.[19] When this money was paid out on 13 February preparations were at last begun for the departure of the imperial armies from Rome. Easily the most potent argument that the imperial leaders had been able to produce for the lansquenets was that Lautrec was advancing with all speed on the kingdom of Naples, and that the loss of Naples would see the cutting-off of the last guarantee that the soldiers would be paid.

Lautrec's arrival in Italy was in many ways a direct threat to the imperialists. He was no novice to Italian campaigns; he had accompanied Louis XII to Italy in 1511 and had been named guardian of the council of Pisa. He had fought at the battle of Ravenna, where he had been left for dead on the battlefield, and he had distinguished himself at Marignano. In 1516 he had been appointed lieutenant-general in Italy. His bravery, justice and loyalty were never in question but, like many of the French commanders, he was both proud and obstinate and found it difficult to take advice from anyone.

Lautrec reached Susa in the first week of August 1527 and began his campaign by the capture of Bosco and Alessandria. Crossing the Ticino, Lautrec occupied Abbiategrasso and restored it to Sforza, with exemplary promptitude. Having joined with the Venetian forces, the French commander then attacked Pavia, which was defended by Ludovico Belioso's Italians, and captured it on 5 October, although it was with considerable difficulty that the league commanders prevented their men from embarking on a systematic sack of the town as a revenge for the battle of Pavia.[20] Their success in doing so is probably largely explained by the fact that Pavia had been fought over, through, and about for so long that it was scarcely worth sacking; but it still gave cause for self-congratulation and comparison with the imperial commanders in Rome to the latter's disadvantage.[21]

On 14 October 1527 Lautrec had moved from Pavia, crossed the Olona and the Lambro to Landriano, and advanced to a point where he might effect a crossing of the Po. Advancing thereafter through Castel San Giovanni to Piacenza, Lautrec was joined on 28 October by Vaudemont, the current French claimant for the throne of Naples. On 7 November the French troops moved south from Piacenza to Firenzuola and Parma, virtually abandoning Lombardy in favour of a Neapolitan expedition. From this point onwards Lautrec, who had effectively taken over from Urbino the direction of the League armies, represented an overt threat to the imperialists in Rome. He had with him, or was joined by, the cream of the league armies: 1000 lances, 1000 light horse, 2000 Italian adventurers and about 10,000 infantry. He had, moreover, the promise of support from the duke of Ferrara.

Este had remained loyal to the emperor until after the sack of Rome when, as the likelihood of Clement's adherence to the imperialists increased daily, Este began to lend a sympathetic ear to the confederates. The duke was well aware that, if necessary, Charles would choose an alliance with Clement VII rather than maintain his obligations to Ferrara, and as early as March Sanchez had prophesied that, were Clement to make peace with the emperor, Este would join the League.[22] Este realized, after the sack of Rome, when the imperialists consistently disregarded his advice, that he was honoured by the emperor only for as long as he was useful. By June the duke was talking of joining the League and becoming a 'good Italian', and the following month he informed the imperialists that under no circumstances would he ever take over the command of the imperial army.[23] On the strength of this, Lautrec approached the duke, asking for a gift of 200,000 ducats. In return, Este demanded from the League protection from the imperialists, absolution for all injuries done either to Clement or to his predecessors, the surrender by the papacy of all rights to Ferrara, Modena or Reggio, restitution of the Polesine,[24] which was in Venetian hands, together with the right to manufacture salt in the Comacchio, and the bishopric of Modena and the archbishopric of Ferrara for his son. On this basis negotiations continued; in October 1527 Venice dispatched one of her most illustrious citizens as ambassador to Ferrara – Gaspare Contarini, the son of a rich Levantine merchant who had studied under some of the best scholars of his age, and had himself become a famous humanist and philosopher. He had previously served as Venetian *proveditor* in the Polesine, where he became an expert on irrigation systems, hydraulics and Ferrarese problems. At Este's court Contarini joined Sir Gregory Casale, the English representative, who had received an ample brief from Wolsey to treat with the duke. After lengthy talks, Ferrara adhered to the League on 14 November, the agreement being published on the following day. Even then, Este can scarcely be described as throwing caution to the winds since, on the same day, he made a formal protest that he had only acted under compulsion for the preservation of his estates. In fact, he was making substantial territorial gains; he was to be granted possession of Ferrara, Modena, Reggio and Rubiera, in which the cardinals at Parma, on behalf of the pope, surrendered all rights; he was granted the right to extract salt from the Comacchio; Francis I promised to do everything in his power to ensure that Ferrara should retain Carpi, and Novi and Cortignola were thrown in as compensation for all the years during which the papacy had retained control of Modena. Venice and Florence promised the restoration of all former Ferrarese property now held by them, and Venice, in addition, promised the surrender of the residence of the papal legate in Venice which had previously belonged to Ferrara and which Venice had been forced to hand over to Julius II. The greatest advantages, however, were a royal bride, Renée of France, for Alfonso's son, Ercole, and the promised promotion of Ippolito d'Este to the Sacred College. In exchange, Este merely promised to provide 100 lances, 2000 cavalry, and 6000 ducats a month for six months to Lautrec; to grant free passage and provisions to the league armies; to prevent the passage of imperial troops, ambassadors and couriers across his territory; and to 'do all he can for the Pope's liberation'.[25]

On 14 December Lautrec finally left Parma for Reggio, Modena and Bologna. This advance was welcomed by Venice, which did not trust Florence and believed that the presence of Lautrec in Tuscany would keep that city faithful to the League,[26] though Florence did in fact welcome the news. The towns of the Church State were, understandably, less enthusiastic. The memory of the passage of the armies of Bourbon and Urbino was only too recent. When Lautrec's troops arrived at Bologna, they were kept out of the city by force.[27] Having sent on his artillery in advance, Lautrec left Bologna for Imola, which, despite heavy rain, he reached two days later. Here the fortress, which had fallen to the imperialists, was recovered and handed over to the papal governor of Imola.[28] On 13 January Lautrec was at Faenza and three days later at Forli. Here a diversion was made to recover Rimini for the pope in the hope that this might induce Clement to declare for the League once more.

For the first time, the League seemed to be having some success, and the imperialists were at last on the defensive. This was primarily because the political initiative had passed from Venice to France and the military initiative from Urbino to Lautrec. The extent to which Venice had lost control of the whole enterprise had been clear from the moment Lautrec first appeared in Lombardy; the wooing of the pope, initiated by Lautrec, the powerlessness of Venice to prevent the departure of the French from Lombardy, though this was contrary to her whole strategy, and even the removal of Sigismondo Malatesta, a Venetian client, from Rimini all showed the decline of Venetian influence. Whatever might be the common pretence, the resistance to the imperialists in Italy was no longer being conducted by a league of Italian states united for the preservation of the 'Liberty of Italy'. The war was being waged now by the French, a war of Valois against Hapsburg, in which the Italians played only a subsidiary role. In January 1528 Lautrec's secretary rightly told the ambassador from Lucca, 'The world now is divided in two and it is necessary that you should make it clear whether you are French or imperial, and if you are French supporters show it and make your monthly contributions as the others do.'[29]

Lautrec hastened south. On 9 February he crossed the Tronto, the northern river-boundary of the kingdom of Naples, and less than a week after entering Neapolitan territory he had reduced the whole of the Abruzzi. L'Aquilà was taken without any resistance, and soon all the towns of Apulia had followed suit by surrendering to Lautrec.

These French successes finally convinced the imperialists, even the recalcitrant lansquenets, that they must leave Rome, for if they they did not do so the whole kingdom of Naples would fall into the enemy's hands. After an occupation which had lasted for eight appalling months, the Spaniards, the Italian infantry and the cavalry left Rome on Sunday, 16 February.[30] The lansquenets left on the following day.[31] Already, in the face of the dangers that lay ahead, the imperial commanders had recovered authority over the troops, and the evacuation of Rome took place in the most orderly fashion. The soldiers were forbidden to sack or pillage; and throughout Rome, on countless improvised gibbets, hung grim reminders that the imperial commanders meant to be obeyed.[32]

But the sufferings of the city of Rome were not yet over. As the lansquenets left, at 11 a.m., the Orsini, under the leadership of the abbot of Farfa and Amico d'Arsoli, broke into the city and subjected it to all the horrors of a second sack.[33] The streets rang with shouts of 'Church, France and the Bear!'[34] as the pillagers rushed through the city, taking reprisals on all stragglers from the imperial army, including the sick, who had been abandoned in Roman hospitals. Boats at Ripa, which were loading property belonging to the Spaniards, were seized and their crews made captive. One boat, already on its way down the Tiber, laden with cannon and the property of Gian d'Urbina, was sunk. Pillaging extended from Rome to Ostia. Fourteen boats which had been bringing much needed corn and wine to Rome, retreated on hearing of Farfa's arrival, although the conservators of the city begged them to return and discharge their cargo. Having exhausted all the possibilities of the private vendetta, the Orsini finally turned their attention to a thorough sack of the ghetto.[35]

Campeggio, the sole remaining papal representative in Rome, implored the Orsini to leave. Clement immediately sent a detachment of troops to try to restore order in the city. Strenuous efforts were made to mitigate the distress in Rome, caused by a scarcity of provisions, and to guard against a renewed onslaught of the plague. Heavy penalties were placed on those who sold corn at extortionate prices, and Andrea Doria was employed to guard the coasts against pirates.

Many sensed that the long months of depredation and destruction were over and that soon papal government would make itself felt once more in the religious capital of Europe. The first prerequisite, however, was the return of the pope from exile. On 3 March a deputation from Rome visited Clement at Orvieto and invited him to return to the city whose desecrated churches had now been purified. Clement replied that scarcity and disorder, combined with the uncertain outcome of the Neapolitan war, made such a move impractical. When the delegates begged that at least the officials of the Rota and the Cancellaria might go back, Clement agreed, after consultation with Campeggio.[36] A few days later, Clement also arranged for Cardinals Gonzaga, de Cessis and Pucci to return to Rome, but because of famine in the city the cardinals and officials in question delayed their departure until the last days of April.[37] In preparation for their arrival, the imperial lodgings above the papal apartments in the Vatican were destroyed. By the end of April, the majority of the officials of the Curia had returned, though the situation in Rome remained very difficult, and Cardinal Campeggio's position was often critical.

Lautrec, meanwhile, was achieving astonishing success in the kingdom of Naples, where the towns of the Abruzzi hailed him as a deliverer. But the usual French delays in backing-up expeditions, by the prompt and regular dispatch of money, together with Lautrec's own natural caution, gave the imperialists time to put the city of Naples in a state of defence. Orange, however, also had his difficulties; he found that the evil reputation of hi troops had preceded him, and the Neapolitans were understandably unwilling to admit the army within their walls, 'saying that they do not want their city to become another Milan'.[38] Then, on 28 April as the French settled into their siege of the city, the imperial fleet, which had been keeping open a supply-route to the city of Naples, was completely destroyed by Filippino Doria off Capo d'Orso, between Amalfi and Salerno; del Guasto and Ascanio Colonna were taken prisoner, and Ferramosca and Moncada were among many who lost their lives. Moncada was scarcely mourned; he had become the Spanish scapegoat for the Colonna raid and was now largely blamed for this naval disaster, 'born, as he is said to have been, under an unlucky star and unusually unfortunate in all his enterprises. Now that he is dead people's troubles and misfortunes may be consisidered at an end, since whatever he undertook seldom turned out well.'[39] Lautrec knew that Naples had not yet been provisioned to withstand a long siege, and was convinced that it would only be a matter of time before the city fell to him, and with it the whole of southern Italy.

Clement VII, himself besieged in Orvieto by ambassadors from almost all the European states, who were more and more importunate with demands that he declare either for one side or the other, watched with deep concern the progress of events in Naples. He was still most anxious to return to Rome, but the disturbed state of the country made that impossible, and he believed that such a return would only be possible once he had regained control of the fortresses of Ostia and Civitàvecchia.[40]

Accordingly, in preparation for a return to Rome on 1 June, the pope moved to Viterbo and was received by the pious and aged

Cardinal Egidio Canisio. At Viterbo the pope was first housed in the fortress and subsequently in the palace of Cardinal Farnese. In the same month, Cardinal Campeggio, who was to go as papal legate to England, was replaced at Rome by Farnese, and Clement spoke of soon going there himself.[41] But renewed disturbances between the Orsini and the Colonna, which necessitated finding money for an escort of infantry and cavalry, again delayed the pope's departure, and it was not until 22 September that Clement dispatched dal Valle and Sanseverino to prepare the city finally for his return.

On 4 June Gaspare Contarini, the Venetian ambassador, arrived at Viterbo, commissioned by his government to embark on the virtually impossible task of persuading the pope to permit Venice to keep Ravenna and Cervia. How hopeless the task was can be guessed from the fact that almost the first action of Clement on regaining his freedom had been to dispatch to Venice the archbishop of Manfredonia to demand the restoration of Ravenna and Cervia.[42] Even before this, on 17 December 1527, Pisano had an audience with the pope at Orvieto, the first direct contact the Venetians had had with the pope since the capture of Rome. Clement spoke then of his desire for a general peace, of the possibility that he might go to Spain, but most fully of his desire that Ravenna and Cervia be restored. On the ambassador's departure, Gambara had warned him of the importance of Ravenna and Cervia to the pope, but Venice had chosen to ignore the warning.[43] On 13 January a papal brief demanded the immediate restoration of the two towns and complained that Venice was appointing to benefices in a way which violated agreements made between that state and Julius II.[44]

Venetian stubbornness over Ravenna and Cervia exasperated her allies and this put a considerable strain on the alliance. Neither England nor France was prepared to accept the Venetian position. On 2 February Pesaro reported to Venice that Lautrec, who had just received a large dose of papal rancour on the subject, had urged that Venice try to accommodate Clement over Ravenna and Cervia.[45] In February letters from Henry VIII and in April letters from Wolsey asked for their immediate restitution.[46] Despite Venetian attempts to explain that the two towns had been taken with the consent of both Francis I and of Casale, the English ambassador, to prevent them falling into imperial hands, and that it was impossible to restore them while the war lasted, the French and English ambassadors pressed almost daily for their return to the pope.[47] Even Sforza, embarrassingly dependent on Venetian subsidies as he was, began to urge the restoration of Ravenna and Cervia, in the hope that Clement would then join the League 'to drive the Spaniards out of Italy; not because he would not rather Venice had the towns than the pope, but for the good of all Italy'.[48]

Although a strong party within Venice always argued in favour of a restoration of Ravenna and Cervia, on the grounds that both justice and utility demanded it, they were invariably overruled in the Venetian senate, and Venice remained unmoved by any pleas either from the pope or from her allies. This was the situation when Contarini arrived in Viterbo. He had been ordered by the Senate to try to persuade the pope to re-enter the Italian League. If Clement raised the question of Ravenna and Cervia, and it was difficult to believe that he would not, Contarini was to try to explain that the Venetian retention of the two towns was, for the present, beneficial both to the pope and to the League. Hopefully, in the same breath, he was to ask for permission to levy troops in the Church State and to tax the Venetian clergy.[49]

In the afternoon of 7 June Contarini received an urgent message informing him that he was to see the pope that evening between five and six o'clock. Hurrying to the papal quarters, he found the pope in his private chamber with the French envoy, Viscount Turenne, Stephen Gardiner of England, Sforza's ambassador, and Cardinals Ridolfi and Sforza. In the presence of this distinguished company Clement once again complained about the Venetian occupation of Ravenna and Cervia, and requested the allied powers to obtain their restitution. It was clear that Venice had little support even from her supposed allies. Turenne delivered himself of the opinion, somewhat unfairly harking back to the terms of the League of Cognac, that his king had waged war in Italy not for his own profit but solely to see everyone in possession of their own territory, and that he had always assumed that the Venetians were fighting for the same reason. Stephen Gardiner, who was only interested in obtaining the annulment of his master's marriage to Catherine of Aragon, and who resented the Venetian attitude, which could only obstruct his mission, spoke very irritably. He told Contarini in no uncertain terms that it was the intention of Henry VIII that Ravenna and Cervia should be restored to the pope, and reminded the poor Venetian that when the cities had first been taken, Venice had assured the French and English kings that she was merely holding them in trust for the Church. Contarini, tied by his instructions, could do not more than make, yet again, the futile request that Venice be allowed to keep Ravenna and Cervia, but Clement dismissed the ambassador agrily with the uncompromising statement, 'I said to you, and now repeat, that I choose no other mode, save that you restore those cities to me.'[50]

The possibility that Venice might succeed in permanently wresting Ravenna and Cervia from the Church depended, as so much in Italy depended, on the fortunes of the war in Naples. Here, both for besiegers and besieged, the situation became more and more squalid. The heat of the summer brought inevitable disease, the greatest scourge of all armies in Italy. Typhoid fever and plague spread with alarming rapidity both inside and outside the city of Naples as news arrived of the event which was probably most decisive in determining the direction of the war in Italy – the alliance between Charles V and the great privateering naval captain, Andrea Doria.

Clement had always warned Francis I not to lose Doria's services, for, until this date, the League had retained control of the sea. Without Doria, even the powerful Venetian fleet was not strong enough to ensure naval supremacy for the League. There was no question of Doria having defected. He had been a consistent supporter of the papal cause, and within days of the sack of Rome had offered a month's free supply of victuals to the league army if they rescued the pope. But the period of the engagement he had entered into with Francis I after the sack of Rome was at an end and he was unable to get France to renew it on terms favourable enough to himself. The nature of Doria's occupation was such that he could not afford to remain unemployed for any length of time; he had to spend 150 ducats a day just to keep his fleet in being. Before coming to his agreement with Charles V, Doria had made serious efforts to persuade the pope to employ him.[51] Clement, who attempted to dissuade Doria from taking service with the emperor, would gladly have engaged Doria but could afford to engage no more than two galleys while Doria insisted on a minimum of eight.[52]

Among the league commanders, Renzo da Ceri was the first to recognize Doria's loss as a major blow to the League. On 14 August, in a strongly worded letter to Francis I, he warned the king that Genoa would almost certainly revert to the imperialists, and he advised him to make immediate provisions against such an occurrence. Da Ceri was soon proved right; by 12 September 1528, Genoa was no longer under French control.[53]

Meanwhile Lautrec made the most strenuous efforts to bring about the fall of Naples, but was defeated by the determination of the imperial defence, by scarcity of supplies and by disease. Lautrec's army was being decimated by plague; Vaudemont, Pedro Navarro and Lautrec himself all fell ill. For French hopes in Italy, raised so high by Lautrec's series of victories, the end was now near. On the night following the Feast of the Assumption, Lautrec died. In Rome the Senate commanded funeral solemnities to be held for the man who was universally regarded as the liberator of the city, and for long afterwards he was remembered in masses for the dead. Vaudemont was also carried off by the disease, leaving Saluzzo in sole command. Realizing that the condition of his army, in which not one of his captains was healthy, was such that he could no longer maintain the siege, Saluzzo ordered a retreat on 29 August 1529. The retreat rapidly became a rout as, pursued by the imperial army, the French hurried back to the comparative security of Rome, where the sick and the dying lay in the streets naked and unfed in their hundreds.[54]

The complete triumph of the emperor was no longer in question. Even the Italian representatives of Charles V, who, ever since the sack of Rome, had been intent on playing down imperial successes in Italy, were inclined to admit this. 'If the imperialists now come to Lombardy,' Sanchez told Charles,

not a single Frenchman will remain in Italy and matters will soon be placed on the old footing. The Florentines, when they hear of the advance of the Neapolitan army, will be happy to sign any conditions His Imperial Majesty may be pleased to impose and, as to the pope, the emperor has no doubt by this time sent instructions to the prince of Orange how to proceed with him. The Venetians . . . are so bewildered that they do not know what to do, except to fortify the towns on the border of Lombardy for fear of an invasion. Now is the time to root out that venomous plant and strike a blow at people who have always been the promoters of discord among Christian princes and the constant abettors of the Turk.[55]

Things were not quite to work out in the way that Sanchez envisaged, but certainly affairs were moving back sufficiently in the imperial favour for Clement to thank God that he had not succumbed to the blandishments of Lautrec and the League. Ever since the sack of Rome, Clement VII had maintained an attitude of strict neutrality. He had expressed himself at length and with impartial bitterness on the subject of both the League and the imperialists. When Venice urged the pope to declare for the League, her ambassador was told that when one of the league armies had won a single victory Clement might consider making such a declaration. The pope greeted Lautrec's expedition into Italy with a singular lack of enthusiasm; as the League had failed to rescue him when he was in prison, there could be no reason for Lautrec to advance on Rome now that he was at liberty, and if the French were coming to invade Naples they were merely jeopardizing the position of Francis's sons in Spain. On the other hand, when the Spanish spoke of an alliance with Charles, Clement replied that he would first like to have his state and his friends, the hostage cardinals, returned to him, 'and I will not bother to mention Rome, because that is completely ruined and more than ten million gold ducats' worth of damage has been done to it'.[56]

Papal diplomacy, at this time, was entirely directed towards a restoration of the states of the Church and the recovery of Florence. There was nothing surprising in this. As Cosimo, the founder of the Medici fortunes in Florence had once remarked, 'States are not maintained by reciting the rosary or the Lord's prayer.' It was all very well for humanists and reformers to affirm that the strength of the papacy ultimately lay in divesting itself of temporal power. It would have required superhuman faith for a sixteenth-century pope to have acted on this assumption. Clement VII, it is clear, had his fair share of human weaknesses and he was, above all things, an Italian prince who wanted to be able to resist any external domination of Italy. In addition, he had to reckon with public opinion which, as even a reformer like Valdés realized, expected that a pope would protect and fight for his own: 'The people of Italy would look down on a pope who didn't wage war. They would think it a great insult if a single inch of church land were lost.'[57]

Clement remained single-minded in his determination to reassert the integrity of the Church State. On Good Friday 1528 he made his position perfectly clear when, in one day, he excommunicated Florence, Venice for her possession of Ravenna and Cervia, and Ferrara for her occupation of Modena and Reggio; at the beginning of May he asked the marquess of Mantua to defend Parma and Piacenza for the papacy against either the League or the emperor.[58] Meanwhile all citizens of the Church State serving in foreign armies were ordered home, a move obviously directed against the duke of Urbino, indubitably a citizen of the Church State and very obviously serving with a foreign army, and stricter control was imposed on all towns within papal territories; the keys of each, normally held by the citizens, were to be handed over to the papal governor.[59]

By August 1528 it was already clear to the pope that, if what he sought was the reintegration of his state, his interests must lie with the emperor. Accordingly Clement decided to anticipate the arrival of a new envoy from Spain, Miguel Mai, and return to Rome, before he had recovered Ostia and Civitàvecchia. On 5 October, having first created Quiñones a cardinal, Clement left Viterbo where he had suffered from a scarcity of all commodities save water. That night the papal court was lodged at Nepi. On 6 October in a severe thunder-storm the pope re-entered Rome, escorted by 200 cavalry and 500 infantry. He went first to St Peter's to pray, and thence to the Vatican. Almost his first action after the return to his capital was to reissue a proclamation forbidding reprisals against any imperial subject in the Church State, his previous instructions on this point having been more frequently honoured in the breach than in the observance, particularly by the Orsini; the abbot of Farfa, who had given refuge to many Guelfs at Bracciano, had occupied himself in the past few months by summarily executing any imperial subject unlucky enough to fall into his hands.[60]

Throughout these months many ecclesiastics had imitated the pope's example and had neglected to cut their beards, as a sign of mourning for the sack of Rome. As a gesture of forgiveness towards the imperialists Clement now issued a proclamation forbidding ecclesiastics to go about the streets of Rome with long beards, although in fact he was never to trim his own throughout the rest of his life. To have shown forgiveness towards the imperialists at this moment must have been truly difficult, and Clement's readiness to do so at least entitles him to the name he had chosen on becoming pope; he was truly Clement. He had always loved the city of Rome and in former and happier days had tried to contribute to its growing beauty. On his return to this once great city, he saw a world of ruins and of empty, desolate houses; even the churches were despoiled both of their ornaments and their artistic beauty. For more than a year, in the capital city of Christendom, mass had been regularly performed in only two churches; those of the German and the Spanish nations. On 24 October Clement wrote to the emperor:

We must rejoice on coming safe to shore, after so great a shipwreck, even if we have lost all things; but our grief for the ruin of Italy, manifest to every eye, still more for the misery of this city and our own misfortune, is immeasurably heightened by the sight of Rome. We are sustained only by the hope that, through your assistance, we may be able to staunch the many wounds of Italy, and that our presence here and that of the Sacred College may avail towards a gradual restoration of the city. For, my beloved son, before our distracted gaze lies a pitiable and mangled corpse, and nothing can mitigate our sorrows, nothing can build anew the city and the Church, save the prospect of that peace and undisturbed repose which depends on your moderation and equity of mind.[61]

CHAPTER XVI

BARCELONA AND CAMBRAI

What a wonderful thing it is that the king of France, from a desire to have his sons back, did not refuse anything; that the king of England, from a wish to disencumber himself of his wife, promised everything; and that Charles, anxious to place the imperial crown on his head, conceded more than anyone asked of him.

Benedetto Varchi

ON the day after his return on 7 October 1528, Clement called together his cardinals and the conservators of Rome in order to discuss the restoration of the city. The pope's first care was to provide for the import of food, of which there was the greatest scarcity. The shortage of grain had an important effect on Clement's policies, for continued famine kept the pope dependent on the goodwill of the emperor, who could license the export of vital grain-suppies from Sicily and Naples to Rome. But even these supplies were barely sufficient. In January letters were still reaching the duchess of Urbino, describing famine conditions at Rome: 'Every day one sees people dying in the streets of hunger and throughout the city one hears nothing but the poor crying out, "Help me for I die of starvation." '[1]

Despite the disastrous food-shortage, Rome gradually began to return to normal; food-shops were reopened and houses were rebuilt. On 14 October Clement summoned the cardinals to return to Rome. They came and installed themselves as well as they could amidst the ruins of their palaces, but court-life was voluntarily restricted: 'His Holiness is not bothered by visits and audiences as much as he was at Viterbo, because he has let these cardinals know that they must be content to stay away from the Vatican, except for consistories and important negotiations, and the pope's request is observed,' wrote Francesco Gonzaga.[2] Within a world of common poverty, life at Rome assumed an aspect of seriousness and gloom, which could not even be relieved by traditional ceremonies, since the churches were completely devoid of ornaments and vestments. But, for all that, Clement was glad to be back in Rome, 'where the authority and dignity of His Holiness is understood better than in any other place'.[3] By the end of the year the regular life of the Curia had been resumed.

Clement, meanwhile, was anxiously awaiting the arrival of Miguel Mai and the return of Quiñones, now Cardinal Santa Croce, from the emperor's court whither he had gone to mediate between Charles and Clement. Navigation experts were consulted, and assured the pope that the weather could not have been more favourable for a speedy voyage between Rome and Spain. That Charles was deliberately delaying the cardinal's return was obvious, and Clement began to suspect the emperor's intentions towards him. He even toyed with the idea of an alliance with the League, and had the League been at all successful in the war against the imperialists there seems little doubt that Clement would have joined it once more.

After the departure of Lautrec for Naples, however, the inadequate league forces in Lombardy had been unable to stem any imperial advance, for all the Venetian troops were tied down in the defence of the Venetian state and, in particular, of Bergamo, which was always a difficult city to defend. In April 1528 imperial reinforcements, under the duke of Brunswick, some 25,000 strong, had entered Italy from Trent. Having crossed the Adige on 14 May, they fanned out through the Veronese as far as Bardolino on Lake Garda, imposing fines and ransoms on every place. Crossing Brescian territory and the River Oglio they entered the Bergamasco, while da Leyva advanced from Milan to join them.

Venice immediately increased her own troops and, in particular, strengthened her light cavalry. To do so she had to cast far afield, yet another indication of the exhaustion of Italian resources; troops were brought from Greece and Dalmatia and 500 cavalry from Turkey, 'and that they [might] not appear to be such [Venice] remitted [to Constantinople] cloth and other accoutrements for them to be dressed in the Albanian fashion'.[4] Francis I was asked to raise an additional 6000 lansquenets, to be paid by Venice.[5] But the Venetian army in northern Italy was now hardly strong enough to protect the Veneto, let alone take offensive action, and the duke of Urbino gradually withdrew behind Venetian borders. It made little difference that Francis I dispatched to the League reinforcements under Francis de Bourbon, count of St Pol, a general with little previous military experience, who was to prove as efficient as any other French general in ruining first a campaign and then an army.

By the end of the summer of 1528 the war in Lombardy was virtually over. In the field confusion among the allies was rife. All the armies in Lombardy had begun to feel the effects of the great scarcity and rise in commodity prices, common throughout the Italian mainland, which, in this year, was totally dependent on imported and hoarded grain.

The continued economic drain of the war exacted a heavy toll at Venice, and the republic found that it was virtually impossible to keep up with payments to armies in the field. Almost all the units in Lombardy were heavily in arrears with their pay. Desertions were common, and none of the infantry companies could be kept at full strength. Continuous recruiting hardly kept pace with losses. Apart from the need to maintain the fleet, and to keep the army in Lombardy up to strength, at a cost of some 67,000 ducats each month, Venice was also committed to sending money for the defence of the towns she still held in the kingdom of Naples, to sending subsidies to Lautrec, and was constantly supplying the ever-bankrupt Sforza with loans.

In August came news of Lautrec's failure before Naples and of the French retreat. On 8 September the Venetian army moved to besiege Pavia,[6] which had been recaptured by the imperialists, even as St Pol received orders from Francis I to go immediately to the kingdom of Naples to try to recover the French losses there. Venice and France were already on the verge of a breach over the restitution of Ravenna and Cervia to the pope and over the question of French subsidies to the league army, and now this instruction was interpreted as outright betrayal. The Venetians pleaded with St Pol not to leave Lombardy, but only the French general's inability to pay his troops prevented him from doing so. Pavia surrendered to the League on 22 September, but this success scarcely compensated for the loss of Genoa to the imperialists on 12 September, as a result of a popular rising in favour of Andrea Doria.

St Pol attempted to recover Genoa but, when there was no pro-French rising in the city, withdrew from its walls and retreated towards Pavia. His troops had been decimated by plague and desertion, and when he reached Alessandria in the second week of October he had no more than 1000 left. Thus, by the autumn of 1528, the League, so arduously held together for three years, was practically in ruins. Militarily, total defeat was in sight. Only St Pol, with his depleted resources, continued to display the French colours in Italy. Genoa and Naples were irrevocably lost and in imperial hands, although Venice still clung bravely to the few coastal towns she held in Apulia. Florence was directly threatened. The imperial commanders seemed more powerful and united than ever.

No wonder, therefore, that the imperialists displayed confidence and even arrogance in their dealings with the pope. Charles showed himself in no hurry to reach agreement with Clement, who had already despaired of Quiñones' return, when he heard that on 17 December 1528 the cardinal had landed at Genoa in the company of Mai, 'a bold, unscrupulous character, wholly devoted to his master's interests'.[7] Mai had been dispatched by Charles as a watchdog for Quiñones for, since the latter had become a cardinal, the emperor had less faith in him. Quiñones reached Rome on 30 December and was immediately housed close by the papal apartments, but, although he was much honoured by the pope, he was destined to disappoint him, for he brought little with him from the emperor other than civil words. In January 1529 Quiñones left again, on his peripatetic services for pope and emperor, this time for Naples, in order to negotiate with the viceroy for the surrender of Ostia and Civitàvecchia, the liberation of the hostages, and an understanding between the emperor and the pope. His place at Rome was taken by Mai, who announced that he had full powers to restore Ostia and Civitàvecchia as soon as he had spoken with the pope, but, before he could do so, Clement was stricken down with a most serious illness.

Undoubtedly the long-term cause of the pope's sickness was the serious strain he had been under during the preceding two years; immediately, the cause was a common cold which had been neglected. By 10 January it was general knowledge that Clement's life was despaired of, and in the evening the pope summoned the members of the Sacred College to his bedside, and nominated as cardinals Ippolito de' Medici and Girolamo Doria.

News of the critical condition of the pope spread rapidly among the Romans and released a flood of popular demonstrations in his favour. This illness of the pope revealed at last to the imperialists, what they had previously been unable to accept: the popular determination of the Catholic world to maintain the independence of the papacy. It was evident that, if Charles had wanted to alienate the princes of the church, he could have devised no more effective means than the sack of Rome and the subsequent treatment of the papacy. The cardinals had rallied to the pope and there had been a distinct change in attitude even in those who had formerly supported the emperor. From Rome, Mai reported back to Spain, 'The majority of the cardinals are unfriendly to us on account of the ruthless havoc committed by our soldiery throughout Italy from Piedmont to Apulia.'[8] Quiñones had always been considered an imperialist but warned Mai that he wished to behave like a good ecclesiastic, since 'if he did not serve God first he could not serve the emperor afterwards'.[9]

The papal doctors had despaired of Clement's life, and the cardinals met for consultation in Palazzo dal Monte. They considered that, as Ostia and Civitàvecchia were still in imperial hands, there would be little hope of a free papal election if the conclave took place in Rome. The cardinals, therefore, indicated as clearly as they were able that, even at the cost of a schism, they would hold their conclave on neutral ground and preserve the Church's independence. The entire discussion was dominated by Farnese, president of the Sacred College, who had been forced into a position of pre-eminence by the dangerous situation. It was Farnese who made it plain that the cardinals were as unwilling to accept French or English pressure as that of the imperialists; he refused to countenance any of the French suggestions that the conclave take place in Avignon. At the same time he infuriated Mai by maintaining the right of the cardinals to hold the conclave where they wished, whatever the emperor might desire.[10]

The firm reaction of the Sacred College, coupled with the attitude of the Roman people, who had already begun to lay in arms in order to resist any external interference, convinced the imperialists that it would be expedient to make some gesture to public opinion, by releasing the cardinal-hostages they still held, and by restoring Civitàvecchia and Ostia to the papacy. Mai was working ceaselessly on the emperor's behalf, even throughout Holy Week, on the somewhat dubious grounds that his time could not 'be better employed than in the imperial interests, which, after all, is God's service'.[11]

Clement had, meanwhile, miraculously recovered from his critical illness, apart from continued stomach-pains and general weakness. He was not strong enough to celebrate mass on Easter Sunday, but insisted on giving the traditional Easter blessing to the city and the world, as usual. On Easter Monday, the pope paid 18,000 ducats into the hands of the imperialists. In return he was to have received the two fortresses of Ostia and Civitàvecchia, but at the last moment a hitch occurred; Don Alonso da Cordova, governor of Civitàvecchia, refused to hand over his fortress to the papal troops since his pay was in arrears, and Orange had to send imperial forces to arrest him and take over the fortress. Anxious to further imperial interests with the pope and to break down his attitude of strict neutrality, Orange asked Clement to select a condign punishment for Cordova, 'which act of courtesy and justice was very agreeable to His Holiness particularly and to all in general'.[12]

In fact, Clement was already being driven into an alliance with the emperor. The disruptive antics of the abbot of Farfa, who had declared himself as an adherent of France and a member of the League, were seriously hampering the restoration of papal authority in the Campagna. At the beginning of March he captured two barges bringing vital supplies of corn to Rome. This action was condemned by the pope and by the entire Sacred College, who threatened to use the Colonna against the abbot. Salviati warned Casale that the outrages committed by Farfa would certainly compel the pope to become an imperialist as they would drive him into the arms of the Colonna.[13]

Undoubtedly, however, the single major cause of reconciliation between pope and emperor was Charles V's promise to bring about a restoration of the Medici to Florence. Here events had suddenly changed dramatically. Clement had continued to hope that he might obtain his ends in Florence by peaceable means and, as long as Capponi remained in power, he had little alternative. A successful move against Florence would have required the active support of such individuals as Vettori, Guicciardini, Ruberto Acciauoli and Filippo Strozzi, on whom any successful Medici restoration must depend. While Capponi remained head of the Florentine state, they would not move against him. But the sudden discovery at Florence that Capponi had long been conducting negotiations with the pope,[14] through the medium of Jacopo Salviati, led to Capponi's fall in April 1529, and his successor, the violent Francesco Carducci, was so opposed to Clement and the Medici that any possibility of accommodation could be ruled out. As far as the aristocrats were concerned, Capponi's dismissal removed from the Florentine republican régime the last shreds of respectability. Henceforward they would work with the pope towards a restoration of the old régime. Carducci's victory over Capponi signified the eclipse of the aristocrats in government, for he was a man of lowly origins.[15] The government of the city became dominated by the republican extremists, who, almost without exception, were elected to magistracies as they fell vacant. Increased bitterness against the Medici was very noticeable, and by November 1529 the government was as tyrannical as ever a Medici government had dared to be.[16] On 20 November the Grand Council sanctioned a forced loan of 1000 ducats from each of forty men and of 500 from another forty, and the sale of one-third of all ecclesiastical property in the city. Within Florence there was little unanimity over questions of finance. Although by law all money acts had to have a two-thirds majority in the Grand Council, it was soon discovered that if this provision were retained it would be impossible to raise money at all. The law had to be amended so that only a bare majority was necessary and 'so that the luke-warmness and the avarice of the less lovable of our citizens could do less harm to the defence of liberty'.[17]

The need for money was great, for as the pope approached agreement with the emperor so Florence intensified military preparations in order to defy both. In these the new republican leaders showed a consummate lack of tact, apparently choosing as commanders of their mercenary forces captains who were guaranteed to be unacceptable to Clement VII; Malatesta Baglione, temporarily joint-ruler of Perugia with Orazio Baglione, but a traditional papal enemy against whom Clement was already working, and Napoleone Orsini, the abbot of Farfa.

Contemporaries were not slow in judging that the fall of Capponi and the increased militancy of Florence with its attendant anti-Medici bitterness were the events which finally brought about the imperial–papal alliance. Hearing of events at Florence, the English representative told Wolsey, 'I have persuaded myself and been assured by Salviati a thousand times that the pope would never join with the emperor. Now I should not be surprised if he did, for the persecution of his relatives and friends will be a great incitement to him. The French ought to prevail upon the Florentines to restrain themselves.'[18]

Clement's final decision to make a formal alliance with the emperor was made in the first week of May 1529, and negotiations moved swiftly towards a conclusion. Such delay as there was resulted from a recurrence of Clement's former illness. His constitution seems to have been permanently weakened by the experiences of the sack of Rome and the exile from the Holy City, and fears revived that the pope would die before an agreement could be signed.[19] On 24 May Clement started drinking the waters of Viterbo from which his doctors, who had diagnosed a liver complaint, hoped much, and although Clement disagreed with the diagnosis[20] the doctors seemed to have been vindicated when the pope recovered and resumed his talks with the imperialists. By the Treaty of Barcelona (29 June 1529) Charles virtually committed himself to creating a Medici principality in Tuscany, for it was agreed that Alessandro de' Medici should marry the emperor's illegitimate daughter Margaret. Charles promised to preserve the integrity of the duchy of Milan, although the whole question of Sforza's guilt was still to be resolved. A total reintegration of the Church State was promised, including Ravenna, Cervia, Modena, Reggio and Rubiera. Ferrara was to forfeit his duchy, and Charles promised to assist Clement in executing this papal sentence. Agreement was reached over the related vexed questions of the tribute (*census*) of Naples and provisions to the Neapolitan bishoprics, the pope handing over to the emperor and his successors the nomination to twenty-four Neapolitan bishoprics.

Peace in Italy as a whole was gradually and painfully approaching but was still many months away and peace resulted as much from war-weariness after long years of profitless conflict as from the sack of Rome. Exhaustion of all the parties concerned, none of whom had proved to have the resources necessary to carry on such a prolonged war, was gradually bringing the fighting in Italy to a close with the imperialists predominant but hardly triumphant. Even the long-awaited arrival of the emperor no longer aroused much enthusiasm among his supporters. In May 1529 Pompeio Colonna had warned Charles that if he landed in Naples he would produce famine throughout the kingdom and would drive the imperial army in Italy to mutiny.[21]

Among the allies of the Italian League suspicions were rife as it was clear that, despite the terms of the League of Cognac, the French and the English were now negotiating separately with the emperor. As early as July 1527 the Venetian ambassador had warned his masters that it was likely Francis would desert Sforza if he could thereby recover his sons. Discussions between imperial and Spanish representatives continued all that summer in Spain and were based on the Treaty of Madrid, which was argued over clause by clause. By the autumn agreement was almost reached on a ransom for the French princes, but matters were not progressing entirely in the emperor's favour, for it was clear that in order to achieve a lasting peace in Italy Charles would have to abandon the dream of recovering the Burgundian inheritance. Encouraged by Lautrec's successes in Italy, the French were also standing firm over Milan, much to Charles V's chagrin, as he still wanted to retain the duchy in his own hands.[22]

Then came the French disasters of 1528, and further fluctuation on the part of Francis I, who could not accept defeat at the hands of his cousin Charles, or the contempt of his cousin of England, who had done so little to promote the success of the campaigns in Italy. By the autumn of 1528 a peace party was predominant at the French court and grew in importance in the following months. It was led by the queen mother, Louise of Savoy, who entered into direct communication with Charles's regent in the Netherlands, the Archduchess Margaret, in order to try to discover a face-saving peace-formula.

Throughout the negotiations the French displayed consummate skill, in an age of faulty security, in concealing their transactions from their allies of the Italian League. It was not until June 1529 that the Venetians began to suspect an imminent peace between France and the emperor. At the end of June they learnt that Francis had left Paris for Cambrai where his mother had been conducting the negotiations. Both Venice and Florence hastened to beg the French king to include them in his talks, which Francis, anxious not to be isolated if the peace talks broke down, readily promised to do.[23]

At Cambrai discussions were protracted. To the anxious Venetians and Florentines it seemed likely that Francis would agree to any terms in exchange for the young princes, and suspicion deepened that the French would abandon Italy entirely. Certainly the French king appeared to have good reasons for doing so. Militarily, total defeat was in sight when news came of yet another French disaster: on 19 June in a surprise attack from Milan the imperialists defeated St Pol at Landriano. The artillery was lost, and St Pol himself was taken prisoner.

Still the Italian ambassadors permitted themselves to be persuaded when, on 10 July, they were assured that there would be no peace without the allies. They became less convinced of the integrity of the French king, and their perturbation increased when they found they could get nothing but evasive replies to their questions about the progress of the negotiations. On 11 July the Venetian and Milanese representatives were joined at Cambrai by Calvacanti from Florence. His fellow-Italians had little reassurance for him, since it was now clear that the only remaining obstacle to an agreement between Francis I and Charles V was the French king's wish to include the other league members. But this the emperor could not accept, as the intractable attitude of Venice both over Milan and over projects for a joint expedition against the Turk was irreconcilable with the French willingness to agree over both matters. Nevertheless, as late as 3 August, Francis again said that he would never agree to a peace which did not include the confederates. Only two days later, to the consternation of all the ambassadors, despite the fact that the agreement meant that at least Italy would no longer be the battlefield of Europe, the peace was published without any mention of the Italian powers. With the exception of Milan, which was partially protected by the papal–imperial agreement at Barcelona, the Italians were abandoned in a state of war with Charles V.[24] Among other provisions the agreements mentioned a ransom of two million gold ducats for the French princes; Francis promised not to interfere in Germany, abandoned Tournai and Arras, agreed to join in a naval expedition against Turkey and to restore the property of Orange and that of Bourbon to his heirs. (The property of Orange was never restored. Francis did restore his property to Bourbon's heirs, but reconfiscated it when the French princes came home from Spain.) From an Italian point of view, however, what was important about the Peace of Cambrai was that it left Italy to the discretion of Charles V, to whom Francis surrendered all his rights in Naples, Milan, Genoa and Asti.[25]

CHAPTER XVII

THE RESISTANCE OF FLORENCE

And certainly our citizens deserve the greatest commendation, for although they are overcome with difficulties, yet it does not seem a hard task to maintain their liberty, the sweetness of which is all the greater the more war has been needed to obtain it.

The Balìa of Florence, 12 March 1530

IN August 1529 the Italians had every reason to believe that all was lost, that the emperor was, and would be for the foreseeable future, all-powerful in Italy. Every cherished dream of independence had collapsed. For two years – that is, until May 1527 – the threat to Italian independence which, after the battle of Pavia, Charles V had come to represent, had held the majority of Italian states to a common purpose. For those two years they had been forced together to work in one final effort to rid the peninsula of 'barbarian power'. The sack of Rome had destroyed the unity of Italy. It was followed by a general loss of morale; the pope and Venice moved into opposing camps, Florence revolted against the Medici, and Sforza became immobilized by fear and bankruptcy. France had deserted the Italians once more in pursuit of higher objects in power politics. It seemed that nothing could prevent the total enslavement of Italy to the emperor's will.

But, in the end, Charles V did not have everything his own way in Italy, since, though ultimately at the expense of Florence, Venice succeeded in checking the more flamboyant of his designs. The Venetian republic retained one major bargaining-counter in the kingdom of Naples where she still held Trani, Barletta and Monopoli. Charles had hoped that French pressure on Venice would lead to their restoration, and eventually Francis duly asked Venice to restore this property to the emperor, 'in order to free the sons of the king'. When the French ambassador suggested that Venice was bound to such an arrangement by the terms of the League of Cognac, Venice caustically replied that the terms of the same League of Cognac had also bound the French king not to make peace without including Venice, 'notwithstanding the fact that we have always desired the restoration of his dearly beloved sons, and to this end, since they have been in Spain, we have spent more than four million in gold between the armies and the navy'.[1]

Charles V was constantly aware that he needed peace with Venice before he could have peace in Italy. At the time of the negotiations at Cambrai, it was already clear that Charles was prepared to talk with Venice if Venice was prepared to talk with him, and Andrea Doria had sent Federico Grimaldi to Venice to offer his services as a go-between for the republic and the emperor. The republic was, at the same time, under pressure both from Mantua and from the pope, and indeed from its own very large peace-party to come to an agreement.

But in the meantime all the indications were that Venice would continue her resistance; if France had deserted her there was one ally on whom the Venetian Republic could still depend. Reports from Charles's brother, the Archduke Ferdinand, were already speaking of a Turkish advance in Hungary that had been clearly instigated by Venice.[2] While the emperor now had a free hand to dispose of Milan, were he to give it to the Archduke Ferdinand Venice would be driven into an open alliance with Constantinople.[3] Steadfastly, throughout all negotiations, the Venetians refused, and went on refusing, to take part in a crusade against the Turk, for they were well aware of the importance of Ottoman trade in the maintenance of the financial stability of Venice, the very stability on which her vast war effort had been based. So negotiation between the imperialists and Venice was difficult, and this was not without its side-effects; as a result the emperor was driven into a close relationship with Clement, whose co-operation could only be purchased by the vigorous prosecution of a war against the Florentine republican régime.

For more than two years, imperial supporters in Italy had looked forward to a golden age which would be inaugurated the moment Charles V set foot in Italy to solve, by his presence, those problems which had for so long defeated the ingenuity of even the most devoted of his servants. As the day of the emperor's arrival grew closer, the encomiums became even more lyrical: 'Once in Italy,' wrote Agostino Grimaldi on 1 May 1529, 'the emperor will soon put down all his enemies, reform the Church, convoke a general council, extinguish the flames of the Lutheran heresy, defeat the intrigues and plots that might be devised against such measures, and unite the forces of Christendom to fight the Turk.'[4] Other Italians were able to recognize that the coming of the emperor and the certainty of peace might bring at least some benefits. News of Charles's imminent arrival reached Milan simultaneously with that of the peace treaties at Cambrai and was greeted with a certain enthusiasm; 'all the people of Milan rejoiced, trusting that God would now ameliorate their condition'.[5] Long anticipated and, by some at least, eagerly awaited, on 12 August 1529 Charles V, with a military escort of 14,000 troops, landed at Genoa where he was welcomed by shouts of 'Long Live the Ruler of the World!' As it seemed likely that Charles would use the fresh troops who accompanied him to subdue Venice, it was natural that the Venetians should react with alarm, 'Finding themselves with very few infantry, the raising of infantry within the Church State being denied to them, and thinking that they would not remain in the field, but retire into their fortresses, but not having had the means to supply them all as was necessary, since the marquess of Mantua had declared himself as an imperialist'.[6] In the meantime, while making herself conspicuous by being the only Italian state not to send ambassadors to Genoa, Venice began to raise fresh troops while, with the courage of the damned, Francesco Sforza of Milan declared that he would rather be cut to pieces in front of the fortress of Cremona than surrender to the emperor.[7]

But if the Venetians, stubborn in their refusal to bow their knee to the emperor, refused to go to Genoa, they would be scarcely missed, so many had crowded there to greet Charles V. On behalf of the pope, Cardinals Farnese, Medici and Quiñones, together with Alessandro de' Medici had been sent to greet the emperor on his arrival. Thither also hastened the most famous of the Italian trimmers, Federigo Gonzaga, arriving four days late, but gratified to be received with the greatest cordiality, escorted into the emperor's presence by the marquess of Astorga, 'one of the most honoured grandees of Spain', and by other prominent Spanish nobles, and welcomed by the emperor so graciously 'that it has given rise to considerable talk at the Court'.[8] The city of Milan elected its own ambassadors to Charles, who left the city on 2 September, 'but with little pomp, because our poor city is now in the most miserable and poverty-stricken condition possible'.[9]

To Genoa there also hastened envoys from Florence, who had come to plead for a postponement of the projected expedition against their city. Charles refused to listen to them, and Gattinara told them plainly that they would have to restore the pope and his relatives. The reasons for this attitude are not difficult to find; it was popularly supposed that the decision of Charles V to bring down the Florentine republican régime was made on the assumption that this would force Clement VII to abandon his attitude of neutrality and tie him firmly to the imperial cause in Italy. In fact, the subjection of Florence and the setting-up of a Medici principality in central Italy was a logical extension of the emperor's Italian policies, and to some degree had been long planned. The tendency of Florence towards France, based on communal trading interests, was notorious and was a constant danger to the emperor. Since 1494 it had been the first concern of every anti-French power in Italy to bolster up a Medici régime in Florence, for if individual Medici might flirt occasionally with the French alliance, and in this Clement was by no means unique, every Florentine republican régime had been totally reckless in pursuing the French alliance through thick and thin. It was clear that the chief supporters of republicanism in Florence, notably the Soderini, were also those most vocal in proclaiming Florentine adherence to the French cause, and that of the *palleschi* only the potential defectors among the Medici supporters, Vettori, Acciauoli and Guicciardini, had been outspoken in defiance of the emperor. As recently as 1512, a Spanish army had restored the Medici to power in Florence, and Ferdinand of Aragon told Guicciardini that it had been done 'because he and the other powers of the League had supposed that the Florentine *gonfaloniere* was so inclined towards the French, and had so much influence in the city, that they could not be secure for as long as he held that office'.[10]

The geographical position of Florence could not be ignored by the emperor, for Florence was vital for communications within Italy. The one lesson which the Italian wars, since 1494, had surely taught was that no one could control Naples and Milan without also controlling Florence and the Church State. The subjection of Florence was, therefore, essential for imperial success in Italy. In addition, Charles V had no sympathy for the city-state; it had been

republicanism which had constantly thwarted him in Italy. Immediately after Pavia, apart from the pope, it had been the republics
of Venice, Florence, Siena and Lucca that were singled out for
punishment. Again, writing on 5 February 1527, the emperor had
instructed Lannoy 'that above everything else he should not
forget the Florentines, for they deserve to be so thoroughly
chastised that they will remember it for a long time'.[11] Immediately
after the sack of Rome, Perez had suggested that the emperor place
a heavy tax on Florence, that he should demolish her fortifications and take Leghorn and Pisa from her; in the following April
Sanchez was urging an attack on Florence to subject it to the
'emperor's rule':[12] and as early as June it was rumoured that
Charles would restore the Medici to Florence by force. Now
Charles was being warned to subject the Florentines before his
coronation, and in a letter to Granvelle a few days later the same
adviser commented on the pronounced pro-French bias of the
Florentines; 'The Florentines will always lean towards the French
and be enemies of the emperor, for as long as one stone rests on
another in their city.'[13] An expedition against Florence was,
therefore, a foregone conclusion even before the emperor left
Spain; and in the gradual recovery of the Florentine state the
natural imperial antipathy to the small unit seems evident.

'Rule Pisa by poverty, Pistoia by factions and Volterra by fortresses' – so ran the traditional Florentine proverb, indicating the
difficulties which had always faced Florence in ruling her subject-
towns. The major weakness of the city-state, and of Florence in
particular, was the narrowness of its political world, where the
dominant city jealously guarded its right to exploit those brought
under its rule. Whenever Florence was threatened, either by
foreign invaders or by internal crisis or, as was common, by both
at once, the subject-towns would seize the opportunity to rebel in
an attempt to regain lost freedoms. By the beginning of the
sixteenth century, in a world of consolidated territorial monarchies,
Florence no longer had the resources to defend both her independence and her subject-territories. The passage of the vast
armies of the emperor and of the League through Tuscany, between 1527 and 1529, the disorganization following the sack of
Rome, weakened every extant political bond, broke down communications and created some form of political change in every

major Tuscan town. Throughout the area there were parallel movements to that which occurred in Florence as the whole area fragmented into the smallest possible political units. As Florence broke away from Rome, so places like Cortona, Arezzo and Pistoia broke away from control by Florence. But the enthusiastic reception at Florence of the virtues of freedom and republicanism did not lead her to accept with equanimity expressions of similar sentiments by the subject-towns. Here it was expected, as it had always been expected, that while none of the subject-towns was accorded a say in government all were to accept the physical and financial consequences of Florentine policy and of changes in the government of Florence.

There were a number of particular reasons why these arrogant Florentine expectations had not been realized. There was little tradition of loyalty to Florence and, least of all, to a republican régime. The Medici had, on the whole, a better tradition of fair government in the Florentine state. It had been a republican régime which had pursued the long and bitter struggle against Pisa at the beginning of the century; indeed recovery of the subject-towns was the only policy which had ever been able to unite republican Florence. Ever since the sack of Rome, Florence had shown little genuine concern for her territories, for, adapting the imperial military strategy, Florence concentrated her entire defence effort on the capital city, abandoning, one by one, Arezzo, Prato and Pistoia. The sack of Prato in 1512 was still remembered, and it was remembered also that Florence had failed to prevent this peculiarly horrid episode but had not hesitated to come to terms when it was a question of saving Florence from a similar fate.

The subject-towns of the Florentine state came to believe that the emperor would help them to achieve independence, but nothing could have been further from the truth. Each Florentine town recovered by the imperialists was to be scrupulously restored into papal hands, and it is probable that this was done not out of deference to Clement VII but because it was on the large unit of the old Florentine state that Charles V hoped to found a new Medici principality.

In fact, as was not uncommon in the emperor's political experience, two strands of his policy were here in conflict. Opposed as he was to Clement as pope, and to the powerful Medici–Orsini complex in the Church State, in Florence the emperor needed to bolster up the Medici régime. From the beginning, therefore, even at Genoa, the only basis for negotiation offered to the Florentines by Charles V was the return of the Medici to their city. It was a fundamental weakness of the republican régime at Florence that it failed to realize adequately the imperial interest in a Medici restoration. In order to initiate negotiations with the pope which would lead towards such an aim, the prince of Orange, now viceroy of Naples, reached Rome at the end of July and was lodged in Salviati's palace in the Borgo. Orange brought with him some 1500 men, and it was clear that, before long, an attack would be made on Perugia and ultimately on Florence.

> At that time one saw nothing in the streets of Rome but soldiers' plumes, and one heard nothing but the sound of drums, and it seemed as if the whole of Italy was full of soldiers and was about to be turned topsy-turvy; and so great was the general desire of the soldiers, particularly the Spanish, to sack Florence, and so certain their belief that they would be able to, that there were those of them who used as a security for debt the gains they would make in the sack of Florence.[14]

Already, on 11 July 1529, Clement had sent an ultimatum to Perugia, ordering the withdrawal of hostile troops from the city and threatening an advance by the imperial troops in the event of the city's disobedience, and a brief on 24 July officially ordered the city of Perugia to return to its traditional obedience to the papal see. But Perugia was being used by the Florentines as an outer bulwark of their defences and was dominated by their forces under Malatesta Baglione, who thus hoped to preserve his position in Perugia. Thus, the city council of Perugia was, as yet, in no position to change its current policy.

For a while it even seemed that Malatesta Baglione might succeed and maintain his rule of force in Perugia. Typically, Orange and the pope had begun their joint enterprise by quarrelling about money. The Treaty of Barcelona, which had arranged for the campaign against Perugia and the recovery of Florence, had contained no provision as to the division of expenditure between pope and emperor, but, although it was obvious that Clement, despite a steep rise in the Roman customs in April,[15] would be unable to finance any large-scale project, Orange also lacked adequate funds. In the end the pope's contribution to the campaign had to be made by Cardinal Pucci, who personally lent the money for the operations out of his own large fortune.

Thus it was that, even before the Florentines had spoken with the emperor at Genoa, the prince of Orange had left Rome with the immediate objective of recovering Perugia and Florence for the pope. The campaign against Perugia proved to be scarcely worthy of the name, for it was shown that neither the lawlessness of the Baglioni family nor the attempts of the Perugian commune to reassert its independence could affect the gradual process by which, since the time of Julius II, the papacy had been acquiring control over Perugia. The events of the preceding months had barely disguised the fact that the relative position of the papacy and Perugia was such that it could only be a matter of time before Baglioni power was permanently eroded. When the papacy was strong, as under Julius II, Leo X or Paul III, such erosion occurred. When it was weak, as during the period immediately following the sack of Rome, there was an apparent resurgence of the Baglioni. The pretensions of both the Baglioni and of the commune had been astutely weakened by successive popes for, by adapting and using the old institutions of government they were incorporating Perugia into the Church State, and these institutions of government gradually became inextricably tied to papal institutions, so that the commune and the papacy stood or fell together. Each military advantage of the papacy over the Baglioni had been followed by the imposition of fresh organs of government until, eventually, by papal intervention, Perugia was provided with a constitution opposed to the Baglioni tyranny and enjoying papal protection.

Consistently, the papacy set itself up as the better and the lawful government. The papal success is largely explained by the weakness of the Baglioni within Perugia, for the basis of their power was very slender. They commanded no popular support, and the family was divided within itself, a fact of some importance in Italy, where family loyalty and solidarity were often vital in securing power. Like all the tyrants of the Church State the

Baglioni were weakened by their own struggles with the exiles of rival families. In Perugia the situation was complicated by the fact that the city ruled a larger state which contained towns of mixed allegiance, never all loyal to the ruling faction in Perugia. It was as leaders of the Guelf faction that the Baglioni first came to power, having the traditional support of the Guelf towns of Spoleto and Camerino. Against them were ranged the Ghibelline Oddi, who commanded the support of such traditional Ghibelline strongholds in Umbria as Foligno and Assisi. Much of the Baglioni energy was directed towards the extermination of Oddi influence inside and outside Perugia, a process which, being by its nature disruptive of peace and order, was regarded with extreme disfavour by the papacy.

Orange gathered his troops in the flat country around Foligno and Spello: 3000 infantry, the remnants of Frundsberg's lansquenets, and 4000 irregular Italian infantry under Pierluigi, the son of Cardinal Farnese, Camillo Marzio, Sciarra Colonna and Giovan Battista Savelli, together with troops provided by the enemies of Malatesta Baglione, the exiled Braccio and Sforza Baglione. Clement contributed three cannon and other artillery from the battery of Castel Sant'Angelo. More troops were being brought from Apulia by del Guasto, and Orange was constantly being joined by Italian mercenaries anxious to profit from another imperial campaign, and hoping, no doubt, to participate ultimately in the sack of Florence.

Assisi was the first of the Umbrian towns to fall to the imperialists, captured after a fierce if short battle in which the defenders were aided by the protection offered by the shrine of St Francis. But Malatesta Baglione had reckoned on the loss of this particular town and had concentrated his defence on Spello, where he had placed his natural brother, Leo, in command.

At the end of August, wearied of waiting for del Guasto, who had still not arrived, Orange launched his attack on Spello, an attack in which the notoriously cruel but able Gian d'Urbina was mortally wounded while reconnoitring the walls. Malatesta had reckoned on Spello holding out for long enough to permit him to put Perugia in a state of military preparedness and to gather in the harvest, but, even as Orange brought up his cannon to bombard the town, 'Monsignor Leo, acting the part of a priest[16] rather than a soldier, and the captains of Malatesta taking no thought for the inhabitants of Spello, thinking more of saving their skins than of their honour', surrendered and fled from the town.[17]

This virtually ended the military resistance of the Perugian state. On 8 September the imperial army crossed the Tiber, joined with del Guasto, who had finally arrived, and pitched camp before Perugia. Four days later Malatesta Baglione was forced by the commune to come to an agreement with Orange. The Perugians, he was told, had no desire to be rebels of the Church or to bring down papal condemnation on themselves. They had already sent a separate embassy to the imperial camp.[18] It was arranged that Malatesta and his mercenaries, together with the 3000 Florentine troops in the city, should leave Perugia, although Malatesta was to remain in the service of Florence. Orange promised that he would not impede the departure of the Florentine troops and that no reprisals would be taken on the property of Malatesta or that of his adherents. Clement was in favour of a policy of reconciliation, and in consequence, with the minimum of trouble, Perugia returned to its previous relations with the Holy See. On 11 September Cardinal dal Monte took possession of the city in the pope's name.

The fall of Perugia meant that the imperial attack could be concentrated on Florence and, reassessing the situation, the Florentines decided that, given the pronounced disaffection of the subject-towns and the poverty of resources, their defence should be concentrated on the city of Florence. After the fall of Perugia, Malatesta Baglione fell back on Montevarchi, leaving no troops to guard the Florentine frontier-towns. Commissioners and representatives of Florence in outlying areas suddenly found themselves abandoned and without any financial resources with which to carry on government. They were driven to make the best bargain they could with whomsoever they could. Whenever possible, the Florentine subject-towns, mindful of the fate of Prato in 1512, and more recently of Rome, came to an independent agreement with Orange. The pope and the imperialists actively exploited the situation. Clement VII and Morone promoted rebellion wherever they could in Florentine territory, as did Orange and the exiled Baccio Valori. When cities rebelled against Florence Clement VII provided an alternative administration, and when the pope failed to do so the want was supplied by the imperialists, their administrators being drawn from the vast number of Florentine exiles in attendance on the imperial army.

Orange crossed the border into the Florentine state on Holy Cross Day, 14 September, and advanced immediately on Cortona, where a small Florentine garrison remained. Although the defending troops put up a brilliant and vigorous defence, their military resistance was not welcome to the citizens of Cortona. Certain of being abandoned by the Florentines, the civic leaders asked Orange for terms, ransomed their city and handed over the Florentine troops.[19] One by one all the frontier towns followed the example of Cortona; Castel Fiorentino, Pietrasanta, Peccioli, Palaia, Forcoli and Arezzo – the last one of the most important of the defectors. Traditionally an imperial town, opposed to Florentine dominion, and particularly to Florentine republican régimes, Arezzo had only come under Florentine control at the end of the fourteenth century and had revolted in 1408, 1431 and again in 1502. By 1527 the town had already been showing marked opposition to Florentine policies which had resulted in April in the sacking by the imperialists of several places within the Aretine *contado*. Close behind Bourbon on the march south came the league army, whose behaviour had no more to recommend it than that of the imperialists. Arezzo took the initiative into its own hands. On 22 April 1527 4000 of the 'Black Bands' were clamouring at the gates of Arezzo for admittance, 'and although they were strong armed men, yet so great was the fame of their evil behaviour and thieving' that Arezzo was reluctant to let them in. Indeed, the Aretines were glad when the arrival of imperial light cavalry gave them an excuse and allowed them to take up arms both against 'bad friends' and the enemy. For as long as the league army remained in the area, Arezzo was forced to supply it; 'Some areas they paid for the supplies, and some they sacked, and their behaviour was worse than that of the enemy.'

The attentions which Arezzo received so unwillingly from passing armies she owed partially to her position as an outpost in the Florentine defences. So important was Arezzo that, in 1529, Florence paid as much attention to the refortification of Arezzo as to that of Florence. Yet this also bred resentment; the operation was financed by Arezzo, 'to the serious inconvenience of the men of the *contado*', and was not even done efficiently. In September, as Orange advanced, it was discovered that there was neither artillery nor ammunition in the city.[20] The financial hardship which this refortification of Arezzo involved contrasted with the normally light load of taxation which subjection to Florence involved, for in a normal year the income to Florence from Arezzo was a mere 2800 ducats and, although this was a larger income than from any of the other subject-towns, it was still a minimal sum in the total Florentine budget.

Thus, for a combination of reasons, all related in some way to the war, by 1529 the disloyalty of Arezzo was so notorious that Florence, not content with garrisoning the city, demanded fifty hostages for good behaviour. Yet, at the critical period, Florence did nothing to ensure the continued loyalty of Arezzo. It was sacrificed for the preservation of Florence. Not only was the city denied military support, as Malatesta Baglione fell back on Florence with his troops, but even the Florentine civic authorities abandoned Arezzo to its own devices. In the evening of 18 September Iacopo Altoviti, the captain, and the commissary, Mariotto Segni, returned the keys of Arezzo to the citizens; and when, on the following day, after a demand from the imperialists for the surrender of the city, the Aretines asked Altoviti what they should do, he virtually renounced all Florentine interest in Arezzo.[21]

Florence thus lost her entire position in Arezzo where, through the old machinery of city government, it was decided to negotiate with Orange on the basis of a demand for self-government. Flags of the republic of Arezzo, which had been secretly manufactured in, and imported from, Siena, were flown once more, and the city embarked on a cautious period of experimentation in self-government. Florentine property in Arezzo was confiscated, new coins were cast and the arms of the emperor were set up throughout the city with the superscription, 'As you have liberated us from the hand of the enemy, we will serve you.'[22]

Beyond Arezzo, Orange advanced very slowly up the Arno valley, thus giving the Florentines time to defend themselves. Clement's great hope was that Florence would submit rather than fight, and he was determined to give the city the opportunity and time to negotiate. His hopes were destined to be shattered. The Florentines seem to have sensed that this would be their last struggle for liberty. In order to deny the imperialists any point of cover, they pulled down the villas and palaces which surrounded the city and which, two years previously, they had refused to sacrifice for the pope. Orchards and gardens around were also destroyed, and trees uprooted. The Florentines sang as they went about their work:

> *Alas, what grief,*
> *To ruin with our hands*
> *The tombs of our fathers,*
> *And Christian houses!*
>
> *Alas, what great sorrow*
> *To think that a pope,*
> *And her own citizen,*
> *Drives his mother country to such a fate!*
>
> *But, pope, you will never boast,*
> *Of holding Florence*
> *Or you will have her dying*
> *And give her holy unction.*[23]

Unfortunately, destruction proved to be an infectious disease and spread to the young men, feeding their hatred of the Medici and their aristocratic allies. It was but a short step from destroying the houses of friends close by the city to destroying the palaces of enemies, even if they were too far from the city-wall to be of military importance. The magnificent Medici palace at Coreggi was burned, and that at Castello was also threatened. Jacopo Salviati's costly villa at Montughi was razed to the ground, and further outrages would no doubt have followed if it had not been for the advance of the imperialists.

All this time negotiations had been going on between Florence and the imperialists, but there was little ground for discussion. The Florentine ruling party consistently chose to ignore the imperial interest in a Medici restoration and refused to negotiate on any basis other than that of the 'freedom of Florence'. They would rather, they declared, see their city in ashes than submit to the Medici.

By the end of September Orange was aware that he would have to face a protracted siege of Florence. He, therefore, lingered in the plain around Ripoli, waiting for the heavy siege-artillery and the batteries which were being brought from Siena and were delayed by torrential rain.[24] The final advance on Florence began on 10 October, and by the end of the week Orange was at the very gates where his Spaniards raised their famous cry, 'Get out your brocades, Florence. We come to measure them with pikestaffs.' The army was spread out in a semi-circle in the hills above the city. By the end of the month the imperial artillery-fire was trained upon the heights of San Miniato and the siege of Florence had begun.[25]

Since April, however, San Miniato had been transformed by Michelangelo, who had been appointed overseer of the Florentine fortifications, into a bulwark of such strength as to be impervious to the fire from Orange's guns. The city was, as yet, besieged on only one bank of the Arno and, 'although Giovanni da Sassatello, Ramazzotto and other heads of the Romagnol factions, all traditional friends and partisans of the Medici, were authorized by the pope to infest the Romagna and the province of the Mugello, and were continually riding almost to the gates of the city',[26] communications with the western Florentine state remained open, and food and military supplies continued to reach Florence in considerable quantities. Most important of all, communication was maintained with the great Florentine military leader Ferruccio, who was operating on behalf of Florence with considerable success, keeping open the vital road between Pisa and the capital.

Spectacular successes of Ferruccio, and the initial success of their defence measures filled the Florentines with fresh courage and optimism and encouraged the extreme republicans. They were convinced that France would not desert them in their hour of need and looked constantly beyond the Alps for aid. War-fever was deliberately drummed up in a traditionally pacific city. Hatred of the Medici was brought to such a pitch that the virtue and life of the young Catherine de' Medici, a mere child of ten, held hostage in a convent, were in constant danger. Popular preachers of the school of Savonarola daily exhorted the citizens of Florence to fresh efforts on behalf of liberty.

Yet already there were signs of weakness in Florence for those who could discern them. Had the Florentines wished to learn from the past, in the way that Machiavelli, the greatest of all Florentines, had tried to teach them, they could have discerned the traditional pattern of disaster which always produced political crisis in Florence; warfare, which always underlined any inherent weakness in government, recurring epidemic disease, and economic weakness resulting from an inflexible taxation system. It was not merely that the thoughts of the rest of Europe were turning towards peace and only Florence seemed bent on resisting the will of Charles V in Italy. Florence itself was really in no position to make war, as a moment's reflection would have indicated. The very constitution, so new and so vaunted, made decision-making difficult and militated against all speed, efficiency or secrecy. With the departure and seclusion of the great ruling aristocrats the government had fallen into the hands of idealistic but incompetent amateurs, without any adequate experience of administration. In consequence, no serious defence measures had been taken; the state of Florence was largely undefended and the fortifications of the capital were only the bare minimum, despite Michelangelo's efforts. In addition, within Florence the seeds of future discord were already sown. The causes of discontent which had provoked a spontaneous revolt against the Medici had not been miraculously removed. By the spring of 1529 the cloth industry had virtually collapsed and, when Genoa fell to the imperialists, it proved impossible thereafter to export to Lyons. As the transit of cloth through Venetian territory was forbidden, the only remaining outlets for Florentine exports were illegally through Mantua and the Brenner pass to Germany and through Ancona and Trieste to Flanders. Much Florentine capital was tied up in Lyons and could not be touched by the republic. There was a constant and living fear that the city would be sacked, and 'the people of Florence began to whisper that they were at war and that under the Medici they had lived in peace'.[27] Most ominous of all was the fact that the city was now so poor that the virtues of poverty had to be positively extolled by preachers and statesmen alike; poverty prevented discord, plots, lasciviousness, luxury and tyranny. It was the only means of preserving the republican spirit and true liberty: 'nothing is sweeter, in fact, that to sit in one's poor cottage and to recount to one's little family one's famous past deeds in the defence of, and for the honour of, one's fatherland'.[28]

CHAPTER XVIII

THE IMPERIAL CORONATION

Italy at this time was thought of as a land belonging to nobody, or as an island in the Pacific, and the legitimate rulers of Italy were thought to be any who could surprise it and subject it.

Sigismondo della Valle

WHILE still in Genoa, Charles V sent a request to Clement that the imperial coronation might be solemnized in the papal city of Bologna, and not, as was normal, in Rome. Acutely aware of Turkish pressure on the eastern borders of his far-flung empire, Charles V was anxious to travel to Germany with all speed, to be as close as possible to the trouble-spot. Reluctantly, unwilling as ever to come to a definite decision without due deliberation, Clement eventually acceded to the emperor's request, and preparations began for the pope's journey north.

The Peace of Cambrai was officially published in Rome on 19 September, and on 7 October Clement left the city, accompanied by Accolti, de Cessis, Cesarini and Ridolfi. They passed through Cività Castellana, Terni, Spoleto and Foligno to Sigillo where they were met by an imperial embassy. The events of the past five years had aged Clement considerably. Thin and shrunken, his complexion permanently sallow as a result of his liver complaint, the pope was almost blind in his right eye and found it more difficult than ever to act decisively. His mind was bent on church reform – indeed, the only way he could come to terms with the sack of Rome was to see it as an agent of reform; but although he spoke much on the subject he was too old to initiate change. His mind dwelt much on old quarrels. He was more bitter than ever against the duke of Ferrara, against the emperor and against the duke of Urbino, who, Clement had come to believe, had deliberately failed to succour the papacy in its hour of greatest need.[1] But it was typical of Clement that he should take no action on the score of these enmities, and that he should remain, as always, a man of moderation, continence and the greatest patience in all things.

This same patience and deliberation was now applied to the new

embassies from Charles V. The emperor had, at last, certain news
that the Ottomans were advancing on Vienna and was, conse-
quently, more than anxious, in the face of hardening attitudes at
Venice, that papal–imperial relations should not be jeopardized.
Accordingly, he declared his willingness to listen to the pope's
advice over Milan.

Passing through Cesana and Forlì, Clement made his solemn
entry into Bologna on 24 October 1529. The road to the great
civic church of San Petronio, a monument to Bolognese pride,
was hung with green garlands and the arms of the Medici. Passing
under triumphal arches and surrounded by his cardinals and the
civic officials, Clement was borne to San Petronio, where he
blessed the crowds which had gathered to greet him, before re-
tiring to the Palazzo Pubblico, on the north side of the square,
where splendid apartments had been prepared to receive him.

Here, on the following day, Clement was visited by Gaspare
Contarini, the Venetian ambassador, who, under instruction from
his Senate, had the unpleasant task of raising, yet again, the subject of Ravenna and Cervia, offering, on behalf of Venice, an
annual tribute for the two towns. Although it was obviously of
the greatest importance that Clement should work closely with
Venice over the question of Milan, the pope's bitterness on the
subject of Ravenna and Cervia had by no means evaporated.
Cardinal Cybo attacked Contarini in public on the subject, and
Clement reminded the Venetian that 'Venice took these cities at a
time when I was in league with her and was a prisoner in Castel
Sant'Angelo; and it was promised that they would be restored to
me as soon as I had escaped out of the hands of the enemy'.[2]
Contarini referred to the long years during which Ravenna and
Cervia had been held by Venice, 'whence it seems that our republic
is right to hold on to them, and not to let anyone take them away
from us, for they are like property which has been inherited from
our fathers and our ancestors'. Here he drew a tactless comparison
between Venice in relation to Ravenna and Cervia, and the
Medici in relation to Florence, but Clement refused to be diverted
from the main topic, and explained that, albeit the Venetians had
obtained Ravenna and Cervia from the Polenta family and had
held them for over a hundred years, the Polenta themselves had
taken the two cities from the Holy See. In despair Contarini was

heard to grumble 'that, if the affairs of states were to be resolved into their origins, today we would find that no one was the true possessor of anything',[3] a remark which could well have been made about most of the subsequent discussions at Bologna. In the meantime Clement concluded the audience very firmly by re-affirming that he was determined to recover the two cities what-ever might happen.

On the following day, Contarini had a second audience of the pope, but found no change in Clement's attitude; and subsequently the Venetian cardinals, Grimani and Pisani, assured the Venetian ambassador that Clement really was determined to have Ravenna and Cervia, and would have the backing of the emperor in his attempts to recover them.

Meanwhile this same emperor, Charles V, was approaching Bologna. Venice still clung to the hope that the Ottoman threat would have the effect of modifying the emperor's position but, even while he was travelling through the Church State, Charles heard of the complete failure of the Ottoman attack on Vienna. Thus Charles's position in Italy was considerably strengthened, although Mercurino Gattinara solemnly assured Contarini that Charles was anxious to make peace with the Venetian republic in order to 'bring peace to this poor, ruined Italy'.[4]

On 5 November the emperor made his state entrance into Bologna, a beautiful city which had been decked out in full Renaissance splendour in order to honour his arrival, with decora-tions far surpassing those which had been provided for the pope. The windows of every house were adorned with tapestries and garlands, and allegorical representations of the emperor's power abounded; at the gate of San Felice, through which Charles entered, was set up, on one side, a triumph of Neptune, sur-rounded by Tritons, sirens and sea-horses and, on the other, Bacchus, in the midst of satyrs, fauns and nymphs, with the in-scription 'Ave Caesar, Imperator invicte!' Many of the great figures of Europe rode with the emperor in procession through the streets of Bologna; the chief nobility of Spain, and among them, borne in the litter to which gout had long since confined him, the great and invincible da Leyva, who had for so long served Charles V honourably and well on the Italian battlefields. Church-men, too, rode with the emperor; Cardinal Campeggio, newly recalled from England, where he had been considering the vexed question of an annulment of the marriage between Henry VIII and the emperor's aunt Catherine of Aragon, and the young and handsome Cardinal Ippolito de' Medici, one of Clement's closest kinsmen. There rode the Admiral Andrea Doria, an old man now, like the pope, and there rode also the last heir of the old emperor of Constantinople, the boy-marquess of Montferrat, Boniface, whose presence in the procession had precluded that of Federico Gonzaga, who refused to give precedence to his cousin of Montferrat and kept away from the proceedings. In the midst of this glittering throng rode the young man on whom all eyes were fixed and whom on this occasion all eyes chose to find agreeable. Charles V, still only twenty-nine, but with the bearing of a king, blonde-haired, blue-eyed, dressed in cloth of gold and sitting on a white horse, was gracious and courteous to all who addressed him, and in particular to the ladies of Bologna, to whom he constantly raised his hat as they sat at their windows to watch him ride past.

In the main square of Bologna, on a wooden platform, covered with crimson cloth, which had been erected in front of San Petronio, the pope awaited the emperor, and it was here that the man ultimately responsible for the sack of Rome came, for the first time, face to face with his most famous victim. Two cardinals escorted the emperor to the pope, and at Clement's feet Charles knelt in humble submission. The pope turned pale, and the tears streamed down his face as he knelt to kiss Charles in forgiveness. Briefly, pope and emperor greeted each other in Spanish; 'Holy Father,' said Charles, 'I have come to kiss the feet of Your Holiness, an act which I have long wished to do, and am at length allowed to accomplish, and I pray God that this may be for the glory of His Service and that of Your Holiness.' To this Clement politely responded, 'We thank God, who has brought us to this day which we have so long desired to see, and hope that Your Majesty may be the means of gaining great things for the service of God and the good of Christendom.'[5] Having risen to his feet, Charles presented the pope with a gift of a purse containing 1000 gold ducats, then was conducted into San Petronio for the singing of a solemn *Te Deum*, while the pope withdrew to his own apartments.

For the next four months Bologna became a festival city, to which visitors from all over Europe flocked. Briefly, the humanistic circles, which had been destroyed by the sack of Rome, revived again. The great patronesses of learning were there; Isabella d'Este, who gave hospitality to the poets Antonio Broccardo and Molza and to Angelo Colucci; and Veronica Gambara, sister to the governor of Bologna, and a lady frequently honoured by visits from Charles V. At her house this winter gathered humanists and poets from all over Italy: Contarini, now the Venetian ambassador, but known and welcomed as much for his great learning; and Bembo, who arrived from Padua in December. In Clement's entourage were to be found the poet Trissino, Francesco Guicciardini, and the historian Paolo Giovio, all three distinguished men of letters, although Guicciardini would have preferred recognition as a politician and as the pope's lieutenant-general.

But Bologna was not given over entirely to festivities. Much solid business had yet to be completed, in order to prepare the way for the imperial coronation on which Charles V had long been bent. Within the municipal palace, Charles V had been lodged in apartments which adjoined those of the pope, and it was within these private apartments that the fate of Italy was being settled. Months of hard bargaining were involved, and Charles, a shrewd politician, did not make the mistake of underestimating the abilities of Clement VII. For each conference with the pope the emperor prepared carefully, noting down on slips of paper all the essential points in discussion.

Much remained to be settled at Bologna, not least the issue between the pope and Venice. Contarini had continued to warn the pope on behalf of the Venetian government that his stubbornness over Ravenna and Cervia, which was certainly delaying peace in Italy, might well prove disastrous. Although the Turks had withdrawn from Vienna, it was common knowledge that Naples and Sicily were considerably weakened and in no state to resist should the Turks invade from the sea. The pope remained unmoved. On the following day, the new datary, Girolamo Schio, informed Contarini that the pope was as firm as ever in his determination to have Ravenna and Cervia restored. Venice was at last forced to give in. On 10 November the Venetian government instructed Contarini to agree to restore the two cities on the conclusion of a peace, the pope promising that no reprisals would be taken on the inhabitants of Ravenna and Cervia for having supported Venice and that Venetian citizens should enjoy any property they still held in the two towns. Clement also had to agree to the right of the duke of Urbino to the possession of his estates. At the same time the Venetian government declared itself ready to evacuate Apulia, although it was not until 26 November that Venice would agree to entering a defensive Italian League principally directed against the Ottomans.[6]

The major outstanding problem in Italian politics was now Francesco Sforza, who still enjoyed the total, unflagging support of Venice, of Clement VII and, surprisingly, of his own Milanese subjects. Negotiations between the pope and the emperor on the subject of Milan had opened in September when the imperial envoys suggested that the duchy be given to Alessandro de' Medici, who, it was presumed, with the backing of Florence, would be powerful enough to resist any eventual French invasion of northern Italy. But not even to aggrandize his family would Clement abandon Sforza, although powerful forces were still working against him. Antonio da Leyva who, apparently on aesthetic grounds, was opposed to the restoration of the effeminate Sforza to Milan, and the Ghibelline faction of the Milanese aristocracy canvassed the candidature of Francesco's brother, Massimiliano. Since the latter was still a prisoner in France and likely to remain one until the end of his days, he would be no impediment to effective power remaining in imperial hands. Others worked towards securing Milan for Federico Gonzaga, and in order to further his own claims Federico hastened towards Bologna. He reached the city on 20 November, but there discovered that Francesco Sforza had already been given a safe-conduct by the emperor to come to Bologna. Rightly recognizing this as an indication that Charles V had relented in his attitude to the errant duke, Federico left Bologna as precipitately as he had arrived. On 23 November Sforza had his first interview with Charles.[7]

Venice was determined that there would be no peace in Italy unless Sforza was restored to Milan, but when, on 14 December, Contarini spoke to Charles on the subject he found that the emperor was not in the most conciliatory of moods. While remarking that nothing could be further from his desire than the 'monarchy of Italy', he managed to suggest that the same could not be said of Venice. He still seemed set against the restoration of Sforza and again referred to the possibility that Alessandro de' Medici might be given Milan. But Contarini remained firm and assured the emperor that any attempt to replace Sforza in the duchy would lead to a renewal of the Italian conflict.[8]

The stubbornness of Venice and the conviction of the pope eventually overcame all resistance; Charles was forced to give way. Agreement was finally reached, as so often in Italian quarrels, on a financial basis; Sforza was to pay 800,000 ducats to the emperor for the investiture of Milan and, as a security for this sum, was to surrender the castles of Como and Milan. On 23 December 1529 Charles signed his agreement with Venice and with Sforza, and the three powers entered into a mutual defence pact. On Christmas Eve a general peace was signed by Charles, Venice, Sforza, the pope, the Archduke Ferdinand's representative, Mantua, Savoy, Montferrat, Urbino, Siena and Lucca. 'Now, indeed', declared Cardinal Pucci, 'we can sing the *Gloria* with the angels, since peace and goodwill are restored to men.'[9]

The emperor's decision to restore Francesco Sforza led to a temporary and uncharacteristic wave of pro-imperialism in Milan where the news was greeted with the greatest possible public rejoicing: 'Pray God', wrote the city's chronicler, 'that in his year of 1530 which is to come God will free us from all our tribulations.'[10] Popular the restoration of Sforza might be throughout Italy, but in letters to his brother and to Margaret of Austria Charles subsequently recorded that it had been the last thing he desired and that only the implacable hostility of Venice to any other solution had persuaded him to it. In June, Giovanni Maria Fregosi had spoken feelingly of Venice's contribution in preserving such Italian independence as was left: 'You have sustained one of the harshest wars in our memory, with immortal praise and have been upholder of the liberty of the whole of Italy.'[11] But this was to be the last decisive political victory of Venice. Exhausted by the economic drain of the war between 1525 and 1529, estimated to have cost between four and five million ducats, which she had embarked on before recovering from the crisis of the war years between 1509 and 1516, Venice was unable to prevent Charles from retaining the duchy of Milan when Sforza died six years later.[12] The republic no longer had the economic resilience to support virtually constant expenditure on defence. The building of complicated new fortresses and the cost of their maintenance – the normal garrison of Bergamo, for instance, was 6000 infantry – the casting of new artillery, the payment of heavy tribute to Constantinople after 1517, the cost of the grain shortage after 1525, had absorbed the entire wealth of the state for ten years. Venice had found it increasingly difficult to fulfil her military engagements and had had to cast further and further afield when raising new troops. From 1508 onwards the Venetian republic was one of the states most exposed to troop movements, and under these conditions the normal flow of merchandise arriving from Alessandria, Syria, Flanders and England through Venetian territories could not be maintained. A depression in the spice-trade coincided with these events and lasted until at least 1531. For several years Venice had been forced to resort to very heavy extraordinary taxation. Within Italy, as the influence of the emperor increased, so that of Venice declined; this decline had been perceptible immediately after the sack of Rome when she had been unable to influence the duke of Ferrara against attacking Modena.

As far as Este was concerned, if there were to be any lasting peace in Italy he would have to be included in the peace talks, but Clement was still most bitter in his attitude to the duke. To the ambassadors of Ferrara he declared expressly that under no circumstances would he allow Alfonso d'Este, whom he held to be personally responsible for the sack of Rome, to take part in the coronation of the emperor.

Already visitors and ambassadors from all over Europe were gathering at Bologna to witness this great event; envoys from only one other state in Italy were needed to complete the emperor's triumph, those of Florence, still openly defiant of pope and emperor. Clement had hoped to include the Florentines in the general peace talks and, as early as December 1529, asked Malatesta Baglione to act as intermediary between himself and Florence. The Florentines reacted with characteristic optimism and, on 6 January, elected ambassadors who hastened to Bologna, accompanied by several young Florentines who, oblivious of the state of war extant between their state and Charles V, were bent on observing the imperial coronation. Among their number was Benedetto Varchi, the historian.

Extraordinarily enough, the Florentines were still convinced that the emperor would favour their cause and restore the liberty of Florence, if only they could approach him in the right way. But even before they entered Bologna their hopes were dashed. Believing themselves to be ambassadors of a sovereign state, the Florentine representatives anticipated an honourable reception. They suffered, instead, a speedy disillusionment, for at the gate of Bologna they were stopped by the police, were examined, interrogated and had their luggage ransacked. Once inside Bologna they were cold-shouldered by everybody and rapidly became the laughing-stock of the entire city. They were unable to detect any change in the pope's attitude to rebellious Florence, and the emperor received them frigidly, curtly ordering them to restore the Medici to their rights. The government of Florence had thoughtfully provided its ambassadors with letters of credence to four of the cardinals, but neither they nor the Florentine cardinals, Medici, Ridolfi, Salviati and Gaddi, could offer any comfort save that the pope, 'was well disposed towards his own city'.[13] Distressed by their reception and bitterly disappointed, the Florentines did not even bother to wait for the imperial coronation but left Bologna on 7 February to report back to Florence that their mission had been not only a failure but a farce.

By the end of the month all the preparations for the double coronation, an honour traditionally accorded to the emperors, were complete. The iron crown of Italy had been sent from Monza, on the instructions of Francesco Sforza, and on 22 February Charles V received it from Clement VII in the first part of the double ceremony. On this occasion the emperor was anointed by, and received communion from, Cardinal Enkevoirt, who still wore his beard long in mourning for the fall and sack of Rome.

The feast of St Matthias, 24 February, being the emperor's birthday and the anniversary of the battle of Pavia, was the day chosen for the imperial coronation itself. To the great delight of the Bolognese the ceremony was as impressive as if it had taken place at Rome, the organization having been master-minded by Antonio da Leyva. Save for an accident to the wooden bridge connecting San Petronio with the Palazzo Pubblico, and a dispute about precedence between the ambassadors of Genoa and Siena, scarcely an incident marred the proceedings, which were conducted with all the splendour of the medieval ceremonies of coronation. One may perhaps be forgiven for wondering what ran through Clement's mind as he placed the ancient imperial crown on Charles's head and repeated the traditional words, 'Receive this symbol of glory and the diadem of the empire, even this imperial crown, in the name of the Father, and of the Son, and of the Holy Ghost, that thou, despising the ancient enemy and guiltless of all iniquity, mayst live in clemency and godliness, and so one day receive from our Lord Jesus Christ the crown of His eternal kingdom.' Humbly the emperor received communion at the hands of Clement, humbly he kissed the pope's forehead and together the two heads of Christendom left the church to ride, with all the panoply of their rank and under the same golden canopy, through the streets of Bologna. Above the procession fluttered the banners of the crusade, the Church and the pope, followed by those of the empire, of the city of Rome, Germany, Spain, the New World, Naples and Bologna. Treasurers flung gold and silver coins to the expectant crowds who thronged the route of the procession until it reached the square in front of the most famous shrine in Bologna, the last resting-place of Saint Dominic, a saint whose character appears to have borne at least more than a slight resemblance to that of Clement VII. It was within the peaceful walls of Saint Dominic's own church and convent that Clement and Charles prayed together at last side by side.[14] Then leaving the pope to his own thoughts, prayers and meditations, Charles, still full of vigour and energy, conferred knighthood on about a hundred persons, before returning to his apartments to prepare for the great coronation banquet which brought the celebrations to an end.

It appeared that Charles V had made good the imperial pretensions which had for so long dominated Italian politics, culture and thought. But tensions remained; problems were still unsolved; Florence was still obstinate, and Ferrara and the papacy unreconciled. On Ferrara, at least, Clement was at last forced to give way, and at the request of the emperor Alfonso d'Este came to Bologna under a safe-conduct. The success of Charles in bringing about agreement, which was finally reached on 21 March 1530, contrasts with the inability of the Italian powers to solve the problem previously. Matters in dispute between Este and the pope were to be referred to the emperor, to whom Este agreed to surrender Modena and its *contado*. Charles was to adjudicate on the matter of the ownership of Modena, Reggio and Rubiera within the following six months, and if, after this lapse of time, he had not done so, the towns were to revert to Este.[15]

As for Florence, well might Clement claim that he wished the city had never existed. Month after month passed; May, June and July had gone, and still the city held out against pope and emperor. It was only in August that events began to move against Florence, after the failure of Francesco Ferruccio, who had emerged as a new Florentine hero, in his vain attempt to raise the siege. On 3 August a decisive battle was fought at Gavinana, in the hills above Pistoia, in which both Ferruccio and Orange met their death. It was this disaster that convinced Malatesta Baglione that the further resistance of Florence was useless, and that, therefore, he had better rapidly set about mending his own relations with pope and emperor in order to preserve his position in Perugia.[16] All subsequent Florentine historians were to accuse Malatesta of treachery, and even the contemporary verdict of the doge of Venice was adverse; 'He has sold that city and the blood of those poor citizens ounce by ounce, and has assumed the cap of the greatest traitor in the world.'[17] In a sense Malatesta was a traitor, but he certainly saved the city from eventual sack. In the early days of August Baglione promised the imperialists that, if the Medici were not restored to Florence, he and his men would leave the city. This promise, at least, was kept; it was to the imperialists and to the pope that Baglione maintained faith and not to the Florentine republic.

In the end, the sheer weight of the emperor's military superiority, Malatesta's treachery and the loss of the rest of the Florentine state forced Florence to come to terms, but, even so, the imperialists could only have their way by agreeing to the fiction that 'liberty be preserved'. The Medici were to be allowed to return as private citizens; their property was to be restored and their supporters released from prison. Many naïvely believed this agreement would be observed, but, in fact, it was only to be a matter of time before there was a full Medici restoration. In this capitulation the Florentines had acknowledged the right of the emperor to stabilize their constitution and thus sealed their own fate. Ominously enough, from the beginning Baccio Valori, the Medici representative in Florence, began to disregard even the appearance of preserving republicanism, reproducing the worst excesses of the period of direct rule by Duke Lorenzo de' Medici. A restoration of the old Medici-dominated government was effected by simple and tried Florentine methods; a *coup d'état* effected by armed force. But worse was to follow. Charles V's method of stabilizing the Florentine constitution was to create Alessandro de' Medici duke of Florence, and this was accepted by the bulk of the Florentine aristocracy.

Although autocratic Medici rule continued to be unpopular with them, the events of the previous three years had ensured the success of the Medici principality, for these events convinced the Florentine aristocrats that, while they did not love the Medici, they could not exist without them. In 1527 the aristocrats had connived at the expulsion of the Medici; and they had accepted the rule of Capponi, who was, ultimately, one of their own. But the fall of Capponi and the emergence of the new régime had brought personal persecution and public disaster. The aristocrats had been excluded from office and had seen the government mismanaged in consequence. The country, which must be at peace if their businesses, on which its prosperity was based, were to flourish, had been plunged into an expensive war. The Florentine state had been lost, the Florentine treasury had been bankrupted. Henceforward the aristocrats would, on the whole, support the Medici régime, even accepting, almost without question, the suppression of their ancient liberties by the emperor and the absorption of Florence into a Tuscan principality.[18]

CHAPTER XIX

THE IMPERIAL VICTORY

The emperor's greatness is our slavery.
Francesco Guicciardini

IT IS impossible to ignore the sack of Rome. That in 1527 the city of the popes was subjected to one of the worst sacks in recorded military history at the hands of the army of Charles V is a fact which sooner or later faces the general historian of the sixteenth century. Not only was it 'one of the most frightful and dramatic events of the century',[1] of a century which was not lacking in frightful and dramatic events, but the effects of the sack were to be felt throughout Europe for years. It was to affect decisively the course of the Reformation in England; it created a mood of distinct unease in Spain; and it contributed greatly to the imposition of a Spanish hegemony in Italy and Europe and, in consequence, to the failure of the Italian reformation.

Of course, one could argue that the sack of Rome made little difference ultimately, that the struggle between Hapsburg and Valois in Italy was already over, leaving the advantage with the former, and that, with the removal of French influence from Italy, the Italian powers could no longer resist an imperial, or, as it turned out, a Spanish hegemony. But, although there is some truth in this argument, it is one that can only be maintained if attention is concentrated exclusively on the struggle between Charles V and Francis I in a general European context. Certainly Italy no longer maintained the position and importance in European affairs which had been hers in the fifteenth century, but if Italy was in decline after the mid-sixteenth century, and even this recent scholarship has begun to question, that decline was by no means inevitable. Italy seems less important in European affairs because, after 1530, it was difficult for any Italian state to pursue a policy independent of that of Spain. Yet domination by Spain was hard-won, on the Spanish side, along a path that has been shown in this work as *not* following an inevitable logic of events; the battle of Pavia, the discovery of Morone's conspiracy, the sack of

Rome, the defection of Doria, the break-up of the Italian League, the Peace of Cambrai, the siege of Florence and the imperial coronation were all, in a sense, from an Italian point of view, avoidable disasters. And, in this sequence of events, the sack of Rome is of paramount importance because of the effect which it had on Italian morale.

Contemporaries, unlike later writers, did not make the mistake of underestimating the effect of the sack of Rome. In writing, in painting, in the minor arts, they hurried to express their horror at the disaster that had befallen them as common children of one city. Even in the narrow world of maiolica painting this great event was allowed to obtrude; Francesco Xanto of Urbino produced two companion pieces which were in fact commentaries on the sack of Rome and the pope's captivity.[2] No subsequent political event made such a deep impression as did the sack of Rome. The blow which the papacy had suffered was so severe that its effects were still being felt a hundred years later. Throughout the Church State and in Rome itself the sack led to a recrudescence of banditry and violence, undoing the work of the previous four pontificates. The economic development of Rome was disastrously interrupted; the whole physical aspect of the city changed and went on changing as a new Rome grew up to replace all that had been lost in the sack. New buildings were erected, old ravages and wounds were made good, and a new defence system remedied the defects of the old. The population of the city changed. Many died in the sack or in its aftermath, many left the city and never returned. The artistic and literary circles, so characteristic of the High Renaissance, were completely destroyed. For Rome, at least, the sack was of the gravest consequence, a scar on her history which was long recalled in the popular and literary tradition of the city.

What reaction Charles V anticipated when he agreed to an attack on Rome is not clear, but what is certain is that the sack of the city produced feelings of hostility towards the emperor in the most unexpected quarters. Everywhere the news was greeted with shock and horror; at Urbino men stood in the streets and wept as they listened to accounts of what had happened at Rome.[3] Despite the subsequent adulation of Charles V in Italy, largely resulting from fear, the attempts to maintain the fiction that the emperor had been in no way responsible for the sack, and a glossing-over of its worst aspects, public opinion throughout Europe was appalled. Few found that they could congratulate Charles on this victory, and those who did tempered their enthusiasm for the victory with criticisms of the way in which it had been brought about; 'The imperial generals', wrote Salazar to Gattinara, 'have made the Emperor absolute master of Italy as we all wished him to be, yet the thing might have been accomplished without so much cruelty and shedding of blood . . . there will be no business done at Rome for a long time and the city itself is so destroyed and ruined that, until 200 years hence, it will not be Rome again.'[4]

For Francis I the sack of Rome presented a golden opportunity for anti-imperial propaganda which the French king was not slow to seize. Brushing aside Charles V's excuses he maintained that it was public knowledge that the emperor had ordered the attack on Rome, and criticized Charles for his praise of Bourbon. 'Besides,' he said, 'it was easy to know who were those who wished for the peace and quietness of Christendom and those who did not. As far as he himself was concerned he aimed not at universal monarchy, knowing very well that it did not belong to him; he only wanted to live in peace within his own kingdom.'[5]

In Spain, where the emperor received the news of the sack at Valladolid while celebrating the birth of his son, Prince Philip, at the beginning of June, it was as unpopular as anywhere. Particularly among the ecclesiastics of Spain, there had always been a large body of influential opinion opposed to a war against the pope. Now the opposition, led by the archbishop of Toledo and the duke of Alva, became embarrassingly outspoken. They were particularly incensed by Bourbon's failure to observe Lannoy's truce, and this was to prove the biggest stumbling-block to the emperor's subsequent attempts at self-justification. It is clear that the government remained sensitive on the subject of the sack of Rome, judging by the affair of Eugenio Torralba, who was arrested by the Inquisition of Cuenca in 1528 on charges of witchcraft. Torralba had been a medical student at Rome in the early years of the sixteenth century and there he had first adopted his own peculiar spirit, Zequiel, who, he claimed, had the ability to transport him through the air at will. In 1527 Torralba betrayed himself, for Zequiel informed him that Rome was about to be sacked by the imperial troops and he asked the spirit to carry him there to witness the horrifying scene. He left Valladolid at eleven o'clock on the night of 5 May and was back by three o'clock the following afternoon to tell his friends what he had witnessed. The fact that the authorities took Torralba seriously and arrested him clearly indicates that the government of Spain was disturbed by any loose talk associated with the sack of Rome.[6]

Close upon the first news of the sack came adverse criticism from Italy, particularly from the emperor's own advisers. Typical of these was Salazar, who told Gattinara that, although a great victory had been achieved, it was not without a 'shade of infamy with which future generations are likely to brand Spain'. The only way in which the bad impression created by the imperial army might be obliterated was by ensuring that these events would now be followed by a reform of the Church.[7] Gattinara's own ideas on the sack of Rome were first written down on 7 June. He saw that public opinion would blame the emperor most severely. He advised Charles to justify himself publicly, but not to repeat the mistakes made after Pavia, and forgo any of the advantages which the capture of Rome and the imprisonment of the pope might bring to the imperial cause. He suggested that the humanist and Erasmian, Valdés, should draft the emperor's public justification and in it draw the moral that henceforth wars in Christendom must be stopped, a general council must be called and the Church reformed.[8]

Church reform was in the minds of many, not least in that of Quiñones, who arrived from Rome towards the end of July and soundly castigated Charles, saying boldly 'that unless his Majesty did his duty by the pope he could no longer be styled "Emperor" but "Luther's Captain", as the Lutherans, in his name, and under his flag, perpetrated all their atrocities'.[9] But Quiñones was perhaps unnaturally irritated with Charles, since his journey from Rome and the atrocities he had viewed there had included an unplanned detour. He had been captured by Moorish corsairs who, in order to extract a substantial ransom, subjected him to the torture he had managed to escape at Rome.

Charles, as advised by Gattinara, was inclined to justify himself on religious grounds and to point to the sack of Rome as a divine judgement on the pope for failing to reform the Church.[10] The sack of Rome he declared to be no doing of his but rather of his soldiers, who had been exasperated by Clement's failure to fulfil his promises. There were many who were prepared to share the emperor's view. Lope de Soria declared the sack to be a punitive visitation from God to demonstrate to the world at large the iniquities of those who obstructed the emperor's messianic purposes in Europe, and wondered 'whether the Italians are aware that all those calamities and troubles have no other source than their own sins and divisions'.[11] Soria concluded that

> the emperor ought now to try to make his peace with the pope and with the rest of the Christian princes, who, perceiving their inability to carry out their wicked purposes, and how favourable Fortune shows itself to the imperial arms, will certainly not refuse his terms. Should the emperor think that the Church of God is not what it ought to be, and that the pope's temporal power emboldens him to promote rebellion and incite the Christian princes to make war on each other . . . it will not be a sin, but, on the contrary, a meritorious action to reform the Church in such a manner that the pope's authority may be confined exclusively to his own spiritual duties.

The official imperial viewpoint was presented by Valdés in the *Dialogue of Mercury and Charon*[12] and in the *Dialogue of Lactantio and the Archdeacon*.[13] These remarkable documents reflect imperial policy and the hope for church reform. They excuse the sack on somewhat contradictory grounds claiming that, although it had not been ordered by the emperor, it had been made inevitable by the intrigues of Clement VII and of Francis I, and that it was a manifestation of God's will, designed to punish evil churchmen for religious abuses. Although Valdés is here expressing official opinion, he was not the only Spanish humanist to be elated by the sack of Rome. For many, the tangible benefits to be gained from the sack were so great that they overrode its more horrifying aspects. To Erasmus, who was appalled by the events at Rome since he believed they would only lead to worse conflict between Christian peoples, Vives wrote on 13 June that, on the contrary, this would be the prelude to the long-awaited reform of the Church.[14]

On the other hand, among the Italians, many shared a fatalistic view of events, particularly in retrospect. They spoke of 'the time when God, by his just judgement, wanted to punish the people of Rome for their sins'.[15] This was a view of events most vigorously contested by Castiglione, hitherto one of the emperor's consistent supporters, a man who had invariably regarded Charles V's actions in the most favourable light. Publicly replying to Valdés' famous *Dialogues* and to that humanist's subsequent justificatory letters, Castiglione argued that the sack of Rome owed nothing to divine intervention, 'And certainly the "permission of God" in this case has been nothing more than in not prohibiting it and allowing this army to exercise its free will.'[16] Valdés, Castiglione argued, would have done better to argue that God permitted the sack of Rome in order that Clement and the cardinals might have a greater reward in heaven, and Valdés's suggestion that the sack was a punishment because the pope had sold church property and cardinals' hats must surely be ironic, given that the money thus raised had been used to pay the imperial army.[17]

Although the Sienese, who had suffered nothing by the sack of Rome, obstinately continued to regard the emperor as the saviour of Italy,[18] in general the sack of Rome brought about one great change in public opinion, an increase in the popularity of the French, even among those who had previously held Francis I in derision. The outrages of the imperial army, 'enemies to God and to his Church',[19] finally killed in all save the most credulous the belief in Charles V and the Spaniards as vindicators of Italian liberty against French oppression. This change in public opinion was carefully fostered by Francis I, who inevitably took the opportunity to emphasize his own virtues at the expense of the emperor. There were many Italians now who would believe Francis; Alberini, for instance, spoke in glowing terms of the French king and swore never to forgive Charles or his army.[20] France and Venice were praised and were supplicated as potential deliverers of the pope, of Rome and of Italy.[21] Some took the opportunity to advocate a united Italy or a revival of the glories of Italy's Roman past, using the sack of Rome to reinforce all the old arguments.[22]

Alberini's views on the sack were bitter, understandably so, for he had suffered considerably by it. What outraged him most, how-

ever, were not his own difficulties but that it was against *Rome* that
the imperial army had been unleashed, 'the common home of all,
which does not shrink from receiving in her bosom and lovingly
embracing those who had taken her captive, robbed, burned and
destroyed her'.[23] An intense love of his city where even the plants,
the trees and the animals had been destroyed made every Roman
suffer doubly, once for himself and once for Rome,[24] and instilled
into eye-witness accounts a bitterness it was impossible to hide.[25]
But the suffering of the individual alone would have been sufficient
to bear. The most neutral, indifferent or even hostile observer in
Rome could still be frankly appalled; Francesco Gonzaga, for
instance, spoke only of the intense compassion to which he had
been moved by the fate of the city – 'it seems to me that the whole
world has been turned topsy-turvy'.[26]

Immediately, people observing the destruction of Rome began
to ask how such a thing had come about. It was easy to survey the
whole sequence of events which led up to the sack of Rome, easy
to point to single errors and mistakes – the failure to prosecute the
attack on Milan and the death of Giovanni de' Medici were two
favourites. For the Venetians it was very simple, the blame must
lie with Clement VII, who had been so credulous in his dealings
with the emperor and the viceroy Lannoy; 'His Holiness has
always believed the viceroy, and put as much faith in him as if he
had been a god, and . . . this has been the ruin of our whole enterprise and of Rome.'[27] But this was only a short-term view. It was
explored and was rejected because it was believed that so great a
tragedy ought to have great causes, and as time passed the sack of
Rome was universally moralized over. Among the most common
of interpretations was that which regarded the sack as a punishment by God, although it was difficult to explain why a pope so
notably virtuous as Clement should have been singled out for so
drastic a punishment, when more conspicuous sinners such as
Alexander VI, Julius II and Leo X had got away scot-free. Some
commentators attempted to get round this particular stumbling-
block by regarding the sack as a punishment for the corruption of
the papal court or of Rome, in which the pope, albeit innocent,
had been caught up.[28] Even Aretino was shaken by the disaster to
which he subsequently referred with some frequency and which he
tended to regard as a deserved punishment, justifying all that he

had ever written about Rome. Although he wrote to the emperor urging him to release the pope and to spare Rome, he also wrote sharply to Clement that he 'who falls, as Your Holiness has done, ought to turn to Jesus in prayer, and not to fate with complaints. It was necessary that the vicar of Christ, by suffering the misery of events, should cancel the debts of the failings of others, nor would the justice by which heaven corrects error be revealed to all the world, without the witness of your prison.'[29]

Eustachio Celebrino, author of the poem *La Presa e Lamento di Roma*,[30] attributed the sack to the internal divisions of Rome, between Orsini and Colonna, and between Guelph and Ghibelline, which had betrayed the traditions of classical Rome;

> '*Oh! my people, you are very wrong*
> *To make war among yourselves like dogs or wolves.*'[31]

Others concentrated on the picture of Rome reduced from the summits of prosperity to the depths of human misery, regarding it as an excellent object lesson in the mutability of fortune, 'and of the fragility of human affairs'.[32] This was the standpoint adopted by Guicciardini,[33] who pointed out how peculiarly vulnerable to Fortune's caprices men were in war. Choosing to place the sack in its proper context, he reviewed all the events which had led up to such 'infinite and universal calamities',[34] and concluded that the disastrous outcome did not prove that the pope was wrong to enter the war in the first place. On the contrary, Guicciardini was convinced that all the dictates of reason had demanded that the pope should attempt to check Charles V. For both Guicciardini and Vettori the years 1525–30 were of the greatest importance, and, in particular, the traumatic experience of the sack of Rome which represented the triumph of *Fortuna* over Reason. The experiences of these years had revealed to the Florentines the limitations of human reason, of human planning and of human power, and had demonstrated how great must be the uncertainty in the world of politics. It was clear that the Italians could not, after all, control their own destiny, for what had happened in Italy was largely the result of what had happened elsewhere in Europe. It was for this reason that Vettori and Guicciardini began to investigate the power of *Fortuna* in history, with the result that 'The strongest, most permanent impression which [Guicciardini's] *History of Italy* imparts . . . is that of the helplessness and impotence of man in the face of fate.'[35]

Inevitably, comparisons were drawn with the previous sack of the city by the Goths, the general consensus of opinion being that the barbarians had behaved rather better than the armies of Charles V.[36] Equally inevitable were the comparisons made with the sacks of Carthage, Jerusalem, Constantinople, Rhodes or such sacks as Italy had witnessed in recent years. It was generally agreed that the sack was worse than that of Genoa[37] or even of Prato. Later on Brantôme compared the sack of Rome and the sack of Antwerp and decided that that of Rome was worse.[38]

In the end the Italians came to terms with the sack of Rome by maintaining the fiction, so convincingly put forward by Charles V, that he had nothing to do with it. All could then be blamed on the emperor's evil servants, on Bourbon, or on Bourbon's mutinous army which was held to have forced the march on Rome onto the unwilling imperial commanders. Thus, the decimation of the imperial armies in Naples by the plague was considered a divine punishment for the sack, and thus Bourbon, despite the official imperial view of his quasi-sanctity,[39] came to personify, in Italian terms, all that was bad, as did Moncada, Lannoy, and to some extent Colonna, who were all held to have acted without the emperor's previous knowledge. Giovio describes the popular rumour that Sessa had been poisoned by Moncada and the Colonna because he refused to sanction an attack on the pope and Rome.[40] Even Clement, in his own mind, seems to have shifted responsibility from the emperor to Bourbon and the duke of Ferrara,[41] whilst some, particularly the Florentines, held that Clement himself must bear the entire responsibility.[42] Alberini even managed to blame Adrian VI, 'a barbarian, from the vile nation of Flanders, and instructor and teacher of Charles V, who, even if he deserved praise for any other reason, for this alone deserves eternal condemnation, that he had such a disciple'.[43] Yet another favoured means of excusing the emperor, among the Italians, was to argue that the sack of Rome had increased European unity against the Turk. The sack of Rome had shown what quarrelling within the Italian community could lead to. It was an object lesson to all Europe, a lesson which Erasmus had been trying to teach for many years. And the emperor, it was argued, had learned that lesson. The monument to the imperial coronation in Bologna emphasized the fact that, after his coronation, Charles went off to Germany to fight against the Ottoman empire.

One thing seemed clear to all Italian observers; the sack of Rome and the subsequent disasters had left the emperor supreme in Italy; 'The emperor's greatness is our slavery,'[44] wrote Guicciardini. It appeared that Charles had made good the imperial pretensions which had, for so long, influenced Italian politics, culture and thought. Charles V's domination of Italy was complete; the monument to the coronation was paid for by the anti-imperial Cardinal Cybo. Although Clement and his successors were, at intervals, to attempt an independent policy, the papacy was now the emperor's client; in 1535 the Florentine exiles, anxious to rid their city of Alessandro de' Medici, realized that this could only be done through the emperor, and placed themselves entirely in his hands. The final agreement imposed on Alessandro de' Medici and the exiles gave the emperor considerable powers of intervention in Florence – judgements in disputes over property of the exiles were to be made by the imperial ambassador, while Alessandro was only permitted to take action against them with imperial approval, and promised not to alter the constitution of Florence without the emperor's consent.

It was soon clear that it was not only the political world that would be controlled by the emperor. The victory of Charles V had an immediate effect on the intellectual life of Italy. According to Venetian sources, as early as April 1528 a commission of cardinals, appointed to look into the annulment of the marriage between Henry VIII and Catherine of Aragon decided against the king, not on grounds of canon law, but 'so as not to displease the emperor'.[45] But canon law had often been twisted to meet the needs and whims of princes; the novelty in 1528 is that this decision was reached in a period of church reform. That it was to be only a Catholic reform movement, with all the consequences this was to have for Europe, can largely be explained by the predominance of imperial Spain in Italy and by the emperor's victory over the pope. Henceforward the Italian princes were too tied to imperial policy to permit offensive unorthodoxy in their states. From the beginning, the Italian reformers had seen this connexion, which explains their very considerable interest in politics. They knew that the continued survival of their ideas depended on the 'liberty of Italy'. In the sense that it did end the reform movement, which had grown alongside and out of the Renaissance, the sack of Rome was indeed 'the death-blow of Renaissance Italy'.[46] And even more was it the death-blow of Renaissance Rome. Though the gracious area of the Borghi now became a slum, new palaces did rise elsewhere from the ruins of Rome. But the city had changed – its intellectual life was more sombre, the Counter Reformation was gaining ground. Certainly Rome was no longer the home of art, of beauty and of free speculation. And, in some cases, even the spiritual life of Rome had suffered; the Theatines, for instance, had abandoned Rome, after escaping from the sack, and had moved to Venice, which to many Italians now seemed the only home of liberty, both political and intellectual.

Powerful as he was, Charles V was the last emperor to be crowned in Italy. Although it had been an international army which had sacked Rome, and although the Italians customarily thought of Charles as emperor and not as king of Spain, it was under Spanish domination that Italy had fallen. Just as Naples, Sicily and Sardinia had been for so long under Spanish influence and, latterly, direct control, so now would be all Italy. When Charles V abdicated, his imperial rights in Italy passed to Philip II and to Spain, by the creation of a perpetual imperial vicariate. In his own person, therefore, Charles had been able to effect a significant change in the course of Italian history. The Peace of Câteau-Cambrésis of 1559 confirmed Philip's authority in Italy, and France surrendered all her rights in Milan and Naples. The period of imperial interference in Italy had ended, the long period of Spanish control was just beginning. This, in itself, permanently solved the problem of Venice from the Spanish point of view, for Venice was, traditionally, the enemy of the Hapsburgs in Austria and not of Spain. It had been imperial preponderance in Italy that she had feared, not Spanish, and against Austria that she hoped to use the Ottomans. Now Venice, like every other Italian power, had to reorientate her foreign policy. When Charles V abdicated he automatically divided the Italian powers and made the creation of another league like the League of Cognac unlikely.

What had united Italy had been the nature and extent of the rule of Charles V. When that personal union ended, Italy was divided, the south caught up in the Spanish complex, the north – Venice in particular – threatened by Austria and the Ottoman empire. Without a common enemy Italy was unable to unite, and without unity the Italians were weak. All their experience in diplomacy, their intelligence, their still considerable wealth, their courage – for the years between 1525 and 1530 saw many acts of bravery both by Italian governments and by individuals – were nothing in confrontation with the great powers of Europe. Although the Italians were only just coming to acknowledge it, even the barbaric country of England was more powerful in Europe than any single Italian state.

The Italians knew their own weakness; some of the most impassioned pleas for Italian unity were made in these years, though always the underlying assumption, except for a few visionaries or eccentrics such as Machiavelli, was that a united Italy would remain a free association of sovereign states living without foreign interference. The Italians knew that disunity had undone them; disagreements between states, disagreements within states, disagreements between families had all played their part. In his plea to continue league co-operation, made on 14 April 1528, the Florentine ambassador rehearsed to the Venetian senate this familiar theme;

> Don't let anyone think . . . that if we have many times seen Italy a prey for the powers beyond the mountains this has been caused by any other power but by the Italians themselves, who have turned on each other . . . one can state categorically that the discord of the peoples of Italy has been that which depressed her, weakened her and finally to a large extent placed her under the yoke of barbarian servitude.[47]

The idea of Italy, however, was too weak, particular interests too strong. In 1526 and 1527 Italy approached closer to unity in action than is generally recognized, but the sack of Rome, symbolic of Charles V's ascendancy in Italy, was the last event in which all the Italian states could feel a common sympathy and interest before the great movement of the Risorgimento. The emperor's dominion spelt the death of the city-states and the independent republics, which had for so long preached, if they had not practised, the virtues of independence preserved by a united Italy. Whatever may be said against them, those republican communes had once clearly provided an atmosphere which was favourable to the development of wide interests, and in them the responsibilities of civic life had stimulated a new patriotism and historical consciousness. The Spanish domination, coupled with the Counter Reformation, which was largely Spanish-controlled, suppressed what was left of the culture supported by the old political order. By the mid-sixteenth century the republic of Venice alone maintained the ancient traditions. 'Today', Alberini wrote as he reflected on the sack of Rome, 'only Venice, which maintains both the form and the reputation of a republic, preserves the honour of Italy.'[48]

GLOSSARY

SOME of the words used in the text may be unfamiliar to English readers. Unless their meaning has been explained in the text they are listed here:

Apostolic Chamber. Governed the finances both of the Church State and of the whole Church. It was also a law-court for cases in which the papacy had a financial interest.

Auditore di camera. The presiding official of the Apostolic Chamber when sitting as a law-court.

Balìa. A committee, supposedly elected in times of crisis in Florence, but used by the Medici to enforce their rule.

Caporioni. Roman municipal officials. There were 13 *rioni* in Rome; each elected its *caporione,* who was responsible for law and order within his quarter.

Census. Financial tribute owed to the pope annually from various towns, countries or persons, and paid on the Feast of Saints Peter and Paul.

Condottiere. A professional military captain, who raised a troop and sold his services to states or princes at war. The word is usually translated by the phrase 'soldier of fortune'. He was said to hold a *condotta.*

Conservators of Rome. Municipal officials in Rome. Nearly always members of the nobility, they called and presided over the Roman councils, supervised the Senator of Rome, watched prices and maintained the city-aqueducts. They acted as intermediaries between Rome and the pope.

Contado. From the Latin *comitatus.* The countryside which surrounded a town and was dependent upon it. Generally it corresponded with the boundaries of the town's bishopric.

Doge. The titular head of the Venetian republic.

Ducat. The gold ducat is the coin in which papal accounts were normally reckoned. There were supposed to be 100 to the *libbra* ('pound').

Giulio. A silver coin, introduced by Julius II in 1504. At that time there were 10 *giulii* to a ducat.

Gonfaloniere. Literally, 'standard-bearer'. It was the title of the titular head of the Florentine republic, but was an office found in other

Italian towns. Eighteenth-century Italian-English dictionaries unhelpfully translated the word as 'Lord Mayor'.

Palleschi. A word employed in Florence to describe those families who were popularly linked with the Medici. They did not always support the Medici, but tended to rise and fall with them.

Proveditor. Literally, 'provider'. Commissary to Venetian troops, or to a town ruled by Venice.

Rione. Administrative division of Rome, or a small alley or lane.

Rota. A papal law-court in Rome, judging all cases, religious and civil, with jurisdiction over both first-instance and appeal cases.

Ruggio. A measure of weight in use in Rome and the Church State, varying from place to place.

Sapienza. The University of Rome.

Scriptoria. A minor office in the papal administration, connected with the drafting and drawing-up of papal documents.

Scudo. A coin, roughly equivalent in value to the papal ducat.

Senator of Rome. President of the Capitol law-court.

Signoria. The chief aristocratic executive board at Florence. It was composed of nine members, the Eight Priors of Liberty, and the Gonfaloniere di Guistizia. The word can also be used to indicate the palace in which the Signoria met.

Staio. A dry measure of varying dimensions used in Rome and the Romagna.

NOTES

ABBREVIATIONS

Albèri, *Relazioni* E. Albèri, *Le relazioni degli ambasciatori Veneti al Senato durante il secolo decimosesto,* 3 series

A.S. Archivio di Stato, Modena

A.S.C. Archivio Storico Capitolino

Baeça, *Don Hugo* G. de Baeça, *Vida de el femoso caballero Don Hugo da Moncada*

Bardi, 'Carlo V e l'assedio di Firenze' A. Bardi, 'Carlo V e l'assedio di Firenze da documenti dell'arch, di Bruxelles'

B.N. Bibliothèque Nationale, Paris

Bonazzi, *Storia di Perugia* A. Bonazzi, *Storia di Perugia,* ed. G. Innamorati

Brandi, *Charles V* K. Brandi, *The Emperor Charles V. The Growth and Destiny and of a Man and of a World Empire,* trans. C. V. Wedgwood

Brantôme, *Œuvres* *Œuvres complètes de Pierre de Bourdeilles, abbé et seigneur de Brantôme,* ed. P. Mérimée

Burigozzo, 'Cronaca' G. Burigozzo, 'Cronaca Milanesi del 1500 al 1544'

Cal. S.P. Milan *Calendar of State Papers and Manuscripts Relating to English Affairs Existing in the Archives and Collections of Milan,* ed. A. B. Hinds

Cal. S.P. Spanish *Calendar of Letters, Despatches, and State Papers, Relating to the Negotiations between England and Spain, Preserved in the Archives at Simancas and Elsewhere,* ed. G. A. Bergenroth, P. de Gayangos, M. A. S. Hume, R. Tyler

Cal. S.P. Venetian *Calendar of State Papers and Manuscripts Relating to English Affairs Existing in the Archives and Collections of Venice and in Other Libraries of Northern Italy,* vols I–V, ed. R. Brown

Canestrini et Desjardins, *Négociations* G. Canestrini et A. Desjardins, *Négociations diplomatiques de la France avec la Toscane*

Castiglione, *Lettere* *Lettere del Conte Baldesar Castiglione ora per la prima volta data in luce e con annotazioni storiche illustrate dell'Abate Pierantonio Serassi*

Catani, *Ricordi* 'Libro de' Ricordi di Iacopo di Maccario di Gregorio Catani Cittadino Aretino'

Cave, *Sac de Rome*	'Le Sac de Rome (1527). Relation inédité de Jean Cave Orléanais', ed. L. Dorez
Cellini, *Autobiography*	*The Autobiography of Benvenuto Cellini*, trans. G. Bull
Cod. Top	*Codice Topografico della Città di Roma*, ed. R. Valentini, G. Zucchetti
Cronache e documenti, ed. Ricci	*Cronache e documenti per la storia Ravennate del secolo,* xvied. C. Ricci
Curiosità Letterarie	*Sceltà di Curiosità Letterarie inedite o rare*, vol. 236
Delumeau, *Rome*	J. Delumeau, *Vie economique et sociale de Rome dans la seconde moitié du XVIᵉ siècle*
'Descriptio Urbis'	D. Gnoli, ' "Descriptio Urbis" o censimento della popolazione di Roma avanti il sacco borbonico'
Direptio Expugnatae Urbis	*Direptio Expugnatae Urbis Romae ab Exercitu Caroli Quinti in Zeitgenossische Berichte uber die Eroberung der Stadt Rome 1527*
Douglas, *Jacopo Sadoleto*	R. M. Douglas, *Jacopo Sadoleto 1477–1547, Humanist and Reformer*
Du Bellay letter	'Guillaume du Bellay à l'amiral Chabot'
G.A.	Gonzaga Archives, Mantua
Gilbert, *Machiavelli and Guicciardini*	F. Gilbert, *Machiavelli and Guicciardini, Politics and History in Sixteenth Century Florence*
Giovio, *Vita Colonna, Vita Leo X*	*Paulus Jovius, De vita Leonis Decimi Pont. Max, libri quatuor, His ordine temporum accesserunt Hadriani Sexti Pont. Max. et Pompeii Columnae Cardinalis vitae etc.*
Giovio, *Vita del Gran Capitanio, Vita Pescara*	P. Giovo, *Le vite del Gran Capitanio e del Marchese di Pescara,* trans. G. Panigada
Guazzo, *Historie*	*Historie di M. Marco Guazzo di tutti i fatti degni di memoria nel mondo successo*
Guicciardini, *Carteggi*	F. Guicciardini, *Carteggi,* vols v–x, ed. P. G. Ricci
Guicciardini, *Scritti inediti*	*Scritti inediti di Francesco Guicciardini sopra la politica di Clemente VII dopo la battaglia di Pavia,* ed. P. Guicciardini
Guicciardini, *Storia d'Italia*	F. Guicciardini, *Storia d'Italia,* ed. C. Panigada
L. Guicciardini, *Sacco di Roma*	L. Guiccardini, *Il Sacco di Roma*
Hierarchia Catholica	*Hierarchia catholica medii (et recentorius) aevi sive summorum pontificum, S.R.E. cardinalium, ecclesiarum antistutum series e documentis Tabularii praesertim Vaticani collecta, digesta, edita,* vol. 2, ed. C. Eubel
L. & P. Henry VIII	*Letters and Papers, Foreign and Domestic, of the Reign of Henry VIII,* ed. J. S. Brewer, J. Gairdner, R. H. Brodie

Lanz, *Correspondenz*   K. Lanz, *Correspondenz des Kaisers Karl V*

Magnuson, *Roman Quattrocento Architecture*   Torgil Magnuson, *Studies in Roman Quattrocento Architecture*

Molini, *Documenti*   G. Molini, *Documenti di Storia Italiana copiata su gli originali autentici e per lo piu autografi esistenti in Parigi*

Monaco, *Camera Apostolica*   M. Monaco, *La Situazione della Reverenda Camera Apostolica nell'anno 1525*

Montluc, *Commentaires*   *Commentaires de Messire Blaise de Montluc, Mareschal de France,* ed. M. Petitot

Nardi, *Historie*   J. Nardi, *Le historie della città di Fiorenza le quali contengono quanto dal'anno 1454 fino al tempo del anno 1531 e successo*

Orano, *Sacco di Roma*   D. Orano, *Il Sacco di Roma del MDXXVII, Studi e Documenti,* vol. I. *I ricordi di Marcello Alberini*

Paruta, *Istorie*   P. Paruta, *Dell'Istorie Veneziane,* in *Degli Istorici delle Cose Veneziane,* vols III, IV. Reference in the text is made to vol. III only

Pastor, *Popes*   L. Pastor, *The History of the Popes from the Close of the Middle Ages,* ed. R. F. Keir

Ridolfi, *Guicciardini*   R. Ridolfi, *The Life of Francesco Guicciardini,* trans. C. Grayson

Roth, *Last Florentine Republic*   C. Roth, *The Last Florentine Republic 1527–30*

Sacco, ed. Milanesi   *Il Sacco di Roma del MDXXVII: narrazioni di contemporanei,* ed. C. Milanesi

Sadoleto, *Letters*   *Jacobi Sadoleto S.R.E. Cardinalis Epistolae quotquot extant proprio nomine scriptae*

Sansovino, *Casa Orsina*   F. Sansovino, *Dei gli Huomini Illustri della Casa Orsina*

Sansovino, *Famiglie d'Italia*   F. Sansovino, *Della origine et de' fatti delle famiglie illustri d'Italia*

Sanuto, *Diarii*   *I Diarii di Marino Sanuto,* ed. F. Stefani

Schulz, *Der Sacco di Roma*   Hans Schulz, *Der Sacco di Roma, Karls V Truppen in Roma 1527–8*

Segni, *Storie Fiorentine, Vita Capponi*   B. Segni, *Storie Fiorentine dell'anno MDXXVII al MDLV colla vita di Niccolò Capponi*

Spadari, *Racconto della ribellione Aretina del 1529*   'Racconto della Ribellione Aretina del 1529 di G. Spadari'

'Suites du Sac de Rome'   'Les Suites du Sac de Rome', ed. H. Omont

Tomassetti, *Campagna Romana*   G. Tomassetti, *La Campagna Romana, antica. medioevale e moderna*

Top. e Urb.   F. Castagnoli, C. Cecchelli, G. Giovannoni, M. Zocca, *Topografiae Urbanistica di Roma*

Valeriano, *De litteratorum infelicitate*   G. P. Valeriano, *De litteratorum infelicitate libri duo,* ed. R. Brydges

Varchi, *Storia Fiorentina*   B. Varchi, *Storia Fiorentina,* ed. G. Milanesi
Vettori, *Sommario*   'Sommario della Storia d'Italia dal 1511 al 1527
                               da Francesco Vettori', ed. A. von Reumont
V.L.   Vatican Library

CHAPTER I. CLEMENT VII AND ROME

1. Pastor, *Popes,* vol. IX, p. 237. See also Albèri, *Relazioni,* 2nd series, vol. III, p. 126.
2. These hopes had never, in fact, been very well grounded.
3. For details of these attempts, see Delumeau, *Rome,* pp. 566–8.
4. Niccolò Machiavelli, *Il Principe,* ch. XI.
5. For a modern account of this attempted *coup,* see Orano, *Sacco di Roma,* pp. 26–7. See also *Enciclopedia Italiana di Scienze, Lettere ed Arti* (Rome, 1929–39) under 'Roma', and Guicciardini, *Storia d'Italia,* vol. III, pp. 118–19.
6. For a contemporary's assessment that Clement's way of thinking was characteristically Florentine, see Albèri, *Relazioni,* 2nd series, vol. III, p. 278. For Florence and this subject in general, see Gilbert, *Machiavelli and Guicciardini,* pp. 30–4.
7. Of 267 artists known to have been working in Rome in 1526, only ten were Roman by birth and, of these, only one, Giulio Romano, was of any distinction.
8. During the sack of Rome many Roman looters made straight for the Vatican Library and, with a sure eye, picked up many valuable works for future resale to the cardinal-librarian.
9. Delumeau, *Rome,* p. 117.
10. A complete census taken of the population of the city just before the sack of Rome has survived and has been printed in 'Descriptio Urbis'. This gives the population as 55,035, but peculiar circumstances had reduced the population: three cardinals were absent, some Romans were in the papal camp, and many of the Colonna adherents were *fuorusciti.*
11. In the February before the sack of Rome Sir John Russell gave this figure as an estimate, but it is more than double the figure given by Alberto Pio at the same date. *L. & P. Henry VIII,* vol. IV, pt 2, p. 1286; Molini, *Documenti,* vol. I, p. 205.

CHAPTER II. POPE AND EMPEROR

1. Pastor, *Popes,* vol. IX, p. 253.
2. V.L. ASV MS. Fondo Pio n.54 f.37*v.*
3. *Cal. S.P. Spanish 1525–6,* p. 347.
4. Castiglione, *Lettere,* vol. II, p. 113.
5. Albèri, *Relazioni,* 2nd series, vol. III, pp. 270–80.
6. Ibid. p. 128.
7. Quoted in T. Pandolfi, 'Giovan Matteo Giberti e l'ultima difesa della libertà d'Italia negl'anni 1521–5', *Archivio della Reale Società Romana di Storia Patria,* vol. XXXIV, which should be consulted for Giberti's career.
8. Castiglione, *Lettere,* vol. II, p. 9.

9. Pastor, *Popes*, vol. IX, p. 502.
10. Ibid. p. 271.
11. For the opinion of some Italians on the consequences of Pavia, see Gilbert, *Machiavelli and Guicciardini*, p. 241. On Gattinara, Brandi, *Charles V*, pp. 90–1, 153–4. M. Bataillon, *Érasme et l'Espagne* (Paris, 1937) pp. 243–6, has a full account of the reaction in Spain to the news of Pavia.
12. *Cal. S.P. Spanish 1525–6*, p. 247.

CHAPTER III. MORONE'S CONSPIRACY AND THE LEAGUE OF COGNAC

1. Guicciardini, *Scritti inediti*, p. 17. The instructions of Charles V to Lannoy after the battle of Pavia are printed in Bardi, 'Carlo V e l'assedio di Firenze', p. 22. See also *Cal. S.P. Venetian 1520–6*, pp. 447.
2. Ibid. p. 474.
3. *Cal. S.P. Spanish 1525–6*, pp. 265, 280, 292, 307; *Cal. S.P. Venetian 1520–6*, pp. 473–4.
4. Sanuto, *Diarii*, vol. XL, pp. 87, 201–2, 220.
5. Giovio, *Vita del Gran Capitanio, Vita Pescara*, p.219.
6. For a discussion of this question, see L. Marini, *La Spagna in Italia nel'Età di Carlo V* (Bologna, 1961).
7. Brandi, *Charles V*, p. 206.
8. F. Chabod, *Lo Stato di Milano nel prima metà del Secolo XVI* (Rome, 1954) p. 27; Castiglione, *Lettere*, vol. II, pp. 11–15, 56.
9. Canestrini et Desjardins, *Négociations*, vol. II, p. 850; Castiglione, *Lettere*, vol. II, p. 82; *Cal. S.P. Venetian 1520–6*, p. 526; A. Luzio, *Isabella d'Este e il Sacco di Roma* (Milan, 1908) p. 15.
10. *Cal. S.P. Spanish 1525–6*, p. 365.
11. Sanuto, *Diarii*, vol. XL, pp. 344–5.
12. Ibid. p. 475; Paruta, *Istorie*, p. 401.
13. *Cal. S.P. Venetian 1520–6*, pp. 509–11.
14. Sanuto, *Diarii*, vol. XL, pp. 772–3.
15. For these negotiations, see V.L. ASV MS. Fondo Pio n.53 ff.128–31, n.54 f.89*v*, 197*v*; *L. & P. Henry VIII*, vol. IV, pt 1, p. 948.
16. V.L. ASV MS. Fondo Pio n.53 ff.130–1*v*; H. Hauser, *Le Traité de Madrid et la Cession de la Bourgogne à Charles-Quint* (Dijon, 1912) p. 5.
17. See V. Ilardi, ' "Italianità" among some Italian intellectuals of the early sixteenth century', *Traditio*, vol. XII, for a partial discussion of this question from one contemporary view. One can also consult Ridolfi, *Guicciardini*, ch. 14.

CHAPTER IV. POPE, EMPEROR AND ROME

1. Lanz, *Correspondenz*, vol. I, pp. 212–16.
2. *L. & P. Henry VIII*, vol. IV, pt 1, p. 1009. V.L. ASV MS. Fondo Pio n.54 f.223. What, in fact, Charles V did or did not owe to the king of England would make the subject of another book.
3. V.L. MS. Chigi G.II 39 f.293.
4. 'Description Urbis', passim; Cellini, *Autobiography*, passim.

5. Copy of the bull *Romanus Pontifex* in V.L. MS. Chigi G.ii f.39.

6. Delumeau, *Rome*, pp. 19–22, 224.

7. Varchi, *Storia Fiorentina*, vol. i, p. 86; Delumeau, *Rome*, pp. 207–11, 849; 'Descriptio Urbis'; P. Pecchai, *Roma nel Cinquecento* (Bologna, 1948) p. 280.

8. Apart from one Italian monograph (Monaco, *Camera Apostolica*), the finances of the pontificate of Clement VII have scarcely been considered; but it can be no accident that the gravest general crisis of the modern Church coincided with its gravest financial crisis.

9. Albèri, *Relazioni*, 2nd series, vol. iii, p. 33.

10. Sanuto, *Diari*, vol. xliii, p. 15; Albèri, *Relazioni*, 2nd series, vol. iii, p. 269.

11. Vettori, in *Sacco*, ed. Milanesi, pp. 423–5.

12. Monaco, *Camera Apostolica*, p. 57.

13. V.L. MS Chigi G.ii 39 f.391.

14. Varchi, *Storia Fiorentina*, vol. i, p. 87; V.L. MS. Chigi G.ii 39 f.327; Albèri, *Relazioni*, 2nd series, vol. iii, pp. 126–7; Delumeau, *Rome*, pp. 244, 828; Orano, *Sacco di Roma*, p. 217; V.L. MS. Vat. Lat. 8251 f.610.

15. Varchi, *Storia Fiorentina*, vol. i, p. 86.

16. Albèri, *Relazioni*, 2nd series, vol. iii, pp. 126–7; *Cal. S.P. Spanish 1527–9*, p. 38.

17. Ibid. p. 13.

18. Varchi, *Storia Fiorentina*, vol. i, p. 86; Monaco, *Camera Apostolica*, p. 64.

19. V.L. ASV AA.ARM. i–xviii. vol. 6522 f.34; *L. & P. Henry VIII*, vol. iv, pt i, p. 1009; Varchi, *Storia Fiorentina*, vol. i, p. 86.

20. Molini, *Documenti*, vol. i, pp. 205–6. For these incidents, see V.L. ASV MS. Fondo Pio n.53 f.154v; Baeça, *Don Hugo*, p. 60; Guicciardini, *Storia d'Italia*, vol. v, p. 40.

21. Lanz, *Correspondenz*, vol. i, p. 217; Castiglione, *Lettere*, vol. ii, p. 56.

22. Brandi, *Charles V*, p. 241; Castiglione, *Lettere*, vol. ii, p. 89.

23. *Cal. S.P. Venetian 1520–6*, pp. 603–4.

24. Castiglione, *Lettere*, vol. ii, p. 61.

25. Sanuto, *Diarii*, vol. xl, p. 174.

26. *Il Cortegiano* itself is full of 'Spanishisms'.

27. Castiglione, *Lettere*, vol. ii, pp. 73–8.

28. Giovio, *Vita Colonna, Vita Leo X*, p. 109.

29. Ibid. p. 88.

CHAPTER V. THE LEAGUE AT WAR

1. Paruta, *Istorie*, p. 409; Sanuto, *Diarii*, vol. xli, pp. 431, 483.

2. Ibid. pp. 415–18, 474, 497, 499, 541, 608–10, 723; V.L. ASV MS. Fondo Pio n.53 f.147v.; Guicciardini, *Carteggi*, vol. ix, p. 69; Burigozzo, 'Cronaca', p. 458.

3. F. Bennato, 'La partecipazione militare di Venezia alla Lega di Cognac', *Archivio Veneto*, vol. lviii, pp. 70–1; V.L. ASV MS. Fondo Pio n.54 f.233, n.53 ff.145, 148; Sanuto, *Diarii*, vol. xli, pp. 541, 594, 715.

4. Guicciardini, *Carteggi*, vol. ix, pp. 36, 236–9; *L. & P. Henry VIII*, vol. iv, pt i, pp. 1019, 1024.

5. V.L. ASV MS. Fondo Pio n.54 f.234.
6. *L. & P. Henry VIII*, vol. IV, pt I, p. 1027; Sanuto, *Diarii*, vol. XLI, p. 701; Guicciardini, *Storia d'Italia*, vol. V, p. 28.
7. Ibid., for Lodron at Pavia, see V.L. ASV MS. Fondo Pio n.54 f.234.
8. Ridolfi, *Guicciardini*, pp. 154-6; V.L. ASV MS. Fondo Pio n.53 ff.149v-150v.
9. *Cal. S.P. Venetian 1520-6*, p. 589; Guicciardini, *Carteggi*, vol. IX, p. 32.
10. Ibid. pp. 5, 32-3.
11. Ibid. p. 19.
12. Ibid. pp. 7-116.
13. Montluc, *Commentaires*, p. 338.
14. Guicciardini, *Carteggi*, vol. IX, pp. 28-30, 104, 197; *Cal. S.P. Venetian 1527-33*, pp. 154-5.
15. Giovio, *Vita del Gran Capitanio, Vita Pescara*, p. 11.
16. Guicciardini, *Carteggi*, vol. IX, pp. 81, 87-9, 115.
17. Ibid. pp. 87, 271.
18. Ibid. pp. 112-16.
19. V.L. ASV MS. Fondo Pio n.54 f.249v; Lanz, *Correspondenz*, vol. I, p. 215.
20. For the Siena campaign, see *La Guerra di Camollia*, in *Curiosità Letterarie*; Guicciardini, *Storia d'Italia*, vol. V, pp. 41-3; B.N. MS. Italien 15; Guazzo, *Historie*, pp. 36-9.
21. Sanuto, *Diarii*, vol. XLII, pp. 354, 544; *L. & P. Henry VIII*, vol. IV, pt 2, p. 1091; Paruta, *Istorie*, pp. 412-15.
22. Sanuto, *Diari*, vol. XLIII, pp. 181-2.
23. Brantôme, *Œuvres*, vol. II, p. 46.
24. J. Heers, *Gênes au XVe siècle* (Paris, 1961); G. Coniglio, *Il Regno di Napoli al Tempo di Carlo V* (Naples, 1951).
25. Sanuto, *Diarii*, vol. XLII, p. 261.
26. Ibid. pp. 261, 544, 555, 763; vol. XLIII, p. 185. V.L. ASV MS. Fondo Pio n.54 f.9; ASV MS. Arm. i-xviii. vol. 6522 f.94.
27. Sanuto, *Diarii*, vol. XLII, pp. 586, 593.
28. Ibid. p. 545. For the siege of Cremona, see also V.L. ASV MS. Fondo Pio n.54 ff.8-9; Guicciardini, *Carteggi*, vol. X.
29. Sanuto, *Diarii*, vol. XLII, pp. 552, 558.
30. Ibid. pp. 571-2, 582.
31. V.L. ASV MS. Fondo Pio n.54 f.5.
32. This letter is quoted in Pastor, *Popes*, vol. IX, pp. 323-4.

CHAPTER VI. THE COLONNA RAID

1. *L. & P. Henry VIII*, vol. IV, pt 2, p. 1111; Sanuto, *Diarii*, vol. XLII, p. 681; Guicciardini, *Storia d'Italia*, vol. V, pp. 75-8; Guazzo, *Historie*, p. 48.
2. Vettori, *Sommario*, p. 368.
3. Baeça, *Don Hugo*, p. 452; *L. & P. Henry VIII*, vol. IV, pt 2, p. 1111. For the numbers involved, see Baeça, *Don Hugo*, pp. 452, 464; *L. & P. Henry VIII*, vol. IV, pt 2, pp. 1111 and 1120; V.L. ASV MS. Fondo Pio n.53 f.12v.
4. Sanuto, *Diarii*, vol. XLII, p. 681.

5. I have not come across any eye-witness accounts of these events. Reference should be made to Sanuto, *Diarii*, vol. XLII, pp. 690, 724; *Cal. S.P. Spanish 1527–9*, p. 516; Guazzo, *Historie*, p. 48; Vettori, *Sommario*, p. 368; Cave, *Sac de Rome*, p. 385; Orano, *Sacco di Roma*, p. 216.

6. Buonaparte in *Sacco*, ed. Milanesi, p. 277. See also Orano, *Sacco di Roma*, p. 225; Sanuto, *Diarii*, vol. XLII, p. 690; Baeça, *Don Hugo*, p. 67.

7. Orano, *Sacco di Roma*, p. 224.

8. Estimates vary as to how many troops were involved on the papal side. The best accounts are to be found in Sanuto, *Diarii*, vol. XLII, pp. 700, 724, 725, 727.

9. Ibid. p. 700; Vettori, *Sommario*, p. 368, states specifically that the wall was broken. The Colonna also had the advantage of attacking from elevated ground. The information that this was a weak point in the defence of the Borgo was clearly passed on to Bourbon.

10. Buonaparte in *Sacco*, ed. Milanesi, p. 277; V.L. ASV MS. Fondo Pio n.53 f.13, MS. Vat. Lat. 8251 pt II f.609.

11. F. G. Mazzuchelli, 'Vita di Francesco Berni', printed in F. Berni, *Orlando Innamorato di Matteo M. Bojardo*, in *Classici Italiani*, vol. 12 (Milan, 1806) p. xxiii.

12. Letter of Girolamo Negri, Secretary to Cardinal Cornaro, printed in Pastor, *Popes*, vol. IX, pp. 332–3.

13. For accounts of the plunder of the Borgo, see V.L. ASV MS. Fondo Pio n.53 ff.13*v*, 127*v*; Sanuto, *Diarii*, vol. XLII, pp. 700, 725–8, 702; Guicciardini, *Storia d'Italia*, vol. v, p. 79.

14. Buonaparte in *Sacco*, ed. Milanesi, p. 279. See also V.L. ASV MS. Fondo Pio n.53 ff.14–16; Varchi, *Storia Fiorentina*, vol. I, p. 58; Guicciardini, *Storia d'Italia*, vol. v, p. 79.

15. V.L. ASV MS. Fondo Pio n.53 f.14*v*, MS. Vat. Lat. 8251 f.610. For these negotiations, see also Sanuto, *Diarii*, vol. XLII, p. 726; Guazzo, *Historie*, p. 48.

16. G. Salvioli, 'Nuovo studii sulla politica e le vicende dell'esercito imperiale in Italia nel 1526–7 e sul sacco di Roma', in *Archivio Veneto*, vol. VII, p. 4; see also Orano, *Sacco di Roma*, p. 226; Sanuto, *Diarii*, vol. XLII. p. 722; Molini, *Documenti*, vol. I, p. 229.

17. V.L. ASV MS. Fondo Pio n.53 f.17.

18. Sanuto, *Diarii*, vol. XLIII, p. 50; *L. & P. Henry VIII*, vol. IV. pt 2, p. 1140; V.L. Arch. Cap. MS. Arm. xiv tom.7 f.2, Cornelius de Fine, 'Diarium', f.83.

19. Sanuto, *Diarii*, vol. XLIII, p. 580.

20. Ibid. vol. XLII, p. 70.

21. 'Memorie Perugine di Teseo Alfani', *Archivio Storico Italiano*, vol. XVI, pt 2, p. 309; Salvioli, 'Nuovi studii . . . sul sacco di Roma', *Archivio Veneto*, vol. XVII, p. 6.

22. Sanuto, *Diarii*, vol. XLII, pp. 682, 699, 700, 741; Guicciardini, *Carteggi*, vol. x, p. 49.

23. Ibid, pp. 52–3.

24. Sanuto, *Diarii*, Vol. XLII, pp. 698, 708–10.

CHAPTER VII. THE WAR AGAINST THE COLONNA

1. *L. & P. Henry*, vol. IV, pt 2, p. 1153; V.L. ASV MS. Fondo Pio n.54 f.18.

2. Sanuto, *Diarii*, vol. XLIII, pp. 152, 199, 447; Salvioli, 'Nuovi studii . . . sul sacco di Roma', *Archivio Veneto*, vol. XVII, pp. 6–7.

3. See the copy of the citation in V.L. Arch. Cap. MS. Arm. xiv. tom.7 ff.102–5*v*.

4. V.L. ASV MS. Fondo Pio n.53 f.45*v*.

5. V.L. Cornelius de Fine, 'Diarium', f.84; Sanuto, *Diarii*, vol. XLIII, pp. 236, 320; Varchi, *Storia Fiorentina*, vol. I, p. 89. Gattinara maintained that the wording of the sentence implied an excommunication of the emperor; Castiglione, *Lettere*, vol. II, pp. 145–6.

6. Salvioli, 'Nuovi studii . . . sul sacco di Roma', *Archivio Veneto*, vol. XVII, p. 11; Guazzo, *Historie*, p. 50; V.L. Cornelius de Fine, 'Diarium' f.83v, ASV MS. Fondo Pio n.53 f.37.

7. V.L. ASV MS. Fondo Pio n.5 f.12*v*.

8. Guazzo, *Historie*, p. 50; Tomassetti, *Campagna Romana*, vol. I, p. 371. After the sack of Rome Ascanio Colonna tried to force Velletri to make reparations, estimating them at 26,000 ducats. On 14 November 1527, after the intervention of Cardinal del Valle, Velletri agreed to pay.

9. V.L. Cornelius de Fine, 'Diarium' f.83*v*.

10. V.L. ASV MS. Fondo Pio n.5 f.12*v*.

11. Ibid. n.53 f.41*v*; *L. & P. Henry VIII*, vol. IV, pt 2, p. 1164.

12. V.L. ASV MS. Fondo Pio n.54 f.19*v*; Sanuto, *Diarii*, vol. XLIII, p. 169.

13. V.L. ASV MS. Fondo Pio n.53 f.46*v*.

14. Ibid.; Sanuto, *Diarii*, vol. XLIII, pp. 218, 234, 270–1, 282, 305.

15. L. Guicciardini, *Sacco di Roma*, pp. 70–1; V.L. ASV MS. Fondo Pio n.53 f.60.

16. Sanuto, *Diarii*, vol. XLII, p. 746; vol. XLIII, p. 311; vol. XLV, p. 75.

17. Ibid, vol. XLIX, p. 31.

18. Ibid, vol. XLIII, pp. 349, 375, 515.

19. V.L. ASV MS. Fondo Pio n.53 f.43.

20. Baeça, *Don Hugo*, p. 451; Brandi, *Charles V*, p. 256. Gattinara's views, described here by Brandi, were shared by many of the emperor's advisers.

21. Salvioli, 'Nuovi studii . . . sul sacco di Roma', *Archivio Veneto*, vol. XVI, p. 280.

22. The Colonna were repaying a debt; Alfonso d'Este had refused to hand over Fabrizio Colonna to the French after the battle of Ravenna.

23. The Este family were notoriously unsqueamish about illegitimacy. Alfonso's own bride had been Lucrezia Borgia.

24. For the negotiations between Clement VII and Alfonso d'Este, the following should be consulted: *Cal. S.P. Spanish 1525–6*; Sanuto, *Diarii*, vols XLI, XLII, XLIII; Salvioli, 'Nuovi studii . . . sul sacco di Roma', *Archivio Veneto*, vols XVI, XVII; Guicciardini, *Carteggi*, vols IX, X; V.L. ASV MS. Fondo Pio n.53.

25. V.L. ASV MS. Fondo Pio n.53 f.49.

26. For this correspondence, see Pastor, *Popes*, vol. IX, pp. 499–501.

27. Canestrini et Desjardins, *Négociations*, vol. II, pp. 846–7, 865, 881, 893.

28. Sanuto, *Diarii*, vol. XLIII, pp. 579–80, 614; *L. & P. Henry VIII*, vol. VI, pt 2, pp. 1187–8, 1210.

29. V.L. ASV MS. Fondo Pio n.53 f.52v; Schulz, *Der Sacco di Roma*, p. 83.

30. *Cal. S.P. Spanish 1527–9*, pp. 40, 514–15; Sanuto, *Diarii*, vol. XLIII, p. 615; *L. & P. Henry VIII*, vol. IV, pt 2, pp. 1202, 1257; V.L. ASV MS. Fondo Pio n.53 f.61v.

31. Sanuto, *Diarii*, vol. XLIII, p. 447; *L. & P. Henry VIII*, vol. IV, pt 2, p. 1207; Pastor, *Popes*, vol. IX, p. 359; *Cal. S.P. Spanish 1527–9*, p. 7.

32. *L. & P. Henry VIII*, vol. IV, pt 2, p. 1209; V.L. ASV MS. Fondo Pio n.53 ff.57–57v.

33. V.L. ASV MS. Fondo Pio n.53 f.58.

34. *Cal. S.P. Spanish 1527–9*, no. 3. For the well-known history of Charles V's letter, see Brandi, *Charles V*, pp. 250–2; and for the unfortunate hopes which the document raised among the Italian reformers, see D. Cantimori, 'L'Influence du manifeste de Charles-Quint contre Clement VII et de quelques documents similaires de la littérature philoprotestante et anti-curiale d'Italie', in *Charles-Quint et son temps* (Paris, 1959).

CHAPTER VIII. THE ADVANCE OF BOURBON

1. Guicciardini, *Carteggi*, vol. IX, p. 81.

2. Sanuto, *Diarii*, vol. XLIII, pp. 433, 477, 565–6; *Cal. S.P. Spanish 1527–9*, pp. 69–70; A. Lebey, *Le Connétable de Bourbon, 1490–1527* (Paris, 1904) p. 396.

3. V.L. ASV MS. Fondo Pio n.54 f.29v; Sanuto, *Diarii*, vol. XLIII, p. 678.

4. The lansquenets had been complaining about their lack of shoes for months; *Cal. S.P. Spanish 1527–9*, pp. 15–16; Sanuto, *Diarii*, vol. XLIII, pp. 618, 690–1; vol. XLIV, p. 141; V.L. ASV MS. Fondo Pio n.54 f.52.

5. *Cal. S.P. Spanish 1527–9*, p. 37.

6. Ibid.; V.L. ASV MS. Fondo Pio n.53 ff.61v–70v.

7. *L. & P. Henry VIII*, vol. IV, pt 2, p. 1276.

8. V.L. ASV MS. Fondo n.53 f.55.

9. Ibid. f.62v; Sanuto, *Diarii*, vol. XLIII, pp. 614, 646.

10. Guicciardini, *Storia d'Italia*, vol. V, p. 103.

11. V.L. ASV MS. Fondo Pio n.54 ff.48v–49.

12. Ibid. ff.60–1.

13. Ibid. ff.55–55v, 60v–61v; Guazzo, *Historie*, p. 53; Sanuto, *Diarii*, vol. XLIV, pp. 212–13.

14. V.L. ASV MS. Fondo Pio n.53 f.81.

15. Guicciardini, *Storia d'Italia*, vol. V, p. 104; V.L. ASV MS. Fondo Pio n.53 f.80.

16. Sanuto, *Diarii*, vol. XLIV, p. 34.

17. *Cal. S.P. Spanish 1527–9*, p. 57; *La Presa e Lamento di Roma*, in *Curiosità Letterarie* p. 122; Varchi, *Storia Fiorentina*, vol. I, p. 92.

18. Luzio, *Isabella d'Este e il Sacco di Roma*, p. 49.

19. Bataillon, *Érasme et l'Espagne*, p. 250.

20. See, for example, the instructions from Spain which reached Bourbon in March, in *Cal. S.P. Spanish 1527–9*, p. 133, and a letter from the Venetian

ambassador in Valladolid written 18 April; Sanuto, *Diarii*, vol. xlv, p. 372; also *Cal. S.P. Spanish 1527-9*, pp. 514-15.

21. Luzio, *Isabella d'Este e il Sacco di Roma*, p. 26.

22. *Cal. S.P. Spanish 1527-9*, p. 71. For the attitude of the soldiers, see Sanuto, *Diarii*, vol. xlv, p. 207; 'The Spaniards have let it be known in the camp that they want to go and sack Florence.' See also ibid. p. 201; A.S. Rettori dello Stato n.8a f.539.

23. On 11 March Sanchez reported that Bourbon had informed him he was going to advance on Rome by forced marches; *Cal. S.P. Spanish 1527-9*, p. 96. For the letters, see ibid. pp. 132-3. Alfonso d'Este is often credited with having suggested the attack on Rome, but Bourbon was quite capable of arriving at the decision himself. Because he was an *Italian* contemporary Italian historians have almost certainly overestimated Este's influence, e.g. Varchi, *Storia Fiorentina*, vol. I, p. 100.

24. These are the figures of the abbot of Najera in *Cal. S.P. Spanish 1527-9*, p. 91. The figure for the infantry is probably too large, for Sanuto, *Diarii*, vol. xliv, p. 267, gives only 4000 Spaniards and 2000 Italians at the beginning of March.

25. Sanuto, *Diarii*, vol. xliv, pp. 57, 198, 203, 210. At the beginning of March the supply of bread came from Correggio; ibid. p. 201.

26. Ibid. pp. 216-17.

27. Luzio, *Isabella d'Este e il Sacco di Roma,* pp 40, 49; Guicciardini, *Carteggi*, vol. IX, p. 199.

28. L. Guicciardini, *Sacco di Roma*, p. 186; Buonaparte in *Sacco*, ed. Milanesi, pp. 255-6.

29. Brantôme, *Œuvres*, vol. I, pp. 301-2, 328-30; *Cal. S.P. Spanish 1527-9*, p. 240.

30. He is said to have told Luther at the Diet of Worms, 'Little monk, thou hast a fight before thee which we, whose trade is war, never faced the like of.'

31. *Cal. S.P. Spanish 1527-9*, p. 241. Varchi remarks how hard it was for a man of his nature to resist risking the whole fortune of Naples on a single battle (*Storia Fiorentina*, vol. I, p. 297). See also Brantôme, *Œuvres*, vol. I, pp. 288-9.

32. *Cal. S.P. Spanish 1527-9*, pp. 90-1.

33. *La Presa e Lamento di Roma*, p. 122; *L. & P. Henry VIII*, vol. IV, pt 2, p. 1233; A.S. Rettori dello Stato n.8a f.544.

34. *Cal. S.P. Spanish 1527-9*, p. 88; A. S. Rettori dello Stato n.8a ff.539, 542, 544.

35. A.S. Rettori dello Stato n.8a ff.557-8; Sanuto, *Diarii*, vol. xliv, pp. 216-17; Salvioli, 'Nuovi studii . . . sul sacco di Roma', *Archivio Veneto*, vol. xvii, p. 17.

36. A.S. Rettori dello Stato n.8a f.561

37. Sanuto, *Diarii*, vol. xliv, pp. 218-19, 245.

38. *Cal. S.P. Spanish 1527-9*, pp. 45, 88, 130-1, 134-5; Guicciardini, *Storia d'Italia*, vol. V, pp. 117-18; Sanuto, *Diarii*, vol. xliv, p. 227; Buonaparte in *Sacco*, ed. Milanesi, p. 291; L. Guicciardini, *Sacco di Roma*, pp. 95-107;

Lanz, *Correspondenz*, vol. I, p. 231. The weather was bad throughout March and April; see, e.g., Burigozzo, 'Cronaca', p. 466.

39. A.S. Rettori dello Stato n.8a ff.511, 513; Sanuto, *Diarii*, vol. XLIII, p. 618; vol. XLIV, pp. 7, 176; Ridolfi, *Guicciardini*, pp. 165–6.

40. Sanuto, *Diarii*, vol. XLIII, pp. 597–8, 614.

41. V.L. ASV MS. Fondo Pio n.54 f.42.

42. A.S. Rettori dello Stato n.8a f.514.

43. Sanuto, *Diarii*, vol. XLIV, p. 52.

44. A.S. Rettori dello Stato n.8a f.539.

45. Sanuto, *Diarii*, vol. XLIII, p. 694; vol. XLIV, pp. 363, 454.

46. A.S. Rettori dello Stato n.8a f.514: 'I do not believe that they can make any impression at all, because all these towns are well guarded and the troops of the League are ready to succour any locality as soon as the need arises.'

47. Guicciardini, *Storia d'Italia*, vol. V, pp. 117–18; *Cal. S.P. Venetian 1527–33*, p. 33; A.S. Rettori dello Stato n.8a ff.534, 539, 542.

48. Sanuto, *Diarii*, vol. XLIV, pp. 295–7, 325; Guicciardini, *Storia d'Italia*, vol. V, p. 119; *Cal. S.P. Spanish 1527–9*, p. 133.

CHAPTER IX. LANNOY'S TRUCE

1. V.L. ASV MS. Fondo Pio n.54 f.53; *Cal. S.P. Venetian 1527–33*, p. 23; *Cal. S.P. Milan*, vol. I, p. 474; Sanuto, *Diarii*, vol. XLIII, p. 604.

2. *L. & P. Henry VIII*, vol. IV, pt 2, p. 1299; and see also Sanuto, *Diarii*, vol. XLIV, p. 210.

3. V.L. ASV MS. Fondo Pio n.53, f.49v.

4. *L. & P. Henry VIII*, vol. IV, pt 2, p. 1209.

5. V.L. ASV MS. Fondo Pio n.53 f.81.

6. Sanuto, *Diarii*, vol. XLIII, p. 580; *L. & P. Henry VIII*, vol. IV, pt 2, p. 1300; *Cal. S.P. Milan*, vol. I, pp. 489–90; *Cal. S.P. Venetian 1527–33*, p. 24.

7. V.L. ASV MS. Fondo Pio n.53 f.61v.

8. Lanz, *Correspondenz*, vol. I, p. 230.

9. The army was to consist of 300 lances, 400 cavalry and 4000 infantry; V.L. ASV MS. Fondo Pio n.53 ff.73–4; *L. & P. Henry VIII*, vol. IV, pt 2, p. 1260.

10. Ibid.; V.L. ASV MS. Fondo Pio n.53 f.75v. Clement told the Venetian ambassador that he was very anxious to conclude a truce as he could no longer afford to make war, but the ambassador warned him that the Venetian senate would strongly oppose any agreement. V.L. ASV MS. Fondo Pio n.54 ff.53–53v.

11. Canestrini et Desjardins, *Négociations*, vol. II, p. 902.

12. V.L. ASV MS. Fondo Pio n.54 ff.53v–54.

13. Guicciardini, *Carteggi*, vol. IX, p. 128.

14. V.L. ASV MS. Fondo Pio n.54 f.63.

15. *Cal. S.P. Milan*, vol. I, p. 489; Sanuto, *Diarii*, vol. XLIV, p. 148.

16. Ibid. pp. 272–3.

17. *Cal. S.P. Venetian 1527–33*, p. 23.

18. V.L. ASV MS. Fondo Pio n.53 ff.100–100v.

19. Sanuto, *Diarii*, vol. XLIV, p. 277.
20. V.L. ASV MS. Fondo Pio n.53 f.99*v*; *Cal. S.P. Spanish 1527–9*, p. 125.
21. V.L. Cornelius de Fine, 'Diarium' f.89*v*.
22. Sanuto, *Diarii*, vol. XLIV, p. 300.
23. V.L. ASV MS. Fondo Pio n.53 ff.104*v*–105*v*.
24. *Cal. S.P. Spanish 1527–9*, pp. 88–91; A.S. Rettori dello Stato n.81 f.597.
25. Ibid. ff.581, 595; *Cal. S.P. Spanish 1527–9*, pp. 130–1.
26. A.S. Rettori dello Stato n.8a ff.589, 597.
27. Ibid. n.8a ff.92, 98, 114, 115, 132, n.9a ff.74–5.
28. Sanuto, *Diarii*, vol. XLIV, p. 245.
29. Ibid. pp. 266–7.
30. Almost all the authorities have an account of this mutiny. See, in particular, Buonaparte in *Sacco*, ed. Milanesi, p. 29; Guicciardini, *Storia d'Italia*, vol. V, p. 119; *Cal. S.P. Spanish 1527–9*, pp. 131–2; Sanuto, *Diarii*, vol. XLIV, p. 293; A.S. Rettori dello Stato n.8a ff.597, 598.
31. *Cal. S.P. Spanish 1527–9*, p. 132; Sanuto, *Diarii*, vol. XLIV, pp. 293, 302.
32. *Cal. S.P. Spanish 1527–9*, p. 132; Guicciardini, *Storia d'Italia*, vol. V, p. 119.
33. Lanz, *Correspondenz*, vol. I, p. 231.
34. This was the accepted contemporary viewpoint. The viceroy's reputation and, by implication, that of the emperor were only rescued by subsequent historians, beginning with Varchi. I do not see any evidence to support this subsequent whitewashing.
35. Sanuto, *Diarii*, vol. XLIV, p. 353.
36. Ibid. p. 354.
37. *Cal. S.P. Spanish 1527–9*, p. 133.
38. Sanuto, *Diarii*, vol. XLIII, p. 516.
39. *Cal. S.P. Spanish 1527–9*, p. 133; Lanz, *Correspondenz*, vol. I, p. 233. The Neapolitans were, of course, placed in a position of some difficulty as there could be no dispute about Lannoy's authority over them, but they may have had other reasons for leaving the army. Del Guasto, for instance, had been quarrelling with Bourbon for months and was in general disagreement with the emperor's imperial ambitions.
40. V.L. ASV MS. Fondo Pio n.53 ff.104–104*v*.
41. *Cal. S.P. Spanish 1527–9*, pp. 518–19.
42. Lanz, *Correspondenz*, vol. I, pp. 231–2.
43. Sanuto, *Diarii*, vol. XLIV, pp. 436–7.
44. Lanz, *Correspondenz*, vol. I, p. 231; *Cal. S.P. Spanish 1527–9*, p. 134.
45. *L. & P. Henry VIII*, vol. IV, pt 2, p. 1292: 'Letters from Bourbon to the viceroy have been intercepted, asking him to come to an agreement with the pope as soon as possible, that he may the sooner send money.'
46. See his letter of 31 March 1527 printed in Schulz, *Der Sacco di Roma*, p. 173.
47. Vettori in *Sacco*, ed. Milanesi, p. 429. The evidence for collusion between Lannoy and Bourbon over the breaking of the truce is diffuse and complicated. Venetian intelligence had been informed of what would happen long before the event (Sanuto, *Diarii*, vol. XLIV, p. 353), and many contemporaries state categorically that Bourbon suborned his own troops

(V.L. ASV MS. Fondo Pio n.53 f.107; Vettori, *Sommario*, p. 375, and in *Sacco*, ed. Milanesi, p. 427; L. Guicciardini, *Sacco in Roma*, p. 63). Circumstantial evidence supports them; Bourbon never lost control of his men even in far worse circumstances, and normally they had to be bribed to advance; they did not mutiny in order to be allowed to. As far as Lannoy is concerned, one should note in the first place that the Colonna did not attempt to observe the truce even for twenty-four hours – and the strange relations which existed between Lannoy and Bourbon afterwards. After Lannoy had removed to Siena the Venetians were sent two reports, 28 April and 1 May (Sanuto, *Diarii*, vol. XLV, pp. 24–6. 39–40). It is obvious that, had he wished to, Lannoy could have used Siena to block Bourbon's advance south. But his demands on that city, as relayed to Venice, reveal him as fully identified with Bourbon's campaign and the extension of imperial power in Italy. He asked the city of Siena for the use of all Sienese troops, both cavalry and infantry, for twenty pieces of artillery for the army, for supplies for the imperial camp, etc. These demands were not altered but merely reiterated by Bourbon on *his* arrival two days later. At the least it is difficult to believe that Lannoy was making much effort to observe his own truce.

48. *Cal. S.P. Venetian 1527–33*, pp. 63–4.
49. Salvioli, 'Nuovi studii . . . sul sacco di Roma', in *Archivio Veneto*, vol. XVII, p. 22.
50. Schulz, *Der Sacco di Roma*, pp. 173–4.
51. *Cal. S.P. Spanish 1527–9*, no. 47.
52. *Cal. S.P. Venetian 1527–33*, p. 33; Paruta, *Istorie*, p. 441.
53. Canestrini et Desjardins, *Négociations*, vol. II, pp. 902–28.
54. Bennato, 'La partecipazione militare di Venezia alla Lega di Cognac', *Arch. Ven.* lviii, pp. 80–1.
55. Sanuto, *Diarii*, vol. XLIV, p. 356.
56. Ibid. pp. 359, 447, 463; *Cal. S.P. Spanish 1527–9*, p. 130; L. Guicciardini, *Sacco di Roma*, p. 160; Salvioli, 'Nuovi studii . . . sul sacco di Roma', *Archivio Veneto*, vol. XVII, p. 22.
57. V.L. ASV MS. Fondo Pio n.53 f.107*v*; Snauto, *Diarii*, vol. XLIV, pp. 329, 359.
58. A.S. Rettori dello Stato n.8a ff.598–9, n.9a f.34; Guicciardini, *Storia d'Italia*, vol. V, pp. 118, 124; Sanuto, *Diarii*, vol. XLIV, pp. 448, 451, 476.
59. Ibid. pp. 473, 477–8, 499, 502, 518; Guicciardini, *Storia d'Italia*, vol. V, p. 127; Salvioli, 'Nuovi studii . . . sul sacco di Roma', *Archivio Veneto*, vol. XVII, p. 24.
60. *L. & P. Henry VIII*, vol. IV, pt 2, p. 1362. Campeggio estimated the damage to his see of Bologna at 4000 ducats.
61. Guazzo, *Historie*, p. 55.
62. L. Guicciardini, *Sacco di Roma*, p. 107; *La Presa e Lamento di Roma*, p. 124.
63. Sanuto, *Diarii*, vol. XLIV, pp. 515, 529, 555; L. Guicciardini, *Sacco di Roma*, pp. 107–9; *La Presa e Lamenta di Roma*, pp. 124–9; Guicciardini, *Storia d'Italia*, vol. V, p. 127.

64. L. Guicciardini, *Sacco di Roma*, p. 110.
65. Sanuto, *Diarii*, vol. XLIV, p. 556.
66. V.L. ASV MS. Fondo Pio n.53 ff.107*v*–108.

CHAPTER X. FROM FLORENCE TO ROME

1. Albèri, *Relazioni*, 2nd series, vol. III, p. 129.
2. Vettori in *Sacco*, ed. Milanesi, pp. 416–17.
3. Instructions quoted in A. von Reumont, *La Jeunesse de Catherine de Medicis* (Paris, 1866), p. 8 n.1.
4. Nardi, *Historie*, p. 173.
5. Ibid. p. 174.
6. Ibid.
7. For this information I am indebted to Mrs Rosemary Pesman of the University of Sydney. For opposition by the Soderini to the Medici in the fifteenth century, see N. Rubinstein, *The Government of Florence under the Medici 1434–1494* (London, 1966) passim.
8. Nardi, *Historie*, 161–79.
9. Giovio, *Vita Colonna, Vita Leo X*, p. 177; Varchi, *Storia Fiorentina*, vol. I, p. 64.
10. Ibid. pp. 174–5; L. Guicciardini, *Sacco di Roma*, p. 99.
11. *Cal. S.P. Spanish 1527–9*, pp. 41, 171.
12. Sanuto, *Diarii*, vol. XLIV, p. 92.
13. The *palleschi* were the members of families popularly linked with the Medici. Although they did not inevitably support Medici policy, they tended to rise and fall with them.
14. Gilbert, *Machiavelli and Guicciardini*, pp. 100–35.
15. Vettori, *Sommario*, p. 349.
16. Vettori in *Sacco*, ed. Milanesi, pp. 417–19; Ridolfi, *Guicciardini*, p. 173.
17. Varchi, *Storia Fiorentina*, vol. I, p. 95; B.N. Italian 15 f.655; Segni, *Storie Fiorentine, Vita Capponi*, p. 297; Ridolfi, *Guicciardini*, p. 172.
18. J. R. Hale, *Machiavelli and Renaissance Italy* (London, 1961) pp. 221–2; Lucci Landucci, *A Florentine Diary,* trans. A. de R. Jervis (London, 1927) p. 291; Varchi, *Storia Fiorentina*, vol. I, p. 96.
19. Sanuto, *Diarii*, vol. XLIV, p. 98; V.L. ASV MS. Fondo Pio n.54 f.41.
20. L. Guicciardini, *Sacco di Roma*, p. 134.
21. Vettori, *Sommario*, p. 378.
22. British Museum Cotton MS. Vitellius B. ix. ff.104–6*v*. By the Treaty of Cognac Florence had been put under the protection of the League, without actually joining it, and that only by a secret clause. Florence now became a formal member with the obligation to maintain 5000 infantry, 250 lances and 500 light cavalry. Urbino at the same time re-acquired St Leo, taken by Florence after 1517.
23. Sanuto, *Diarii*, vol. XLV, p. 232.
24. Ibid. pp. 39–40.
25. Gattinara in *Sacco*, ed. Milanesi, pp. 495–6; V.L. Cornelius de Fine, 'Diarium' f.95.
26. Gattinara in *Sacco*, ed. Milanesi, p. 496.

CHAPTER XI. THE SACK OF ROME

1. L. Guicciardini, *Sacco di Roma*, p. 174; Buonaparte in *Sacco*, ed. Milanesi, p. 330. Brandano's bizarre career did not end with this imprisonment but rather went from strength to strength. He had a very large popular following, and in parts of Italy he was venerated as a saint. After the sack of Rome he went to Spain on pilgrimage where, not surprisingly, he managed to fall foul of the Inquisition. He subsequently returned to Siena where between 1550 and 1552 he ran a campaign against the building of the Spanish fortress, resorting in the end to direct action against the builders. He died in 1554 during the siege of Siena.

2. A.S.C. MS. Arm. xiv. tom.7 f.1.

3. L. Guicciardini, *Sacco di Roma*, pp. 174–7. For a description of the last event, written three days after it occurred, see Sanuto, *Diarii*, vol. xli, p. 143.

4. L. Guicciardini, *Sacco di Roma*, p. 177. Guicciardini disliked Rome and the Romans intensely.

5. *Cal. S.P. Spanish 1527–9*, p. 173.

6. The most recent example was da Leyva's refusal to permit the sack of Milan in 1526. Guicciardini, *Storia d'Italia*, vol. v, p. 25.

7. Sanuto, *Diarii*, vol. xliii, pp. 633, 646.

8. *Cal. S.P. Spanish 1527–9*, p. 173.

9. Vettori in *Sacco*, ed. Milanesi, p. 435.

10. V.L. ASV MS. Fondo Pio n.53 f.65, n.54 f.34*v*; *Cal. S.P. Spanish 1527–9*, pp. 12–13, 42, 162, 170; Sanuto, *Diarii*, vol. xliii, pp. 548, 700; vol. xlv, pp. 60, 338; Lebey, *Le Connétable de Bourbon*, p. 426 n.1; V.L. Cornelius de Fine, 'Diarium' f.95.

11. Orano, *Sacco di Roma*, pp. 239–40. In the Middle Ages the Senate met there; it was there that Charles of Anjou convoked the Roman parliament; there the defence against Henry VII was organized; Cola di Rienzo held his meetings there.

12. V.L. Cornelius de Fine, 'Diarium' f.95, implies that it was 4 May. See also Orano, *Sacco di Roma*, p. 238; Sanuto, *Diarii*, vol. xlv, p. 60.

13. Orano, *Sacco di Roma*, pp. 244–5; Sanuto, *Diarii*, vol. xlvi, pp. 129–30.

14. Orano, *Sacco di Roma*, pp. 245–6; *Cal. S.P. Spanish 1527–9*, p. 174.

15. Sanuto, *Diarii*, vol. xlv, p. 91; vol. xlvi, p. 129; Vettori in *Sacco*, ed. Milanesi, p. 431; Gattinara in ibid. p. 499; *Cal. S.P. Spanish 1527–9*, p. 137.

16. Cellini, *Autobiography*, p. 70; Sanuto, *Diarii*, vol. xlv, pp. 186–7.

17. Orano, *Sacco di Roma*, pp. 256–7.

18. *La Presa e Lamento di Roma*, p. 142. See also V.L. Cornelius de Fine, 'Diarium' f.95; Guazzo, *Historie*, p. 50.

19. Orano, *Sacco di Roma*, p. 252; V.L. Cornelius de Fine, 'Diarium' f.95*v*; *La Presa e Lamento di Roma*, pp. 143–4, 152.

20. Guicciardini, *Storia d'Italia*, vol. v, p. 138; L. Guicciardini, *Sacco di Roma*, p. 156; *La Presa e Lamento di Roma*, p. 136; Schulz, *Der Sacco di Roma*, p. 104; letter printed in Pastor, *Popes*, vol. ix, p. 503; Sanuto, *Diarii*, vol.

xlv, p. 232; *Alfonso de Valdés and the Sack of Rome*, ed. John E. Longhurst (Albuquerque, 1952), p. 57; *Cal. S.P. Spanish 1527–9*, p. 196; Du Bellay letter, p. 410; Vettori in *Sacco*, ed. Milanesi, p. 432; V.L. Cornelius de Fine, 'Diarium' f.95.

21. Buonaparte in *Sacco*, ed. Milanesi, p. 320. The harangue of a commander before battle was a set piece according to certain rules. It rarely varied. There are several versions of Bourbon's on this occasion. None seems likely to have been accurate.

22. Sanuto, *Diarii*, vol. xlv, p. 232. See also Schulz, *Der Sacco di Roma*, p.104; Guazzo, *Historie*, p. 66; Brantôme, *Œuvres*, vol. i, p. 308.

23. Cave, *Le Sac de Rome*, p. 395; V.L. Cornelius de Fine, 'Diarium' f.96.

24. Buonaparte in *Sacco*, ed. Milanesi, p. 333.

25. Du Bellay letter, p. 410; Schulz, *Der Sacco di Roma*, p. 104; L. Guicciardini, *Sacco di Roma*, pp. 180–3.

26. Vettori, *Sommario*, p. 379.

27. L. Guicciardini, *Sacco di Roma*, pp. 178–80; *La Presa e Lamento di Roma*, pp. 141–3; Sanuto, *Diarii*, vol. xlv, pp. 185–6, 214, 232; Cave, *Le Sac de Rome*, p. 396; letter printed in Pastor, *Popes*, vol. ix, p. 505.

28. Cave, *Le Sac de Rome*, p. 397.

29. Guazzo, *Historie*, p. 66.

30. Letter printed in Pastor, *Popes*, vol. ix, p. 505; L. Guicciardini, *Sacco di Roma*, pp. 184–7; Vettori, *Sommario*, p. 379; Orano, *Sacco di Roma*, p. 258; Sanuto, *Diarii*, vol. xlv, p. 232.

31. Ibid. vol. xlv, pp. 91, 233; vol. xlvi, p. 130; *Cal. S.P. Spanish 1527–9*, p. 212; L. Guicciardini, *Sacco di Roma*, p. 187.

32. Guazzo, *Historie*, 68.

33. Sanuto, *Diarii*, vol. xlv, pp. 91, 123, 165–7, 186; L. Guicciardini, *Sacco di Roma*, p. 189; Cave, *Le Sac de Rome*, p. 346; *La Presa e Lamento di Roma*, pp. 147–52; Guazzo, *Historie*, pp. 67–8; 'Descriptio Urbis', p. 463.

34. *Cal. S.P. Spanish 1527–9*, p. 195.

35. Giovio, *Vita Colonna, Vita Leo X*, p. 191; *Cal. S.P. Spanish 1527–9*, p. 195; Sanuto, *Diarii*, vol. xlvi, p. 131.

36. Buonaparte in *Sacco*, ed. Milanesi, p. 353.

37. Sanuto, *Diarii*, vol. xlv, pp. 167, 186; Cave, *Le Sac de Rome*, p. 398.

38. Sanuto, *Diarii*, vol. xlv, pp. 91, 219; Orano, *Sacco di Roma*, p. 261; L. Guicciardini, *Sacco di Roma*, pp. 197–9; Vettori, *Sommario*, p. 380; Pastor, *Popes*, vol. ix, p. 505.

39. Sanuto, *Diarii*, xlv, p. 145.

40. Ibid. p. 219.

41. V.L. MS. Vat. Lat. 7933 f.57*v*.

42. *Cal. S.P. Spanish 1527–9*, no. 71.

43. Orano, *Sacco di Roma*, pp. 81–3, 261–2, 281.

44. Como in *Sacco*, ed. Milanesi, pp. 472–3.

45. Como in ibid. p. 474.

46. At least 600 people in dal Valle's palace were found to be worth ransoming (A.S.C. MS. Arm. tom. xiv, 7 ff.123*v*–131). They came from all ranks of society, though most notably from the Roman nobility and clergy; but

there were also servants, prostitutes, one baker, a smith, three tailors, four lawyers, a surgeon, a herbalist and a bookseller. Eight Jews were also named.

47. A.S.C. MS. Arm. tom. xiv. 7 ff.123*v*–136; V.L. ASV MS. Fondo Pio n.53 ff.126–126*v*; Como in *Sacco*, ed. Milanesi, pp. 475–6; Sanuto, *Diarii*, vol. xlv, p. 216.

48. Como in *Sacco*, ed. Milanesi, p. 478.

49. Ibid. pp. 482–4.

50. V.L. ASV MS. Fondo Pio n.53 f.123*v*.

51. Bourbon was Isabella's nephew also.

52. Como in *Sacco*, ed. Milanesi, p. 481.

53. Sanuto, *Diarii*, vol. xlv, p. 237.

54. L. Guicciardini, *Sacco di Roma*, p. 171.

55. V.L. ASV MS. Fondo Pio n.53 f.122*v*.

56. V.L. MS. Vat. Lat. 7933 ff.55–60.

57. Sanuto, *Diarii*, vol. xlv, p. 133.

58. V.L. MS. Vat. Lat. 7933 f.61.

59. Sanuto, *Diarii*, vol. xlv, p. 166; S. Muzzi, *Annali della Città di Bologna* (Bologna, 1844) vol. vi, p. 219; V.L. ASV MS. Fondo Pio n.53 f.123; L. Guicciardini, *Sacco di Roma*, p. 202; Como in *Sacco*, ed. Milanesi, p. 485.

60. Buonaparte in *Sacco*, ed. Milanesi, p. 378.

61. Letter quoted in Pastor, *Popes*, vol. ix, p. 506.

62. Buonaparte in *Sacco*, ed. Milanesi, p. 380; L. Guicciardini, *Sacco di Roma*, p. 227.

63. V.L. MS. Vat. Lat. 8251 pt II f.229; Orano, *Sacco di Roma*, pp. 85–7, 99. Clement ordered a special commission of cardinals to try each case, but so many were pending before the court that in 1535 the Alberini family still had not obtained judgement.

64. L. Bianchi, *Carissimi, Stradella, Scarlatti e l'Oratorio Musicale* (Rome, 1969) p. 70.

65. Gattinara in *Sacco*, ed. Milanesi, p. 504. It is difficult to establish an accurate chronology. Certainly Cardinal Como was not right in claiming that Orange had little success in restoring order (Como in ibid. pp. 471, 489). Como was not in Rome but at Civitàvecchia. Angelo Sanuto, also writing from Civitàvecchia on 19 May, said that the sack only lasted for three days (Sanuto, *Diarii*, vol. xlv, p. 217). Salazar says nine or ten days (*Cal. S.P. Spanish 1527–9*, p. 196). See also Colla Colleine, a Roman from Trastevere, in A.S.C. MS. Arm. tom. xiv. 7 f.2. The most probable sequence of events would seem to be a sack lasting for about a week, and that the army was brought back under some kind of military discipline after the three days which custom allowed for in the sack of a town.

66. Como in *Sacco*, ed. Milanesi, pp. 477, 484.

67. Buonaparte in *Sacco*, ed. Milanesi, pp. 390–1.

68. Orano, *Sacco di Roma*, pp. 92, 284–5.

69. Contemporary guesses are wild and do not seem to be based on any accurate lists. The situation was complicated by the fact that many people

did manage to escape from the city, and refugees from Rome turned up all over Italy in the following months.

70. V.L. MS. Vat. Lat. 8251 pt II f.229.

71. Sanuto, *Diarii*, vol. XLV, pp. 166–8; Sadoleto, *Letters*, p. 195; Cave, *Le Sac de Rome*, pp. 373–4. For Colucci's library, see Francesco Flamini, *Il Cinquecento* (Milan, 1903) p. 102.

72. Cave, *Le Sac de Rome*, p. 374; Como in *Sacco*, ed. Milanesi, p. 487; Delumeau, *Rome*, p. 689; Sanuto, *Diarii*, vol. XLVI, p. 137; *Cal. S.P. Spanish 1527–9*, p. 200.

72. Cave, *Le Sac de Rome*, p. 374; Valeriano, *De litteratorum infelicitate*, p. 18; Giovio, *Vita del Gran Capitano, Vita Pescara*, p. 7.

73. *Direptio Expugnatae Urbis*, p. 39; Como in *Sacco*, ed. Milanesi, p. 487; Delumeau, *Rome*, p. 689; Sanuto, *Diarii*, vol. XLVI, p. 137; *Cal. S.P. Spanish 1527–9*, p. 200; Cave, *Le Sac de Rome*, pp. 365–72; Monaco, *Camera Apostolica*, p. 23.

74. *Cal. S.P. Spanish 1527–9*, pp. 510, 512, 516. See also Pandolfi, 'Giovan Matteo Giberti e l'ultima defesa della libertà d'Italia negl'anni 1521–5', p. 181, for the loss of Alexander's correspondence.

75. Sanuto, *Diarii*, vol. XLVI, p. 137; Como in *Sacco*, ed. Milanesi, pp. 487–8.

76. On Boccadiferro, see 'Benedetto Varchi e l'aristotelismo del Rinascimento', in *Convivium*, n.s., vol. III (1963) pp. 280–311.

77. For Raffaelo, his losses during the sack and the repercussions, see *Carteggio inedito d'artisti dei secoli XIV, XV, XVI*, ed. G. Gaye (Florence, 1840) vol. II, pp. 192–3, 195, 203.

78. Flamini, *Il Cinquecento*, p. 95; Muzzi, *Annali della Città di Bologna*, vol. VI, p. 220; G. Vasari, *Lives of the Painters*, trans. Mrs J. Foster (London, 1851) pp. 109, 167, 300, 312, 363–4, 477, 505; Castiglione, *Lettere*, vol. II, p. 9; A. Renaudet, *Érasme et l'Italie* (Geneva, 1954) p. 76; 'Descriptio Urbis', pp. 447, 516.

79. Cave, *Le Sac de Rome*, pp. 393–4; Sanuto, *Diarii*, vol. XLVI, p. 138; vol. XLV, p. 233; V.L. MS. Vat. Lat. 7933 f.580; Valeriano, *De litteratorum infelicitate*, p. 68; L. Guicciardini, *Sacco di Roma*, p. 237. On the other hand, because of the extensive loss of life, some money buried at the time was not recovered for centuries. In 1705 a chest buried before the sack was dug up and was found to contain 60,000 gold ducats.

80. V.L. MS. Vat. Lat. 7933 f.580; *Direptio Expugnatae Urbis*, p. 41; Sanuto, *Diarii*, vol. XLV, pp. 90, 196; *Cal. S.P. Spanish 1527–9*, p. 198.

81. Sanuto, *Diarii*, vol. XLVI, p. 137.

CHAPTER XII. ROME AFTER THE SACK

1. Even during a conclave the *auditore di camera* usually continued his work.

2. Gattinara in *Sacco*, ed. Milanesi, pp. 517–18.

3. Gattinara in ibid. p. 528.

4. *Cal. S.P. Spanish 1527–9*, p. 535.

5. Sanuto, *Diarii*, vol. XLVI, p. 132.

6. Ibid. vol. XLV, p. 163; Orano, *Sacco di Roma*, 265.

7. V.L. ASV MS. Fondo Pio n.53 f.115.

8. Sanuto, *Diarii*, vol. XLV, p. 133.
9. V.L. ASV MS. Fondo Pio n.53 f.123*v*.
10. Sanuto, *Diarii*, vol. XLV, pp. 164, 183, 206; V.L. ASV MS. Fondo Pio n.53 ff.114–114*v*.
11. Sanuto, *Diarii*, vol. XLV, p. 208.
12. Orano, *Sacco di Roma*, p. 95.
13. V.L. MS. Vat. Lat. 7933 f.60.
14. V.L. ASV MS. Fondo Pio n.53 f.112*v*.
15. *Cal. S.P. Spanish 1527–9*, pp. 479–81. The letter was written in December.
16. Orano, *Sacco di Roma*, pp. 92–3.
17. Sanuto, *Diarii*, vol. XLV, p. 313.

CHAPTER XIII. THE LOSS OF THE CHURCH STATE

1. Quoted in Ridolfi, *Guicciardini*, p. 58. For the kind of authority which a governor did exercise, see Guicciardini's governorships in ibid. pp. 64–84, and see A.S. Rettori dello Stato n.8a ff.601–2.
2. Castiglione, *Lettere*, vol. II, p. 13; A.S. Rettori dello Stato n.9a f.12.
3. Sanuto, *Diarii*, vol. XLIII, pp. 526, 654.
4. Ibid. p. 654.
5. Sanuto, *Diarii*, vol. XLIV, pp. 331, 216–17, 329, 454, 476; vol. XLVI, p. 489.
6. Ibid. vol. XLIV, p. 496.
7. E. Benoist, *Guichardin* (Marseilles, 1862) p. 410; A.S. Rettori dello Stato n.9a ff.161–3, 172, 191–2; Gattinara in *Sacco*, ed. Milanesi, p. 526; *Cal. S.P. Spanish 1527–9*, pp. 255, 299; Varchi, *Storia Fiorentina*, vol. I, p. 247.
8. Sanuto, *Diarii*, vol. XLVI, pp. 170, 302, 326, 327, 336, 337.
9. *Cal. S.P. Spanish 1527–9*, p. 292; Sansovino, *Famiglie d'Italia*, p. 97.
10. Sanuto, *Diarii*, vol. XLVI, p. 337; *Cal. S.P. Venetian 1527–33*, p. 133; *Cal. S.P. Spanish 1527–9*, p. 421; Sansovino, *Famiglie d'Italia*, p. 97.
11. V.L. ASV MS. Fondo Pio n.53 ff.123*v*–124.
12. *L. & P. Henry VIII*, vol. IV, pt 2, p. 1481.
13. Ibid. p. 1539.
14. Sanuto, *Diarii*, vol. XLVI, p. 608.
15. *L. & P. Henry VIII*, vol. IV, pt 2, p. 1460.
16. A.S. Rettori dello Stato n.8a ff.518–21, 545–6, 549, n.9a f.46.
17. Salvioli, 'Nuovi studii . . . sul Sacco di Roma', *Archivio Veneto*, vol. XVII, p. 30; Guicciardini, *Storia d'Italia*, vol. V, pp. 148–9; Varchi, *Storia Fiorentina*, vol. I, p. 253; A.S. Rettori dello Stato n.9a ff.153–5, n.8a f.98; *Cal. S.P. Spanish 1527–9*, p. 249.
18. Salvioli, 'Nuovi studii . . . sul Sacco di Roma', *Archivio Veneto*, vol XVII, p. 29.
19. Sanuto, *Diarii*, vol. XLV, p. 111.
20. Ibid. p. 211.
21. Ibid. pp. 212–13.
22. Canestrini et Desjardins, *Négociations*, vol. II, pp. 950, 955–7; *Cal. S.P. Venetian 1527–33*, p. 69.
23. Sanuto, *Diarii*, vol. XLV, p. 283.

24. *Cronache e Documenti*, ed. Ricci, pp. 59–68; Sanuto, *Diarii*, vol. XLV, pp. 160, 197, 325, 334, 348, 374; Paruta, *Istorie*, pp. 457–8.

25 Varchi, *Storia Fiorentina*, vol. I, p. 81; Benoist, *Guichardin*, p. 410; Sanuto, *Diarii*, vol. XLVI, p. 506.

26. 'Memorie Perugine di Teseo Alfani', *Archivo Storico Italiano*, vol. XVI, pt 2, pp. 309–19.

27. Roth, *Last Florentine Republic*, p. 41.

28. Albèri, *Relazioni*, 2nd series, vol. V, p. 420; Vettori, *Sommario*, p. 381.

29. For the date, see Roth, *Last Florentine Republic*, p. 40, and *Cal. S.P. Venetian 1527–33*, p. 64, which makes it clear that the news did not become generally known until twenty-four hours later.

30. In the following narrative of events at Florence I have tried to meet the problems traditionally faced by scholars writing in English about this highly sophisticated political system by observing the following conventions:

    (i) When talking about a 'republican régime', I refer to the type of governments which existed in Florence between 1494 and 1512 and again between 1527 and 1530. It is, of course, true that, technically, Florence was also a republic under the Medici between 1434 and 1494 and between 1512 and 1527, but clearly contemporaries knew the difference between the 'free governments' (1494–1512, 1527–30) and Medici rule.

    (ii) I refer to the upper, traditional ruling class of Florence throughout as the aristocrats, unless quoting contemporary sources. It is a usefully vague term to describe a group which it is impossible to define by any kind of modern sociological analysis.

    (iii) The names of the magistracies I have translated wherever this is feasible, but certain terms like *Gonfaloniere* and *Signoria* have no acknowledged English equivalent, so that I have used them, giving a brief explanation of the function of these offices.

31. Salvioli, 'Nuovi studii . . . sul Sacco di Roma', *Archivio Veneto*, vol. XVII, p. 29.

32. Segni, *Storie Fiorentine, Vita Capponi*, pp. 302–5; Roth, *Last Florentine Republic*, p. 44.

33. They were held by foreign captains directly dependent on the Medici and in their name. The citadel at Pisa was a new one.

34. Sanuto, *Diarii*, vol. XLV, pp. 155–6; Roth, *Last Florentine Republic*, p. 45.

35. Niccolò Machiavelli, *Discorsi sopra la prima deca di Titio Livio*, bk I, ch. 8.

36. Further information on the constitution of Florence and Medici controls, how they manipulated the elections, etc., can be found in N. Rubinstein's great book, *The Government of Florence under the Medici*.

37. It was composed of nine members – eight Priors of Liberty (*Priori di Libertà*) and the *Gonfaloniere di Giustizia*, the official head of the Florentine Republic. Two of the Priors came from each quarter of the city. Seven members of the board had to come from the Greater Guilds (*arti maggiori*) and two from the Lesser Guilds (*arti minori*). The Signoria made the final decisions on all questions of policy.

38. For the way in which the Medici government was organized, reference should be made to Rubinstein, *Government of Florence under the Medici*, and to Gilbert, *Machiavelli and Guicciardini*.
39. Sanuto, *Diarii*, vol. XLV, pp. 156, 137–9; Roth, *Last Florentine Republic*, p. 46; Varchi, *Storia Fiorentina*, vol. I, p. 147; Albèri, *Relazioni*, 2nd series, vol. V, p. 413.
40. Varchi, *Storia Fiorentina*, vol. I, pp. 178–9.
41. Ibid. p. 139.
42. For Vettori and Guicciardini, see Gilbert, *Machiavelli and Guicciardini*, passim; Varchi, *Storia Fiorentina*, vol. I, pp. 138–61; Roth, *Last Florentine Republic*, pp. 52–3.
43. Volterra, for instance, was virtually depopulated by the plague.
44. Varchi, *Storia Florentina*, vol. I, pp. 368–71; vol. II, pp. 319, 355; B.N. MS. Italien 15 f.661; Roth, *Last Florentine Republic*, p. 75; Segni, *Storie Fiorentine, Vita Capponi*, pp. 42–3, 321; Nardi, *Historie*, pp. 201–3.
45. By 1529 they included Ruberto Acciauoli, Domenico Canigiani, Palle Rucellai, Giovanfrancesco Ridolfi, Alessandro and Luigi Cappei and Antonfrancesco degli Albizzi, all of whom had originally been prominent in the rebellion against the Medici.
46. Sanuto, *Diarii*, vol. XLV, p. 418.
47. Ibid. p. 316.
48. Pastor, *Popes*, vol. IX, p. 423.
49. Sanuto, *Diarii*, vol. XLV, pp. 317, 390; A.S.C. MS. Arm. xiv. tom.7 ff.116–19; *Cal. S.P. Spanish 1527–9*, pp. 231–3.

CHAPTER XIV. THE POPE ESCAPES

1. *Cal. S.P. Spanish 1527–9*, pp. 138, 167.
2. Ibid. p. 242.
3. Varchi, *Storia Fiorentina*, vol. I, p. 210.
4. V.L. ASV MS. Fondo Pio n.53 f.119*v*; Tomassetti, *Campagna Romana*, vol. III, p. 118.
5. *Cal. S.P. Spanish 1527–9*, p. 429.
6. V.L. ASV MS. Fondo Pio n.53 f.113.
7. Delumeau, *Rome*, p. 534; Tomassetti, *Campagna Romana*, vol. I, p. 213; V.L. ASV MS. Fondo Pio n.53 f.119*v*; Molini, *Documenti*, vol. II, p. 21.
8. A.S.C. MS. Arm. xiv. tom.7 f.2; Sanuto, *Diarii*, vol. XLVI, pp. 186, 222–3.
9. Ibid. vol. XLV, pp. 223, 300.
10. Ibid. vol. XLVI, pp. 280, 293; *Cal. S.P. Spanish 1527–9*, pp. 427–9.
11. Sanuto, *Diarii*, vol. XLV, pp. 296–7.
12. *Cal. S.P. Spanish 1527–9*, pp. 467–8.
13. Ibid. pp. 473–4.
14. Molini, *Documenti*, pp. 273–7; Sanuto, *Diarii*, vol. XLVI, p. 361; Schulz, *Sacco di Roma*, pp. 177–87.
15. *Cal. S.P. Spanish 1527–9*, p. 475.
16. Ibid. p. 476.
17. Varchi, *Storia Fiorentina*, vol. I, p. 261.
18. *Cal. S.P. Spanish 1527–9*, p. 490.

19. Ibid. p. 494.

CHAPTER XV. THE POPE IN EXILE

1. Varchi, *Storia Fiorentina,* vol. I, pp. 261–2.
2. Pastor, *Popes,* vol. x, p. 3.
3. *L. & P. Henry VIII,* vol. IV, pt 2, p. 1819.
4. Sanuto, *Diarii,* vol. XLVII, p. 488.
5. He returned to Rome in February 1529 but did not stay.
6. For the impact of these reforms, see Sanuto, *Diarii,* vol. XLIX, p. 161.
7. Quoted in Pastor, *Popes,* vol. x, p. 16. The reference is to I Samuel, XXI 6.
8. Sanuto, *Diarii,* vol. XLVII, p. 235.
9. *Cal. S.P. Spanish 1527–9,* p. 635.
10. Sanuto, *Diarii,* vol. XLIX, p. 18.
11. *Enciclopedia Italiana;* Varchi, *Storia Fiorentina,* vol. I, p. 228; *Cal. S.P. Spanish 1527–9,* p. 393; Sansovino, *Famiglie d'Italia,* pp. 98–9.
12. *Cal. S.P. Spanish 1527–9,* p. 538.
13. Sanuto, *Diarii,* vol. XLVI, pp. 445–6; 'Suites du Sac de Rome', pp. 20–1.
14. 'Suites du Sac de Rome', pp. 23–8.
15. *Cal. S.P. Spanish 1527–9,* p. 534.
16. This included money borrowed from the son of Agostino Chigi, on a security of estates in the Regno; *Cal. S.P. Spanish 1527–9,* pp. 534, 545, 559, 581; 'Suites du Sac de Rome', pp. 28–30.
17. *Cal. S.P. Spanish 1527–9,* p. 558.
18. Ibid. p. 583.
19. Ibid. pp. 582, 592; 'Suites du Sac de Rome', pp. 30, 37; Sanuto, *Diarii,* vol. XLVI, p. 602.
20. Varchi, *Storia Fiorentina,* vol. I, p. 236; Segni, *Storie Fiorentine, Vita Capponi,* vol. I, p. 44; *Cal. S.P. Spanish 1527–9,* pp. 418–19.
21. Sanuto, *Diarii,* vol. XLVI, pp. 173–4.
22. *Cal. S.P. Spanish 1527–9,* pp. 94–5.
23. *L. & P. Henry VIII,* vol. IV, pt 2, p. 1460.
24. The Polesine had been obtained by Venice in 1483, and good government had endeared the population of that province to Venetian rule. After the battle of Vailà the Polesine had been occupied by Alfonso d'Este but was recovered by Venice within six months. In 1513 Este once more took over the Polesine with the assistance of Cardona's Spanish troops; Alviano recaptured it for Venice in 1514.
25. *Cal. S.P. Spanish 1527–9,* pp. 457, 462, 604–5; *L. & P. Henry VIII,* vol. IV, pt 2, p. 1610; Sanuto, *Diarii,* vol. XLVI, p. 329.
26. Sanuto, *Diarii,* vol. XLVI, pp. 409–10.
27. Ibid. p. 459.
28. Ibid. p. 468.
29. M. Berengo, *Nobili e mercanti nella Lucca del Cinquecento* (Turin, 1965) p. 16.
30. Sanuto, *Diarii,* vol. XLVI, p. 645.
31. Ibid. pp. 619, 645.
32. Orano, *Sacco di Roma,* p. 350. Alberini saw Gian d'Urbina hang three pillagers from a shop sign.

33. Sanuto, *Diarii*, vol. XLVI, p. 646; 'Suites du Sac de Rome', p. 39.
34. The bear was the heraldic sign of the Orsini.
35. Sanuto, *Diarii*, vol. XLVI, pp. 646–7; 'Suites du Sac de Rome', pp. 39–40; Orano, *Sacco di Roma,* pp. 39–40; Varchi, *Storia Fiorentina,* vol. I, p. 266.
36. 'Suites du Sac de Rome', p. 46; Sanuto, *Diarii*, vol. XLVII, pp. 96–7, 235; *Cal. S.P. Spanish 1527–9,* p. 626.
37. Sanuto, *Diarii*, vol. XLVII, p. 235.
38. Ibid. p. 210.
39. *Cal. S.P. Spanish 1527–9,* p. 715.
40. Pastor, *Popes,* vol. X, pp. 17–20; Sanuto, *Diarii*, vol. XLVII, p. 359.
41. Ibid. vol. XLVIII, pp. 127–8.
42. *L. & P. Henry VIII,* vol. IV, pt 2, p. 1651.
43. Sanuto, *Diarii*, vol. XLVI, pp. 394–3.
44. Ibid. pp. 489–90.
45. Ibid. p. 558.
46. Sanuto, *Diarii*, vol. XLVII, pp. 238, 289, 363; *L. & P. Henry VIII,* vol. IV, pt 2, p. 1772.
47. Sanuto, *Diarii*, vol. XLVII, pp. 289, 334, 474; *Cal. S.P. Spanish 1527–9,* p. 685; *Cal. S.P. Venetian 1527–33,* p. 139.
48. Sanuto, *Diarii*, vol. XLVIII, p. 139.
49. *Cal. S.P. Spanish 1527–9,* p. 685; *Cal. S.P. Venetian 1527–33,* p. 138.
50. Ibid. pp. 151–2.
51. Molini, *Documenti*, vol. II, p. 36.
52. Ibid. p. 38; Sanuto, *Diarii*, vol. XLVIII, p. 302. This was the number he held from Francis I.
53. It had fallen to the French in the previous August.
54. Sanuto, *Diarii*, vol. XLVIII, pp. 440–60.
55. *Cal. S.P. Spanish 1527–9,* p. 793.
56. Sanuto, *Diarii*, vol. XLVI, p. 383.
57. *Alfonso de Valdés and the Sack of Rome,* ed. Longhurst, p. 34.
58. Sanuto, *Diarii*, vol. XLVII, pp. 426, 438; Varchi, *Storia Fiorentina,* vol. I, p. 247.
59. Sanuto, *Diarii*, vol. XLVII, p. 85.
60. Ibid. vol. XLVIII, p. 128; Varchi, *Storia Fiorentina,* vol. I, p. 353; Albèri, *Relazioni,* 2nd series, vol. III, p. 262; *Cal. S.P. Venetian 1527–33,* p. 172; *Cal. S.P. Spanish 1527–9,* p. 827; Molini, *Documenti*, vol. II, p. 21; Guazzo, *Historie,* p. 69.
61. Quoted in Pastor, *Popes,* vol. X, pp. 30–1.

CHAPTER XVI. BARCELONA AND CAMBRAI

1. Letter printed in part in Pastor, *Popes,* vol. X, p. 32 n.2.
2. Sanuto, *Diarii*, vol. XLIX, p. 134.
3. Ibid.
4. *Cal. S.P. Venetian 1527–33,* pp. 134, 136; *Cal. S.P. Spanish 1527–9,* p. 695; Paruta, *Istorie,* p. 499; Sanuto, *Diarii*, vol. XLVII, p. 354. Albanians also accounted for a large part of the regular Venetian army: F. Braudel, *La*

Mediterranée et le Monde mediterranéan à l'époque de Philippe I (Paris, 1949) p. 25.

5. *Cal. S.P. Venetian 1527–33*, p. 134.
6. Ibid. pp. 469, 471.
7. Pastor, *Popes*, vol. x, p. 38.
8. Ibid. p. 41.
9. *Cal. S.P. Spanish 1527–9*, p. 945.
10. Ibid. pp. 946–7; Canestrini et Desjardins, *Négociations*, vol. ii, pp. 1043–4.
11. *Cal. S.P. Spanish 1527–9*, p. 965.
12. Ibid.; Sanuto, *Diarii*, vol. L, pp. 45, 125–6.
13. *Cal. S.P. Venetian 1527–33*, p. 202.
14. Sanuto, *Diarii*, vol. L, p. 197.
15. Segni, *Storie Fiorentine, Vita Capponi*, vol. i, p. 138; Roth, *Last Florentine Republic*, p. 133.
16. Segni, *Storie Fiorentine, Vita Capponi*, vol. i, pp. 127, 157; Varchi, *Storia Fiorentina*, vol. ii, p. 172; Ridolfi, *Guicciardini*, p. 194.
17. Nardi, *Historie*, p. 209.
18. Roth, *Last Florentine Republic*, p. 138; Segni, *Storie Fiorentine, Vita Capponi*, pp. 158–9.
19. Sanuto, *Diarii*, vol. L, p. 378.
20. Ibid. 385; Molini, *Documenti*, vol. ii, p. 204.
21. Ibid. p. 200.
22. *Cal. S.P. Venetian 1527–33*, pp. 79–80, 92–4.
23. Molini, *Documenti*, vol. ii, pp. 204–8, 214; Canestrini et Desjardins, *Négociations*, vol. ii, p. 1071; Varchi, *Storia Fiorentina*, vol. ii, p. 3.
24. Canestrini et Desjardins, *Négociations*, vol. ii, pp. 1081–1102.
25. Molini, *Documenti*, vol ii, pp. 241, 243, 247. Francis also agreed that Venice must be forced to give up the territories she still held in Naples.

CHAPTER XVII. THE RESISTANCE OF FLORENCE

1. Molini, *Documenti*, vol. ii, pp. 246–7.
2. See, for example, the instructions of the Venetian senate to the ambassador in Constantinople of 25 August 1529; Pastor, *Popes*, vol. x, p. 69; Paruta, *Istorie*, p. 581; *Cal. S.P. Spanish 1527–9*, p. 657.
3. Brandi, *Charles V*, p. 256.
4. *Cal. S.P. Spanish 1527–9*, p. 994.
5. Burigozzo, 'Cronaca', p. 497.
6. Molini, *Documenti*, vol. ii, p. 241.
7. Ibid. p. 243.
8. G.A. busta 2132.
9. Burigozzo, 'Cronaca', p. 498.
10. Guicciardini, *Carteggi*, vol. i, p. 106.
11. Bardi, 'Carlo V e l'assedio di Firenze', pp. 22–3.
12. *Cal. S.P. Spanish 1527–9*, pp. 204, 655.
13. Bardi, 'Carlo V e l'assedio di Firenze', pp. 40, 45. The adviser was de Praet. See also Sanuto, *Diarii*, vol. xlv, p. 317, for the rumours in June.
14. Varchi, *Storia Fiorentina*, vol. i, p. 36.

15. Sanuto, *Diarii*, vol. L, p. 154.
16. He was a Roman Catholic priest.
17. Varchi, *Storia Fiorentina*, vol. II, pp. 90–7.
18. Catani, *Ricordi*, pp. 224–5.
19. Nardi, *Historie*, pp. 109–12.
20. Catani, *Ricordi*, pp. 222–5.
21. Ibid. pp. 225–6; Spadari, *Racconto della Ribellione Aretina del 1529*, p. 245.
22. Varchi, *Storia Fiorentina*, vol. II, pp. 116 ,186–7.
23. Ridolfi, *Guicciardini*, p. 200.
24. Varchi, *Storia Fiorentina*, vol. II, pp. 130–45; Nardi, *Historie*, p. 209. The siege-train consisted of 4 cannon, 1 colubrine and 3 small pieces.
25. Traditionally it was held to have begun on 12 October.
26. Nardi, *Historie*, p. 209.
27. Sanuto, *Diarii*, vol. XLVII, p. 156.
28. Oration of Luigi Alemanni to the Florentine militia, printed in M. Fancelli, *Orazioni Politiche del Cinquecento* (Bologna, 1941) pp. 1–6. See also the Balìa to Baldassare Carducci, 12 March 1530, in *Carteggio inedito d'artisti dei secoli XIV, XV, XVI*, ed. Gaye, vol. II, p. 211.

CHAPTER XVIII. THE IMPERIAL CORONATION

1. Albèri, *Relazioni*, 2nd series, vol. III, pp. 265–7; Sanuto, *Diarii*, vol. L, p. 476.
2. Albèri, *Relazioni*, 2nd series, vol. III, pp. 154–5.
3. Ibid. p. 155.
4. Ibid. pp. 160–1.
5. From a letter written by Isabella d'Este to her niece, Renée of France, and printed in translation in J. Cartwright, *Isabella d'Este* (London, 1915) vol. II, pp. 297–301.
6. Albèri, *Relazioni*, 2nd series, vol. III, pp. 161–71; Paruta, *Istorie*, p. 577; Pastor, *Popes*, vol. X, p. 87.
7. Varchi, *Storia Fiorentina*, vol. II, pp. 175–7; Albèri, *Relazioni*, 2nd series, vol. III, pp. 183, 205; Pastor, *Popes*, vol. X, p. 86; Guicciardini, *Storia d'Italia*, vol. V, pp. 284–5.
8. Albèri, *Relazioni*, 2nd series, vol. III, pp. 178, 205.
9. The peace treaties were ratified on 6 January 1530. Venice restored to the emperor the towns she still held in the kingdom of Naples, promised a pardon to all Venetian subjects who had supported the imperialists since the time of Maximilian, and the restoration of their property, agreed to pay Charles 25,000 ducats still owing under the 1523 agreement and to assist in the defence of Naples. Paruta, *Istorie*, pp. 577–9; Molini, *Documenti*, vol. II, pp. 263, 265; Bardi, 'Carlo V e l'assedio di Firenze', p. 39; Pastor, *Popes*, vol. X, p. 88.
10. Burigozzo, 'Cronaca', p. 501.
11. F. Chadbod, 'Venezia nella politica Italiana ed Europea del Cinquecento', in *La Civiltà del Rinascimento* (Venice, 1957) p. 42; Bardi, 'Carlo V e l'assedio di Firenze', p. 33; Sanuto, *Diarii*, vol. L, p. 473.
12. Sforza's death without an heir was a disaster. It led to another Franco-

Spanish war, the occupation of Savoy and Piedmont by Spanish and French troops for almost twenty years and the investiture of Philip II with the duchy of Milan.

13. Varchi, *Storia Fiorentina*, vol. II, pp. 202–12.
14. Memorial in the cloister of San Domenico at Bologna.
15. *Cal. S.P. Venetian 1527–33*, p. 240; Pastor, *Popes*, vol. x, p. 97. For *his* loyalty to the imperialists Federigo Gonzaga was created duke of Mantua.
16. Malatesta asked specifically for a pardon for all subjects of the Church State who had fought in Florence and for the restoration of their con-fiscated property. He himself was to be permitted to return to Perugia and he was to make substantial personal property gains. Varchi, *Storia Fiorentina*, vol. II, pp. 324, 337, 373–5.
17. Roth, *Last Florentine Republic*, p. 334.
18. For a discussion of the role of the aristocrats 1527–32, see F. Gilbert, 'Alcuni discorsi di uomini politici fiorentini e la politica di Clemente VII per la restaurazione medicea', in *Archivio Storico Italiano*, vol. II, pp. 3–24. See also Nardi, *Historie*, pp. 227–8; Ridolfi, *Guicciardini*, pp. 209–15; F. Guicciardini, *Dall'assedio di Firenze al secondo convegno di Clement VII e Carlo V*, ed. A. Otetea (Aquilà, 1927) pp. 6–8.

CHAPTER XIX. THE IMPERIAL VICTORY

1. F. C. Spooner in *The New Cambridge Modern History* (1962) vol. II, p. 344.
2. J. V. G. Mallet, 'Maiolica at Polesden Lacey III: a new look at the Xanto problem', in *Apollo*, March 1971.
3. Sanuto, *Diarii*, vol. XLV, p. 189.
4. *Cal. S.P. Spanish 1527–9*, pp. 243–5.
5. Ibid. p. 639.
6. H. Kamen, *The Spanish Inquisition* (1965), pp. 205–6.
7. *Cal. S.P. Spanish 1527–9*, pp. 243–5.
8. Brandi, *Charles V*, p. 256.
9. *Cal. S.P. Venetian 1527–33*, p. 76. There is a MS. copy of this letter in British Museum Add. MSS. 28576 f.304.
10. E.g. *Cal. S.P. Spanish 1527–9*, p. 297; Brandi, *Charles V*, p. 259. See also Charles's letter to the commune of Rome in A.S.C. MS. Arm. xiv. tom.7 ff.113–115*v*.
11. *Cal. S.P. Spanish 1527–9*, p. 715.
12. Alfonso de Valdés, *Dialogo de Mercurio y Caron*, ed. Jose F. Montesinos (Madrid, 1929).
13. *Alfonso de Valdés and the Sack of Rome*, ed. Longhurst.
14. Renaudet, *Érasme et l'Italie*, p. 191.
15. V.L. MS. Vat. Lat. 7933 f.56; F. Berni, *Orlando Innamorato di Matteo M. Bojardo* (Milan, 1806) vol. I, p. 273.
16. Castiglione, *Lettere*, vol. II, p. 187.
17. Ibid. pp. 187–93.
18. *La Guerra di Camollia*, p. 43.
19. Orano, *Sacco di Roma*, p. 225.
20. Ibid. p. 327: 'I had in my house at that time four of those insatiable

devourers living continually at my expense, and God knows with what inconveniences and difficulties. I will never forgive either Charles or his servants for it.'

21. *La Presa e Lamento di Roma*, p. 365; *Lamento d'Italia*, in *Curiosità Letterarie*, pp. 405–14, written by Guicciardini. For Guicciardini's authorship, see A. de Ruboli, 'Francesco Guicciardini e la Censura Toscana', in *La Bibliofilia*, vol. LI, pp. 86–91.

22 *La Presa e Lamento di Roma*, p. 397; G. Guiddicioni, *Rime,* ed. E. Chiorboli (Bari, 1912) pp. 5–8.

23. Orano, *Sacco di Roma*, p. 195.

24. e.g. Sadoleto, *Letters*, p. 209.

25. e.g. the account of P. Corsi in *Mélanges d'Archéologie et d'Histoire* (1896) pp. 421–32.

26. Pastor, *Popes*, vol. IX, pp. 503–4; Orano, *Sacco di Roma*, p. 116.

27. Sanuto, *Diarii*, vol. XLV, p. 418.

28. Vettori, *Sommario*, pp. 380–1; Sadoleto, *Letters*, p. 178; Varchi, *Storia Fiorentina*, vol. I, p. 127.

29. P. Aretino, *Il Primo Libro delle Lettere* (Bari, 1913) vol. I, pp. 13–16.

30. Printed in *Curiosità Letterarie*, vol. 236, pp. 356–69. See also *Romae Lamentatio* in ibid. pp. 369–83.

31. Ibid. p. 359.

32. Paruta, *Istorie*, pp. 449–51; Sanuto, *Diarii*, vol. XLV, p. 133; *Romae Lamentatio*, in *Curiosità Letterarie*, vol. 236, p. 371; *Lamento di Roma* in ibid. p. 383.

33. In 'Giustificazione della politica di Clemente VII', printed in F. Guicciardini, *Scritti Politici e Ricordi*, ed. R. Palmarocchi (Bari, 1933) pp. 198–211.

34. Ibid. p. 198.

35. Gilbert, *Machiavelli and Guicciardini*, pp. 253–301; R. Ramat, *Il Guicciardini e la Tragedia d'Italia* (Florence, 1953), especially pp. 94–117. This was a point of view shared by many contemporaries, e.g. the comment of the doge in March 1527 that '*Fortuna* wants to ruin the Pope'; Sanuto, *Diarii*, vol. XLIV, p. 356. See also ibid. vol. XLVII, pp. 130–3, for an elegant inquiry into the role played by *Fortuna* in events leading up to the sack of Rome.

36. Pastor, *Popes*, vol. IX, p. 507; Paruta, *Istorie*, p. 450; Nardi, *Historie*, p. 195; Sadoleto, *Letters*, pp. 244–5; L. Guicciardini, *Sacco di Roma*, p. 23; *La Presa e Lamento di Roma*, p. 364; Sanuto, *Diarii*, vol. XLVI, p. 136.

37. Ibid. vol. XLV, pp. 219, 237; L. Guicciardini, *Sacco di Roma*, p. 23.

38. Brantôme, *Œuvres*, p. 322.

39. Alfonso de Valdés, *Dialogo de Mercurio y Caròn*, ed. Montesinos p. 77; *Cal. S.P. Spanish 1527–9*, p. 639.

40. Giovio, *Vita del Gran Capitanio, Vita Pescara*, p. 7.

41. Albèri, *Relazioni*, 2nd series, vol. III, p. 267.

42. Sanuto, *Diarii*, vol. XLVII, p. 429.

43. Orano, *Sacco di Roma*, p. 203.

44. Guicciardini, *Scritti inediti*, p. 62.

45. Sanuto, *Diarii*, vol. XVLII, p. 354. For the views of another scholar who

agrees that there was a change in the intellectual life of Europe at this time and that the change is clearly reflected in the way the Catherine of Aragon case was dealt with, see H. Kamen, *Spanish Inquisition*, p. 82.

46. C. M. Ady, E. M. Jamison, K. D. Vernon, C. S. Terry, *Italy, Medieval and Modern* (1919) p. 237.

47. Sanuto, *Diarii*, vol. XLVII, pp. 228–32.

48. Orano, *Sacco di Roma*, p. 193. See also William Bouwsma, 'Paolo Sarpi e la tradizione rinascimentale', *Rivista Storica Italiana*, vol. LXXIV (1962) pp. 697–716; and Judith Hook, 'Italy and the Counter-Reformation', *History Today*, November 1970. Caetano Cozzi, *Il doge Niccolò Contarini* (Venice and Rome: Istituto per la Collaborazione Culturale, 1958).

BIBLIOGRAPHY

This is not an attempt at an exhaustive bibliography. I have restricted myself to listing those sources and secondary works to which reference is made in the text or which I have found indispensable. Such a selection must be arbitrary, but I hope that nothing of real importance has been omitted.

I. SOURCES

As source material I have included not only correspondence and accounts which are strictly contemporary, but also a number of later histories and records. Many of the authors of these must have known people who were eye-witnesses of the sack of Rome and the events which led up to it. They had access to an oral and, in some cases, a written tradition which is now lost. Since there is a distinction between material written before and after the imperial coronation I have preserved the distinction here. This list of sources is divided into three parts: a list of manuscripts, a list of printed sources compiled or written before the imperial coronation, and a list of printed works written between 1530 and 1600. Where material in the last two categories overlaps I have invariably included it in the first.

(i) MANUSCRIPT SOURCES
(a) *Vatican Library*

ASV AA.ARM. i–xviii. vol. 6522. Letters of cardinal-legates, ambassadors, and other public and private figures to the secretary, the datary and to Salviati 1525–32.

ASV MS. Fondo Pio n.5. Conclaves of the popes.

ASV MS. Fondo Pio n.53. Letters of ministers of the Holy See 1526–7.

ASV MS. Fondo Pio n.54. Letters of Guicciardini and Gambara 1526–7.

Cod. Chigi G.II. 39, 40. Sigismundi Titii, 'Historiarum Senensium', vols IX, X. Both these volumes contain valuable printed contemporary material. Sigismondo Tizio was born at Castiglione in 1455 and graduated at Siena in 1497. He wrote a lengthy manuscript history of Siena, taking much of his material from the archives of Siena.

Cod. Ottob. Lat. 1613. Cornelius de Fine, 'Diarium'. The diary covers the years 1511–31.

MS. Vat. Lat. 7933. Chronicle of Orsola Formicini.

MS. Vat. Lat. 8251. Notes on the great families of Italy.

(b) *Archivio Storico Capitolino*

MS. Arm. xiv. tom.7. Diaries and other materials for the history of Rome in the sixteenth century, vol. i.

(c) *Archivio di Stato, Modena*

Rettori dello Stato nn.8a, 9a. Letters of Nerli, the papal governor.

(d) *Bibliothèque Nationale, Paris*

B.N. MS. Italien n.13. Conclaves of the popes.

B.N. MS. Italien n.15. 'Edificazione di Firenze'. This is a manuscript history of Florence apparently written in the time of Duke Cosimo.

(e) *Gonzaga Archives, Mantua*

(ii) PRINTED SOURCES COMPILED BEFORE THE IMPERIAL CORONATION

Albèri, E., *Le relazioni degli ambasciatori Veneti al Senato durante il secolo decimosesto*, 3 series (Florence, 1839–55).

Alfani, Teseo, 'Memorie Perugine di Teseo Alfani', in *Archivio Storico Italiano,* vol. xvi (1851) pp. 247–319.

Alfonso de Valdés and the Sack of Rome, ed. John E. Longhurst (Albuquerque, 1952).

Aretino, Pietro, *Il Primo Libro delle Lettere* (Bari, 1913).

Baeça, G. de, *Vida de el femoso caballero Don Hugo da Moncada,* in *Coleccion de Documentos inéditos para la historia de Espana,* vol. xxiv (Madrid, 1854). This contains some of the original correspondence of Moncada.

Bardi, A., 'Carlo V e l'assedio di Firenze da documenti dell'arch. di Bruxelles', in *Archivio Storico Italiano,* 5th series, vol. xi (1893) pp. 1–85.

Bontempi, Giovanello, 'Ricordi della città di Perugia dal 1527 al 1530 di Giovanello Bontempi', in *Archivio Storico Italiano,* vol. xvi, pt 2 (1851) pp. 323–401.

Burigozzo, G., 'Cronaca Milanesi del 1500 al 1544', in *Archivio Storico Italiano,* vol. iii (1842) pp. 421 ff.

Calendar of Letters, Despatches, and State Papers, Relating to the Negotiations between England and Spain, Preserved in the Archives at Simancas and Elsewhere, ed. G. A. Bergenroth, P. de Gayangos, M. A. S. Hume, R. Tyler (London, 1862–1916).

Calendar of State Papers and Manuscripts Relating to English Affairs Existing in the Archives and Collections of Milan, ed. A. B. Hinds (London,

1912). With all the Calendars, as with the *Letters and Papers of the Reign of Henry VIII*, I have sometimes found it necessary to refer to the original source material. On the very few occasions where I have found that it was essential I have given the manuscript reference in the notes.

Calendar of State Papers and Manuscripts Relating to English Affairs Existing in the Archives and Collections of Venice and in Other Libraries of Northern Italy, vols I–V, ed. R. Brown (London, 1864–73).

Canestrini, G., 'Documenti per servire alla storia della milizia italiana dal XIII secolo al XVI raccolti negli archivi della Toscana', in *Archivio Storico Italiano*, vol. XV (1851).

Canestrini, G., and Desjardins, A., *Négociations diplomatiques de la France avec la Toscane* (Paris, 1861).

Captivité du Roi François I, ed. A. Champollion-Figeac (Paris, 1847).

Castiglione, Baldassare, *Lettere del Conte Baldesar Castiglione ora per la prima volta data in luce e con annotazioni storiche illustrate dell'Abate Pierantonio Serassi* (Padua, 1769).

Catani, Iacopo, 'Libro de' Ricordi di Iacopo di Maccario di Gregorio Catani Cittadino Aretino', in *Raccolta degli Storici dal cinquecento al millecinquescento ordinata da L. A. Muratori. Nuova edizione riveduta, ampliata e corretta,* ed. G. Carducci and V. Fiorini, vol. XXIV, pt 1. *Annales Arretinorum Maiores et Minores.*

Cave, Jean, 'Le Sac de Rome (1527). Relation inédité de Jean Cave Orléanais', ed. L. Dorez, in *Mélanges d'Archéologie et d'Histoire de l'École Française de Rome* (1896) pp. 324–409.

Codice Topografico della Città di Roma, ed. R. Valentini and G. Zucchetti (Rome, 1953).

Cronache e documenti per la storia Ravennate del secolo XVI, ed. C. Ricci, in *Scelta di Curiosità letterarie inedite o rare,* vol. 192 (Bologna, 1882).

Direptio Expugnatae Urbis Romae ab Exercitu Caroli Quinti in Zeitgenossische Berichte uber die Eroberung der Stadt Rome 1527 (Halle, 1881).

Du Bellay, Guillaume, 'Guillaume du Bellay à l'amiral Chabot', printed in *Mélanges d'Archéologie et d'Histoire de l'École Française de Rome* (1896) pp. 410–14.

Fancelli, M., *Orazioni Politiche del Cinquecento* (Bologna, 1941).

Fragmento de carta sobra el asalto y saco de Roma en Mayo de 1527, in *Coleccion de Documentos inéditos para la Historia de Espana,* vol. VII (Madrid, 1845) pp. 448–64.

Gnoli, D., ' "Descriptio Urbis" o censimento della popolazione di Roma avanti il sacco borbonico', in *Archivio della Reale Società Romana di Storia Patria,* vol. XVII (1894) pp. 375–520.

Granvelle, Cardinal de, *Papiers d'État du Cardinal de Granvelle,* ed. C. Weiss (Paris, 1841–52).

La Guerra di Camollia, printed in *Sceltà di Curiosità Letterarie inedite o rare,* vol. 236 (Bologna, 1890) pp. 30–110.

Guicciardini, Francesco, *Carteggi,* vols v–x, ed. P. G. Ricci (Rome, 1954–62).

—, *Dall'assedio di Firenze al secondo convegno di Clemente VII e Carlo V. Lettere inédite a Bartolomeo Lanfredini,* ed. A. Otetea (Aquilà, 1927).

—, *Scritti inediti di Francesco Guicciardini sopra la politica di Clemente VII dopo la battaglia di Pavia,* ed. P. Guicciardini (Florence, 1940).

—, *Scritti Politici e Ricordi,* ed. R. Palmarocchi (Bari, 1933).

Guicciardini, L., *Il Sacco di Roma* (Paris, 1564).

Istruzioni e Relazioni degli Ambasciatori Genovesi, ed. R. Ciasca, vol. 1 (Rome, 1951).

Landucci, Lucci, *A Florentine Diary, Continued by an Anonymous Writer till 1542, with Notes by Iodoco del Badia,* trans. A. de R. Jervis (London, 1927).

Lanz, K., *Correspondenz des Kaisers Karl V* (Leipzig, 1844).

Letters and Papers, Foreign and Domestic, of the Reign of Henry VIII, ed. J. S. Brewer, J. Gairdner, R. H. Brodie (London, 1862–1932).

Machiavelli, Niccolò, *Il Principe,* ed. L. A. Burd (Oxford, 1891).

—, *Lettere,* ed. F. Gaeta (Milan, 1961).

—, *Opere complete, novamente collazionate sulle migliori edizioni e sui manoscritti originali e arricchite di annotazioni de un compilatore dell'Archivio Storico Italiano* (Florence, 1857).

Molini, G., *Documenti di Storia Italiana copiata su gli originali autentici e per lo piu autografi esistenti in Parigi* (Florence, 1836–7).

Orano, D., *Il Sacco di Roma del MDXXVII, Studi e Documenti,* vol. 1. *I ricordi di Marcello Alberini* (Rome, 1911).

Il Sacco di Roma del MDXXVII: narrazioni di contemporanei, ed. C. Milanesi (Florence, 1867). This contains: *Il Sacco di Roma descritto da Luigi Guicciardini,* pp. 1–244; *Il Sacco di Roma, ragguaglio storico attribuito a Jacopo Buonaparte,* pp. 245–408; *Il Sacco di Roma, descritto in dialogo da Francesco Vettori,* pp. 409–68; *Del Sacco di Roma, lettera del Cardinale di Como al suo segretario,* pp. 469–90; *Del Sacco di Roma, lettera di un ufficiale dell'esercito del Borbone a Carlo Quinto,* pp. 491–530. From internal evidence it is clear that this letter was written by Giovanni Bartolomeo Arboreo da Gattinara.

Sadoleto, Jacopo, *Jacobi Sadoleto S.R.E. Cardinalis Epistolae quotquot extant proprio nomine scriptae* (Rome, 1759).

Sanuto, Marino, *I Diarii di Marino Sanuto,* ed. F. Stefani (Venice, 1879–1902).

Sceltà di Curiosità Letterarie inedite o rare, vol. 236 (Bologna, 1890). This volume contains a number of poetical accounts of the sack of Rome, including: *La Presa e Lamento di Roma;* the *Lamento d'Italia,* written by

Francesco Guicciardini; the *Lamento di Roma*; the *Romae Lamentatio*; and *La Presa e Lamento di Roma* by Eustachio Celebrino.

Spadari, G., 'Racconto della Ribellione Aretina del 1529 di G. Spadari', in *Raccolta degli Storici dal cinquecento al millecinquecento ordinata de L. A. Muratori, Nuova edizione riveduta, ampliata e corretta*, ed. G. Carducci and V. Fiorini, vol XXIV, pt 1. *Annales Arretinorum Maiores et Minores*.

'Les Suites du Sac de Rome', ed. H. Omont, in *Mélanges d'Archéologie et d'Histoire de l'École Française de Rome* (1896) pp. 13–58. These are notes, written day by day, by a young scriptor in the apostolic penitentiary, beginning on 6 December 1527.

Tommasseo, N., *Relations des Ambassadeurs Vénitiens sur les Affaires de France au XVIᵉ siècle*, vol. 1 (Paris, 1838).

Valeriano, G. P., *De litteratorum infelicitate libri duo*, ed. R. Brydges (Geneva, 1821).

Vettori, Francesco, 'Sommario della Storia d'Italia dal 1511 al 1527 da Francesco Vettori', ed. A. von Reumont, in *Archivio Storico Italiano*, vol. VI (1848) pp. 263–387.

(iii) PRINTED SOURCES COMPILED BETWEEN *c.* 1530 AND *c.* 1600

Ballino, M. G., *De' Designi delle più illustri città et fortezze del mondo* (Venice, 1569).

Berni, F., *Opere Burlesche* (Milan, 1806).

—, *Orlando Innamorato di Matteo M. Bojardo* (Milan, 1806).

Brantôme, *Œuvres complètes de Pierre de Bourdeilles, abbé et seigneur de Brantôme*, ed. P. Mérimée (Paris, 1858).

Cellini, Benvenuto, *The Autobiography of Benvenuto Cellini*, trans. G. Bull (London, 1961).

Fourquevaux, R. B. de, *The 'Instructions sur le faict de la guerre'*, ed. G. Dickinson (London, 1954).

Giovio, Paolo, *Paulus Jovius, De Vita Leonis Decimi Pont. Max. libri quatuor, His ordine temporum accesserunt Hadriani Sexti Pont. Max. et Pompeii Columnae Cardinalis vitae etc.* (Florence, 1549).

—, *Le vite del Gran Capitanio e del Marchese di Pescara*, trans. G. Panigada (Bari, 1931).

Grolerius, C., *Historia expugnatae et direptae Romae* (Paris, 1637).

Guazzo, Marco, *Historie di M. Marco Guazzo di tutti i fatti degni di memoria nel mondo successo* (Venice, 1546).

Guicciardini, Francesco, *Storia d'Italia*, ed. C. Panigada (Bari, 1929).

Guidiccioni, G., *Rime*, ed. E. Chiorboli (Bari, 1912).

Historia del Conde Pedro Navarro por Don Martin de los Heros, in *Coleccion de Documentos inéditos para la Historia de Espana*, vol. XXV (Madrid, 1854).

Montluc, Blaise de, *Commentaires de Messire Blaise de Montluc, Mareschal de*

France, ed. M. Petitot, in *Collection des Mémoires relatifs à l'histoire de France*, vol. xx (Paris, 1821).

Nardi, J., *Le historie della città di Fiorenza le quali contengono quanto dal'anno 1494 fino al tempo del anno 1531 e successo* (Lyons, 1582).

Paruta, P., *Dell'Istorie Veneziane*, in *Degli Istorici delle Cose Veneziane*, vols III, IV (Venice, 1718). Reference in the notes is made to vol. III only.

Sansovino, F., *Dei gli Huomini Illustri della Casa Orsina* (Venice, 1565).

—, *Della origine et de' fatti delle famiglie illustri d'Italia* (Venice, 1609).

Segni, B., *Storie Fiorentine dell'anno MDXXVII al MDLV colla vita di Niccolò Capponi* (Milan, 1805).

Varchi, B., *Storia Fiorentina*, ed. G. Milanesi (Florence, 1857).

Vasari, G., *Lives of the Most Eminent Painters, Sculptors and Architects*, trans. Mrs J. Foster (London, 1850-2).

II. SECONDARY AUTHORITIES

Ady, C. M., *The Bentivoglii of Bologna. A Study in Despotism* (London, 1937).

—, *A History of Milan under the Sforza*, ed. E. Armstrong (London, 1907).

Ady, C. M., Jamison, E. J., Vernon, K. D., and Terry, C. S., *Italy, Medieval and Modern. A History* (Oxford, 1917).

Barbieri, G., *Economia e politica nel ducato di Milano* (Milan, 1938).

Bataillon, M., *Érasme et l'Espagne* (Paris, 1937).

Beloch, K. J., *Bëvolkerungsgeschicte Italiens* (Berlin, 1965) vol. II.

Berengo, M., *Nobili e mercanti nella Lucca del Cinquecento* (Turin, 1965).

Bonazzi, A., *Storia di Perugia*, ed. G. Innamorati (Città di Castello, 1959-60).

Brandi, Karl, *The Emperor Charles V. The Growth and Destiny of a Man and of a World Empire*, trans. C. V. Wedgwood (London, 1965).

Braudel, F., *La Méditerranée et le Monde mediterranéan à l'époque de Philippe II* (Paris, 1949).

Bronziero, G., *Istoria delle origni e condizioni de luoghi principali del Polesine di Rovigo* (Venice, 1747).

Burn, R., *Rome and the Campagna: an Historical and Topographical Description of the Site, Buildings, and Neighbourhood of Ancient Rome* (Cambridge, 1871).

Castagnoli, F., Cecchelli, C., Giovannoni, G., and Zocca, M., *Topografia e Urbanistica di Roma* (Bologna, 1958).

Chadbod, F., *Lo Stato di Milano nel impero del Carlo V* (Rome, 1934).

—, *Lo Stato di Milano nella prima metà del secolo XVI* (Rome, 1954).

—, 'Venezia nella politica Italiana ed Europea del Cinquecento', in *La Civiltà del Rinascimento* (Venice, 1957).

Chambers, D., *Cardinal Bainbridge in the Court of Rome* (London, 1965).

Charles-Quint et son temps (Paris, 1959).
La Civiltà Veneziana del Rinascimento (Venice, 1957).
Coniglio, C., *Il Regno di Napoli al Tempo di Carlo V* (Naples, 1951).
—, *Il Viceregno di Napoli nel secolo XVII* (Rome, 1955).
Crisis and Change in the Venetian Economy in the Sixteenth and Seventeenth Centuries, ed. B. Pullan (London, 1968).
Croce, B., *La Spagna nella vita Italiana durante la rinascenza* (Bari, 1917).
Delumeau, J., *Vie economique et sociale de Rome dans la seconde moitié du XVIe siècle* (Paris, 1957).
Dizionario Biografico degli Italiani (Rome, 1960–).
Douglas, R. M., *Jacopo Sadoleto 1477–1547, Humanist and Reformer* (Cambridge, Mass., 1959).
Drei, G., *I Farnese, Grandezza e Decadenza di una dinastia italiana* (Rome, 1954).
Elton, G. R., *Reformation Europe 1517–1559* (London and Glasgow, 1963).
Enciclopedia Italiana di Scienze, Lettere ed Arti (Rome, 1929–39).
Flamini, F., *Il Cinquecento* (Milan, 1903).
Fossati-Falletti, C., *Clemente VII e l'impresa di Siena, il sacco di Roma, l'assedio di Napoli* (Siena, 1879).
Froude, J. A., *Lectures on the Council of Trent, Delivered at Oxford, 1892–3* (London, 1896).
Gaury, G. de, *The Grand Captain* (London, 1955).
Giannone, P., *The Civil History of the Kingdom of Naples,* trans. J. Ogilvie (London, 1729).
Gilbert, F., 'Alcuni discorsi di uomini politici fiorentini e la politica di Clemente VII per la restaurazione medicea', in *Archivio Storico Italiano,* vol. II (1935) pp. 3–24.
—, *Machiavelli and Guicciardini, Politics and History in Sixteenth Century Florence* (Princeton, 1965).
Gilmore, M. P., *The World of Humanism* (New York, 1952).
Hale, J. R., *Machiavelli and Renaissance Italy* (London, 1961).
Hauser, H., *Le Traité de Madrid et la Cession de la Bourgogne à Charles-Quint* (Dijon, 1912).
Heers, J., *Gênes au XVe siècle* (Paris, 1961).
Hierarchia catholica medii (et recentorius) aevi, sive summorum pontificum, S.R.E. cardinalium, ecclesiarum antistutum series e documentis Tabularii praesertim Vaticani collecta, digesta, edita, vol. 2, ed. C. Eubel (Monasterii, 1924), vol. 3, ed. G. van Gulik and C. Eubel (Monasterii, 1923).
Historiographie de Charles-Quint, ed. A. Morel-Fatio (Paris, 1913).
Ilardi, V., ' "Italianità" among some Italian intellectuals in the early sixteenth century', in *Traditio,* vol. XII (1956) pp. 339–67.
Jacqueton, G., *La politique estérieure de Louise de Savoie* (Paris, 1892).

Jedin, H., *A History of the Council of Trent,* trans. Dom. Ernest Graf, O.S.P. (London, 1957).

Kamen, H., *The Spanish Inquisition* (London, 1965).

Keen, M., *The Laws of War in the Middle Ages* (London, 1965).

Larner, J., *The Lords of the Romagna* (New York, 1965).

Lebey, A., *Le Connétable de Bourbon, 1490–1527* (Paris, 1904).

Luzio, A., *Isabella d'Este e il Sacco di Roma* (Milan, 1908).

Luzzato, G., *Storia Economica di Venezia dall'XI al XVI secolo* (Venice, 1961).

Magnuson, Torgil, *Studies in Roman Quattrocento Architecture* (Stockholm, 1958).

Marini, L., *La Spagna in Italia nell'Età di Carlo V* (Bologna, 1961).

Mattingly, G., *Renaissance Diplomacy* (London, 1965).

Merriman, R. B., *The Rise of the Spanish Empire in the Old World and the New* (New York, 1918).

Mignet, F., *Rivalité de François I et de Charles-Quint* (Paris, 1886).

Monaco, M., *La Situazione della Reverenda Camera Apostolica nell'anno 1525* (Rome, 1960).

Monacallero, G. L., *Il Cardinale Bernardo Dovizi da Bibbiena, Umanista e Diplomatico (1470–1520)* (Florence, 1953).

Muzzi, S., *Annali della Città di Bologna* (Bologna, 1844).

Nibby, A., *Analisi Storico-Topografico-Antiquario della carta de' dintorni di Roma* (Rome, 1837).

Nouvelle Biographie Générale (Paris, 1855–66).

Pandolfi, T., 'Giovan Matteo Giberti e l'ultima difesa della libertà d'Italia negl'anni 1521–5', in *Archivio della Reale Società Romana di Storia Patria,* vol. XXXIV (1911) pp. 131 ff.

Partner, P., *The Papal State in the Reign of Martin V* (London, 1958).

Pastor, L., *The History of the Popes from the Close of the Middle Ages,* ed. R. F. Keir (London, 1899–1910).

Pecchai, P., *Roma nel Cinquecento* (Bologna, 1948).

Pieri, P., *La crisi militari del rinascimento* (Naples, 1934).

Ramat, R., *Il Guicciardini e la Tragedia d'Italia* (Florence, 1953).

Renaudet, A., *Érasme et l'Italie* (Geneva, 1954).

Reumont, A. von, *Le Jeunesse de Catherine de Medicis* (Paris, 1866).

Ridolfi, R., *The Life of Francesco Guicciardini,* trans. C. Grayson (London, 1967).

—, *The Life of Niccolò Machiavelli,* trans. C. Grayson (London, 1963).

Romani, M., *Pellegrini e Viaggiatori nell'economia di Roma dal XIV al XVII secolo* (Milan, 1948).

Roth, C., *The Last Florentine Republic 1527–30* (London, 1925).

Rubinstein, N., *The Government of Florence under the Medici* (London, 1966).

Salvioli, G., 'Nuovi studii sulla politica e le vicende dell'esercito imperiale in Italia nel 1526–7 e sul sacco di Roma', in *Archivio Veneto*, vol. XVI (1878) pp. 272–98, vol. XVII (1879) pp. 1–34.

Santoro, C., *Gli Uffici del dominio Sforzesco* (Milan, 1947).

Schulz, Hans, *Der Sacco di Roma, Karls V Truppen in Roma 1527–8* (Halle, 1894).

Tocco, V. di, *Ideali di Indipendenza in Italia durante la preponderanza spagnuola* (Messina, 1927).

Toffanin, G., *Il Cinquecento* (Milan, 1929).

Tomassetti, G., *La Campagna Romana, antica, medioevale e moderna* (Rome, 1910).

Tonduzzi, G. C., *Historie di Faenza* (Faenza, 1675).

Urgurgieri della Berardenga, *Gli Acciauoli di Firenze nella luce dei loro tempi* (Florence, 1962).

Wind, E., *Pagan Mysteries in the Renaissance* (London, 1967).

INDEX

LAFRERY'S MAP OF ROME, 1557, SEEN FROM THE NORTH-EAST